Community
and Solitude

TRANSITS:
LITERATURE, THOUGHT & CULTURE 1650–1850

Series Editors
Greg Clingham, Bucknell University
Kathryn Parker, University of Wisconsin—La Crosse
Miriam Wallace, New College of Florida

Transits is a series of scholarly monographs and edited volumes publishing beautiful and surprising work. Without ideological bias the series seeks transformative readings of the literary, artistic, cultural, and historical interconnections between Britain, Europe, the Far East, Oceania, and the Americas during the years 1650 and 1850, and as their implications extend down to the present time. In addition to literature, art and history, such "global" perspectives might entail considerations of time, space, nature, economics, politics, environment, gender, sex, race, bodies, and material culture, and might necessitate the development of new modes of critical imagination. At the same time, the series welcomes considerations of the local and the national, for original new work on particular writers and readers in particular places in time continues to be foundational to the discipline.

Since 2011, sixty-five *Transits* titles have been published or are in production.

Recent Titles in the Series

Fire on the Water: Sailors, Slaves, and Insurrection in Early American Literature, 1789–1886
Lenora Warren

Community and Solitude: New Essays on Johnson's Circle
Anthony W. Lee Ed.

The Global Wordsworth: Romanticism Out of Place
Katherine Bergren

Cultivating Peace: The Virgilian Georgic in English, 1650–1750
Melissa Schoenberger

Intelligent Souls? Feminist Orientalism in Eighteenth-Century English Literature
Samara Anne Cahill

The Printed Reader: Gender, Quixotism, and Textual Bodies in Eighteenth-Century Britain
Amelia Dale

For a full list of *Transits* titles go to https://www.bucknell.edu/script/upress/series.asp?id=33

Community and Solitude

NEW ESSAYS ON
JOHNSON'S CIRCLE

Edited by
ANTHONY W. LEE

LEWISBURG, PENNSYLVANIA

Library of Congress Cataloging-in-Publication Data
Names: Lee, Anthony W., editor.
Title: Community and solitude : new essays on Johnson's circle / edited by Anthony W. Lee.
Description: Lewisburg [Pennsylvania] : Bucknell University Press, [2018] | Series: Transits : literature, thought & culture | Includes bibliographical references and index.
Identifiers: LCCN 2018029479| ISBN 9781684480234 (cloth) | ISBN 9781684480227 (pbk.).
Subjects: LCSH: Johnson, Samuel, 1709–1784—Friends and associates. | Johnson, Samuel, 1709–1784—Contemporaries. | Johnson, Samuel, 1709–1784—Influence. | England—Intellectual life—18th century. | Authors, English—18th century—Biography. | Intellectuals—England—Biography. | English literature—18th century—History and criticism.
Classification: LCC PR3533 .C66 2018 | DDC 828/.609 [B]—dc23
LC record available at https://lccn.loc.gov/2018029479

A British Cataloging-in-Publication record for this book is available from the British Library.

This collection copyright © 2019 by Bucknell University Press.
Individual chapters copyright © 2019 in the names of their authors.

All rights reserved

No part of this book may be reproduced or utilized in any form or by any means, electronic or mechanical, or by any information storage and retrieval system, without written permission from the publisher. Please contact Bucknell University Press, Hildreth-Mirza Hall, Bucknell University, Lewisburg, PA 17837-2005. The only exception to this prohibition is "fair use" as defined by U.S. copyright law.

♾ The paper used in this publication meets the requirements of the American National Standard for Information Sciences—Permanence of Paper for Printed Library Materials, ANSI Z39.48–1992.

www.bucknell.edu/UniversityPress

Distributed worldwide by Rutgers University Press

Manufactured in the United States of America

To Thomas and Dylan

CONTENTS

Abbreviations ix

Introduction 1
ANTHONY W. LEE

PART ONE: Personal Relationships:
Letters and Conversation

1 Connecting with Three "Young Dogs":
Johnson's Early Letters to Robert Chambers,
Bennet Langton, and James Boswell 9
JOHN RADNER

2 James Elphinston and Samuel Johnson:
Contact, Irritations, and an "Argonautic" Letter 31
CHRISTINE JACKSON-HOLZBERG

3 The Case of the Missing Hottentot: John Dun's
Conversation with Samuel Johnson in *Tour to the
Hebrides* as Reported by Boswell and Dun 53
JAMES J. CAUDLE

PART TWO: Literary Relationships:
Major Texts and Topics

4 Oliver Goldsmith's Revisions to *The Traveller* 79
JAMES E. MAY

CONTENTS

5 "Down with Her, Burney!": Johnson, Burney, and the Politics of Literary Celebrity 108
MARILYN FRANCUS

6 In the First Circle: The Four Narrators of the *Life of Savage* 132
LANCE WILCOX

7 "Under the Shade of Exalted Merit": Arthur Murphy's *A Poetical Epistle to Mr. Samuel Johnson, A.M.* 153
ANTHONY W. LEE

8 Johnson, Burke, Boswell, and the Slavery Debate 167
ELIZABETH LAMBERT

9 Samuel Johnson and Anna Seward: Solitude and Sensibility 191
CLAUDIA THOMAS KAIROFF

10 Johnson, Warton, and the Popular Reader 214
CHRISTOPHER CATANESE

Acknowledgments 233

Bibliography 235

About the Contributors 249

Index 253

ABBREVIATIONS

CJ	Frances Burney, *The Court Journals and Letters of Frances Burney*, gen. ed. Peter Sabor (Oxford: Clarendon Press, 2011–), 4 vols. to date.
Dictionary	Samuel Johnson, *A Dictionary of the English Language* (London, 1755), 2 vols.
ELJ	Frances Burney. *The Early Journals and Letters of Fanny Burny*, ed. Lars E. Troide, with Stewart J. Cooke and Betty W. Rizzo (Montreal and Kingston, ON: McGill-Queen's University Press, 1988–2012), 5 vols.
FYC	James Elphinston, *Fifty Years' Correspondence, Inglish, French, and Lattin, in Proze and Verse; Between Geniusses ov Boath Sexes, and James Elphinston . . . .* (London, 1794), 8 vols.
Letters	Samuel Johnson, *The Letters of Samuel Johnson*, ed. Bruce Redford (Princeton, NJ: Princeton University Press, 1992–1994), 5 vols.
Life	James Boswell, *The Life of Samuel Johnson, LL.D.*, ed. George B. Hill, with rev. ed. Lawrence F. Powell (Oxford: Clarendon Press, 1934–1964), 6 vols.
Lives	Samuel Johnson, *The Lives of the Most Eminent English Poets: With Critical Observations on Their Works*, ed. Roger H. Lonsdale (Oxford: Oxford University Press, 2006), 4 vols.
LRS	Samuel Johnson, *The Life of Mr Richard Savage*, ed. Nicholas Seager and Lance Wilcox (Peterborough, ON: Broadview Press, 2016)
Poems	Samuel Johnson, *The Poems of Samuel Johnson*, ed. David Nichol Smith and Edward L. McAdam, rev. J. D. Fleeman, 2nd ed. (Oxford: Clarendon Press, 1974).
Yale *Works*	Samuel Johnson, *The Yale Edition of the Works of Samuel Johnson*, gen. ed. Robert DeMaria, Jr. (New Haven, CT: Yale University Press, 1958–2018), 23 vols. to date.

Community
and Solitude

INTRODUCTION

Anthony W. Lee

In a character not published until after his death, Sir Joshua Reynolds wrote of Samuel Johnson: "Solitude to him was horror; nor would he ever trust himself alone but when employed in writing or reading. He has often begged me to accompany me home with him to prevent his being alone in the coach. Any company was better than none; by which he connected himself with many mean persons whose presence he could command."[1] Johnson's horror of solitude manifested itself early in his life, as when he was a child reading *Hamlet* alone, "till coming to the Ghost scene, he suddenly hurried up stairs to the street door, that he might see people about him"; it extended to his very end, when he took comfort from the around-the-clock attention offered by watchers at his deathbed.[2] The implications of this horror are complex—Johnson was an eminently social creature—and his friendships—and antagonisms—allowed him to openly develop and exhibit his brilliant mind and conversation in ways that otherwise, at least from his own tortured perspective, would languish in vacuity.

Taking its cue from his horror of being alone, this volume celebrates the fruits of Johnson's aversion by tracking and illuminating his recourse to the tangible social and cultural world about him. Just as the child "hurried up stairs to the street door, that he might see people about him," the man hurried himself into company and slowed others from leaving it, in the process forging personal relationships and intertextual encounters that illuminate many signal aspects of the brilliant period that is sometimes called "the age of Johnson." His instinctive and deliberate gravitation toward friendship stands as an operational polarity to his shunning of solitude: see, for example, his advice to Reynolds that "a man, Sir, should keep his friendship *in constant repair*" and his rebuff of Sir John Hawkins as "a most *unclubable* man!"[3]

If this emphatic sociability perhaps robbed us of more of his original writings than we in fact possess (the list of his projected but unfinished literary endeavors is tantalizingly full[4]), it established a rich community of friendships—and antagonisms—that can be excavated and partially recovered. That is the brief of this book. Each of the essays collected here—all specifically commissioned for

[1]

the occasion—assemble important work on Johnson and key members of his circle in an effort to exemplify and promote this recovery. The collection clarifies the great influence Johnson exerted upon his age by examining specific relationships and analyzing some of the literary productions emanating from them; in the process, it explores some of the larger aesthetic and cultural domains these relationships and texts represent and illuminate. Therefore, Johnson and many of his friends—and sometimes foes, as in the case of Anna Seward—are brought into greater clarity. However, the volume hopes to succeed in exploring broader areas that will be of interest to a more general readership of eighteenth-century scholars and students. Some of these include the public role of private correspondence, the phenomenon of literary celebrity, the transmission of texts through revisionary practices, the nature of eighteenth-century intertextuality and literary mentoring, public and private debates over the slave trade, the transformation of "Augustan" literary and cultural values to those of sentiment and sensibility, and the shift from an elite to a popular readership and the consequent modulation of emphasis from writer to audience. In these and many other ways, *Community and Solitude: New Essays on Johnson's Circle* constitutes a rich and deeply informed contribution to our current understanding of many aspects integral to the study of the eighteenth century.

The collection falls into two parts. Part I, "Personal Relationships: Letters and Conversation," contains three chapters. The letters Johnson wrote to Boswell from 1763 to 1772, and his failure to write more despite Boswell's efforts to coax responses, both disappointed and puzzled his young friend. In order to better appreciate these texts, as well as Johnson's sustained silences, John Radner's "Connecting with Three 'Young Dogs': Johnson's Early Letters to Robert Chambers, Bennet Langton, and James Boswell" contextualizes Johnson's correspondence during this same period with two younger men whom Johnson befriended eight or nine years before he met Boswell. The letters Johnson wrote to these—applauding their abilities and potential, trying to resolve their doubts and confusions, and seeking to correct their deficiencies—suggest key differences in the ways he regarded each of the three. An appendix offers a year-to-year table charting Johnson's correspondence with Chambers, Langton, and Boswell—and another intimate correspondent, Hester Thrale—from 1754 to 1784.

"James Elphinston and Samuel Johnson: Contact, Irritations, and an 'Argonautic' Letter," considers a less intimate but far longer friendship, that between Johnson and one of the many Scots he embraced, a friendship that began in the late 1740s and survived, or perhaps thrived on, mutual irritations and differences for almost four decades. It is mapped out here by Christine Jackson-Holzberg, whose study of Elphinston's correspondence—which includes an exchange of only nine letters with Johnson, but reveals in many others, for example, a surprising number of shared acquaintances—and other evidence traces not only the course and significance of this friendship, but also a curious episode involving a bottle, Johnson's best-known letter to Elphinston, and its long-forgotten published translation into French by the latter.

Many have debated the veracity of James Boswell's conversational reporting in his *Hebrides* and *Life of Johnson*, and much debate between 1965 and 2017 about the relevance of these two masterworks of biography has centered on how accurately Boswell was able to report Johnson's conversation. In the final chapter of Part I, James Caudle's "The Case of the Missing Hottentot: John Dun's Conversation with Samuel Johnson in *Tour to the Hebrides* as Reported by Boswell and Dun" uses fresh evidence to look at the understudied (yet rather public) debate between Boswell and Boswell's former childhood tutor, Reverend John Dun. The two men wielded verbal arms over the words which Johnson used to rebuke Dun during a heated exchange over religion. Carefully sifting through all available documentary evidence, Caudle successfully engages a number of central issues, such as the truth underlying Johnson's "Hottentot" remark and the nature of Boswell's methods of recording conversation. Ultimately, the chapter teases out Johnson's attitudes toward race and culture and how these exemplify the conflictive relationship between Scotland and England and their rival national churches in the eighteenth century.

Part II, "Literary Relationships: Major Texts and Topics," comprises the remainder of the volume. Although we recognize that Goldsmith was praised in his day for a clear and elegant style, characterizations of his career have not sufficiently weighed the extent to which writing for Goldsmith was actually *rewriting*. Most of his works recast what others had written in English and foreign languages. Nor has sufficient attention been paid to the record of his revisions—a glaring omission, given the extraordinary pains Goldsmith took in revising his major works. James E. May's "Oliver Goldsmith's Revisions to *The Traveller*" importantly redresses this neglect. Proposing that the best text for examining Goldsmith's revisions for insights into his practice is *The Traveller; or, a Prospect of Society*, May performs a careful textual analysis of this poem that presents a solitary author engaging societies in the pursuit of truths about happiness; he concludes that when reviewers, including Samuel Johnson, praised, criticized, and quoted the poem, they provided Goldsmith with considerations that importantly influenced his revisions.

Marilyn Francus's "'Down with her, Burney!': Johnson, Burney, and the Politics of Literary Celebrity" analyzes Johnson and Burney's struggles with literary celebrity in ways that reveal shifts in literary value, cultural capital, and authorship at the end of the eighteenth century. Francus focuses upon the heady months after Burney's *Evelina* thrust her into the London literary scene in 1778. Burney became an overnight sensation and attracted the attention of Johnson, who at the time was writing his *Lives of the Poets*. Francus charts Johnson's attempts to guide his young friend through the literary landscape even as he was fighting his own battles within it. Burney, who agonized over public attention, resisted Johnson's vision of the world of letters as warfare. The disagreement between the younger and the older literary celebrities illuminates shifting patterns within this new and evolving landscape.

Lance Wilcox's "In the First Circle: The Four Narrators of the *Life of Savage*" illuminates the Johnson Circle by looking at Johnson's participation in an earlier one. This "First Circle" centered not around Johnson but Richard Savage, the mercurially brilliant but inevitably self-destructive public figure who mesmerized a Johnson new to the London literary world. This earlier grouping, as fluidly unstable as Savage himself, included such figures as Richard Steele, James Thomson, Alexander Pope, and Aaron Hill. Wilcox interrogates Savage's circle and Johnson's varying attitudes toward it through the prism of the 1744 masterpiece, *The Life of Savage*. His chapter identifies four narrators in that biography: The Sage, the Historian, the Memoirist, and the Friend. Wilcox deploys these narrative articulations to enrich and complicate our understanding of Savage while also demonstrating that, decades later, the experience of knowing and writing about Savage would inform and shape the constitution of Johnson's better-known Circle.

Protégés of major authors endeavor to flourish under their mentor's large shadow in various ways: inventive deviation from the earlier path, as in the case of Oliver Goldsmith; surface homage laced with carefully disguised resistance, as in the case of James Boswell; furiously open defiance, as in the case of an aggrieved Percival Stockwell; or devoted dedication to honoring and extending the *manes* of the great precursor—this last being the path followed by Arthur Murphy. My own contribution to this book, "'Under the shade of exalted merit': Arthur Murphy's *A Poetical Epistle to Mr. Samuel Johnson, A.M.*," uses a little-studied 1760 poem that Murphy addressed to Johnson in order to more closely examine his own attempts to cope with his mentor's influence. Analysis of Murphy's best Johnsonian poem reveals how he productively responds to the immense weight of Johnson's "exalted" literary merit by deftly crafting an intertextual "imitation" of both Boileau's *Epître à Molière* and Pope's *Epistle to Arbuthnot*. These precursive models allow Murphy to give Johnson, the greater writer, his merited due, even while subtly insisting upon Murphy's own aspirational ambitions.

Elizabeth Lambert's "Johnson, Burke, Boswell, and the Slavery Debate," triangulates these three members of the Literary Club through the volatile and still resonant topic of slavery. At the end of his 1775 *Taxation No Tyranny*, Johnson took his most pointed shot at the rebellious American colonists: "How is it we hear the loudest yelps for liberty among the drivers of Negros?" Johnson was among the predominant literary and political figures of the day who opposed slavery as immoral, and he was quick to support the abolition movement of the 1770s. Edmund Burke, one of Johnson's closest friends despite their political differences, was also unremitting in his condemnation of slavery. Yet Boswell, an intimate of Johnson's and a want-to-be intimate of Burke's, steadfastly justified and defended the peculiar institution. Lambert describes how Boswell insinuated his opinions of slavery into the *Life of Johnson* and delineates the ways Johnson and Burke were of one mind on this subject. While there is no record of the two men specifically discussing either abolition or slavery, Burke's convictions and his contribution to the abolitionist movement demonstrate the validity of Johnson's repeated evaluation of him as "a great man by nature."

Claudia Thomas Kairoff's "Samuel Johnson and Anna Seward: Solitude and Sensibility" reappraises the Seward-Johnson relationship. While these two scions of Lichfield were on fairly decent terms throughout much of Johnson's life, after his death Seward demonstrated pointed hostility, especially toward *The Lives of the Poets*. Seward was apparently motivated by what she interpreted as Johnson's attacks on British poets at a time when the literary canon seemed critical to the development of British patriotism. Her disparagement of Johnson as "a very indifferent reader of verse" was therefore rooted in her generational and professional perspectives as much as in her different temperament, religious and political views, class, and gender. Kairoff's chapter pursues this theme through a sensitive and nuanced exploration of travel writings—including Johnson's *Journey to the Western Islands*—and Seward's verse, suggesting that perhaps the chief underlying cause of Seward's animus hinged upon their contrasting views of sensibility, manifested in their respective correspondence, literature, and criticism.

The concluding chapter, "Johnson, Warton, and the Popular Reader," explores the epochal nature of the anxiety over popular readerships through a comparison of Johnson with his friend Thomas Warton, an academic who was largely insulated from the market forces that Johnson navigated. As a writer situated outside the "academic bowers" of scholarly retreat and working within the commercial system of the London book trades, Johnson was directly engaged with the rapidly changing literary market, and especially the inexorable growth of what would eventually come to be understood as a mass reading public. Juxtaposing Johnson's vigorously defensive self-fashioning in the *Rambler* with Warton's literary histories and with the heterodox but ascendant aesthetics of romance, Chris Catanese foregrounds the degree to which Johnson's shrewd negotiation of the "popular" anticipates the tactics of a later generation of Romantic writers in coming to terms with the commercialization of literary form and the demands of a new reading public.

In conclusion, all the contributors to this volume make vibrantly vital contributions in their areas of engagement. *Community and Solitude: New Essays on Johnson's Circle* intends therefore to recommend to the interested reader some of the best thinking and writing currently available within the contours of its subjects of inquiry. It thus is presented not only as a primer of criticism upon Johnson and key members of his circle, but also as a parliament of explorations that will serve as a point of departure for possible future critical inquiry.

NOTES

1. Sir Joshua Reynolds, *Portraits by Sir Joshua Reynolds*, ed. Frederick W. Hilles (New York: McGraw-Hill, 1952), 76. The portrait was part of a cache of manuscripts discovered only in the twentieth century (see Frederick W. Hilles, *The Literary Career of Sir Joshua Reynolds*. [Cambridge: Cambridge University Press, 1936; repr. Hamden, CT: Archon Press, 1967], 13). However, the passage quoted here was transcribed and included in the biography *The Life and Times of Sir Joshua Reynolds*, by Charles Robert Leslie and Tom Taylor (London, 1865), 2:455. Probably written for inclusion in Boswell's *Life of Johnson*, it eventually found its way into G. B. Hill's edition of 1887. See James Boswell, *The Life of Samuel Johnson, LL.D.*, ed. George B. Hill, with rev. ed. Lawrence F. Powell (Oxford: Clarendon Press, 1934–1964) (hereafter cited *Life*, by volume:page).
2. Samuel Johnson, *Johnsonian Miscellanies*, ed. George B. Hill (Oxford: Clarendon Press, 1897), 1:158. For the deathbed scene, see *Life*, 4:406–407; *Journal Narrative Relative to Doctor Johnson's Last Illness Three Weeks before his Death, Kept by John Hoole*, ed. O M Brack Jr. (Iowa City:Windhover Press, 1972); and Stephen Miller, "The Death of Johnson," in *Three Deaths and Enlightenment Thought* (Lewisburg: Bucknell University Press, 2001), 86–122.
3. *Life*, 1:27n2; Frances Burney, *The Early Journals and Letters of Fanny Burney*, ed. Lars E. Troide with Stewart J. Cooke and Betty W. Rizzo (Montreal and Kingston, ON: McGill-Queen's University Press, 1988–2012), 3:76 (hereafter ctied *ELJ*, by volume:page).
4. For the extensive list of unwritten titles, see *Life*, 4:381n1; Paul Tankard, "'That Great Literary Projector': Samuel Johnson's *Designs*, or Catalogue of Projected Works," *Age of Johnson: A Scholarly Annual* 13 (2002): 103–80; and his "Nineteen More Johnsonian Designs: A Supplement to 'That Great Literary Projector,'" *AJ* 23 (2015): 141–57.

Part One

PERSONAL RELATIONSHIPS

Letters and Conversation

1

CONNECTING WITH THREE "YOUNG DOGS"

Johnson's Early Letters to Robert Chambers, Bennet Langton, and James Boswell

JOHN RADNER

> It is now long since we saw one another, and whatever has been the reason neither You have written to me, nor I to you. To let friendship dye away by negligence and silence is certainly not wise. It is to throw away one of the greatest comforts of this weary pilgrimage. . . . Do not forget me, You see that I do not forget You. It is pleasing in the silence of solitude to think, that there is One at least however distant of whose benevolence there is little doubt, and whom there is yet hope of seeing again.
> —Samuel Johnson, Letter to Bennet Langton[1]

ON AUGUST 18, 1763, twelve days after he and Johnson parted on the beach at Harwich, a distraught James Boswell cried out for help from the man who had praised and encouraged him during his last six weeks in London. Seven weeks later, no longer despairing, Boswell wrote again, describing what he had achieved by reading Johnson's *Rambler* essays. But he had to wait more than two additional months before receiving a response that delighted him with its length and upbeat support, but that puzzlingly redefined their friendship.[2]

When Boswell, at twenty-two years old, had come to London the previous November, he knew Johnson as the author of the *Dictionary*, the *Rambler*, and *Rasselas*. He had heard David Hume repeat stories others had told him about Johnson, and he had also heard Thomas Sheridan describe Johnson's marvelous conversation and how he frequently visited till two or three in the morning, before leaving for other engagements. Then, starting on June 25, 1763, when he and Johnson spent the first of many tavern evenings together, they had become friends. Johnson reassuringly reported having once been "a talker against religion," that he "never believed what [his] father said," and that he had been "greatly

[9]

distressed" with melancholy. Boswell's journal and letters also report Johnson repeatedly declaring his "love" for Boswell, and his eagerness to reconnect once Boswell returned from abroad. Johnson also offered to accompany Boswell to Harwich, where he would board the ship to Holland, and where—according to the *Life*—Johnson declared, "Sir, it is more likely that you should forget me than that I should forget you."[3]

Four months later, responding to Boswell's two letters, especially his October anxiety at Johnson's silence, Johnson wrote, "You are not to think yourself forgotten or criminally neglected that you have had yet no letter from me." But after declaring his hope "not to gratify [his] indolence by the omission of any important duty or any office of real kindness," and before addressing Boswell's "dissipation of thought," Johnson seemed eager to modify their friendship. Despite having spent many hours talking about his own experiences as well as Boswell's hopes and fears, Johnson would write only to instruct or advise. "To tell you that I am or am not well, that I have or have not been in the country . . . I seldom shall think worth communication[;] but if I can have it in my power to calm any harassing disquiet to excite any virtuous desire to rectify any important opinion or fortify any generous resolution you need not doubt but I shall at least wish to prefer the pleasure of gratifying a friend much less esteemed than yourself before the gloomy calm of idle Vacancy" (*Letters*, 1:237–38).

Pleased that Johnson had finally written, even if much less companionably than anticipated, Boswell quickly sent a "noble" response, and wrote again in March 1764. But when he left Utrecht in June, Boswell still had not heard again from Johnson. Nor did Johnson respond to the "joint Letter from two of your distant friends" that Boswell got Giuseppe Baretti to write in July 1765.[4] In fact Johnson next wrote only in January 1766, when Boswell would soon pass through London on his way home from the Continent. Then over the next six years, despite repeated attempts to coax responses, Boswell received only six additional letters from Johnson. Also, only in June 1771 did Johnson's letter to Boswell begin to share news and to confess some of his failings, and only the next year did a letter talk about his health.

In *Johnson and Boswell: A Biography of Friendship*, I tried to explain Johnson's initial delay in writing Boswell, his long silences, the relative guardedness of his early letters, and the major changes starting in 1773, when Johnson fully embraced Boswell's plan to write his biography, by carefully examining all the information available concerning this friendship, much of it from Boswell's journals. Here I would like to highlight some of the distinctive features of this developing friendship by comparing Johnson's early letters to Boswell with those he wrote during the same years—as well as earlier—to Robert Chambers and

Bennet Langton, both of whom, like Boswell, saved all the letters they received from Johnson.

Johnson met Chambers, who, like Langton, was three years older than Boswell, in 1754; soon after this young Newcastle man enrolled in the Middle Temple, and Johnson helped persuade Chambers also to enroll in Oxford. About the same time, or perhaps a bit later, Johnson became acquainted with Langton, heir to an ancient Lincolnshire estate, who was preparing for his own matriculation at Oxford. By the time Johnson first encountered Boswell in Tom Davies's Bookshop, both Chambers and Langton had long been members of his inner circle, and Johnson surely had them in mind in when he praised Boswell as "very forward in knowledge, for [his] age," and then added that he "had not six above [him]. Perhaps not one. He did not know one."[5] Johnson saw Chambers regularly in London or Oxford every year through 1773. He saw Langton, too, during most of the years, but not so regularly, especially toward the end, so his letters to Langton occasionally worked harder than those to Chambers at developing and nurturing this friendship. In contrast, Johnson saw Boswell in only six of the eleven years from 1763 through 1773. His letters to Boswell had even more work to accomplish; and his long silences are both puzzling and suggestive.

Johnson's letters to Chambers, Langton and Boswell—all men who had great potential, but in different ways needed guidance and encouragement—suggest key differences in how he befriended each, as well as in the satisfactions each friendship offered, the different worries or frustrations each produced. I am not interested in determining which of the three Johnson loved most, but in noticing what these letters, by themselves, show about how differently Johnson applauded each young friend's abilities, resolved his doubts and confusions, responded to what he saw as his deficiencies. How did Johnson connect with each in those moments when he wrote, and how did writing to each engage him? How did he live vicariously through each of these young friends, and how did he hope to live in their minds? Also, do these early letters indicate changes in each of these friendships?

1754–1763: NOTES AND LETTERS TO CHAMBERS

The eleven letters and notes Johnson wrote to Chambers through 1763, and the five he wrote to Langton during this same period, provide a useful framework for an assessment of his first letter to Boswell. Based on these letters and notes, Johnson's friendship with Chambers was the easiest to maintain, because Johnson regularly saw Chambers in London or Oxford. He requested information, asked other favors, occasionally offered advice, and frequently called for replies, sustaining contact when he and Chambers were not together. But his notes and letters—especially the early ones—reveal less of how Johnson and Chambers interacted when together than those to Langton and Boswell do.

Johnson's first letter, written soon after Chambers had begun studying at Oxford, asked him to pass on to Thomas Warton a detailed request concerning several manuscripts, hoped Chambers did not regret the move from London to Oxford, reported that Baretti and Anna Williams—both daily participants in Johnson's London life—were well, and concluded, "we shall all be glad to hear from you, whenever you shall be so kind as to write" (*Letters*, 1:86–87). The next year, after a visit to Oxford, Johnson left a note thanking Chambers for his "company and kindness," and three days later wrote asking Chambers to pay the barber for a week's shaving, and to "call at Mrs. Simpson's for a box of pills which [he] left behind . . . and [was] "loath to lose" (*Letters*, 1:112–14). A more substantial letter in July 1756 thanked Chambers for a contribution to the *Literary Magazine,* which Johnson "sent . . . to the press, unread," requested other "performances from Oxford," and cautioned Chambers not to tell anyone that Johnson was editing this publication, "For though it is known conjecturally I would not have it made certain." After reporting that Robert Levett and Anna Williams were well, instead of simply asking for news Johnson concluded with this playful allusion to the new war with France: "I think much on my friends, and shall take pleasure to hear of your operations at Lincoln College, when I am unconcerned about the marches and countermarches in America, therefore pray write sometimes to, Dear sir, your affectionate servant, SAM. JOHNSON" (*Letters*, 1:138–39).

In April 1758, when Chambers applied for one of the first Vinerian scholarships to study law at Oxford, Johnson quickly sent several letters of recommendation, for Chambers to read and distribute as he pleased. He wrote again six days later, "long[ing] to hear how you go on in your solicitation, and what hopes you have of success." But Johnson also began reflecting, as he would have done at length had he and Chambers had a chance to talk, whether "these new benefactions," with restrictions on Chambers's time, would be "worth the acceptance of any practical Lawyer" (*Letters*, 1:160–62). Seven weeks later, after expressing his delight that Chambers's application was unopposed, Johnson urged his young friend to "consider how much will be expected from one that begins so well," and to "take care not to break the promise you have made"; he added that Rev. Francis Wise, to whom he had addressed one of his recommendations, had responded "with high commendations" of Chambers (*Letters*, 1:164–65).

At the very end of 1760, Johnson asked Chambers for a detailed report on the condition of Sir John Philips, the "chief friend of Miss Williams," who was "ill of a mortified leg at Oxford," and concluded this request by wishing Chambers "many happy years, for I am, Dearest Sir, you most affectionate servant: SAM: JOHNSON" (*Letters*, 1:195). Two years later he assigned the twenty-five-year-old Chambers a much more delicate investigation. After writing to a schoolmaster about preparing George Strahan, son of his publisher and friend William Strahan, for admission to Oxford, Johnson received an answer "written in so unscholarlike a manner" that he began to doubt the schoolmaster's skill and learning, so he asked Chambers "to make some enquiry into his abilities by such means as may not hurt him" (*Letters*, 1:210–11). Five months later (March 15, 1763), two months before Johnson first met Boswell, after asking Chambers speedily to inquire whether Rev. Thomas Warter "has yet proceeded to take his degree of B. D." and to "make my compliments to the Gentlemen of your College," Johnson noted that Bennet Langton, whom Chambers had met at Oxford in 1757, if not before, had just returned from abroad (*Letters*, 1:218).

1755–1760: LETTERS TO LANGTON

Like Chambers, Langton was frequently in London from 1754 through 1763. But he also spent long stretches at his family estate and at Oxford. Also, before going abroad in 1762–63, he traveled through parts of England. So, Johnson's letters, though much less frequent than those to Chambers, were generally much more substantial.

In the uncharacteristically labored-over opening of his first letter (May 6, 1755), Johnson praised Langton as a lenient judge of his failure to respond promptly to his friend's two letters: "It has been long observed that men do not suspect faults which they do not omit; your own Elegance of manners and punctuality of complaisance did not suffer you to impute to me that negligence of which I was guilty, and which I have not since attoned." Then Johnson explained why he could not immediately visit Langton's family home as he had promised, even though he was now "at liberty," the *Dictionary* having been published. He assumed Langton would approve his "true reason" for postponing the visit: his duty to his aging mother, "who has counted the days to the publication of my book in hopes of seeing me." Having "very seldom received an offer of Friendship which [he] so earnestly desire[d] to cultivate and mature," Johnson promised that "when the duty that call[ed] [him] to Lichfield [was] discharged, [his] inclination [would] hurry [him] to Langton," where he would "delight to hear the ocean roar or see the stars twinkle, in the company of men to whom nature does not spread her volumes or utter her voice in vain." Then in the final paragraph, Johnson repeated

[13]

his desire to visit Langton and his family: "I have known you enough to love you, and sincerely to wish a further knowledge, and I assure you once more that to live in a house which contains such a Father and such a Son will be accounted a very uncommon degree of pleasure by, Dear sir, Your most obliged and most humble servant, SAM. JOHNSON" (*Letters*, 1:105–7).[6]

Johnson's next four letters to Langton—three written between June 1758 and January 1759 while Langton was at Oxford, the fourth in October 1760—continued to woo Langton with wise counsel and leisurely playfulness, while regularly apologizing for not having written, as he never had to do with Chambers. When Chambers went to Oxford in 1754, Johnson simply hoped he did not regret the decision to combine academic study with his work at the Inner Temple. Four years later, a month after he reminded Chambers "how much will be expected from one that begins so well," Johnson encouraged Langton—before Oxford became familiar—to record how he had earlier "imagined . . . an academical life" and "conceived . . . the manners, the views, and the conversation of men devoted to letters, how they would chuse their companions, how they would direct their Studies, and how they would regulate their lives." Since he knew nothing "more pleasant or more instructive than to compare experience with expectation, or to register from time to time the difference between Idea and Reality," Johnson urged Langton to "Let me know what you expected and what you have found"—or at least to "record it to yourself before custom has reconciled you to the scenes before you" (*Letters*, 1:165–66).

Three months later, having heard—perhaps from Langton, perhaps from newspapers—that Major General Alexander Drury, the husband of Langton's mother's sister, had died in battle, Johnson seized the occasion "to try what reflection will suggest to mitigate the horrors of a violent <death which is> more formidable at the first glance than <on> a nearer and more steady view." He sought to comfort Langton, Langton's family, and also himself, by working out at length "why we lament more him that dies of a wound than that dies of a fever." After five sentences contrasting dying in battle with dying by an "accident," or because of "a cold or consumption," or "by the miseries of age," or simply because "life . . . is burnt out," Johnson ended the letter echoing many of his *Rambler* essays: "Let us endeavour to see things as they are, and then enquire whether we ought to complain. Whether to see life as it is will give us much consolation I know not, but the consolation which is drawn from truth, if any there be, is solid and durable, that which may be derived from errour must be like its original fallacious and fugitive" (*Letters*, 1:166–67).

Fourteen weeks later—again behind in this correspondence—Johnson opened with genial self-deprecation to the friend he continued to see as a tolerant judge: "None of your suspicions are true, I am not much richer than when you left me, and what is worse, my omission of an answer to your first letter will prove that I am not much wiser. But I go on as I formerly did, designing to be some time or other both rich and wise, and yet cultivate neither mind nor fortune" (*Letters*, 1:171).

After reflexively urging Langton to "take notice of my example, and learn the danger of delay"—"when I was as you are now, towering in <the> Confidence of twenty one little did I suspect that I should be a<t> forty nine what I now am"—Johnson immediately noted that Langton did not "seem to need [these] admonitions." For he was "busy in acquiring and in communicating knowledge, and while you are studying enjoy the end of Study, by making others wiser and happier." Much pleased with Langton's "tale . . . of being tutor to [his] Sisters," Johnson confessed his "innocent envy" of those, like Langton, "who may be said to be born to friends," noting that this "original amity" is "more frequently thrown away with levity or lost by negligence, than destroyed by injury or violence." (Two weeks later, shortly after his mother's death, Johnson wrote in his journal, "The dream of my brother I remember.")[7]

Since Langton planned not to return soon to Oxford or London, Johnson entertained him with the news of their mutual friends' activities that he would have reported had Langton just come to town—more detailed information than he ever needed to send Chambers. First, he described how he had attended the opening night of Richard Dodsley's tragedy *Cleone*, "and supported it as publickly as I might, for Doddy, you know, is my patron, and I would not desert him." The play was "well acted by all the characters," especially George Ann Bellamy, who "left nothing to be desired," and once its success was assured, "Doddy . . . went every night to the Stage side, and cry'd at the distress of poor Cleone." Johnson then reported having "left off housekeeping," so he had given the pheasant Langton had sent to Samuel Richardson, the Bustard to Dr. Thomas Lawrence, and the sausage to Miss Williams, "to be eaten by myself." He added that Joshua Reynolds had just raised his price for portraits "to twenty guineas a head," that his sister, Frances, "is much employed in Miniatures," and that Arthur Murphy's *Orphan of China* was about to be performed. "I wish I could tell you of any great good to which I was approaching," Johnson concluded, "but at present my prospects do not much delight me, however I am always pleased when I find that you, dear Sir, remember Your affectionate, humble servant, SAM JOHNSON" (*Letters*, 1:171–74).

Twenty-one months later (October 18, 1760), responding to Langton's account of his travels in England—"I should be glad to have all England surveyed by you, if you would impart your observations in narratives as agreeable as your last"—Johnson wrote: "While you have [been] riding and running, and seeing the tombs of the learned, and the camps of the valiant"—and while their mutual friend Topham Beauclerk "went away to Cheshire, and has not yet found his way back [and] Chambers passed the vacation at Oxford"—he had "only staid at home, and intended to do great things which [he had] not done." Concerned for "the preservation or recovery" of Langton's father's sight, Johnson passed along Samuel Sharp's opinion that a cataract "may be removed as soon as it is formed," thus saving "a long and uncomfortable delay." He faulted Langton for writing nothing about his mother, whose wisdom and goodness Johnson had praised in the year before (*Letters*, 1:172). Also, as usual, he asked to hear again from Langton, "wherever you are, or whatever you are doing, whether you wander or sit still plant trees or make Rusticks, play with your Sisters, or muse alone." In "return," Johnson reported Sheridan's success playing Cato and Richard III, and analyzed at length the strengths and especially the "very many" faults of this Irish actor and rhetorician, who was still Johnson's friend, and who the next year would for awhile became Boswell's "Socrates" (*Letters*, 1:192–94).[8]

DECEMBER 8, 1763: JOHNSON'S FIRST LETTER TO BOSWELL

In many ways—including the insistence that he would not gossip, not write about his health and activities, not write "only for the sake of writing"—Johnson's first letter to Boswell was strikingly different from any he had written Chambers and Langton. He warmly encouraged Chambers' success at law and applauded Langton's involvement with his family. But because Boswell—unlike Chambers and Langton but like Johnson himself—was prone to depression, Johnson was reluctant to embrace this friendship. Despite the intentions spelled out in his first two paragraphs, he had not responded to the "harassing disquiet" of Boswell's first letter, which he now claimed, "hardly admitted or deserved an answer," and he had waited two months before fortifying the "generous resolution" described in Boswell's second letter. So, Johnson felt guilty, especially since Boswell, unlike Langton, *had* imagined himself "forgotten or criminally neglected" and worried that Johnson had ceased to care. But Johnson was defensive rather than apologetic" (*Letters*, 1:237–8).

His long letter was generously helpful but guarded: a *Rambler* written expressly for Boswell. After explaining that Boswell's "dissipation of thought" was "nothing more than the Vacillation of a mind suspended between different motives and changing its direction as any motive gains or loses Strength" and urging him to "keep predominant any Wish for some particular excellence or attainment," Johnson offered a comic version of Boswell's "story": the tale of a gentleman who "thought that all appearance of diligence would deduct something from the reputation of Genius," and who was led by "long habits of idleness and pleasure" to conclude "that Nature had originally formed him incapable of rational employment" (*Letters*, 1:239–40).

Then Johnson roused Boswell to action with short, imperative sentences that seem addressed to himself as well as his new friend: "Resolve and keep your resolution. Chuse and pursue your choice." He encouragingly noted that the task would grow easier, but warned that the struggle would continue. "Depravity is not very easily overcome. Resolution will sometimes relax and diligence will sometimes be interrupted. But let no accidental surprize or deviation whether short or long dispose you to despondency." Johnson concluded with a sentence unlike any he had written Chambers or Langton, blending affection, exasperation, and earnest hope: "This my Dear Boswell is advice which perhaps has been often given you, and given you without effect, but this advice if you will not take from others you must take from your own reflections, if you propose to do the dutys of the station to which the Bounty of providence has called you" (*Letters*, 1:240).

Having indicated at the start that Boswell remained part of his everyday life—"I drank your health in the Room in which we sat last together, and . . . all your acquaintance continue to speak of you with their former kindness"—Johnson ended by commissioning Boswell to fill his journal "with many observations upon the country in which [he] reside[d]," to send "books in the Frisick Language" and to discover "how the poor are maintained in the Seven Provinces" (*Letters*, 1:237–40). But he waited twenty-five months before writing again; and only ten years later would he write Boswell as he had written Chambers and especially Langton from the start, combining advice and encouragement with news of mutual friends, reports on his health, and other personal reflections.

1766: CONNECTING WITH ALL THREE

Johnson wrote to none of the three in 1764 or 1765—years when he saw Chambers regularly in London, saw Langton in London and also at his family estate, but did not see Boswell. Then in 1766, a year he saw each of the three, he sent each two letters, several different from any he had earlier written.

Responding in January to what Boswell had written from Corsica, Johnson acknowledged having for more than two years been "a sparing an ungrateful correspondent," and reassured Boswell that "nothing ha[d] lessened" his "esteem or love," that he remained Boswell's "unaltered and I hope unalterable friend." He praised the "wise and noble curiosity" that led Boswell to the remote island "where perhaps no native of this Country ever was before." About to reconnect with Boswell after two and a half years, Johnson mainly reflected—for his young friend but also for himself—on the risks of meeting after a long separation: "No man loves to frustrate expectations which have been formed in his favour; and the pleasure which I promise myself from your journals and remarks is so great that perhaps no degree of attention or discernment will be sufficient to afford it" (*Letters*, 1:261).

Johnson also feared "we shall find it difficult to keep among us a mind which has been so long feasted with variety." But he urged Boswell to "Come home . . . and take your chance. I long to see you and to hear you, and hope that we shall not be so long separated again. . . . Let us try what esteem and kindness can effect" (*Letters*, 1:261–62).

Since Boswell's latest letter had mentioned his father's illness, Johnson in closing cited this additional reason for Boswell's speedy return: "The longer we live and the more we think, the higher value we learn to put on the friendship and tenderness of Parents" (*Letters*, 1:262). Though very different in tone from his earlier letter to Boswell, this, too, was unlike any Johnson had sent either Chambers or Langton.

If Boswell had surprised Johnson by traveling to Corsica instead of Spain, as Johnson had recommended, Langton in 1766 surprised Johnson by not writing. On March 8, soon after Boswell left London for Edinburgh, Johnson for the first time complained to Langton about *his* silence—his neglecting Johnson and all his other friends in London. Instead of scolding, however, Johnson tried to coax a response. "Since you will not inform us where you are, or how you live," he teased, "I know [not] whether you desire to know any thing of us." But Johnson kept writing, assuring Langton that he had not forgotten him. He reported that the Club, formed two years earlier with Langton as one of nine members, continued to meet, and later detailed which members were "constant" in attendance. After noting that Edmund Burke's speeches for repealing the Stamp act had "filled the town with wonder"—"Burke is a great man by Nature, and is expected soon to attain civil greatness "—Johnson added, "I am grown greater too," for his edition of Shakespeare had "maintained the newspapers" for weeks. "What is greater still," he added, only partly facetiously, "I have risen every morning since New years day at about eight," finally fulfilling a resolution he had made repeatedly since 1753. "When I was up I have indeed done but little," he confessed; "yet it is no slight advancement to obtain for so many hours more the consciousness of being." Having noted this achievement, which Boswell did not report having heard about during his brief time in London the previous month, Johnson added an intimate comment that seems unique to his correspondence with Langton:

"I wish you were in my new study. I am now writing the first letter in it. I think it looks very pretty about me" (*Letters*, 1:264–66).[9]

Two months later, responding late to Langton's news that his uncle Peregrine had died, Johnson wrote that he had loved Peregrine "at once by instinct and by reason," and had "seldom indulged more hope of any thing than of being able to improve our acquaintance to friendship." He wanted to "preserve . . . his example of Piety, and economy," especially how he managed to live "in plenty and elegance upon an income which to ma[n]y would appear indigent and to most, scanty." So, he pressed Langton to make enquiries, before the "little things which distinguish domestic character" were forgotten, and to write what he discovered, so it would be useful to others. Johnson also enquired about the rest of Langton's immediate family, and again reported that the "Club holds very well together." Then in closing Johnson again addressed Langton as a confessor and judge, noting that he had continued to rise "tolerably well," and that when awake now he "read more than [he] did. I hope something will yet come on it" (see *Letters*, 1:266–67). Only in 1783, nine years after Chambers had sailed to India, would Johnson write him like this (*Letters*, 4:125–27).

Johnson wrote this way to Boswell sooner, but not yet—certainly not on August 21, 1766, when a copy of Boswell's thesis finally got the depressed Johnson's attention. Instead of apologizing for not responding to Boswell's letters, Johnson reacted aggressively to being forced into activity: first asking why Boswell had dedicated the thesis to "a man whom I know you do not love,"[10] then "punish[ing]" him by noting errors in his Latin Dedication. Only then did he address Boswell's resolution to please his father, his reservations about practicing law, and his projected book about Corsica.

On the first two topics Johnson wrote as both a judge and a fellow resolver and melancholic, blending encouragement with hard-earned warnings. While "sincerely approv[ing]" Boswell's resolve to obey his father, he cautioned him not "to enchain your volatility by vows," which can "leave a thorn in your mind which you will perhaps never be able to extract or eject. Take this warning it is of great importance." He agreed that the study of the law was "copious and generous," and he highlighted the key gain for depressives like Boswell (and himself): "Security from those troublesome and wearysome discontents which are always obtruding themselves upon a mind vacant unemployed and undetermined"— an idea Johnson intensified later, noting "that all the importunities and perplexities of business are softness and Luxury compared with the incessant cravings of Vacancy and the unsatisfactory expedients of idleness." In cautioning Boswell, Johnson was also writing to himself, addressing needs Chambers or Langton seemed not to have had. Finally Johnson advised Boswell not to write about

Corsica—"Mind your own affairs and leave the Corsicans to theirs"—a curious request, since even writing the "History of Corsica," for which Boswell had "no materials which others have not or may not have," would help fill time not spent at law (*Letters*, 1:271–73). Also, six months earlier Johnson had advised Boswell to "give us as many anecdotes as you can."[11]

Having early in 1766 applauded Boswell's bold exploration of Corsica, though he later discouraged him from writing about the island, and having coaxed Langton to resume writing letters and called for a detailed account of his uncle, Johnson ended the year by criticizing Chambers's failure to write lectures and offered to help. In May, at age twenty-nine, Chambers had become the second Vinerian Professor of Law, a position that required him to deliver sixty lectures each year. But Chambers had let a whole term pass without delivering any, despite Johnson's month-long fall visit to help him plan a series that would not simply duplicate William Blackstone's. In the second of two notes asking Chambers for legal information, Johnson responded to what his young friend was experiencing. Instead of scolding, Johnson genially imagined Chambers "dining and supping, and lying in bed." Then he offered to assist. "Come up to town, and lock yourself up from all but me, and I doubt not but Lectures will be produced. You must not miss another term." "Come up and work, and I will try to help you," Johnson repeated two sentences later. "You asked me what amends you could make me," he added, alluding to an earlier conversation or perhaps an earlier letter, and simply replied, "You shall always be my friend" (*Letters*, 1:276–77).

This letter formally invited what became Johnson's major literary collaboration. Despite his diligence and learning, Chambers had "no heart," as Johnson later complained to Hester Thrale, (*Letters*, 1:320), meaning no "courage, spirit" (the sixth definition of "heart" in Johnson's *Dictionary*).[12] So, until all the lectures were completed in 1770, he required Johnson's regular assistance and encouragement. After years of living vicariously through Chambers's academic success, Johnson now directly shared his work.[13]

1767–1772: LETTERS TO CHAMBERS AND LANGTON

Because of these lectures, Johnson spent even more time than usual with Chambers in the years from 1767 through 1772, especially in 1767–1770, and each of his six letters to Chambers point ahead to their next time together. On January 22, 1767, for instance, shortly after they began working together, Johnson wrote: "I hope you are soon to come again, and go to the old business, for which I shall expect great abundance of materials and to sit down very close, and then there will be no danger, and needs to be no fear" (*Letters*, 1:278). Eight months later (October 6, 1767), writing from Lichfield, where his mother's former servant, Catherine Chambers, was dying, Johnson wrote Chambers that he did not "design" to stay at Oxford "longer than may consist with our necessary operations. Let me therefore know immediately how soon it will be necessary for us to be together. If I cannot immediately go with you to Oxford, you must be content to stay a little while in London." (Johnson put off responding to the "great enquiry" in Chambers's witty "Epistle from R. C. to Doctor Samuel Johnson on the Choice of Life" until they could discuss it—"and much more"—"at leisure," whether in Oxford or London.)[14]

On March 24, 1770, three months before Chambers, for the first time, delivered a complete set of lectures, Johnson wrote from London, "I see nothing that needs hinder me from going with you for a few days to Oxford, and therefore intend to do it" (*Letters*, 1:336). But a year later (April 6, 1771), when Chambers invited Johnson to Oxford for a friendly visit, Johnson comfortably postponed their connecting for a few weeks: "As You are to come hither so soon, why should we make journeys for that which will be had without them. . . . We can live together in town, and dine in chambers or at the mitre, and do as well as at New inn hall. . . . Come hither as soon as You can" (*Letters*, 1:358).

The following year (April 11, 1772), when a "kind letter" from Chambers excited Johnson's "desire of [Chambers's] company," a "little business"—the revision of the *Dictionary*—put it "out of [Johnson's] power to gratify [him]self without more inconvenience than [Chambers] desire[d] [him] to incur." Since Chambers would not soon be in London, "We must . . . be content for some time to live apart." "In the meantime," Johnson added, "you need not forget me. I shall be glad to hear any good of my old friends at University College, or any other house" (*Letters*, 1:390). Eight months later, noting an announcement that Chambers had just begun another series of lectures, Johnson wrote from Lichfield that he "would come through Oxford" the following week, and asked Chambers please "to order beds" for himself and his servant (*Letters*, 1:413).

Johnson saw Langton less regularly than Chambers from 1767 to 1772, especially after Langton's marriage in May 1770. Four of Johnson's six letters to Langton seek to arrange contact, or explain why connecting was impossible. On October 10, 1767, four days after writing Chambers about meeting in Oxford or London for their "necessary operations," Johnson regretted his "long stay in the country" while Langton was in London, and hoped his friend would "not leave the town before [his] return" (*Letters*, 1:288). Three years later (October 24, 1770)—years during which he and Langton had no trouble connecting—Johnson reported being free to visit Langton and his new wife, "if Lady Rothes shall be pleased to honour me with her commands" (*Letters*, 1:352). The following August, however, Johnson wrote that since an earlier letter from Langton had mentioned his "design of visiting Scotland," he had put his "Journey to Langton out of [his] thoughts," and now—his "summer wanderings . . . over"—he was engaged "in a very great work the revision of [his] Dictionary, from which [he knew] not at present how to get loose." Still he highly valued "the honour of [Lady Rothes's] invitation, which it [was his] purpose to obey as soon as [he was] disengaged" (*Letters*, 1:381–82). Eight months later (April 13, 1772), Johnson responded to Langton's news that he was in town by offering to "pass wednesday Evening" with him "at whatever place he shall appoint" (*Letters*, 1:391).

Johnson also continued to give Langton news of "Our club." In October 1770, he described how Oliver Goldsmith "has been at Paris with the Hornecks, not very delightfully to either side," how Anthony Chamier has also returned from France, and how Edmund Burke's wife Jane was "quite well" after a long illness; and the following March he told of Thomas Percy's "long Ballad in many *Fits*" (*The Hermit of Workworth*), and of Goldsmith's traveling to Bath with Lord Clare (*Letters*, 1:352, 356). In March 1771, Johnson also wrote at length about the eventual publication of *Thoughts on the Falkland Islands*, and Lord North's stopping the sale ("His reasons I do not distinctly know you may try to find them in the perusal." [*Letters*, 1:356]). In August 1771, Johnson asked Langton to let him know of "any errors or omissions" in the *Dictionary*, which he was revising; he also responded sympathetically to news of Lady Rothes's earlier miscarriage, and hoped "to hear often of her Ladyship and every day better news and better, till I hear that you have both the happiness, which to both is very sincerely wished, by, Sir, your most affectionate and most humble servant, SAM. JOHNSON" (*Letters*, 1:382). The following spring, he congratulated Langton and his wife on the birth of their first child, George, and "hope[d] you will all be many years happy together." But in the same letter he reported that Langton's sister Elizabeth, who thought she was dying, had the day before asked Johnson to "talk . . . on such subjects as suit her condition," and had asked her Aunt "to receive the Sacrament with her" (*Letters*, 1:387).

Even when Johnson could not see Chambers and Langton, his letters make clear that long before 1772 both had become what Johnson would later call "friends of easy conversation and familiar confidence" (*Letters*, 4:126). Boswell eventually became such a friend. But at the start of this period (1767–1772), during which he made only three visits to London, Boswell's status was far different.

1768–1772: LETTERS TO BOSWELL

Three of Johnson's six letters to Boswell during these years, like his first letter in 1766, were written as if they were to reconnect: two after long periods when Johnson had wholly failed to write, the third nine months after Johnson's most recent letter. All three of these letters, especially the first two, were different from Johnson's earlier letters to Boswell, or his letters to Chambers, Langton, or anyone else. Johnson's long silences were also unusual, especially the first, since Boswell wrote frequently starting in November 1766, and in 1767 carefully arranged to have both Tom Davies and Baretti nudge Johnson to respond.[15] In 1771–1772, however, Johnson began to write more regularly, and inched toward writing Boswell as he usually wrote Langton, which he finally did on February 24, 1773.

Since Johnson had urged abandoning the Corsica project, Boswell's writing the book became an act of defiance, especially after he decided to include—without permission—much of the letter where Johnson promised his "unaltered and . . . unalterable" friendship. A month after he received his copy in mid-February 1768, along with news that Boswell would soon be in London, Johnson anticipated Boswell's arrival, and hinted his response to the book, in a short but remarkably enthusiastic and affectionate letter, which Boswell received only after he had reconnected with Johnson in Oxford.

While acknowledging his failure to write for "a long time . . . without knowing very well why," Johnson playfully cited Boswell's having published his earlier letter as a reason to cease writing, "for who would write to men who publish the letters of their friends without their leave? Yet I write to you in spite of my caution," he continued, "to tell you that I shall be glad to see you, and that I wish you would empty your head of Corsica, which I think has filled it rather too long. But, at all events, I shall be glad, very glad to see you." The repetition of "glad . . . glad, very glad" shows an eagerness to reconnect. Boswell clearly was special. Instead of initially addressing Boswell as "Dear Sir," as in his previous three letters—and as in all those he had sent Chambers, and most of those to Langton—Johnson addressed the young author as "My dear Boswell." Then in closing, instead of signing off as "your most affectionate servant" (December 8, 1763, *Letters*, 1:240), or "Your affectionate humble Servant" (January 14, 1766, *Letters*, 1:262), or "Your most humble servant" (August 21, 1766, *Letters*, 1:273), Johnson simply wrote, "Yours affectionately" (*Letters*, 1:298).

Johnson next wrote Boswell on September 9, 1769, fifteen months after Boswell had returned to Edinburgh and just days after Johnson—in Brighton with the Thrales—heard from Boswell that he had come to London to hear Johnson's advice about his impending marriage. Johnson's first sentence—"Why do you charge me with unkindness?"—indicates that Boswell had faulted Johnson's behavior. Whether Boswell was upset because Johnson as usual had failed to respond to his letters, or because—as in 1768—he was not in London as Boswell had expected, his non-specific complaint prompted Johnson to write a long paragraph praising *An Account of Corsica,* which he had aggressively failed to discuss in Oxford where he first saw Boswell in 1768, though he had applauded it five weeks later when he returned to London.[16] Johnson's comments were specific and emphatic. "Your History is like other histories but your journal is in a very high degree curious and delight[t]ful . . . . You express images which operated strongly upon yourself and you have impressed them with great force upon your readers. I know not whether I could name any narrative by which curiosity is better excited or better gratified" (*Letters*, 1:329). Johnson had praised Langton's travel narratives and Chambers's verses, and had probably praised Chambers's lectures, but never this strongly.

Then Johnson wrote how "glad" he was that Boswell was about to be married, while making clear that he still regarded this young friend as a work in process. "What I can contribute to your happiness I should be very unwilling to withhold for I have always loved and valued you and shall love you and value you still more as you become more regular and useful effects which a happy Marriage will hardly fail to produce." (Johnson's letters to Chambers or Langton never hinted that either needed to be "more regular and useful.") But in contrast to 1766 and 1768, Johnson was not eager to reconnect. He cautioned that he would perhaps stay "a fortnight longer" in Brighton, and teasingly added, "a fortnight is a long time to a lover absent from his Mistress. Would a fortnight ever have an end?" (*Letters*, 1:328–29).

Two months later (November 9), a day before Boswell was finally about to return home to his fiancé, Johnson again seemed willing not to have a final meeting with Boswell, whom he had seen frequently between September 28 and October 31, but not afterwards. Responding to Boswell's request that he come to town from Streatham, the Thrales' estate near London, to see him off, Johnson somewhat formally wrote, "Upon balancing the inconveniencies of both parties, I find it will less incommode you to spend your night here, than me to come to town. I wish to see you, and am ordered by the lady of this house to invite you hither." Then since this would be the last note before Boswell's marriage, Johnson once again, "with great sincerity . . . wish[ed him] happiness" (*Letters*, 1:330–31).

When Johnson next wrote to Boswell (June 20, 1771), he for the first time felt no guilt at not having written. For two months earlier, when Boswell finally wrote Johnson fifteen months after his marriage, he had accepted Johnson's claim that a failure to write did not indicate a diminution of love (*Life*, 2:139–40).

Delighted that Boswell now forgave what his anxious letters had regularly complained about, and having experienced the only sustained period in eight years when he did not owe Boswell a letter, Johnson wrote with more ease than usual, and more openly and comfortably identified with this young friend.

"Much pleased" with Boswell's account of his life since his marriage, Johnson "sincerely hope[d], that between publick business, improving studies, and domestick pleasures, neither melancholy nor caprice will find any place for entrance." He no longer imagined Boswell threatened by "the incessant cravings of Vacancy, and the unsatisfactory expedients of idleness," as he had five years earlier. But "melancholy" and "caprice" remained dangers for Boswell, as they were for Johnson but never for Chambers or Langton. "Our minds cannot be empty; and evil will break in upon them, if they are not pre-occupied by good." Johnson urged Boswell—and himself—to "mind [his] studies, mind [his] business, make [his] lady happy, and be a good Christian." Then in response to Boswell's mention of their long-nurtured plan to travel to the Hebrides, Johnson anticipated a shared adventure much richer than dining with Chambers either "in chambers or at the Mitre," much more strenuous and heroic than "hear[ing] the ocean roar or see[ing] the stars twinkle, in the company of" Bennet Langton and his father. "If we perform our duty, we shall be safe and steady . . . whether we climb the Highlands, or are tost among the Hebrides; and I hope the time will come when we may try our powers both with cliffs and water" (*Letters*, 1:362–63).

Responding to Boswell's question about a mutual friend, Patrick Murray, fifth Baron Elibank, Johnson even edged toward confession: "I see but little of Lord Elibank, I know not why; perhaps by my own fault." And he closed this relaxed letter by volunteering for the first time the sort of personal information he had earlier declared off-limits: "I am this day going into Staffordshire and Derbyshire for six weeks" (*Letters*, 1:328–29). Johnson still wrote nothing about his health, however, as he regularly did in his letters to Chambers and Langton.[17] But his health featured prominently in each of his next three letters to Boswell.

On March 15, 1772, in answer to Boswell's hope that they might fix a date for their Hebrides trip, Johnson mentioned that his health "grows better, yet I am not fully recovered. I believe it is held, that men do not recover very fast after three-score." So, while he had "not given up the western voyage," he and Boswell should "try to make each other happy when we meet, and not refer our pleasure to distant times or distant places" (*Letters*, 1:389).

Earlier in the letter, because Boswell had reported he would soon be in London to defend a client whose victory in the Scottish Court of Session was being appealed to the House of Lords, Johnson reported being "very glad" that Boswell would soon be in town, and "still more glad" he was coming as a lawyer, since "nothing is more likely to make your life pass happily away, than that consciousness of your own value, which eminence in your profession will certainly confer." Because Boswell had asked for Johnson's assistance—"It is a general question and not a point of particular law"—Johnson assured him he would "give . . . any collateral help" he could.[18] But he curiously added, "[m]y kindness for you has neither the merit of singular virtue, nor the reproach of a singular prejudice. Whether to love you be right or wrong, I have many of my side: Mrs. Thrale loves you, and Mrs. Williams loves you, and what would have inclined me to love you, if I had been neutral before, you are a great favourite of Dr. [James] Beattie" (*Letters*, 1:388), the Scottish philosopher who had come to London the previous summer with a letter of introduction from Boswell. Asking whether loving Boswell was "right or wrong" seems odd after all Johnson had earlier written about his love and esteem. But probably his offer to help with the appeal recalled his much more extensive collaboration with Chambers, and his talk with Chambers about Boswell, who in 1768 had met Chambers in Oxford. In fact, a month later, on the evening Johnson had set aside for work on Boswell's brief, he wrote Chambers that he expected soon "to hear [Boswell] come in, with his noisy benevolence" (*Letters*, 1:390).

On August 31, 1772, about the time Boswell expected Johnson to arrive in Edinburgh for the long-anticipated trip through the Highlands to the Hebrides, Johnson wrote that "the course of things"—his still-unfinished revision of the *Dictionary*—made his coming impossible, then added that "such has been . . . the state of my body, that it would not well have seconded my inclination. My body, I think, grows better, and I refer my hopes to another year; for I am very sincere in my design to pay the visit and take the ramble." Johnson also fully identified with the appeal for which he had dictated a brief, writing first, "I am glad if you got credit by *your* cause," and continuing, "and am yet of opinion, that *our* cause was good, and that the determination ought to have been in your favour." Also knowing that Boswell would be disappointed, and probably worried that "melancholy" or "caprice" might seize control, Johnson suggested that he use the months set aside for their trip exploring "the antiquities of the feudal establishment" in Scotland: "Do not forget a design so worthy of a scholar who studies the laws of his country, and of a gentleman who may naturally be curious to know the condition of his own ancestors" (*Letters*, 1:393–94; emphasis mine).

FEBRUARY 20, 1773: RECONNECTING WITH BOSWELL

On February 20, 1773, two months after Boswell finally replied to Johnson's postponing the Hebrides trip, Johnson wrote Boswell a fuller, more relaxed letter than any he had previously sent, resembling those he had sent Langton from the start. "Glad to find [him]self not forgotten," Johnson thanked Boswell for "the elegant Pindar" he had sent (as requested), and the "testimonies of affection" he had passed along from Beattie and others in Scotland. He expressed his regret that the Court of Session had rejected Boswell's arguments concerning *vicious intromission*," for which Johnson had written a supporting brief, but his delight that Boswell had "gained reputation even by [his] defeat." He reported that the new edition of his "great Dictionary" had been published: "Some superfluities I have expunged, and some faults I have corrected, and here and there have scattered a remark; but the main fabric of the work remains as it was." He told how Baretti and Davies, both friends of Boswell, "have had a furious quarrel; a quarrel, I think, irreconcileable"; and he described at length Goldsmith's new comedy, in "which a lover is made to mistake his future father-in-law's house for an inn. . . . The dialogue is quick and gay, and the incidents are so prepared as not to seem improbable." Also for the first time Johnson wrote in detail about his health, which "in general seems to improve," though for weeks he had been "troubled . . . with a vexatious catarrh": "I have not found any great effects from bleeding and physick; and am afraid that I must expect help from brighter days and softer air" (*Letters*, 2:8–10).

Johnson still wrote as a mentor, however. Having read or heard about Boswell's attendance at a masquerade in Edinburgh, he somewhat critically noted that he "would not have been one of the *first* masquers in a country where no masquerade had ever been before." He also encouraged his young friend to keep his father's "precept in [his] mind, and endeavour to consolidate in [his] mind a firm and regular system of law, instead of picking up occasional fragments." In addition, Johnson remained somewhat detached. Though both his recent letters had connected his health with the Hebrides trip, he curiously wrote nothing here about this ambitious ramble. Nor did he wonder whether Boswell might visit London in time to see Goldsmith's new play. Instead he closed by asking Boswell to "Write to me now and then, and whenever any good befalls you make haste to let me know if it, for no one will rejoice at it more than, dear Sir, Your most humble servant, SAM. JOHNSON" (*Letters*, 2:43). Johnson anticipated keeping in touch through letters, as earlier he had wholly failed to do. But he did not seem eager for more contact.

Clearly Johnson did not anticipate that Boswell would soon come to London for a five-week visit, during which Johnson would allow him to be with him throughout his usually private Good Friday and would invite him to Easter dinner, would secure his election to the still-exclusive Club, and would commit once again to the Hebrides adventure. Nor did Johnson imagine that in August, as he

TABLE 1. Samuel Johnson's Letters to Selected Correspondents

Year	Robert Chambers (1737–1803)	Bennet Langton (1737–1801)	James Boswell (1740–1795)	Hester Thrale (1741–1821)
1754	1			
1755	2	1		
1756	1			
1757				
1758	3	2		
1759		1		
1760	2	1		
1761				
1762	1			
1763	1		1	
1764				
1765				1
1766	2	2	2	
1767	2	1		4
1768			1	12
1769			2	5
1770	1	1		9
1771	1	2	1	15
1772	2	2	2	15
1773	4		7	38
1774	1	1	11	2
1775		2	11	47
1776		1	14	19
1777		3	13	33
1778		2	4	7
1779	1		6	26
1780			3	29
1781		1	1	22
1782		1	7	34
1783	2	3	4	39
1784		6	10	16
TOTAL	27	33	100	373

SOURCE: *The Letters of Samuel Johnson*, ed. Bruce Redford, 5 vols. (Princeton, NJ: Princeton University Press, 1992–1994).

was about to head to Edinburgh, instead of wondering whether loving Boswell was "right or wrong," he would write, "think only when you see me, that you see a man who loves you, and is proud and glad that you love him" (*Letters*, 2:43). Nor could Johnson have guessed how twelve weeks of traveling with Boswell and regularly sharing travel journals would transform their friendship, after which his trickle of letters to Boswell—only nine in the first ten years—would for several years become a steady stream.[19]

Johnson's February 1773 letter to Boswell, so different in key ways from those he had sent before, suggests he was ready for these changes. But his earlier letters to Boswell, especially when compared with those he wrote Chambers and Langton, suggest that his future letters would probably not be as untroubled and radically comfortable as those to these others had been or would perhaps continue to be. However, a detailed comparison of what Johnson wrote to each of these no-longer-young friends from 1773 through 1784—focusing on how he delighted in their successes, sympathized with their disappointments and losses, worried whether each was accomplishing all that he might, and occasionally feared having been forgotten—must wait for another article.

NOTES

1. Samuel Johnson, March 20, 1782, in *The Letters of Samuel Johnson*, ed. Bruce Redford (Princeton, NJ: Princeton University Press, 1992–1994), 4:22–23 (hereafter cited *Letters*, by volume:page).
2. John B. Radner, *Johnson and Boswell: A Biography of Friendship* (New Haven, CT: Yale University Press, 2012), 27–30.
3. James Boswell, *The Private Papers of James Boswell from Malahide Castle in the Collection of Lt.-Colonel Ralph Heyward Isham*, ed. Geoffrey Scott and Frederick A. Pottle (Privately printed, 1928–1934), 1:70, 84, 128–29; Boswell, *London Journal 1762–1763*, ed. Gordon Turnbull (New York: Penguin, 2010), 250–51, 271, 287, 316–17; and *Life*, 1:472.
4. *Catalogue of the Private Papers of James Boswell at Yale University*, ed. Marion S. Pottle et al. (Edinburgh: Edinburgh University Press, 1993), 2:403–4, C72. While in Venice, Boswell saw the long, comfortable letters Johnson had written Giuseppe Baretti in 1761–1762, filled with news of mutual friends, self-deprecating comments on his own activities, and earnest, uncondescending advice about marriage (*Letters*, 1:196–201, 205–7).
5. Boswell, *London Journal*, ed. Turnbull, 393. For Johnson and Robert Chambers, see Thomas M. Curley, *Sir Robert Chambers: Law, Literature, and Empire in the Age of Johnson* (Madison, WI: University of Wisconsin Press, 1998), 1:19–127. For Johnson and Bennet Langton, see James Boswell, *The Correspondence of James Boswell with Certain Members of the Club*, ed. Charles N. Fifer (New York: McGraw-Hill, 1976), lii–lxxii; and Lyle Larsen, "Dr. Johnson's Friend, the Worthy Bennet Langton," *Age of Johnson* 20 (2010): 145–72.
6. Johnson's deletions and additions as he started this letter are indicated in *Letters*, 1:105–7nn3–5.
7. Samuel Johnson, *Diaries, Prayers, and Annals*, ed. Edward L. McAdam Jr. et al. (New Haven, CT: Yale University Press, 1958), 67.

8. Boswell identified "Rusticks" as "Essays . . . written about this time by Mr. Langton, but not published" (*Life*, 1:358n1). For Thomas Sheridan as Boswell's "Socrates," see James Boswell, *The General Correspondence of James Boswell, 1757–1763*, ed. David Hankins and James J. Caudle (Edinburgh: Edinburgh University Press, 2006), 111.
9. For Johnson's recommendation of Spain, see Boswell, *London Journal*, ed. Turnbull, 251, 293–94. For his resolutions to rise early, see Johnson, *Diaries*, 50, 54, 56, 71, 74, 78, 92, and 95. For Boswell's conversations with Johnson in February 1766, see his *Boswell on the Grand Tour: Italy, Corsica, and France, 1765–1766*, ed. Frank Brady and Frederick A. Pottle (New York: McGraw-Hill, 1955), 281–87, 295–97.
10. Boswell dedicated his thesis to John Stuart, Lord Mountstuart, the eldest son of the Earl of Bute, who had traveled with Boswell in Italy and was a possible future patron.
11. Boswell, *Grand Tour*, 283; see also Radner, *Johnson and Boswell*, 51–52.
12. "Heart" s.v. in Samuel Johnson, *A Dictionary of the English Language* (London, 1755), in 2 vols. (hereafter cited *Dictionary*, by "word").
13. See Curley, *Sir Robert Chambers*, 43–187.
14. *Letters*, 1:287–88. For Chambers' poem and the job-offer that may have prompted it, see Curley, *Sir Robert Chambers*, 74–75.
15. See Radner, *Johnson and Boswell*, 53–55. On November 14, 1768, Johnson made a note "To write . . . Boswell" (*Diaries*, 120).
16. James Boswell, *Boswell in Search of a Wife, 1766–1769*, ed. Frank Brady and Frederick A. Pottle (New York: McGraw-Hill, 1956), 146–49, 165–66.
17. "My Friends tell me that I am pretty well, and I hope you are well too," Johnson had written Chambers in April 1771 (*Letters*, 1:358), having a year earlier reported being "out of order with the rheumatism," which, though "painful," is "an evil much more easily born than my former complaints" (*Letters*, 1:336)—including his "old melancholy," which he reported in 1767, had "laid hold upon [him] to a degree sometimes not easily supportable" (*Letters*, 1:287). In October 1770 he had written Langton, who in 1766 had witnessed Johnson's paralyzing depression, which Boswell learned about only in 1784 (*Boswell: The Applause of the Jury, 1782–1785*, ed. Irma S. Lustig and Frederick A. Pottle [New York: McGraw-Hill, 1981], 246), "I am, for me, not amiss. I believe that I can set acorns, and hope to mend by breath by walking about" (*Letters*, 1:351–52).
18. James Boswell, *Boswell for the Defence, 1769–1774*, ed. William K. Wimsatt Jr. and Frederick A. Pottle (New York: McGraw-Hill, 1959), 26.
19. For the transformative impact of the Hebrides trip, see Radner, *Johnson and Boswell*, 113–48. Table 1 of "Johnson's Letters to Selected Correspondents" shows this increase in letters to Boswell, but also notes how much more often he wrote to Hester Thrale during these years, sustaining their conversation whenever they were not together.

2

JAMES ELPHINSTON AND SAMUEL JOHNSON

Contact, Irritations, and an
"Argonautic" Letter

CHRISTINE JACKSON-HOLZBERG

IN EARLY MAY 1787, the three-man crew of a French fishing boat came upon a small object floating in the sea some five or six nautical miles off the Normandy coast. The find turned out to be a well-corked bottle, its contents a letter written in English to an address in Marylebone, London. Handed over, as required by law, to the nearest admiralty office (in this case at Bayeux), the fishermen's catch became a matter of record memorable not only for the hydrographic conclusions drawn from it and published in 1788 by the French writer and scientist Jacques-Henri Bernardin de Saint-Pierre, but also for some correspondence which arose more immediately from efforts at the Bayeux admiralty to ensure that the letter reached its addressee, a Mrs. Elphinston. Eighteen months on, that exchange formed the basis of a pamphlet assembled by her husband, which also included the text, in English and in French, of a letter he himself had received some thirty-eight years previously from Samuel Johnson. The husband in question was James Elphinston, the teacher, translator, poet, educationalist, grammarian, and committed spelling reformer whose personal relations with Johnson spanned a period of more than three decades. While their friendship was never an especially close one, with the frequency and intensity of contact between them varying over the years, it remains discernible now at a number of points in Boswell's *Life of Johnson* and is also clearly traceable among the 1,700 and more pages which Elphinston himself edited and published in late 1791 as *Forty Years' Correspondence Between Geniusses ov Boath Sexes, and James Elphinston*.[1] The original texts were rendered to conform to the somewhat taxing system of orthography Elphinston himself had devised years previously, but perseverance uncovers in these volumes, over and above their four letters from Johnson and five addressed to him, scattered references and casual remarks which often augment or supplement the minutiae of Johnson's biography already familiar from other sources. In some cases, moreover,

[31]

such passages afford glimpses of what was not always an entirely harmonious friendship, yet one to a certain extent typical of both. The insights given occasionally illustrate, for example, Sir Joshua Reynolds's observation that, in arguments, Johnson "did not trouble himself much with circumlo[cu]tion, but opposed his antagonist['s] *opinion in an abrupt manner that was offensive to those* [who] *were not used to his manner*; he fought with all sorts of wheapons; . . . if all faild, with rudeness overbearing." and Elphinston's own letters, as also his writings, suggest that he, like Johnson, was someone who "thought it necessary never to be worsted in argument."[2]

The presence of Elphinston within the wider circle of company drawn to and ever sought by Johnson—of a man, that is, whose own literary aspirations and scholarly theories often met with scathing ridicule from contemporary critics and whom even a loyal friend characterized as "a Quixote"[3]—seems deserving of closer attention, not least because this particular friendship was variously linked to the circulation and reception of writings penned by Johnson.

FIRST CONTACT, CONSOLATION, AND THE *RAMBLER*

The earliest clear sign for us that the two men were acquainted is Johnson's letter to Elphinston of April 20, 1749,[4] sent from London to the other's home in Edinburgh.[5] This was written in reply to one which Johnson had "long" since received from Elphinston, and in it he observed, from his "recluse kind of Life," "how sensible I am of the kindness you have always expressed to me, and how much I desire the cultivation of that Benevolence which perhaps nothing but the distance between us has hindred from ripening before this time into Friendship."[6] There had, it seems, been more than one previous opportunity for Elphinston to express "kindness," and it is possible that the advertisements in late March and April 1747 announcing Johnson's work on an "English Dictionary" prompted the language enthusiast in the north to introduce himself by letter.[7] There existed, however, a more obvious connection, one which may even have facilitated their meeting in person during a visit by Elphinston to London in early 1748. His sister Margaret lived there, married since 1738 to the London-based Scottish printer William Strahan, and her brother is known to have been staying at the couple's home in February 1748.[8] Strahan—a man later numbered among Johnson's "most intimate friends"[9]—certainly knew the latter socially by September 1750, and his professional connection with Johnson was then already long established.[10]

Elphinston hoped in 1748 to stay more permanently in London, but, called home to care for his ailing mother, he returned to teaching in Edinburgh. In

May 1750, he became the driving force behind the publishing there of the twice-weekly *Rambler* essays—the Scottish issues began to appear on or immediately before June 1—and of the first eight-volume Edinburgh edition (1750–1752).[11] He stated in his advertisement for the individual issues that he, the "Scottish Editor," had "prevailed" upon the author of the originals "to renew in *Scotland* his *Rambles* at half the *London* price."[12] Any prevailing required can only have taken place in a letter or letters now lost, and this possible surge in communication, together with Elphinston's attested "zeal" regarding the *Rambler*, can be seen as persistent efforts to overcome the obstacle of "distance" twice noted by Johnson himself (*Letters*, 1:42, 57). Such attentions were rewarded when, some two weeks after the death on September 10, 1750 of Elphinston's mother, Johnson sent him a letter of condolence dated September 25, written after he had read "with tears" the accounts sent to Margaret Strahan by her brother.[13]

The letter, one that is numbered by Bruce Redford among Johnson's "earlier messages of consolation . . . which resemble quasi-public homilies of a sententious amplitude" (*Letters*, 1:xi), nevertheless—or for that very reason—left Elphinston, as he described in his reply of October 4, "filled . . . widh a transpoart ov grattitude and admiracion, hwich stil almoast totally deprives me ov dhe power ov speaking it. Dhe first sentiment I waz capabel ov expressing, waz a rapture ov thankfoolnes to' dhe grait Creator . . . dhat stil such a frend remained . . . and dhen, dhat I, hoo can plead so small a claim, . . . shood pozes such a share in a frendship, hwich orrators hav preached, poets hav painted, and princes hav wished in vain!"[14]

He had already shown Johnson's letter to friends, and those were insistent that it be printed in the *Scots Magazine* "for dhe bennefit ov my contry" and for "dhe consolacion it might convey to' thouzands, hoo cannot boast such a correspondent." Persuaded by "certain scrupels" to refuse this demand (but hinting too that those were simply a matter of having the "Authors leve"), Elphinston now hoped to "prevail widh yoo, Sir, to' favor dhe pubblic widh an Essay, comprizing dhe principal thaughts ov dhe letter, and purposely adapted to' stil more extensive utillity" (*FYC*, 1:33). Thirty-nine years later, he would claim that Johnson had both granted permission to publish his letter and been prevailed upon "to' dilate dhe sollemn subject into' various eddifying papers subsequent to' dhe fiftieth [*Rambler*]."[15] Grief and consolation were indeed discussed by Johnson in two of the *Ramblers* (52 and 54), but the focus there bears little resemblance to that of the letter which Elphinston received, and the two essays (September 15 and 22, 1750) in fact predate that; the letter of condolence, moreover, would not appear in the *Scots Magazine* (or elsewhere) until 1785.[16] If Johnson did authorize anything, then probably only posthumous publishing of his text. Whatever the truth of the matter, the letter was to occupy a special place in Elphinston's correspondence, an episode to which we shall return below.

The Scot's editorial work on the *Rambler* in its collected form evidently included some idiosyncratic suggestions which his zeal, a perceived growing familiarity between himself and Johnson,[17] or perhaps simply his pronounced inner corrector, emboldened him to make. Writing to a friend on November 9, 1791, Elphinston would reject Johnson's view of modern European languages as "mere *barbarous degenneracions*" (*FYC*, 7:81)[18] and argue that, if anything, it was the widespread and needless use of certain elements that made English "*barbarous*" in the first place—"transplants . . . almoast transplants . . . mistaken impoarts . . . random-formatives," not to mention "such a sesquipedalian, az dhe yet les warranted *transcendental*": "Such a set I wonce clustered in a letter to' Jonson, hwile I waz pubblishing hiz *Rambler* at Eddinburrough; and ov hwich, even in my fondest Jonsonianism, I did wish to' unbarbarize hiz classical diccion. Nay, my boldnes went so far az to' ask him, hweddher he ment such terms for dhe lerned onely, or for dhe ladies also. Dhis question, probably imputed to' yoothfool pettulance, waz (I remember) dhe singuel passage ov my epistel, dhat obtained no anser" (*FYC*, 7:82).[19]

Johnson proved more receptive when it came to his Greek and Latin *Rambler* mottoes and other quotations, specifically to the translations provided by Elphinston at the back of the first six volumes which, with two further, comprised the first and second Edinburgh editions. The overlapping chronology of the Edinburgh and London collected *Ramblers* is complex and compounded in this context by Elphinston's decision in 1752 to show in his final two volumes (*Ramblers* 159–208) the translations already chosen for those essays by Johnson himself, none of which came from his Edinburgh editor. Thankfully, the details have been documented by David Fleeman, and Johnson's actual use of Elphinston's versions has been examined elsewhere,[20] so that I can confine myself here to some simple statistics. Of the 184 translations which Johnson could have borrowed for *Ramblers* 1–158, only forty were taken from the Edinburgh texts; thirty-six of those were duly attributed to Elphinston, two were not (45 and 67), one (19) was shown as the work of Francis Lewis alone although two of the six verses were taken from Elphinston, and one, a rendering of the title-page motto, very soon disappeared from the London editions. In all, twenty-three (counting the title page) were shown unchanged apart from minor variations in punctuation or spelling, while Johnson made alterations to the wording of the other thirteen—in one case (130) drastically so—but still ascribed them to Elphinston. In very approximate terms: Johnson used less than one-quarter of Elphinston's translations and, of the total Edinburgh offerings, liked only one-eighth enough to let them stand.

The "*ingenious Mr.* James Elphinstone"[21]—himself not above at least one modification of Johnson's original text[22]—noted somewhat puzzlingly in 1791 that he had "he translated not anoddher motto, after he understood dhat dhe Author had sold dhe propperty" (*FYC*, 1:35). Either unaware of or impervious to Johnson's obvious reservations regarding his translations,[23] he did finish the editions he had begun, and we also find him using the *Rambler* to test the skills of the students attending his French classes during the early 1750s. One John Wilson, for example, managed to translate *Rambler* 134 into French on October 12, 1751, in only the second month of his weekly four hours.[24] The appearance of the final *Rambler* essay on March 14, 1752 was, wrote Elphinston to Johnson on March 26, mourned by "all dhe sensibel and dhe wordhy ov dhis kingdom," while congratulations were also in order because the author's "labors hav ended az dhey began" (*FYC*, 1:37).

That same letter was also a response to the news which had reached Elphinston one day previously through Margaret Strahan, who informed him that Johnson's wife had died on March 17: "Yoor tender frendship and exalted genius flew unasked to' my aid, hwen I lost my (dhen) nearest and dearest relacion: oh! dhat I cood now minnister equal comfort to' yoo, bereft ov a nearer and dearer" (*FYC*, 1:36). Elphinston, married himself since April 1751, stressed that he could thus all the more "partiscipate yoor sorrow" (*FYC*, 1:36) but observed that it would be "az bold az unnessessary for me to' offer anny hints edher ov consolacion or counsel to' a sufferer, hoo haz so powerfoolly taught dhe pubblic in genneral, and me in particcular, to' indulge Nature widhin dhe limmits ov Rezon, and to' exalt dhe Man into' dhe Christian" (*FYC*, 1:37). The passage which then follows suggests that Johnson's "moddesty" had "prompted" his grief "to'seek dhe aid it uzed to convey," or that Elphinston had understood something written by his sister to indicate such a need or even request. The best answer he could offer, however, was to point to the "linniments" offered in Johnson's very own "pubblic" and "private productions" (*FYC*, 1:37).

CLOSER CONTACT, SHARED ACQUAINTANCES

The hopes expressed by Johnson in early 1752 that he and his Scottish editor in Edinburgh might one day "have a more ready way of pouring out our hearts" (*Letters*, 1:57)[25] became a very real possibility when, in 1753, Elphinston and his wife Clementina moved to London. They opened an academy for boarders in their Brompton house "*One Mile West from Hyde-Park Corner*"[26] and would run that until June 1776 (but moving in January 1760 to Kensington).[27] The correspondence later selected by Elphinston for publication includes many letters to and from former pupils, painting what is probably an idealized picture of life at his academy,[28] but also documenting for us Johnson's interest in the school he openly supported in 1756 with a footnote on the very first page of his fourth *Rambler* edition, where readers were told that the man to whom he was "indebted for many elegant translations of the mottos . . . now keeps an academy for young gentlemen, at Brompton."

One of the earliest pupils was placed there by his father William Drummond, the Edinburgh bookseller and Jacobite known personally to Johnson.[29] The boy, Alexander-Munro Drummond, and his brother James who followed on in the 1760s, were given "dhe onnor . . . ov peculiar countenance" by Johnson: "He exhorted parentally dear *Jem* (at parting) nevver to' looz dhe scollar, in dhe merchant. He enjoined him to' remember, dhat a litterate merchant, not onely made a dubbel figgure in commerce; but had evvery advantage ov a scollar, widhout dhe envy, too often attending dhe carracter."[30] Both Elphinston and Johnson took an active interest in the further education of Alexander and urged his father, albeit unsuccessfully, to allow "Sandy" to study medicine in Edinburgh rather than be apprenticed to a physician in Cupar (Fife).[31] On December 28, 1758, two weeks after reaching the "disagreabel" village and beginning his training, Alexander requested of Elphinston that he send copies of "Mr. *Jonsons* propozals for pubblishing Shakspear . . . for I hav som prospect ov guetting Subscribers" (*FYC*, 1:64–65). The "*Verses, by* Pupils" shown in *FYC*, 5:84–100 include his translation of Horace, *Odes*, 1.22—"a version, hwich Dr. *Sammuel Jonson* preferred to' hiz own" (*FYC*, 5:85)—and his brother James's 1768 poem celebrating the Elphinstons' wedding anniversary, verses which Johnson at first "cood not creddit" but, when told it was true, "ardently prezented dhe yong Poet widh a coppy ov hiz abridged diccionary; havving previously inscribed it widh hiz own hand."[32]

Johnson, to whom the school owed its enrollment of at least one "verry plezing pupil,"[33] described Elphinston in April 1771 as a teacher more suitable "for the sons of citizens, who are to learn a little, get good morals, and then go to a trade" than for any boy "intended for a man of learning."[34] This assessment and his contact with the Drummond boys suggest that he had some first-hand experience of lessons and life at the school, and it is certainly evident that he occasionally dined at the house.[35] Elphinston's own wide circle of acquaintances included a number of Americans, a connection which stemmed not only from his own family ties, e.g., to Rhode Island, where he had a clergyman cousin involved in the Society for the Propagation of the Gospel, but probably also from William Strahan's friendship with Benjamin Franklin. It may have been Strahan, for instance, who had recommended his brother-in-law's academy to Franklin when the latter arranged for his grandson William Temple Franklin to be enrolled there in the late 1760s.[36] While the grandfather dined at least once with the Elphinstons— on January 8, 1774, Franklin expressing "verry real sattisfaccion" at the boy's progress (*FYC*, 2:103)—the letters in *Fifty Years' Correspondence* make no mention of any encounters between Johnson and either Franklin or his grandson.[37] It is clear, however, that, through Elphinston Johnson met Loyalists also known to Franklin: the lawyer Martin Howard, from 1767 until 1775 Chief Justice of North Carolina, and the poet Jonathan Odell can be seen reminiscing in 1770 about their "good frends at dhe Acaddemy" (*FYC*, 1:242), and Johnson regularly featured in Elphinston's letters to and from each.[38] Odell, who came to England around 1763, worked for a time as assistant teacher at the school in Kensington before being ordained as deacon in 1766 and receiving full orders in 1767; letters from the years 1773 and 1774 show his keen interest in the news that Johnson was revising his *Dictionary*—"I rejoice in dhe prospect, ov seing hiz diccionary rendered more perfet; and consequently more wordhy, ov its author and ov posterity" (*FYC*, 2:119)—and he would himself write an essay intended as an introduction for Jonathan Boucher's supplement to the *Dictionary*.[39] It was Odell who introduced William White, later Bishop of Pennsylvania, to Elphinston and thus to Johnson; White, who was to correspond with the latter, is known to have dined with both at the school, probably in late 1771 or 1772, and to have kept (or, like Sir Joshua Reynolds, been persuaded to keep)[40] Johnson company "on the stage-coach" afterwards (*Life*, 2:499).

Elphinston was also acquainted with the Mr. Bond to whom Johnson entrusted "a packet" on his departure for America in March 1773 (*Life*, 2:207) and who, in February 1773, the Scot was sure would return there "an ornament" and "a boolwark" to his country (*FYC*, 2:52). A brief exchange in November 1792 shows that the man who "desired [of Boswell] that his name might not be transcribed at full length" (*Life*, 2:207) was indeed the later "Consul-General for the Middle and Southern States of America" (*Life*, 2:498), i.e., the younger Phineas Bond, also that he was at the time in England: Elphinston hoped that Bond would pay him a visit together with "my belovved Pupil W. T. Franklin" (*FYC*, 7:171).

Scottish guests at the academy in Brompton and later Kensington included, certainly before 1756, "the brilliant Colonel Forrester" (*Life*, 3:22), author of *The Polite Philosopher*, and governor from 1762 until 1763 of the British-occupied Belle-Île. His letter to Elphinston of June 8, 1762 shows him regretting that he would not be able to meet Elphinston and Johnson "at dhe social hour ov three" on the date suggested as he would be leaving for the island on that very day.[41]

More momentous, perhaps, was the occasion "about Christmas, 1774" when Elphinston introduced Johnson to the Gaelic scholar William Shaw, whose

[37]

Memoirs of the Life and Writings of the Late Dr. Samuel Johnson—published in early June 1785—was to rely for its "principal, and most valuable communications" on Elphinston, those, in turn, based on a long "correspondence of the greatest intimacy."[42] One of the "communications" (we shall be looking below at the letters provided by Elphinston) shows Johnson explaining his "strong prejudice against Lord Bute" over dinner at the Elphinstons' home "but a few days before the pension was proposed": "He gave the king a wrong education. He had only taught him . . . to *draw a tree*."[43] On learning "not above a day or two after this" that a pension had been granted, Elphinston "hastened to congratulate his friend," who "related the matter circumstantially," mentioning one unnamed lord who had been "abundantly sarcastic on [Johnson's] character" and argued that "his political principles" were "inimical to the House of Hanover," but whose objections had been swiftly countered by Bute.[44]

The volumes published by Elphinston in 1791 show that he corresponded between 1768 and 1778 with the Edinburgh author Henry Mackenzie, following closely the other's literary career.[45] Questions about Johnson and references to his works often crop up in these letters, for example when Mackenzie asked in December 1758, having seen "som late performances against him, equally stupid and abusive," whether Johnson was "quite sattisfied" with a reputation which now ensured him "dhe obloquy ov dulnes," the kind of encomia, that is, which "an authors vannity shood wish" (*FYC*, 1:169). Elphinston assumed in 1779 that Johnson's *The False Alarm* would appeal to Mackenzie, who replied that it was "such az might be expected" from such an eminent and singular "advocate ov Administracion" (*FYC*, 1:215). The brief meeting that took place in Edinburgh between Johnson and Mackenzie in November 1773, on the former's "return from dhe north" (*FYC*, 2:98), was one that Elphinston claimed to have arranged for his "frend *dhe Man ov Feeling*" (*FYC*, 2:105).

Letters to and from those of Elphinston's friends who would themselves never meet Johnson still betray his presence and the pride Elphinston took in his connection with such eminence. This becomes clear in passing references to the famous friend's health—for example, "I am sorry Dr. *Jonsons* helth iz declining. I suspect he haz not been modderate in hiz studdies" (*FYC*, 1:162)—and in Elphinston's activities as a sort of self-appointed agent. We see him sending the "*Ramblers*" from London to Philadelphia in 1754 (the Edinburgh edition, of course), and in May 1770 he reported to a friend in Rhode Island that Johnson had produced *The False Alarm*, a new "master-piece . . . tending (moast laudably) to' promote pece and order, in dhis madding contry" (*FYC*, 1:210). One of Elphinston's cousins in Scotland voiced the following reaction on May 9, 1770 to the same pamphlet: "Yoor frend Dr. *Jonson* iz com too late, to' stop dhe torrent. If hiz admirable Essays cood not prevent it in its soarce, by dheir influence on private manners; it iz not to' be expected, dhat a temporary warning, drowned by dhe stronguer voice ov clamorous sediscion, can now avail annithing. Dhe onely comfort dhat remains, iz; dhat *we*, perhaps, shal be taken away from dhe evil to' come" (*FYC*, 1:202). *The False Alarm* and *Thoughts on the Late Transactions Respecting Falkland's Islands* were nevertheless both recommended by Elphinston to another Scottish cousin on March 25, 1771 as affording the "*truest nocion in dhe noblest way*" when it came to current politics (*FYC*, 1:256). And in 1775, he expressed to his former pupil Jem Drummond that their mutual friend's "masterly pamphlet, entitled, *Taxacion no tyrranny* . . . may anser dhe benevolent authors intension, by conducing to' duty and harmony on boath sides dhe Atlantic" (*FYC*, 2:151).

One final shared and somewhat perplexing acquaintance: By late 1756 or early 1757, Elphinston had clearly met the author Charlotte Lennox and been requested by her to provide English versions of a small number of verse quotations found in the French work she was currently translating, La Beaumelle's *Mémoires et Lettres de Madame de Maintenon* (the five-volume English text was published in March 1757). It may have been Johnson, Lennox's friend and mentor, who introduced the two, but it could also have been either Samuel Richardson or William Strahan.[46] Whose idea it was, moreover, that Elphinston's services should be obtained, or precisely why another translator was even deemed necessary, is also something of a mystery, unless we can believe the explanation given by Elphinston himself in 1763: that he was "prevailed on to take in the work" and thus accorded "an honor (perhaps needlessly) devolved by Modesty upon Friendship."[47] In the event, the 1757 choice proved to be an unfortunate one: three years earlier, Elphinston's own *Religion, a Poem: From the French of the Younger Racine* (1754) had been dismissed as "moderately executed" (with examples given in order to preclude any accusation of "partiality"), and one critic who reviewed Lennox's *Memoirs for the History of Madame de Maintenon* promptly singled out "*Elphingston*" as having contributed as a "specimen of ingenuity" which did not merit "great regard."[48]

IRRITATIONS, ACID, AND ALKALI

One might wonder whether the reviewers' comments served in part as sly digs at Johnson, given his prominent naming in the *Rambler* of the "*ingenious*" translator. Elphinston himself quite possibly read them as such, deeming the criticism of his own work in any case wholly unwarranted. While Johnson would scarcely have risen to the bait, the maligned Scot quite soon did: after seeing his own verse and prose subjected to rising levels of scathing ridicule, Elphinston launched an attack against his reviewers in 1763 with the above-mentioned cryptic and unpalatable *Apology*. Not only did the "ingenious Translatress" Lennox, who had accorded "her Friend" Elphinston the "honor" of seeing their names joined, find her "arraigned" taste defended there,[49] but Johnson, too, saw himself championed with an obscure rebuttal of Owen Ruffhead's review of *The Prince of Abissinia*;[50] moreover, Johnson's conjoining of Horace, himself, and Elphinston in *Rambler 3* was an "honor" now celebrated by reprinting on pages 87–90 the entire text of the essay (including the substantive modification its author had made to the original Edinburgh translation of its motto).

Elphinston's reactions to all criticism of his own writings and talent remained persistently indignant, vehement, and vociferous throughout his life,[51] just as the quality of his poems was consistently poor and his prose challenging. His friend Dallas circumscribed this with a benevolent characterisation: "A Quixote in whatever he judged right . . . the force of custom made no impression upon him; the only question with him was, *should it be, or should it not be?* . . . untainted and unbroken . . . he lived upon the square with the world."[52] Johnson, who apparently never doubted that Elphinston had "a great deal of good about him" and was "a man of good principles"(*Life*, 2:171; 3:379) nevertheless had certain reservations: his friend was "also very defective in some respects. His inner part is good, but his outer part is mighty aukward" (*Life*, 2:171). While not seen in 1772 as a hindrance to the teaching of boys destined to "go to trade" (*Life*, 2:171), Elphinston's "defective" parts later gave rise to a more damning view, with Johnson declaring him "very fit for a travelling governour" because "there would be no danger" that a single pupil "should catch his manner;" that being "so very bad, that it must be avoided. In that respect he would be like the drunken Helot" (*Life*, 3:379). Elphinston had, moreover, "the most *inverted* understanding of any man whom I have ever known" (*Life*, 3:379).

The exasperation palpable in all this was, as Elphinston's correspondence occasionally reveals, quite often felt on both sides. Frequent references are made in the 1773 letters, for example, to hopes that Johnson would return from Scotland with "a more favorabel idea, dhan he carried dhiddher" (*FYC*, 4:281), but the impressions then published in 1775 included "obnoxious passages," things that were "exceptionabel" and which Elphinston, "in all dhe ardor ov frendship," took upon himself to mention in conversation with Johnson (*FYC*, 4:286). The complaints were allegedly received "kindly" because they were couched in "happy" terms agreeable to Johnson's "good-nature, (hwich iz grait)" (ibid.), but Elphinston privately asked the historian William Tytler to list "elucidating and certifying obzervacions" on the offending passages "before annoddher ediscion," simply as a favour to Johnson, even if the latter "be too much an Inglishman" to know how much he and the volume needed such help (*FYC*, 4:286–87). Tytler, who had read the work "with very great pleasure" and found its "few errours . . . of no great importance" (*Life*, 2:305), excused himself as regards any list, but did feel that Johnson's "remarks, on dhe authentiscity ov *Ossians* poems, ar verry strong; but not always just": while James Macpherson "might hav altered dhe dres considderably," Tytler himself had heard some of the poems "chanted" by West Highland families in 1748, "long before Macpherson waz evver herd ov" (*FYC*, 4:289). Johnson's verdict with regard to Ossian was all the more of a disappointment for Elphinston because others were encouraged to espouse "so damnabel a herresy" (*FYC*, 2:136). Another of his correspondents was told that the published *Journey* would have been "fautles, and perhaps dhe author; wer he not so inveterately an Inglishman" and had he enjoyed "an opener erly edducacion" (*FYC*, 2:151). And even Henry Mackenzie's above-mentioned meeting with Johnson in Edinburgh—one which left the Scottish novelist feeling "instructed and entertained" as well as pleased that Johnson was coming away with "a verry favorabel idea" of the Highlanders and their hospitality (*FYC*, 2:98–99)—caused Elphinston to niggle that, although both had evidently enjoyed their encounter, Mackenzie had expressed his pleasure "more strongly" than Johnson: the younger man had, of course, wanted "to' hear" Johnson and been thus the more willing to sacrifice "self-lov, to' hwat he found such enjoyment" (*FYC*, 2:105).

Another bugbear was Johnson's steadfast resistance to Elphinston's ideas regarding language, pronunciation, and spelling. "Inglish Orthoggraphy waz no more known to' [Johnson], dhan to' moast ov my oddher Correspondents" (*FYC*, 7:16); a stranger "to the System, even of English Sounds," Johnson followed in the *Dictionary* "the only Rule he possessed; that of keeping as near each parental [sc. etymological] pattern . . . as possible" and chose "the Symbols but by habit and remembrance" (*FYC*, 7:143, in a letter sent on July 9, 1792 to the editor of the *St James's Chronicle*).[53] Hoping in October 1791 that an acquaintance would order a copy of his *Fifty Years' Correspondence*, Elphinston even boasted that every one of his correspondents, "*Jonson*, and dhe rest," had "simmilarly aimed" at an orthography which "ascertained dhe picture ov our Speech," but had "moddestly left its ascertainment" to him (*FYC*, 7:77).

It does seem likely that Elphinston continued the attempts begun during his work on the Edinburgh *Ramblers* to proselytize and unbarbarize Johnson, who himself considered Elphinston lacking in "that nice critical skill in languages, which we get in our schools in England" (*Life*, 2:171), and their discussions of these and all sensitive matters may sometimes have been quite spirited. In 1771,

Elphinston reminded his American friend Martin Howard of a scene the other had witnessed in the mid-1760s, a conversation with Johnson "hwich to' yoo waz rude on my part; to' me, on hiz"; in 1791, he added the following footnote: "Ov dhis notthing can be remembered by won, hoo iz in no dainger ov forguetting, dhat *Jonson*s conversacion had always an alcaline, hdat sheadhed anny ascid" (*FYC*, 2:280). The combination must often have been an explosive one: on Elphinston's part the conviction with which he upheld his own theories, publishing on undeterred, and his "simplicity of character,"[54] which manifested itself in well-meaning pedantry; on Johnson's side the tendency to argue "on every occasion as if his whole reputation depended upon the victory of the minute" and, when contradicted, to cling "stubbornly" even to opinions voiced "perhaps first at random" rather than "to acquiesce."[55] It was apparently Johnson who put out the fires, however, being often "the first to seek after a reconciliation" when an "antagonist resented his rudeness,"[56] or, as Elphinston put it, to bring a mediating, alkaline quality into play.

THE TROUBLE WITH MARTIAL

There was at least one potentially caustic irritation for which Johnson knew the best alkali to be simple avoidance. In 1778, when Elphinston's *Proposals for Printing by Subscription . . . the Epigrams of M. V. Martial* were printed in London,[57] Johnson's reaction to the samples offered of the translations the Scot had been working on since 1776 was to comment, in Hester Thrale's company, that there was "too much folly for madness . . . and too much madness for folly" in the renderings shown (*Life*, 3:258n3). However, unlike David Garrick, who said that he had advised Elphinston not to go ahead with the project, thinking him "crazy," and in contrast to William Strahan, who offered to double the £50 already paid out for a subscription if his brother-in-law "would not publish" (*Life*, 3:258), Johnson declined to intervene:

> JOHNSON: "He did not ask my advice, and I did not force it on him, to make him angry with me."
> GARRICK: "But as a friend, Sir—." Johnson. "Why, such a friend as I am with him—no." (*Life*, 3:258)

An attempt to dissuade Elphinston would, Johnson thought, "hurt his vanity, and do him no good. He would not take my advice" (*Life*, 3:258), and he was doubtless not far wrong. On July 30, 1791, after reading the *Life*, Elphinston wrote to Boswell and informed him that Johnson, "hwen I first intimated my translacion ov Marsial," had "warmly" declared, "I am sorry I waz not yoor first subscriber"; as, moreover, "for Garrics vaporing on dhe subject," Elphinston denied ever having "consulted him on anny subject," let alone having "prostitute[d] to' hiz critticism, hwat I nevver wood submit to' hiz masters (*FYC*, 7:17). The friends' reactions to the *Proposals* were justified, however: when finally published in 1782,[58] both Elphinston's verse translation of Martial and his prose preface were lambasted as utterly unintelligible, with one critic finding the language such "as could only have been expected from a Laputan compositor, who puts his words together by the assistance of a machine."[59]

THE "ARGONAUTIC EPISTEL" AND AN INNOCENT VICTIM OF THE FRENCH REVOLUTION

In mid-1785, four letters written by Johnson to Elphinston between 1749 and 1778—they remain the only extant ones—were published by Shaw,[60] among them the condolences sent in September 1750 on the death of Elphinston's mother, the text, that is, which the addressee had considered publishing at the time in the *Scots Magazine*. Johnson had also written when Elphinston's wife died in July 1778, the sympathy expressed this time coloured by the writer's own experience of loss:

> I well know the weight of your distress, how much you have need of comfort, and how little comfort can be given. A loss, such as yours, lacerates the mind, and breaks the whole system of purposes and hopes.... But in the condition of mortal beings, one must lose another. What would be the wretchedness of life, if there was not something always in view, some Being, immutable and unfailing, to whose mercy man may have recourse.... The greatest Being is the most benevolent. We must not grieve for the dead as man without hope, because we know they are in his hands. We have, indeed, not leisure to grieve long, because we are hastening to follow them.[61]

Of the two letters, the earlier and less personal one was considered suitable for printing in the *Gentleman's Magazine* of October 1, 1785, it being "*a very good commentary on the much-agitated part of the Meditations.*"[62] One month later, the text also appeared in the *European Magazine & London Review*, the *Weekly Entertainer*, and the *Scots Magazine*, in each case, however, no longer marked as a contribution to the discussion of Johnson's posthumously published *Prayers and Meditations*.

Elphinston himself may or may not not have been directly involved in the appearance of the magazine versions, but one printed text of the letter he received from Johnson on September 25, 1750, was later to trigger a chain of events which briefly turned an international spotlight on his friendship with Johnson. On August 17, 1787, one James Falconar, first mate on a British ship bound for India, learned that another vessel was about to pass and would be able to deliver mail to England. He quickly penned a short letter to his sister in London, mentioning in it that, earlier in the day, he had been reading a letter of condolence from Dr. Johnson to Mr. Elphinston on the loss of his mother—newsworthy in this case because Falconar's sister Charlotte had married the widower Elphinston in October 1785. However, her brother managed in the end to miss the other ship and so, on a whim, immediately placed his own letter inside a bottle, corked that, and tossed it into the Bay of Biscay.

About nine months later, the bottle, by this time shell-encrusted, was broken open by the fishermen mentioned at the beginning of this chapter, and its contents landed in the admiralty registry at Bayeux; the curiosity which had led the men to damage their find would normally have ended in a sizeable fine, but they had left the seal on Falconar's letter intact and so escaped punishment. An admiralty secretary was given orders to contact the addressees ("Mrs." being read as "Messieurs"), and an intrigued James Elphinston, who could think of no explanation for all this, wrote back (in French) requesting that the letter be sent to London. This reply, or specifically its rapturous opening remarks on the most natural and sacred bonds between the two countries, prompted a more senior official, Jean François Philippe, Sieur de Delleville to take the matter in hand, he himself being a native of Normandy and thus, as he wrote, all the more sensible of their oneness. There remained, nonetheless, a certain amount of legal red tape to be overcome, all complicated by the Elphinstons' departure in July 1788 for a two-month visit to Scotland and the need, therefore, to have any further correspondence go through their old charge (and Johnson's young friend) James Drummond; even the Lord Provost of Edinburgh was dragged into the affair as a witness to the proxy issued by Mrs. Elphinston authorizing a French merchant to pick up the letter in her place. Finally, however, on November 15, 1788, James Elphinston was able to thank both the merchant and Philippe de Delleville for the floating letter his wife had now finally received, as well as to explain how it had come to be in the bottle[63] and to ask how best he could have a copy of his new book on English orthography conveyed to Bayeux. (He had introduced himself to Philippe de Delleville back in July 1787 as someone who, having previously translated Martial into English, edited the Roman poet's Latin texts,[64] then done in England for the English language what the Academie Française had done for

French, i.e., introduce and establish a new system of spelling, was now heading to Scotland to repeat that success.)

By January 4, 1788, Elphinston had decided that the letter, "hwich, from floting on Christian coasts, haz becom dhe instrument ov uniting nacions and individduals by dhe moast blessed bonds" and the correspondence to which it had given rise were "too impoartant to' be concealed from dhe eye ov dhe pubblic" (*FYC* 3:238–39). A good ten months later, he had the "Bottel-pamphlet" (*FYC* 3:277) privately printed as *Correspondance Française-Anglaise causée par une lettre trouvée en mer dans une bouteille sur la côte normande; avec la lettre même*.[65] The original plan had probably been to show twelve letters, each in French and in English (using for the latter Elphinston's orthography): the toing and froing between Bayeux and London (May 10 to November 15, 1787), James Falconar's "foundling" letter (August 17, 1786), the letter of consolation mentioned in that[66] together with Elphinston's reply to Johnson (September 25 and October 4, 1750). In the end, two further letters were included: one (May 20, 1788) in which Philippe de Delleville informed Elphinston that the bottle's journey now featured in the fourth volume which Jacques-Henri Bernardin de Saint-Pierre had added to the third edition of his *Études de la nature* (1788).[67] A brief newspaper report about the finding of the bottle (*Mercure de France*, January 12, 1788) had caught Bernardin de Saint-Pierre's eye and, furnished with the more precise details supplied by Philippe de Delleville through a mutual friend, he deduced from the latitudes, longitudes, dates, and distances that the current had first carried the bottle south to the Azores (or beyond), and that it had been borne northwards again after the September equinox, thus illustrating his theory that the tides and currents were ruled by the fusion of the ice at the poles (and, he thought, disproving Newton's gravity-based explanation). Elphinston being Philippe de Delleville's own source for the specifics, his name also appeared in these deliberations, which Bernardin de Saint-Pierre placed in the foreword to his new volume, by way of responding to previous critics. The final letter selected by Elphinston for his pamphlet was his own response (July 25, 1788) to Philippe de Delleville's news: the Scot longed to see a copy of Bernardin de Saint-Pierre's book and thought that the theory "may be az sollid az dhat ov Newton: dhe polar ices, like dhe polar Beirs, may hav az much influence on dhe Sea, az dhe Moon."[68] Both Elphinston and his friend at the admiralty in Bayeux were apparently unaware that the main body of the text in the volume was the first edition of Bernardin de Sainte-Pierre's hugely successful novel *Paul et Virginie*.[69]

Elphinston noted in the introduction to (each part of) his pamphlet that some critics might find the "foundling" letter somewhat simple, but that "nevver did *Jason* from dhe *Argo* dismis a more native epistel" than Falconar from his ship:

"if dhe Argonautic Epistel, hwatevver in itself, and howevver conveyed, hav braught wonce more togueddher a Jonson and a Delleville; nedher nacion wil be sorry to' witness dhe meeting of such Geniusses."[70] Philippe de Delleville himself, when finally able to peruse the booklet in late May 1789, found that Johnson's 1750 letter to Elphinston and the reply contained "som of dhose sentimental truiths, dhat seem adapted to' evveriboddy" (*FYC*, 4:74). His copy was one of three hundred which were sent to Bayeux with the request that they be disseminated first in Normandy and the remainder posted to Paris. On July 18, 1789 (!), Philippe de Delleville told Elphinston that the pamphlets would at any other time have been "eguerly snatched from hand to' hand," but now lay "widhout mocion; heds and harts being fixed on dhe crittical juncture" (*FYC*, 4:103). He did eventually send copies to a friend in Paris who passed a number of them on, but commented that writings on public affairs were still "engrocing all attension, and cauzing evvery oddher reading to' be neglected" (*FYC*, 7:41).[71] As Elphinston himself would observe on January 30, 1792, his pamphlet became an "innocent victim ov dhe French regenneracion";[72] undaunted, however, he ensured that the texts thus lost in France were all "regennerated in dhe *quadradgenary Correspondence*" (*FYC*, 7:104).[73]

EPILOGUE

The volumes of correspondence published by Elphinston support his own claim in 1789 that he "always found hiz interest, hiz glory, hiz joy, in cultivating truly-grait men"[74] and show that being known as a friend of Johnson's, as the recipient, for example, of the "pure Bennevolence" (ibid., 8) which induced the other to send his eloquently phrased condolences, was a source of considerable personal pride. His collection points to a certain acerbity, an edge to the "glory" and "joy." The unbounded public praise of his "onnored frend" Johnson (*FYC*, 2:82),

> In speech a *Tully*, and a *Pope* in song;
> As *Moses* learned, and as *Samson* strong;
> To friends or foes, whate'er he speak or write,
> He thunders truth, and deluges delight[75]

stands in contrast to the occasional argumentative, acid turn conversations between the two appear to have taken and to some resentful, even faintly rancorous remarks made in private to others about the man. That, however, seems wholly in keeping with Elphinston's well-documented tendency to be opiniated when it came to his own literary or scholarly productions and ambitions, and it serves as a good example of what Johnson meant when he explained why he would on no account advise his friend against going ahead with his translation of Martial: for fear of making the man "angry with me," of "hurt[ing] his vanity," in the certainty that he "would not take my advice" anyway (*Life*, 3:258). Those reasons, in turn, illustrate quite perfectly what Johnson had long since written on the offering of advice or well-meant criticism:

> I have often known very severe and lasting malevolence excited by unlucky censures, which would have fallen without any effect, had they not happened to wound a part remarkably tender. . . . Thus are the fondest and firmest friendships dissolved, by such openness, and sincerity, as interrupt our enjoyment of our own approbation, or recall us to the remembrance of those failings, which we are more willing to indulge than to correct.[76]

While Elphinston's appearance alongside Johnson, Arthur Murphy, and other of his coeval "rhyming brethren" in Cuthbert Shaw's 1765 satire *The Race*—he rates there as an also-ran who "Broke thro' all pedant rules of mood and tense, / And nobly soar'd beyond the reach of sense"[77]—may well primarily have aroused a proud sense of being recognized in all of twenty-four verses as one of the "brethren," we should perhaps not assume that the long years of being ridiculed in reviews and failing to find acceptance for his ideas really did leave him "untainted and unbroken"[78] and without "a part remarkably tender."

Johnson's own private observation about Elphinston's "*inverted* understanding" and the "manner . . . so very bad" that he could well serve as "the drunken Helot" (*Life*, 3:379) seems quite harsh, even if one allows that the Helot may simply have been introduced for effect. In combination, however, with his reluctance to provoke the other by giving advice that would only touch a nerve and anger, it helps to explain what Johnson meant when he said of himself "such a friend as I am with [Elphinston]" (*Life*, 3:258). Even in a more casual than intimate friendship, Johnson was willing to accept the other with all his faults, not perhaps because "any company to him was better than none,"[79] but because his own good nature was indeed, as Elphinston stressed, "grait" (*FYC*, 4:286).

NOTES

1. *In Six Pocket-Vollumes*: *Foar ov Oridginal Letters, Two' ov Poetry* (printed in London at Elphinston's own expense and sold by various booksellers in London and Edinburgh). These were supplemented in 1794 with two further volumes numbered 7 and 8, but showing as title James Elphinston, *Fifty Years' Correspondence, Inglish, French, and Lattin, in Proze*

and Verse; Between Geniusses ov Boath Sexes, and James Elphinston. . . . (again printed privately in London, 1791), in 8 vols. (hereafter cited *FYC*, by volume:page).
2. Frederick W. Hilles, *The Literary Career of Sir Joshua Reynolds* (Cambridge: Cambridge University Press, 1936; repr. Hamden, CT: Archon Press, 1967), 164.
3. Robert Charles Dallas, "Biographical Memoir of James Elphinston, Esq.," *European Magazine* 56 (1809): 366. The account was also printed in *Gentleman's Magazine* 79 (1809): 1057–63; *Literary Panorama* 7 (1810): 529–42; and *Monthly Magazine, or, British Register* 28 (1809): 484–91. Dallas (1754–1824), formerly one of Elphinston's pupils, was himself "a prolific author, in a variety of genres." See James Watt, "Dallas," s.v. *Oxford Dictionary of National Biography Online* (*ODNB*), http://www.oxforddnb.com/. See also n19 below.
4. Old Style; [*sic*] also in the following all dates prior to September 1752.
5. On Elphinston (1721–1809), see Dallas, *Memoir*, 361–68; also see Joan C. Beal, "Elphinston" s.v. *ODNB*; both are supplemented here with details scattered throughout *FYC*. Born and educated in Edinburgh, he studied briefly at the university there, but took up employment as a tutor in late 1738; he left Scotland in early 1743 to travel with the English historian and Jacobite Thomas Carte through Holland and the Low Countries, then on to France, where he stayed in Carte's Paris home, thus able to improve the spoken and written French already acquired in Edinburgh. In November 1743, he returned to Scotland and to working as a tutor, his pupil in 1744, for instance, the son of a man with known Jacobite leanings. Elphinston's own background explains these connections, his father William (d. 1723) having been a non-juring minister with an accordingly troubled career; see *Fasti Ecclesiae Scoticanae: The Succession of Ministers in the Church of Scotland from the Reformation*, ed. Hew Scott, 2nd ed. (Edinburgh: Oliver and Boyd, 1915–1981), 4:355–56.
6. *Letters*, 1:42.
7. *London Evening Post* 3034, April 16, 1747, from an advertisement declaring the planned two volumes already "*in good Forwardness.*" See also David Fleeman, *A Bibliography of the Works of Samuel Johnson*, ed. James McLaverty (Oxford: Clarendon Press, 2000), 1:415.
8. See the letter from his mother in Edinburgh, *FYC*, 1:5–7.
9. Arthur Murphy, *An Essay on the Life and Genius of Samuel Johnson, LL.D* (London, 1792), 108.
10. See, for example, Fleeman, *Bibliography*, 1:66. One reason for Elphinston's 1748 stay in London was undoubtedly the serial publication of a translation he was preparing: Jacques Benigne Bossuet, *An Universal History* (London, 1748); advertised in early February as forthcoming, the first of four volumes available by late April.
11. Probably also of the second Edinburgh edition (1751–1753). See Fleeman, *Bibliography*, 1:199–204.
12. Cited here as found in Dallas, *Memoir*, 363 (the text there was taken from Elphinston's papers). The words seem to corroborate what Boswell would later write: "With a laudable zeal at once for the improvement of his countrymen and the reputation of his friend, he [sc. Elphinston] suggested and took the charge of an edition . . . at Edinburgh, which followed progressively the London publication" (*Life*, 1:210). The "*London* price" was 2*d.*; only *Ramblers* 1–104 were sold singly in Edinburgh, "the remainder were published in vols. only" (Fleeman, *Bibliography*, 1:202).
13. *Letters*, 1:45. See *FYC*, 1:20–25, for Elphinston's letters to "Peggy" Strahan of September 11 and 13, also n73 below.
14. *FYC*, 1:31–32. Elphinston was expressly responding on October 4 to two letters received from Johnson: one (now lost) regarding which he had been doubting his own "abillity ov making a suitabel return" when the other with its "next to' inspired excellence" had arrived; he refers to the second one as "last Sundays," but there can be no doubt that he means the letter of Tuesday, September 25.

15. *Correspondence French and Inglish* (London, 1789), 7. See pp. 43–46.
16. See pp. 00–00 ["The 'Argonautic Epistel' and an Innocent Victim of the French Revolution"].
17. Elphinston was clearly here, too, the driving force, with Johnson admitting in early 1752 "the failures of [his] correspondence" (*Letters*, 1:57).
18. See *Rambler*, 169, §6; Samuel Johnson, *The Yale Edition of the Works of Samuel Johnson*, gen. ed. Robert DeMaria Jr. (New Haven, CT: Yale University Press, 1958–2018), 6:135 (hereafter cited Yale *Works*, by volume:page).
19. The offending sesquipedalian only appeared once—in *Rambler* 131 of June 18, 1751, offering a possible *terminus post quem* for the lost quibbles. Elphinston's published aversion to all the above is already noticeable in his *The Analysis of the French and English Languages* (London, 1756). If "pettulance" played a part in his letter to Johnson, then hardly just the "yoothfool" kind. On August 7, 1776, Elphinston would write to Edward Gibbon congratulating him on the first volume of his *Decline and Fall*, but remarking that there were some small stylistic details he would be happy to discuss with the other in person: see British Library, Add. MS 34886, fol. 82, a letter not included in Elphinston's own collection (no response found). Tellingly perhaps, his pupil Dallas would alienate Lord Byron by "suggesting alterations to his work" (Watt, "Dallas," s.v. *ODNB*).
20. Fleeman, *Bibliography*, 1:199–208. Ellen Douglas Leyburn, "The Translations of the Mottoes and Quotations in the *Rambler*," *Review of English Studies* 16 (1940): 169–76; numbers in the following differ slightly from Leyburn's count.
21. As credited by Johnson in the 1752 *Rambler* 1:A2r.
22. The Edinburgh and London texts of *Rambler* 8, §13 show some variations in what had presumably always been Johnson's own translation of the Greek cited there. See also C. B. Bradford, "The Edinburgh 'Ramblers,'" *Modern Language Review* 34 (1939): 241–44, esp. 243–44, on possible corrections made by Elphinston to Johnson's English text.
23. See Leyburn, "Translations," 171–72, on "Elphinston's pompous dullness as a poet," but also 170: "in supplying to Johnson the idea of using translations, Elphinston did really enrich the *Rambler*."
24. Text of "Le Rodeur" 134, printed by Elphinston in *FYC*, 8:53–60; see also *FYC*, 8:45–53 for a William Matthew's French version of *Rambler* ("Le Coureur") 102.
25. An undated letter in which Johnson mentions that he has already "transcribed the mottos."
26. *London Evening Post* 4081, January 8, 1754, advertising the school as "*Lately Opened.*" Elphinston's brochure for interested parents, "Dhe Plan ov Edducacion" [curriculum, daily routines] shows the date 1753 (see *FYC*, 8:72–81).
27. The "Plan" for that (*FYC*, 8:81–104).
28. The degree of affection on both sides is often striking, with the childless husband and wife seeing themselves and regarded as "oddher" parents to their charges (*FYC*, 2:150). If Elphinston practiced the ideas described in his four-book 1763 poem *Education*, however, the avoidance of excess in all things (especially diet), the instilling of strict obedience, and, "where the most wisely-charming charmer fails" (see James Elphinston, *Education, in Four Books* [London, 1763], bk. 3, line 102), fear (drawing if necessary "the salutary tear": bk. 3, line 131) were also the order of the day.
29. Possibly since 1745 or 1746. See *Life*, 2:26–27; and, for example, *Life*, 5:385; also *Letters*, 1:168–69.
30. *FYC*, 1:183; similar *FYC*, 2:60–61.
31. See *FYC*, 1:55–69; and *Letters*, 1:168–69. "Sandy" went on to become a physician of some renown, but died in 1782 "by a fall from hiz horse at Napels" (*FYC*, 3:110). Elphinston's last known letter to Johnson (March 30, 1784, *FYC*, 3:110–11) came with a prescription which James Drummond had found among his late brother's papers; the remedy being

"remarkably succesfool abraud," James was wondering whether it could be "ov dhe smallest use" to Johnson or whether he thought that "it may in Lattin, Inglish, or boath, be worth guivving to' dhe world."

32. *FYC*, 5:93. The gift, a copy of the 1766 abridged edition, was inscribed "To Mr. James Drummond in acknowledgement of pleasure received from his verses, this Book was given by Sam: Johnson May 22 1769" (Fleeman, *Bibliography*, 1:493). See also the mention of "yoor, and my old frend Jonson" in Elphinston to James Drummond, August 15, 1776 (*FYC*, 2:202).
33. *FYC*, 2:82; in 1773. See also *Letters*, 2:25.
34. *Life*, 2:171. See *ibid.*, n2 for Thomas Carlyle's more damning reference to Elphinston's "Jacobite seminary," from which a friend had emerged, "his body starved, and his mind also," with "hardly a word of Latin."
35. Dallas noted that, "as a pupil" he was introduced to Johnson (*Memoir*, 365).
36. Either in 1767 or 1768; in 1771, the boy was found by Elphinston to be "daily more prommising" and thus "doutles" destined to "proov wordhy hiz distinguished frends" (*FYC*, 1:284); he stayed at the school until 1775.
37. Dallas met not only Johnson (see n35 above), but also Benjamin Franklin and the divine John Jortin, probably on separate occasions; Johnson appears not to have been personally acquainted with the clergyman and church historian Jortin (see *Life*, 4:161).
38. See *FYC*, 1:158–161, 174, 180, 241–242, 280–81; 2:19 and 85. Odell, a friend of Benjamin Franklin's son William, could in theory also have recommended that William Temple Franklin be placed there). Elphinston possessed manuscript versions of some early poems by Odell and printed those in *FYC*, 5:101–42, together with one of his own (a response) and two by Odell's daughter Mary. A number of those are known from other sources, but not all.
39. Jonathan Odell, *An Essay on the Elements, Accents, and Prosody of the English Language* (London, 1805).
40. See Hilles, *Literary Career*, 163: Reynolds was "often beg'd . . . to accompany [Johnson] home . . . to prevent his being alone in the coach."
41. *FYC*, 1:96. See also James Forrester, *The Polite Philosopher* (Edinburgh, 1736); and *FYC*, 5:18, Elphinston's 1756 poem for Forrester ("Hwile unsown Curnels crown dhis golden age / Not in each soil a Forrester iz found").
42. William Shaw, *Memoirs of the Life and Writings of the Late Dr. Samuel Johnson*, in *The Early Biographies of Samuel Johnson*, ed. O M Brack Jr. and R. E. Kelley (Iowa City: University of Iowa Press, 1974), 137–38.
43. Ibid., 171.
44. Ibid.
45. Henry Mackenzie's half-brother James (also Mackenzie) was a pupil at Elphinston's school around 1772; see *FYC*, 2:20–22.
46. Both were involved in the printing of the 1752 novel for which Lennox became famous, *The Female Quixote*. For Elphinston's acquaintance with Richardson, see *FYC*, 1:39. For Johnson's mentoring of Lennox, see Anthony W. Lee, *Dead Masters: Mentoring and Intertextuality in Samuel Johnson* (Bethlehem, PA: Lehigh University Press, 2011), 110–17.
47. James Elphinston, *Apology for the Monthly Review, with an Appendix in Behalf of the Critical* (London, 1763), 95–96.
48. James Kirkpatrick, Review of *Religion, a Poem: From the French of the Younger Racine*, by James Elphinston, *Monthly Review* 10 (1754): 306; and Tobias Smollett, Review of *Memoirs for the History of Madame de Maintenon*, by Charlotte Lennox, *Critical Review* 3 (1757): 361.
49. Elphinston, *Apology*, 95.
50. Owen Ruffhead, Review of *The Prince of Abissinia*, by Samuel Johnson, *Monthly Review* 20 (1959): 428–37.

51. After two more decades of merciless reviews, the *Apology* was followed in by Elphinston's *The Hypercritic* (London, 1783); Lennox and Elphinston's work for her featured there once more, but Johnson was spared.
52. Dallas, *Memoir*, 366. Even Dallas admitted, however, that the poetry could be "unharmonious, and sacrificed, not only to sense, but too often to rhyme, in which he allowed no licence," also that in his prose, Elphinston "had early habituated his pen to an inverted arrangement" (ibid., 367–68).
53. See also Elphinston's letter of January 10, 1774 to Jonthan Odell, in which he notes that he has not looked at Johnson's revised edition of the *Dictionary*, but that it "must be prefferabel to' dhe former" (*FYC*, 2:105).
54. Shaw, *Memoirs*, 368.
55. Reynolds, quoted in Hilles, *Literary Career*, 158–59.
56. Ibid., 165.
57. James Elphinston, *Proposals for Printing by Subscription . . . the Epigrams of M. V. Martial* (London, 1778).
58. The list of subscribers included (besides Johnson, various Strahans, and an alarming number of bishops and noblemen) Henry Mackenzie, Arthur Murphy, Sir Joshua Reynolds, and William Shaw, but not James Boswell, David Garrick, or Hester Thrale.
59. Edmund Cartwright, in the *Monthly Review* 67 (1782), 380.
60. Shaw, *Memoirs*, 160–62; 178–79.
61. Johnson to Elphinston, letter of July 17, 1778, in Shaw, *Memoirs*, 179.
62. Johnson to Elphinston, letter of July 27, 1778, in Shaw, *Memoirs*, 179.
63. Elphinston told both that the letter had been entrusted to the crew of a vessel heading for England and cast bottled into the sea by them, but later revised this version after his brother-in-law had returned from India.
64. The 1782 English text had been followed in 1783 by an annotated edition of the original epigrams, on which Charles Burney commented that there was "no *other possible method* which [Elphinston] could have adopted of rendering his translation intelligible" (*Monthly Review* 70 [1784], 482).
65. James Elphinston, *Correspondance Française-Anglaise causée par une lettre trouvée en mer dans une bouteille sur la côte normande; avec la lettre même . . . .* (London, 1789) (to be sold by booksellers there and in Edinburgh). The French texts form the first part of the brochure, the second, English part shows the title *Correspondence French and Inglish: Occazioned by a Letter Found Floting in a Bottel on dhe Coast ov Normandy: Widh dhe Letter Itself* and has its own pagination.
66. This, Elphinston was sure, would not "be found les authentic, or les excellent" here because shown in "an Orthoggraphy unknown in its Authors time" (*Correspondence*, 8).
67. Jacques-Henri Bernardin de Saint-Pierre, *Études de la nature* (Paris, 1788).
68. Elphinston, *Correspondence*, 43.
69. Elphinston would remark in 1790 that the "lerned . . . author ov dhe *Studdies ov Nature*" seemed, "in dhe impoartant career ov *Edducacion*, to hav' lost sight, at wonce ov Nature and ov Art; in order to' roam at large widh dhe crac-brained *Jon-James Rousseau*" (*FYC*, 4:267).
70. Elphinston, *Correspondence*, 7.
71. Philippe de Delleville's lengthier letters to Elphinston (the last one printed in *FYC* dates from November 27, 1792) offer quite vivid accounts of events in France from the storming of the Bastille on: see esp. *FYC*, 4:87–103 (July 18, 1789), and 116–50 on his own trial and acquittal in late 1789 (the charge: facilitating the escape of a nobleman). He went on to become a member of the National Convention and the Council of Five Hundred.
72. Elphinston did gift copies to friends in Britain, and a very few have survived (e.g., in the British Library).

73. Johnson's condolences of September 1750, together with Elphinston's reply were included among the six letters which Dallas had published as a supplement to his *Memoir*. See the *European Magazine* 56 (1809): 457–61 (also printed in the magazines mentioned in n3 above); among the six were one of the letters to Margaret Strahan which had moved Johnson to tears, also Elphinston's own condolences to Johnson of March 26, 1750 and February 22, 1759.
74. Elphinston, *Correspondence*, 7–8.
75. Elphinston, *Education*, 3:367–70; see also the Elphinston-spelling version in *FYC*, 6:42.
76. *Rambler*, 40; Yale *Works*, 3:217, 219
77. Mercurious Spur, [Cuthbert Shaw] *The Race* (London, 1765), 6, 26.
78. Shaw, *Memoir*, 366.
79. Reynolds, quoted in Hilles, *Literary Career*, 163.

3

THE CASE OF THE MISSING HOTTENTOT

John Dun's Conversation with Samuel Johnson in *Tour to the Hebrides* as Reported by Boswell and Dun

JAMES J. CAUDLE

> Before I quit this subject, I think it proper to say, that I have suppressed every thing that I thought could really hurt any one now living. With respect to what *is* related, I thought it my duty to "extenuate nothing, nor set down aught in malice;" and with those lighter strokes of Dr. Johnson's satire, proceeding from a warmth and quickness of imagination, not from any malevolence of heart, and which, on account of their excellence, could not be omitted, I trust that they who are the object of them have good sense and good temper enough not to be displeased.
> —James Boswell, *Journal of a Tour to the Hebrides*.[1]

THERE ARE VERY FEW INSTANCES in James Boswell's *The Journal of a Tour to the Hebrides* (1785) or *Life of Samuel Johnson* (1791) for which the same conversation is preserved by Boswell and another person present. Although Boswell spent significant portions of his *Life of Johnson* attacking the accuracy and general credibility of his most powerful rivals for the informal title of greatest Johnsonian biographer, Sir John Hawkins and Hester Lynch Piozzi,[2] he generally did not do so by citing occasions for which they were both present at a social event with Johnson, and had written differing memories of what was said at that same event. We do have several standard scholarly accounts of Boswell's method of reporting conversation that detail individual instances of divergence between Boswell's version and another variant account by other letter-writers, diarists, and anecdotalists. These variant perceptions of what was actually said include observations by Thomas Blacklock, Joseph Cradock, Thomas Campbell, Charlotte Burney, Anna Seward, Mary Knowles, and Hester Lynch Thrale Piozzi.[3] Many such specific instances have been deployed as evidence in a wider scholarly debate, conducted from 1950 onwards, questioning or defending the accuracy of Boswell's records of Johnson's conversations.[4]

However, there has been, to my knowledge, no critical discussion of a similar differing with the clergyman John Dun over the phrasing of Johnson's conversation in Boswell's *Journal of a Tour to the Hebrides*. That disagreement over Johnson's exact words spoken in 1773 led to a literary quarrel between Boswell and Dun in 1789–1791 that, although not well known, is revealing of Boswell's biographical methods by which he developed his work from memoranda or notes into fully written journal, into published book, and onward to revision into second and third editions. The incident also confirms Boswell's stubborn confidence in his own memory and his after-the-fact notes whenever he was confronted with another person's variant memory, or even his own variant memory, of a shared event.

THE QUARREL OF JOHNSON AND DUN AT AUCHINLECK MANSE, NOVEMBER 5, 1773

The passage in question occurs in the description of Johnson and Boswell's visit to Auchinleck on November 5, 1773. Auchinleck was the parish in Ayrshire in which Auchinleck House, the hereditary country seat of the Boswell family, stood. During that visit, the parish minister, John Dun, aged about fifty, invited the two travelers to dine with him at the manse, the village church's rectory or parsonage.[5] This invitation to join the parish minister for what would now be called lunch was accepted. Boswell did not say so in the patching-text for the *Hebrides Journal* which he used to augment days for which there was never any fully written manuscript journal, but Johnson and Boswell had already dined with Dun (and Bruce Campbell, as well) on the preceding day (November 4). So, Johnson had previously met Dun and shared a meal with him—at an intimate dinner with only four named gentlemen present—when Johnson went to the manse.[6] (It is reasonable to surmise that this dinner on the fourth was the occasion on which Dun asked the two to dine with him the following day.)

Boswell was entirely capable of cunningly setting up a social experiment to see how men of diametrically opposite politics would interact. After all, fewer than three years later, he would connive an invitation for Samuel Johnson to come along for a dinner at the Dilly Brothers on May 15, 1776, an event to which one of Johnson's archenemies, John Wilkes, had already been invited. Boswell solicited that invitation for Wilkes from the Dillys knowing full well that Wilkes and Johnson, who had "attacked one another with some asperity in their writings," might well clash in a manner that might potentially ruin his friends' and publishers' jovial dinner.[7] However, we see no anterior suggestion that Boswell intended the dinner with Dun to provoke a social confrontation between advocates of Whig and Tory politics, or partisans of Presbyterian and Anglican churchmanship. That was precisely what *did* happen, but it was not (as far as we know) *planned* to happen.

Yet, as Johnson demonstrated in his showdown with Lord Auchinleck at Auchinleck House, his conversations could take a sudden wrong turn into angry and even brutal verbal attacks on his Scottish hosts. In the revised *Hebrides Journal* for October 29, 1773, Boswell mentioned Johnson's "impatience, and spirit of contradiction," which he unleashed not just on obvious dunces, but on mild-mannered intellectual luminaries such as Adam Smith. Boswell compared Johnson's savage mode of arguing when disagreeing in polite society to a "battery of cannon."[8] He was hardly the only person within Johnson's social circle who held such an opinion.

Boswell, knowing Johnson's propensity for verbal irritability when contradicted, had made him pledge on November 2, 1773, when visiting the Boswells' country seat "to avoid three topics, as to which they [Johnson and Boswell's father, Lord Auchinleck] differed very widely: Whiggism, Presbyterianism, and—Sir John Pringle." Johnson, rather than resisting this restriction on his freedom of speech, had "courteously" agreed. "I shall certainly not talk on subjects which I am told are disagreeable to a gentleman under whose roof I am; especially, shall not do so to *your father*" (*Life*, 5:376). (Note that Johnson will have broken this vow within three days of his arrival.)

Day one of the visit (November 2) had gone as planned; Lord Auchinleck and Johnson discussed the fine collection of Greek and Latin classics in the Auchinleck House library, which was certainly one of the greatest private libraries in the southwest of Scotland and was probably among the finest collections in the entirety of Scotland and the Borders.[9] Day two (November 3) had been depressingly rainy, "that incommodiousness of climate in the west," but the Ayrshire gentlemen Alexander Farquhar (d. 1779) of Gilmilnscroft and James Chalmers (d. 1783) of Fingland had been to dinner (presumably at Auchinleck House) and the latter had stayed for supper that evening, joined by Bruce Campbell (1734–1813) of Mayfield and Milrig.[10]

Indeed, it was not until some later day—Boswell "cannot be certain" if it was November 6, or "a former" day—that "Dr. Johnson and [Boswell's] father came in collision" during a discussion of commemorative medals, one featuring Oliver Cromwell, upon which "they became exceedingly warm, and violent . . . [in] an altercation . . . [of] intellectual gladiators" (*Life*, 5:382). Johnson on that day flatly denied (as he had done earlier in Boswell's presence, on September 23, 1773, at Talisker) that the Church of Scotland's "Presbyterian ministers" had produced "any theological works of merit" since the Scottish Reformation, with the implication that in the eras when the Church of Scotland was Episcopalian or—in the centuries before the Reformation created separate "national" churches—Roman Catholic in form, it was more amenable to and encouraging of erudition.[11] "In the course of their altercation, Whiggism and Presbyterianism, Toryism and Episcopacy, were terribly buffeted . . . Sir John Pringle, never having been mentioned, happily escaped without a bruise" (*Life*, 5:251–52, 376, 382–84). That confrontation between Boswell's father and his mentor is closely linked thematically to the one with Dun, as we shall see, although Boswell's muddled memory does not allow us to determine if the confrontation with Lord Auchinleck was temporally the cause or the effect of the altercation with Dun.

At any rate, the stage was set for something to go wrong at Dun's on November 5, if for no other reason than that Boswell had felt he had had to warn Johnson on November 2 to mind his manners in conversation, and avoid religion and politics. Who heard their quarrel, besides Boswell, who witnessed the combat of Johnson and Dun? Neither Boswell's nor Dun's accounts inform us if the clergyman and his guests were joined by Dun's wife Deborah, their baby Alexander Boswell Dun, or Dun's two daughters from his first marriage.[12] Certainly the family—and the assistant parish minister—were to be asked to join the guests at another lunch, on September 2, 1780: "Mr. Millar, Mr. Dun's assistant, and his daughters and son were at dinner. Mrs. Dun was ill and did not appear till tea."[13] Surviving textual evidence for November 5, 1773 in Boswell's papers supplies only the names of two other diners at Dun's manse that day, Alexander Mitchell of Hallglenmuir and someone named Usher or perhaps Askew.[14] One notes that both of these names are omitted from the account of this day in the published *Hebrides* book in 1785 and from Dun's letter to the *Whitehall Evening Post* in 1791 discussing the events.[15] They were important in other stories, but they were not central to the Dun-Johnson quarrel.

THE GAPS IN BOSWELL'S JOURNALS FOR OCTOBER 23–NOVEMBER 22, 1773

Any discussion of what actually happened at Auchinleck manse on November 5, 1773 must begin with the severe problems of the source material for the version of the incident which Boswell published in 1785. When they wrote the majority of the book version of Boswell's *Tour to the Hebrides*, Boswell and friend and collaborator Edmond Malone were abridging, expanding, and adapting what the *Catalogue* of the Boswell Manuscripts refers to as "fully written journal," the section now referred to as J33. The latter begins with the tentative sketch notes jotted down from August 18–20 (Edinburgh to Montrose) as Boswell was feeling his way toward the project. Its core, however, is the fully written journal of August 21–October 22, 1773, taking the travelers from Laurencekirk to the morning of the sailing to Oban. Boswell worked to finish up the journal *post facto* in 1779–1782, and finished the text from October 22 up to 26, from the notes, moving the narrative forward to the visit to Sir James Colquhoun's home on the banks of Loch Lomond. Yet he proceeded at a snail's pace and only completed the work during the composition of *Hebrides* as a book project. J33 is in poor condition, "mounted on gauze; with many defects caused by crumbling, some of them extensive." Still, these days are the heart of the Hebrides journey and the part most readers pay the most attention to. Before the Boswell-Malone revisions, J33 originally consisted of some 355 leaves (thirty-seven of which have gone missing), of which 677 numbered sides had been written on by the time the revisions for press had concluded. From manuscript evidence, we know that some sides—an estimated 3.3 percent (20/607) of the total sides available—were originally intentionally left blank in 1773 when Boswell wrote the ur-journal.[16]

By contrast, its predecessor as source-material, J32, containing the notes for the journal August 14–17, 1773 with the earliest events of Johnson's stay in Edinburgh, is far less satisfactory. J32 consists only of thirteen sides on eight pages of "Rough notes with many abbreviated words."[17] Whatever J32's faults, it is far superior in its provision of thirteen sides for four days (roughly three sides per day) to the surviving ur-manuscript for the October 22–November 5 segment of the *Tour*.[18] As Pottle explains in the *Catalogue* of the Boswell Papers, "The first leaf consists of very brief notes for Friday 22 Oct. to Friday 5 Nov.," since "the fully written journal was discontinued in the middle of the entry for 22 Oct. at Lochbuie. From these leaves, in 1779, 1780, 1781, and 1782, JB posted [completed] the journal (J33) through the first two paragraphs of the entry for 26 Oct." Pottle noted that "In 1785, when preparing the journal for publication, he returned to them and brought the narrative down to 22 Nov.," which is remarkable, since there is no surviving evidence of any original journal texts covering the dates November 6–9 or November 12–22 at all. "This small packet of leaves," of which the bulk covers just the two days of November 10–11, "appears to have formed the whole of the record that JB made in 1773, after the fully written journal was discontinued in the middle of the entry for 22 Oct. at Lochbuie."[19]

There are, as we have seen, only the brief and heavily abbreviated notes on one scrap of paper in Boswell's hand recording these days October 22–November 5,

[57]

1773. Boswell scholars such as Marion S. Pottle concluded from such absence of fully written journal, and from Boswell's own statements regarding his journalizing in 1773, that this lonely scrap is all the journal that ever existed. One concludes that when Boswell and Malone came to write the passages for these days, they primarily relied on Boswell's memory, as sparked by these few names and key words. Furthermore, we cannot know what relation the first edition's printed passages on the Dun-Johnson quarrel on November 5 bore to the Boswell-Malone manuscript printer's copy submitted for the first edition. The fair-copy text for these days which Boswell developed with Edmond Malone—the clean manuscript copy which Boswell would have sent to the printers for this date—is missing from the surviving, heavily water- and rot-damaged, *Hebrides* 1785 manuscript. The Boswell-Malone fair copy for the press in M132 and the proof-sheets and revises of the first edition in P84 are the closest evidence we have to the original MS.[20]

WHAT THE SURVIVING SOURCES TELL US ABOUT THE JOHNSON-DUN SPAT

In what follows, it should be recalled that the text regarding the events on November 5, published by Pottle and Bennett in their landmark trade edition of the 1773 manuscripts (1937, 1961), is not based on the surviving manuscript at all, but simply follows as copy-text the published text of the third (rather than the [expected] first) edition, thus omitting the diurnal text of the scrap for October 22–November 5, 1773.[21] In Boswell's abbreviated notes for October 22–November 5, and full journal for November 10–11, from which he would eventually fabricate or fashion his journals (which were not fully written at this time), the entire entry for November 5 read as follows: "Friday 5 Hallglen[muir] & ?Usher—They went with us & dined at Mr Dun's. Know no more of our church than a Hottentot."[22] Boswell's groundwork in his 1773 manuscripts was only these twenty-one words. In the *Hebrides/Life*, the final text runs to around 205 words.

The Boswell-Malone text which the duo prepared for the printers to use in 1785—here seen in Peter S. Baker's and Anna Keller's meticulous transcription for the Yale Boswell Editions—offers a much fuller account, close in number of words to the published book, and with few variations from the first edition:

> The Reverend Mr. Dun, our Parish Minister, who had dined with us yesterday with some other company insisted that Dr. Johnson and I should dine with him to-day. This gave me an opportunity to shew my Friend the road to the Church made by my Father at a great expence "for three above three miles" through a range of well disposed farms with

hedge & ditch & a row of trees on each side. He called it the *via sacra* and was very fond of it. [I and my tenants "I hope shall ever" keep it in good repair as if he were surveying it.]²³

      Mr. Dun, though a man of sincere good principles, as a presbyterian Divine discovered such narrowness of information concerning the dignitaries of the Church of England amongst whom may be found Men of the greatest learning virtue piety and assiduity of instructing men of a truly apostolick character. He talked before Dr. Johnson of fat Bishops and lazy Deans, and in short, seemed to believe the scoffings [of sob::rists {?sophists}] equally illiberal and profane of professed satyrists or vulgar railers. Dr Johnson said to him Sir you know no more of our church than a Hottentot.—I was sorry that he brought this upon himself. [But I hoped it would do him good.]²⁴

In the first edition of *Hebrides Tour*, published in October 1785, Boswell told the tale of the altercation in this manner:

Friday, 5th November.
The Reverend Mr. Dun, our parish minister, who had dined with us yesterday, with some other company, insisted that Dr. Johnson and I should dine with him to-day. This gave me an opportunity to shew my friend the road to the church, made by my father at a great expence, for above three miles, through a range of well enclosed farms, with a row of trees on each side of it. He called it the *Via sacra*, and was very fond of it. Mr. Dun, though a man of sincere good principles, as [he is] a presbyterian divine, discovered a narrowness of information concerning the dignitaries of the Church of England, among whom may be found men of the greatest learning, virtue, and piety, and of a truly apostolick character. He talked before Dr. Johnson, of fat bishops and drowsy deans; and, in short, seemed to believe the illiberal and profane scoffings of professed satyrists, or vulgar railers. Dr. Johnson was so highly offended, that he said to him, "Sir, you know no more of our Church than a Hottentot."—I was sorry that he brought this upon himself.²⁵

The 1785 *Hebrides* text has, probably wisely, lost the wish expressed in M132 for the alteration to have had a beneficial effect on Dun.

BOSWELL'S TWO UNSATISFACTORY REVISIONS OF THE DUN EPISODE IN *HEBRIDES*

When *Hebrides* appeared in a second "revised and corrected" edition in December 1785, under what Pottle described as "Malone's able editorship," at least four diplomatic changes had been made to the book; three in the main text and a fourth which was sufficiently complex as to justify an appendix.[26] Boswell wrote of these changes in a second edition footnote appended to his first edition's apology for publishing Johnson's rude or cruel remarks. He explained that, "Having found, on a revision of this work, that, notwithstanding my best care, a few observations had escaped me, which arose from the instant impression, the publication of which might perhaps be considered as passing the bounds of a strict decorum, I immediately ordered that they should be omitted in the present edition. If any of the same kind are yet left, it is owing to inadvertence alone, no man being more unwilling to give pain to others than I am."[27]

For the second edition (1785, 481), directly after the topographical *Via Sacra* passage, but before the account of Dun's "narrowness," Boswell added an encomium to Johnson's eirenic spirit, and attesting to his admiration of certain Church of Scotland and English Presbyterian divines. "Dr. Johnson, though he held notions far distant from those of the Presbyterian clergy, yet could associate on good terms with them. He indeed occasionally attacked them" (*Life*, 5:380). One notes how the added text that Boswell wrote to patch over the transition in topics from the paternal road to the kitchen debate is slightly clumsy in its attempt to be diplomatic. Boswell first gives the reader the idea that Johnson was a good example of Christian ecumenicism, given that he often could be pleasant to Presbyterian clergy, whose lack of formal liturgy and whose theology he despised. Yet Boswell must then, in the next sentence, do an about-face, and prepare the reader for Johnson's brutal attack on Dun (which remains the same as in the first edition), with the phrase "He indeed occasionally attacked them." The statement about the infrequency of the attacks will presumably have been meant to mitigate the reader's impression of the severity or brutality of them.

The most striking change for November 5 in the revised second edition is that the damn-with-faint-praise description of Dun as "Mr. Dun, though a man of sincere good principles . . . a presbyterian divine" disappears. That description is simply replaced by an anonymized "One of them," placed after the aforementioned sentences regarding Johnson's attitudes and behavior toward "the presbyterian clergy." This was Boswell's one concession to Dun's request to modify the offensive anecdote. An attentive reader of the second or third edition might have naturally and forgiveably concluded that the textual placement of the concealed "One of them" clergyman a few sentences after the mention of the lunch with "The Reverend Mr. Dun, our parish minister" meant that the presbyterian cleric in question was most probably none other than Dun himself. It was not a very helpful cover-up. Whether Boswell maintained this passage in the interest of a more precise veracity, or in some schoolboy's long-delayed revolt against his childhood tutor, cannot be known.

In a third edition, whose "Advertisement" was dated "London, 15th Aug. 1786," Boswell remarked that "it has been my study to make it [the text] as perfect as I could in this edition, by correcting some inaccuracies which I discovered myself, and some which the kindness of friends or the scrutiny of adversaries pointed out." He added defensively that "A few notes are added, of which the principal object is, to refute misrepresentation and calumny." There was a peculiar spikiness to Boswell's statement that "to the animadversions in the periodical Journals of criticism, and in the numerous publications to which my book has given rise, I have made no answer."[28] (We shall see how this refusal to retort against a verbal assault is paralleled in Dun's own statement about his demurral from making any answer to Johnson's abuse.) The account of the passage about Dun and the Hottentot conversation was identical to that in the second edition.

The third edition of 1786, reissued in 1791, revisited Boswell's second edition apology about "a few observations [which] had escaped me" whose publication had "pass[ed] the bounds of a strict decorum." In this revision, he added a line that "I was pleased to find that they did not amount in the whole to a page" in total. He added some clarification that "a contemptible scribbler [probably "Peter Pindar"] . . . has impudently and falsely asserted that the passages omitted were *defamatory*, and that the omission was not voluntary, but compulsory." Offended by the idea that he had possessed the *mens rea* to defame, Boswell offered "an obvious and certain mode of refuting" the contention that "the passages omitted were *defamatory*." (Though, *contra* Boswell, one should note that this hermeneutical method could not have guaranteed that the deletions were "voluntary," rather than "compulsory"; an author can be forcibly compelled to retract an innocent, non-libelous statement, after all.) He observed that "Any person who thinks it worth while to compare one edition with the other will find that the passages omitted [repairing flaws corrected in the main text regarding Macdonald of Sleat, Dun, and Alexander Fraser Tytler, and, in an appendix, a clarification regarding Rev. Thomas Blacklock] were not in the least degree of that nature, but exactly such as I have represented them in the former part of this note, the hasty effusion of momentary feelings, which the delicacy of politeness should have suppressed."[29]

Dun, however, was not satisfied with these revisions—mainly published in 1785 and 1786—even though he was one of only three or four people honored with concealment of name and rewriting of the account. His request for a retraction took place within a context of some more general misunderstandings and dissonances with James and Margaret Boswell. In a letter to his wife of December 5, 1788, James Boswell wrote, "Mr. Dun's behaviour is to be regretted. I feel for you as to *preaching*. I do not intend to settle anybody till there is a vacancy." Lustig and Pottle in their note on this letter opined that Dun "had become increasingly cranky and quarrelsome with years (occasionally, it seems, with good cause)."[30] An item in Boswell's personal *Register of Letters* observed for March 9, 1789 that he had received a letter protesting the text from Dun. "Received: Rev. Mr. Dun insisting that Dr. Johnson did not use the word *Hottentot* to him, and *expecting* that I will say I am told so by him in another edition of my *Tour* or in my *Life of Johnson* to prevent his publishing a denial of it."[31] Boswell enclosed this letter (now presumed missing) in a letter to his wife Margaret, dated from London, March 9, 1789: "I enclose a foolish letter from Mr. Dun which came today, and my answer to it, of which I desire Euphemia may make a fair copy for me, and let them both be returned to me. He seems to grow worse and worse. It is painful that an old preceptor and parish minister should be such a man."[32] Boswell replied to Dun on March 9, 1789, in a letter also presumed missing, but recorded by the *Register of Letters*. "Sent: Rev. Mr. Dun that I am perfectly certain as to the *Hottentot*. To let the matter rest as it is" (That much of the evidence in this case has been known to readers of the Hill-Powell edition of *Hebrides*, and the trade edition of Boswell's journal completed in 1989).[33]

JOHN DUN'S VERSION OF THE STORY

I have recently discovered a public-private letter from Dun to Thomas Paine in the *Whitehall Evening Post* that sheds additional light on this famous disputed passage. The letter itself is dated Auchinleck Manse, Ayrshire, N[orth] Britain [i.e., Scotland], July 15, [1791], so it postdates the April 1791 reissue of the 1786 "third edition, revised and corrected" of *Hebrides Tour* by about three months. It is part of a broader sequence of four letters to the newspaper printed in August 30–September 15, 1791.[34] Dun addressed one of them (written July 9, 1791) to Boswell's former friend and clubfellow Edmund Burke in response to his *Reflections on the Revolution in France* (November 1790). The other three (written July 15, 19, and 21, 1791), Dun addressed to "Thomas Paine, Esq.," in response to Paine's *Rights of Man* (March 1791).[35] In the first letter, Dun observes to Paine,

> You shine while confining yourselves to your own sphere, but when you go out of it, allow me to say to you, as Dr. Johnson said to me with *great good breeding*, as [i.e., when he was] under my roof and to dine [i.e., dining] with me. When I was urging that virtuous nervous-writing bigot with arguments against the Prelatic Constitution, he said, "Sir, you know nothing of the matter." I became silent for some time, and did not resent such an answer; for even the Arabian [Bedouin observing the code of *diyâfa*] will restrain himself while the traveller is under his roof.

I pray God that your publication, Sir, may not set the whole *British earth* in a flame.

Here, in the *Whitehall Evening Post* letter to Paine, we finally have Dun's version of the infamous "Hottentot" exchange. In Boswell's account, Dun insultingly speaks "of fat bishops and drowsy deans" in terms reminiscent of "the illiberal and profane scoffings of professed satyrists, or vulgar railers." Dun is presented as ignorant, his opinions predicated on "narrowness of information." The host is seen to be at fault in provoking his innocent guest Johnson. Yet in Dun's version of this story, Johnson is the one who is the religious "bigot," even if a "virtuous" one, and Dun is the one presenting careful and rational "arguments against the Prelatic Constitution." Johnson, a bad guest, is implied to be at fault in provoking Dun. Dun represents himself as a Scottish version of the honorable and chivalrous Arabian Bedouin, preferring to remain silent and let the insult pass rather than to commit any violence, even if merely verbal violence, against his honored guest Johnson, however hostile that visitor might have been toward him or his faith.

It is at this point that the dispute over phraseology begins. In Boswell's version, the retort by the "highly offended" Johnson is the hyperbolic "Sir, you know no more of our Church than a Hottentot." Dun's version of Johnson's remark in the *Whitehall Evening Post* is less "Johnsonese" than Boswell's and in some ways more dignified: we have no mention of the metaphor of the "Hottentot," merely "Sir, you know nothing of the matter." The manner in which this retort was delivered is open to interpretation, as well. Is the text "Dr. Johnson said to me with *great good breeding*" Dun's good Scottish sarcasm? Or is it meant sincerely? The italicization of the phrase suggests that it might be an allusion. We find those words used to comic effect in the 1755 Tobias Smollett translation of *Don Quixote* ("Both mother and son were struck with his [Quixote's] uncouth figure, and he, alighting from Rozinante, with great good breeding, begged leave to kiss the lady's hands"), and unironically in 1762 in the anonymous *Life of Richard Nash* by Oliver Goldsmith ("Some of the nobility regarded him as an inoffensive, useful companion, the size of whose understanding was in general level with their own; but their little imitators admired him as a person of fine sense, and great good breeding.").[36] Note that a few words later, Johnson is called a "virtuous nervous-writing bigot." "Nervous" here holds the older definition that was preferred in Johnson's *Dictionary*, that of "well strung; strong; vigorous," but "bigot" means much the same as it does now, though primarily focused in this period on prejudices based on religion rather than ethnicity. Moreover, Dun's version adds that in the wake of Johnson's insult to his knowledge of the neighboring established church over the border, he (Dun) "became silent for some time." By contrast, Boswell abruptly ends the account of the dinner with Dun with Johnson's retort. Boswell, unlike Dun himself, ignores the latter's reaction. That disregard for Dun's response is a rather unusual move for Boswell, who is normally so concerned with theatrical "scenes" such as the famous account of the Wilkes and Johnson dinner at Dilly's, in which the verbal and emotional reactions of the antagonists are the heart of the appeal. Boswell instead shifts into condescending pity by stating, "I was sorry that he brought this upon himself," which confirms that, for Boswell, Dun was legitimately chastised by Johnson rather than verbally assaulted. Dun concludes his own account by saying that he "did not resent such an answer." It cannot be completely determined from the text whether he did not resent it from agreeing with Boswell that he had earned a sharp retort, or from Christian forbearance of the sort exhibited by the Independent (Congregationalist) minister Dr. Henry Mayo, who was called "The Literary Anvil" by Boswell for his ability to take the pounding verbal abuse of Johnson's hammer without breaking.[37] However, Dun's additional statement that "even the Arabian will restrain himself while the traveller is under his roof" makes it far more likely that he meant to say that he was piously forbearing under an unjustified insult because of laws of hospitality.

Ministers of the Gospel could not, professionally speaking, take the recourse of British gentlemen and aristocrats, that of challenging those who had insulted them to a duel. Parish ministers were expected to turn the other cheek when affronted. By contrast, Alexander Macdonald (c. 1745–1795), Lord Macdonald of Slate, had been so seriously offended by his portrayal in *Hebrides Tour* that he and Boswell nearly dueled. Boswell in his entries for September 2, 1773 had portrayed him as a stingy and miserly host who had abandoned and betrayed those ancient clan traditions of hospitality to guests which Boswell and Johnson felt that he was obliged, as the chieftain of Clan Macdonald of Sleat (*Clann Ùisdein*), to provide. He demanded in what Boswell termed a 'most shocking, abusive letter' dated November 27, 1785 that he retract the passage. Of this letter, Boswell noted, "I thought made it indispensable for me to fight him." The quarreling author and peer almost faced each other with pistols at the ring in Hyde Park on December 10, 1785. The peace treaty that averted the duel involved Boswell sending a letter of apology and pledging to remove the offensive comments from the second edition, on the condition that Macdonald would never print his insults to Boswell, although he might publish Boswell's own letter of clarification and apology.[38] Samuel Collings and Thomas Rowlandson mocked this encounter in their satirical print "Revising for the Second Edition" (June 1786). This caricature print showed Boswell's home, which is being invaded by Lord Macdonald dressed in a folkloric

Highlander's feathered blue bonnet, tartan kilt, and tartan hose. Macdonald is grasping a terrified Boswell by the neck with his left hand, and pointing with a riding crop in his right hand to page 169 of the first edition of *Hebrides* (the monument to Sir James Macdonald in the parish church, September 5, 1773), lying open on Boswell's escritoire, open to pages 168–69, which record the visit on September 4–5 to "the English-bred Chieftain." Pages [164-]65 (September 2, the tepid reception by Macdonald at Armidale) and [166-]167 (September 3) already have been torn out, and lay on the floor at Boswell's feet. Boswell is understandably panicked at the prospect of being horsewhipped, and is praying for mercy.[39] John Wolcot (writing as "Peter Pindar") joked about the dispute in the verses of his *Poetical and Congratulatory Epistle to James Boswell, Esq.* (which was reviewed by the *Monthly Review* in April 1786):

> Let Lord Macdonald threat thy breech to kick,
> And o'er thy shrinking shoulders shake his stick;
> Treat with contempt the menace of this Lord,
> Tis Hist'ry's province, Bozzy, to record.

(Collings and Rowlandson took the first two lines as one of the mottoes for their satirical print.) In a mock-scholarly footnote to that section of his verses, "Pindar" observed, "A letter of *severe* remonstrance was sent to Mr B., who, in consequence, omitted, in the second edition of his Journal, what is so generally pleasing to the public, viz. the *scandalous passages* relative to this nobleman."[40]

Another gentleman who felt he had been made to look ridiculous in the first edition of *Hebrides*, the advocate (lawyer in the Scots legal system) Alexander Fraser Tytler (1747–1813), demanded that Boswell retract the story of Tytler's conversation with Johnson about the debate on the authenticity of Macpherson's Ossian "translations." The result of their correspondence was that Boswell agreed to conceal Tytler's name in future editions of the work, though as with the case of Dun, Boswell refused to eliminate the unsavory and humiliating anecdote altogether, as he might easily and more generously have done.[41]

The rediscovered letter to Paine in the *Whitehall Evening Post* sheds new light on Dun's warning over two years earlier, on March 9, 1789, when he had insisted in a letter to Boswell "that Dr. Johnson did not use the word *Hottentot* to him." Dun, we recall, threatened that he would have to "publish . . . a denial of it" if Boswell failed to "say I am told so [of the inaccuracy of the reported conversation's wording] by him," whether in the forthcoming *Life of Johnson* or in "another edition of my *Tour*."[42] (One might take from the wording of this admonition that Dun was prepared to allow Boswell to republish the story itself, as long as he appended something in the main text or a footnote alerting the reader that Dun disputed his guest's account.) In the event, Dun was not mentioned directly or indirectly in the *Life* when it was published in May 1791, so the mention in the letter to Paine cannot be a response to his reaction to that work's appearance. The third edition of *Hebrides* had been published almost five years earlier, in October 1786, although the "corrected" third edition appeared, again without Dun's name but again still with the Hottentot story, in April 1791, three months before the date of the letter to Paine.[43]

Dun had no contractual grounds to think that his former pupil would have excised the offending passage in the 1791 version; there had been no promises of authorial protections or erasures from Boswell in 1773–1791. After all, the last known communication on the matter was back in March 9, 1789, by means of a letter in which Boswell had sullenly stood his ground: "I am perfectly certain as to the *Hottentot* . . . let the matter rest as it is."[44] It is possible, however, that Dun was responding to the renewed public interest in *Hebrides Tour* in the wake of the *Life*, had expected Boswell would have heeded his warning, and was disappointed when he saw in the newest edition that the corrections for the supposedly new and improved third edition had not spared his reputation any more than the second edition or original third edition had. Since Boswell had not followed Dun's advice to "say I am told so by him in another edition of my *Tour*," by the terms of his letter of warning, Dun was justified in "publishing a denial of it" in a London newspaper. Since Boswell had moved to London in 1786 (abandoning his town house in Edinburgh, but not his country seat of Auchinleck), a London newspaper such as the *Whitehall Evening Post* was the best way for Dun to garner Boswell's, and his readers', attention.

SHOULD WE BELIEVE BOSWELL OR DUN?

So, with the rediscovery of the *Whitehall Evening Post* letter to Paine, we now know not just that Dun denied that Johnson ever called him a man as ignorant of the Church of England as a Hottentot, but we also know the exact words he thought he heard, viz., "Sir, you know nothing of the matter." But knowing that, we face this puzzle: which of our two alternatives was the sentence Johnson actually said? Was it "Sir, you know no more of our Church than a Hottentot," or "Sir, you know nothing of the matter"? Boswell's quotation *sounds* more like the Johnson of legend familiar to us. Yet that is mainly because the Johnson of legend was popularized by Boswell and his rivals Hawkins and Piozzi, by the slew of other and even more minor Johnson biographers, and by those satirists such as Churchill and Campbell who mocked "Dr. Pomposo" and "Lexiphanes," respectively. The mythical Johnson, the sesquipedalian ogre-khan of Tobias Smollett's "Great Cham of literature" (1759), Archibald Campbell's *Lexiphanes* (1767),[45] Philip Melton's "Mr. Oddity" (1777),[46] Peter Pindar's "Great Caliban, the giant Johnson" (1778),[47] Charles Churchill's (1762) and then James Gillray's "Dr. Pomposo" (1783),[48] or Pasquale de Paoli's "Polyphemus" (1784)[49] had already emerged in the public imagination years before Johnson's three or four major biographers had printed a word of recollection of the great man, whether *pro* or *contra*, in the years from 1784 to 1791.

The power and prevalence of that version of Johnson—or constellation of versions (*Ursa Major*)—which was emergent in 1760–1784 produced a remarkable effect in his audiences in taverns and drawing rooms. In his final quarter-century of life, contemporaries' experience and memory of the real-life Johnson as a man and a speaker was shaped by these stereotypes and spoofs, to varying degrees, depending on how well they got acquainted with him in any depth or intimacy.[50] Even for those such as Boswell and Hester Thrale Piozzi who came to know him very intimately in his later years, there was still a risk that even their experience of Johnson would be filtered in part through the mythical Johnson of pamphlets, farces, verses, cartoons, and even animal or monster metaphors. In these recensions, his natural (or cultivated) manner of speaking was rendered into an even more "Johnsonese" versions of his utterances, a form of speech often based on his more formal and Latinate published writings such as the *Rambler* papers.

This condundrum brings us back to the essential problem we began with, that of how accurately Boswell reported conversation. Piozzi, Burney, and Macaulay described him as a frenetic transcriber of notes on the spot whose pinpoint accuracy was never in question any more than his pinprick impertinence; Pottle and William R. Siebenschuh stressed his allegedly astounding memory, which Pottle asserted was nearly phonographic if properly cued by a written record; Pittock, following Donald Greene, has essentially called Boswell a liar who made up the persona of Johnson by suppressing some facts and exaggerating others for purposes of "making Johnson up," and Bell described the *Life* as a "supreme fiction"[51] In literary-critical circles, the more technical questions of how and how accurately Boswell recorded conversation devolved, from the late 1960s onwards, into what has been described as the "Truth versus Art" or "Fact versus Art" debate. Was Johnson in Boswell's *Life of Johnson* more of an accurate historical record of how Johnson sounded and what he said? Or was Boswell's Johnson rather a fictionalization or docudrama, fairly far removed from the original historical Samuel Johnson, whether one believed him to have been transformed by Boswell into an excessively pure Platonic Christian hero or an excessively foul pantomime grotesque?[52]

I myself have argued that Boswell reconstructed speeches through jotted verbal cues in his notes made soon after conversations. He then expanded these keywords through a mode of versimilitudinous reconstruction of typical speech, rather than by means of total recall or cued phonographic memory. (The method was time-honored, and had previously been used by Thucydides and other historians.)[53] Boswell could not, even with the power of memory, recall 100 percent of the *ipsissima verba*, any more than Truman Capote, who would claim in the 1960s to possess a same gift or skill of near-total recall, might have been able to do. He could only write legitimate simulacra of the way people spoke, in order to add flesh to the skeletons of memoranda, and months- or years-old memory. This view of how Boswell recorded conversation will be familiar, since it is essentially a variant of the theories of Geoffrey Scott (1929), Marshall Waingrow (1968), and Frank Brady (1984), in their foundational works on Boswell's method of recording conversation. Waingrow described "local verbal precision" in "key words and phrases" rather than a stem-to-stern *verbatim* stenographical recording of what Johnson had said.[54] However, such a theory does differ from two popular views of Boswell's accuracy. First, it rejects the view of Greene that Boswell was a uniquely bad, dishonest, and inaccurate biographer. Second, it pushes away from the theories of those literary critics who stressed that the *Life* was more valuable or significant as Art than as Fact, or was some unusual and rare successful hybrid of documentary and drama rather than a more conventional biography, even by Georgian standards.[55]

Short of traveling back to the eighteenth century to record the exchange at the Auchinleck manse on the night of the November 5, 1773, we cannot know with absolute certainty whose recollection was correct. We could only determine the matter were we to apply Frederick Pottle's theory that Boswell's memory was of a prodigious strength and capacity, so that in the case of him or someone else remembering differently, Boswell is probably right. On the other hand, in the interest of fairness, we could as easily apply Greene's rubric that if Boswell reports Johnson as saying something and Hawkins, Piozzi, Burney, or Campbell, or probably anyone else, really, report it differently, Boswell must be misreporting or distorting, and the other(s) must be the truer witness. However, as these two hermeneutic premises cancel each other out, they can be of no possible good in resolving what happened.

What is more useful is to note that Boswell was not simply or solely relying on his memory when he contradicted Dun. This view takes into account the textual problem, discussed in detail earlier in this essay, that much of the final segment of the *Hebrides Journal*, as published in 1785, is of far weaker textual authority as a retelling of what actually happened than the segments of near-contemporary journal which Boswell composed up to the entry for October 22, 1773. Nonetheless, as this scrap was presumably generated in these weeks as the duo completed their tour, it is the closest textual record of the words Boswell heard Johnson say. The words "know no more of our church than a Hottentot" are the only multi-word snatches of all of his conversations that Boswell chose to record on his one sheet of journal notes for October 22–November 5 which he carried from Oban to Auchinleck. That ill-scribbled scrap confirms that Boswell's core memory of the Dun and Johnson exchange was, as he retorted to Dun, that Johnson used the word "Hottentot" to demean Dun's knowledge of the Church of England. The fragments for these days were clearly precious to him, and presumably he was able to draw upon this sheet when he opposed Dun's memory of the exchange in 1789. By contrast, there is no similar brief account which Dun had possessed to prompt his recollections in 1785, 1789, or 1791; the letter to Paine suggests that Dun was relying on memory years after the fact, rather than on diaries or letters. Simply observing a lack of contemporary textual record does not disqualify Dun's memory from validity, of course. Furthermore, the Boswell and Dun accounts of November 5 are, despite all the bitterness Boswell and Dun generated on debating their wording, much the same in basic theme and plot: Dun criticizes the Church of England and its episcopal system, and Johnson replies that Dun is ignorant of the Church of England. Given that we seem much surer now that 'Know no more of our church than a Hottentot' was probably something that Johnson said to Dun in 1773, what remains?

The remaining puzzle is why Boswell did not simply do an old mentor a favor, and withdraw the Hottentot story from the second and subsequent editions of *Hebrides Tour*. Granted, the passage is an important element in Boswell's portrayal, sustained in both *Hebrides Tour* and *Life*, of Johnson as a champion and a doctor of the Church of England, perhaps even a saint of sorts. In the Appendix to the former, just after the extended discussion of what Blacklock said or did not say to Johnson as variably remembered by Boswell and Blacklock, Boswell offers a principle which is foundational to his stubborn response to Dun and Blacklock both:

> If this book should again be reprinted, I shall with the utmost readiness correct any errours I may have committed, in stating conversations, provided it can be clearly shewn to me that I have been inaccurate. But I am slow to believe, (as I have elsewhere observed,) that any man's memory, at the distance of several years, can preserve facts or sayings with such fidelity as may be done by writing them down when they are recent: And I beg it may be remembered, that it is not upon *memory*, but upon what was *written at the time*, that the authenticity of my Journal rests.[56]

At any rate, with assurance we can add Dun's festive November 5 dinner with Johnson and Boswell to a long historical list of social lunches gone horribly wrong. If Dun's memory was accurate, it was a rather silent "dinner" after the point at which Johnson condemned Dun's ignorance of Anglicanism, with not much conversation left to record.

THE IMPORTANCE OF THE "HOTTENTOT" IN BOSWELL'S FLEMISH PORTRAIT

Even if we cannot know what Johnson said, we can know with certainly that Boswell bought the newspaper which contained Dun's letter to Paine, presumably with the intention of reading it. We can also know that he asked Charles Dilly, his publisher, bookseller, and friend, to acquire all of the issues of the *Whitehall Evening Post* which contained Dun's counterpoints to Burke and Paine.

Boswell's accounts with Charles Dilly show this entry in 1791:

                Paid for Whitehalls containing}
ept.   1   Mr Dun's Letters   }[57]

The shilling and twopence paid would certainly have covered the price of four fourpenny *Whitehall Evening Post*s.

Did Boswell eventually repent of his stubbornness with Dun in 1789–1791 over the issue of one petty Johnsonian insult? That, unfortunately, is unknowable, since there were no more chances after the third edition of 1791 (which was a trivial variant of the third edition of 1786, plus a new map) for Boswell to revise *Hebrides* before he died in London in 1795, only in his mid-fifties. He had last travelled in July 1794–January 1795 to the parish in which the Boswells of Auchinleck had been and would continue to be lairds and lay patrons. The former parish minister, Dun, had died in 1792, around sixty-eight years in age, and Boswell had done his duty in 1793 as lay patron in heeding the advice and consent of the kirk session in appointing Dun's replacement, John Lindsay.[58] Danziger and Brady remarked that in October 1792, "back in London, Boswell was further depressed by the news that the Rev. John Dun, his old teacher and the parish minister at Auchinleck for almost forty years, had died after a long illness."[59]

The offending "Hottentot" text remains in all authoritative editions of *Hebrides Journal*, though the ones by Pottle and Bennett and Ronald Black note Dun's objections.[60] Only in those editions such as Fitzgerald's (1874) which employed the first edition as copy-text is Dun's name revealed elsewhere than the footnotes as the clergyman whom Johnson opined knew no more of the Church of England than a Hottentot.

Boswell was a "feudal," "Tory" gentleman and a "clubable" man who valued friendship and conviviality. He wished to give proper regard to due social reticence and Georgian British standards of politeness demanding that respectable people not publish malicious gossip or undermining, defamatory tales. Yet he had a sort of compulsion to include most (though not all) of the scraps of conversation which he had heard during his roughly four hundred days in Johnson's company. In the *Life*, he observed that "I acquired a facility in recollecting, and was very assiduous in recording, his conversation, of which the extraordinary vigour and vivacity constituted one of the first features of his character. . . . I am fully aware of the objections which may be made to the minuteness on some occasions of my detail of Johnson's conversation. . . . I am . . . exceedingly unwilling that any thing, however slight, which my illustrious friend thought it worth his while to express, with any degree of point, should perish" (*Life*, 1:26, 33).

That observation goes some way to explain why Boswell was willing to damage or even destroy old friendships in order to publish a Johnsonian conversation, and insist on preserving the very wording Johnson used, no matter how abusive or insulting to living persons' reputations it might be. To us, it might seem fungible whether Johnson said "Hottentot" or not. To Boswell, it was an essential touch in his "Flemish Portrait" of his late friend and mentor.

NOTES

1. In the third edition, which provided the copy-text for the *Life*, ed. Hill and Powell, Boswell added the line, "Vanity and self-conceit indeed may sometimes suffer." He also changed "the object of them" to "the subject of them." James Boswell, *The Journal of a Tour to the Hebrides*, 1st ed. (London, 1785), 523–24; cf. *Life*, 5:416.
2. See O M Brack, Jr., "Attack and Mask: James Boswell's Indebtedness to Sir John Hawkins' *Life of Samuel Johnson*," in *The Interpretation of Samuel Johnson*, ed. J. C. D. Clark and Howard Erskine-Hill (Basingstoke, UK: Palgrave Macmillan, 2012), 43–71; Frederick A. Pottle, "The Dark Hints of Sir John Hawkins and Boswell," *Modern Language Notes* 56, no. 5 (May 1941): 325–29; William Yarrow, "Boswell's Debt to Mrs. Piozzi," paper presented at the East-Central/American Society for Eighteenth Century Studies Annual Conference, Philadelphia, 1992; Mary Hyde Eccles, *The Impossible Friendship: Boswell and Mrs. Piozzi* (Cambridge, MA: Harvard University Press, 1972), passim.
3. See "Appendix No. 1," on Thomas Blacklock (first published in James Boswell, *The Journal of a Tour to the Hebrides, The Second Edition, Revised and Corrected*, [London, 1785], 529–32), *Hebrides*, *Life*, 5:417–19; Joseph Cradock, *Literary and Miscellaneous Memoirs* (London, 1826), 237–38; *Johnsoniana, or, Supplement to Boswell: Being Anecdotes and Sayings of Dr. Johnson . . .* , ed. John Wilson Croker (London, 1836), 214–15; Thomas Campbell, *Dr. Campbell's Diary of a Visit to England in 1775, Newly Ed. From the MS.*, ed. James L. Clifford (Cambridge: Cambridge University Press, 1947), ix–x, 72–74; James Boswell, *Boswell: The Ominous Years, 1774–1776*, ed. Charles Ryskamp and Frederick A. Pottle (New

York: McGraw-Hill, 1963), 114n3, 123–24; Donald Greene, "Do We Need a Biography of Johnson's 'Boswell' Years?," *Modern Language Studies* 9, no. 3 (Autumn 1979): 133; Charlotte Ann Burney, April 7, 1781, writing April 10, 1781; BL Egerton MSS 3700 B, published in James Boswell, *Boswell: Laird of Auchinleck, 1778–1782*, ed. Joseph W. Reed and Frederick A. Pottle (New York: McGraw-Hill, 1977), 309–12, 309n7; James D. Woolley, "Johnson as Despot: Anna Seward's Rejected Contribution to Boswell's *Life*," *Modern Philology* 70, no. 2 (November 1972): 140–45; James L. Clifford, "The Authenticity of Anna Seward's Published Correspondence," *Modern Philology* 39, no. 2 (November 1941): 113–22; Donna Heiland, "Swan Songs: The Correspondence of Anna Seward and James Boswell," *Modern Philology* 90, no. 3 (February 1993): 381–91; Judith Jennings, *Gender, Religion, and Radicalism in the Long Eighteenth Century: [Mary Knowles] The "Ingenious Quaker" and Her Contemporaries* (Aldershot, UK: Ashgate, 2006), see chapters: "Confronting Samuel Johnson," 49–72; and "Defying James Boswell," 99–120.
4. See Richard B. Schwartz, "Epilogue: The Boswell Problem," in *Boswell's Life of Johnson: New Questions, New Answers*, ed. John A. Vance (Athens, GA: University of Georgia Press, 1985), 248–59; Louis Baldwin, "The Conversation in Boswell's *Life of Johnson*," *Journal of English and Germanic Philology* 51, no. 4 (October 1952): 492–506; D. Greene, "Do We Need a Biography?" 128–36; Paul Korshin, "Johnson's Conversation in Boswell's *Life of Johnson*," in *New Light on Boswell: Critical and Historical Essays on the Occasion of the Bicentenary of the Life of Johnson*, ed. Greg Clingham (Cambridge: Cambridge University Press, 1991), 174–93; Catherine N. Parke, "Johnson and the Arts of Conversation," in *The Cambridge Companion to Samuel Johnson*, ed. Greg Clingham (Cambridge: Cambridge University Press, 1997), 18–33.
5. John Dun (1724–1792) had served as chaplain in the family of Lord Auchinleck and had been young Boswell's first tutor, who had assigned him the *Spectator* papers as improving reading, and offered a more rational vision of Heaven which stressed the promise of meeting good and wise people rather than the threat of Hellfire. Licensed to preach in 1750 (presbytery of Irvine), he was called and ordained in the parish of Auchinleck in 1752, a post in which he remained until his death in 1792. He published a two-volume collection of his sermon, *Sermons, in Two Volumes, by John Dun, V.D.M.* (Kilmarnock, 1790). He was also the author of the *Statistical Account* survey of Auchinleck published after his death (*Statistical Account of Scotland*, ed. Donald J. Withrington, Donald and Ian R. Grant [East Ardsley, UK: E. P. Publishing, 1982], 6:13–17; repr. ed. Sir John Sinclair, 1791–1799). See Richard B. Sher, "Dun, John (1723/4–1792)." s.v. *Oxford Dictionary of National Biography Online* (2004). http://www.oxforddnb.com/; *Fasti Ecclesiæ Scoticanæ: The Succession of Ministers in the Church of Scotland from the Reformation*, ed. Hew Scott; 2nd ed. (Edinburgh, Oliver and Boyd, 1915–1981), 3:4.
6. "Thursday [November] 4, Bruce Camp[bell] & Jo[hn] Dun dinner" (Beinecke Rare Book & Manuscript Collection. Yale University Library, New Haven, CT, Boswell MSS J 33.1).
7. *Life*, 3:64–78. The Johnson-Wilkes dinner, as recounted in the journal and then revised for the *Life*, is addressed in Bruce Redford, *Designing the Life of Johnson: The Lyell Lectures, 2001–2* (Oxford: Oxford University Press, 2002), 103–9. A more innocent and wholesome example of an event which Boswell staged for effect was his escorting Sam Johnson on November 20, 1773 to the Scottish castle where Ben Jonson had been a guest of William Drummond of Hawthornden in the winter of 1618–1619; see James J. Caudle, "'O Rare Sam Jonson': James Boswell's Journal of a Tour to Hawthornden Castle with Samuel Johnson and Ben Jonson, 1773," *Age of Johnson: A Scholarly Annual* 22 (2012): 23–71.
8. *Life*, 5:371; see also Journal, October 29, 1773; *Boswell's Journal of a Tour to the Hebrides with Samuel Johnson, LL.D., 1773*, ed. Frederick A. Pottle and Charles H. Bennett, 2nd ed. (New York: McGraw-Hill, 1961), 364–65.

9. For the library, see Terry Seymour, *Boswell's Books: Four Generations of Collecting and Collectors* (New Castle, DE: Oak Knoll Press, 2016).
10. *Life* 5:377; *Boswell's Journal of a Tour to the Hebrides*, 371. "Tuesday 2 Auchin[leck] to dinner [i.e., arrived at Auchinleck before dinner]. Alone Wednesday 3 Wet. Gilmil{n}sc[roft] & Fing[land] dinner Fing[land] supper—& Bruce Camp[bell]]" (Notes November 2–3, 1773, Beinecke Library, Yale, Boswell MSS J 33.1). The local gentlemen were ?Alexander Farquhar (d. 1779) of Gilmillscroft, ?James Chalmers (d. 1783) of Fingland, "a man of moderate understanding and some taste, very honest and very obliging," and ?Bruce Campbell (1734–1813), of Mayfield and Milrig, "a rough, blunt, resolute young fellow with much common sense, and is very obliging to his friends" (James Paterson, *History of the County of Ayr: With a Genealogical Account of the Families of Ayrshire* [Edinburgh, 1847; repr. 1895]); Journal, September 14 and 19, 1762 [Chalmers], Journal, October 18, 1762 [Campbell]), in James Boswell, *London Journal, 1762–1763, Together with Journal of my Jaunt, Harvest, 1762*, ed. Frederick A. Pottle, deluxe ed. (London: Heineman, 1951), 44, 54, 85.
11. Johnson's comments at Talisker on September 23, 1773 are revealing and insulting in equal parts: "'The clergy of England,' said Johnson, 'have produced the most valuable books in support of religion, both in theory and practice. What have your clergy done, since you sunk into presbyterianism? Can you name one book of any value, on a religious subject, written by them?' We were silent. 'I'll help you. [Bishop] Forbes [William Forbes, 1585–1634, first Bishop of Edinburgh from 1634] wrote very well; but I believe he wrote before episcopacy was quite extinguished" (*Life*, 5:252).

    A detailed account of Johnson's intense religious bigotry against Presbyterianism and Calvinism may be found in Murray G. H. Pittock, "Johnson and Scotland," in *Samuel Johnson in Historical Context*, ed. Jonathan Clark and Howard Erskine-Hill (Basingstoke, UK: Palgrave Macmillan, 2002), 184–96.
12. Dun's wife Deborah (about forty-one years old), would presumably have been busy with their new baby, only a year and four months old. Little Alexander Boswell Dun had been named in honor of Boswell's father, Dun's ecclesiastical lay patron, who had made Dun's ecclesiastical career through appointing him to the church (although the congregation had rights of advice and consent over the lay patron's choice). Dun's two daughters from his first marriage were Elizabeth, then about age fifteen, and Isabella, then about age thirteen (Sher, "Dun, John")
13. Journal, September 2, 1780, in *Boswell: Laird of Auchinleck*, 237–39.
14. "Hallglen[muir] & ?Usher—They went with us & dined at Mr Dun's" (Notes November 5, 1773, Beinecke Library, Yale, Boswell MS J 33.1). Alexander Mitchell of Hallglenmuir is extensively mentioned in Boswell's journals. Usher is an unclear reading; possibly Askew?
15. In Journal, October 1, 1773, Boswell refers to "my friend Hallglenmuir" (*Boswell's Journal of a Tour to the Hebrides*, 240).
16. *Catalogue of the Private Papers of James Boswell at Yale University*, ed. Marion S. Pottle et al. (Edinburgh: Edinburgh University Press, 1993), 1:15–18
17. Ibid., 1:15–18.
18. Beinecke Library, Yale, Boswell MSS, J33.1
19. *Catalogue of the Private Papers of James Boswell*, ed. Pottle et al., 1:15–18
20. Beinecke Library, Yale, Boswell MS P84.
21. The textual rationale given by Pottle and Bennett for their editorial decision is baffling: "Our text up to the point at which the journal becomes fully written, and from the point at which the journal lapses, was that of Boswell's third edition, the last which he revised. When, however, the published *Tour* was used for filling in defects in the manuscript, the

first edition was chosen, because its phraseology was likely to be closer to that of the original record" (*Journal of a Tour to the Hebrides with Samuel Johnson*, xxii–xxiii [quoted], *Boswell's Journal of a Tour to the Hebrides with Samuel Johnson, LL. D., now first published from the original manuscript*, ed. Frederick A. Pottle and Charles H. Bennett [New York: Viking Press, 1936], xii–xiii). Pottle and Bennett prepared that edition in 1936 for the aborted Viking edition of Boswell's journals. Their 1961 text for the Yale Boswell Editions "trade edition" published by McGraw-Hill and Heinemann is a revision and expansion of *Boswell's Journal of a Tour to the Hebrides with Samuel Johnson, LL.D., 1773*, 2nd ed. (1961), xxii–xxv.

22. Notes November 5, 1773, Beinecke Library, Yale, Boswell MS J 33.1. Alexander Mitchell of Hallglenmuir is extensively mentioned in Boswell's journals. Usher is an unclear reading: possibly Askew?
23. Beinecke Library, Yale, Boswell M132.704
24. Ibid., M132.704
25. Boswell, *Journal of a Tour to the Hebrides*, 1st ed. (1785), 478–79.
26. Boswell, *Journal of a Tour to the Hebrides*, 2nd ed. (1785); preface signed "J. B.," dated "London, 20th Dec. 1785." The problem passage was now found on pp. 481–82. See Frederick A. Pottle, "General Notes on the Journal of a Tour to the Hebrides," in *The Literary Career of James Boswell, Esq.; Being the Bibliographical Materials for A Life of Boswell* (Oxford: Clarendon Press, 1929), 121–22.
27. Boswell, *Journal of a Tour to the Hebrides*, 2nd ed. (1785), 527 n*.
28. James Boswell, *The Journal of a Tour to the Hebrides with Samuel Johnson, LL.D. By James Boswell. . . . The Third Edition, Revised and Corrected*. 3rd ed. (London, 1786), iv–v; the problem passage about Dun was now found on 398–99; see Pottle, *Literary Career*, 121–23.
29. Boswell, *Journal of a Tour to the Hebrides*, 3rd ed. (1786), 435n*.
30. James Boswell to Margaret Montgomerie Boswell, December 5, 1788, in *Boswell: The English Experiment, 1785–1789*, ed. Irma S. Lustig and Frederick A. Pottle (New York: McGraw-Hill, 1986), 259–60, and 260n2.
31. James Boswell, *Register of Letters*, March 9, 1789, transcribed by Jerry Weng for the Yale Boswell Editions, unpublished edition.
32. James Boswell to Margaret Montgomerie Boswell, March 9, 1789, in *Boswell, the English Experiment*, 275–76, and 275n2.
33. *Life*, 5:381–82, and 569n4. The research edition is still ongoing.
34. "To Thomas Paine, Esq., Letter I" (dated Auchinleck Manse, Ayrshire, N[orth]. Britain, July 15, [1791]), published in *Whitehall Evening Post* 6720 (September 8–10, 1791).
35. "To Edmund Burke, Esq. on his 'Reflections'" (dated Auchinleck Manse, Ayrshire, North Britain [July 9, 1791], publishing in *Whitehall Evening Post* 6716 (August 30, 1791-September 1, 1791); "Mr. Dun's Letter to T. Paine is unavoidably postponed till our next," *Whitehall Evening Post* 6719 (September 6–8, 1791); "To Thomas Paine, Esq., Letter I" (dated Auchinleck Manse, Ayrshire, N. Britain, July 15), published in *Whitehall Evening Post* 6720 (September 8–10, 1791); "To Thomas Paine, Esq., Letter II" (dated Auchinleck Manse, Ayrshire, N. Britain, July 19), published in *Whitehall Evening Post* 6721 (September 10–13, 1791); "To Thomas Paine, Esq., Letter III" (dated Auchinleck Manse, Ayrshire, N. Britain, July 21), published in *Whitehall Evening Post* 6722 (September 13–15, 1791). [mentions letter to Burke in September 1 issue].
36. Miguel Cervantes, *The History and Adventures of the Renowned Don Quixote*, trans. Tobias Smollett (London, 1755), 2:102; Anonymous [Oliver Goldsmith], *The Life of Richard Nash Esq.; Late Master of the Ceremonies at Bath . . . The Second Edition* (London, 1762), 29.

37. "The two had a heated argument on toleration which led Boswell to dub him Johnson's literary anvil" (John Stephens, "Henry Mayo," s.v. *Oxford Dictionary of National Biography Online* [2008] http://www.oxforddnb.com/).
38. During the Highlands and Islands Tour of 1773, he was still Sir Alexander Macdonald of Sleat (in Scotland), Bart., but in 1776 he had been raised to the Irish peerage as Baron Macdonald of Slate, in the County of Antrim. The challenge to a duel is in James Boswell to Lord Macdonald, December 10, 1785 (Beinecke Library, Yale, Boswell MSS).
39. Samuel Collings, "Revising for the Second Edition," in *Picturesque Beauties of Boswell Parts I and II*, engraved by Thomas Rowlandson (London, 1786).
40. Peter Pindar [John Wolcot], *A Poetical and Congratulatory Epistle to James Boswell, Esq. on his Journal of a Tour to the Hebrides. With the Celebrated Dr. Johnson.* (London, 1786), 16n*.
41. The latest and most comprehensive account of this dispute is the currently unpublished Richard B. Sher, "Appendix 3: Boswell, Forbes, and the Quarrel with 'Young Mr. Tytler,'" which has been written expressly for the new edition of Boswell's heretofore unpublished correspondence with Sir William Forbes, exchanged during 1772–1794. Their solid friendship is one of the best-documented of Boswell's final decade. Until such time as Sher's comprehensive account, based on new evidence from the Fettercairn manuscripts at the NLS, is published, the reader should consult Claire Lamont's still-important "James Boswell and Alexander Fraser Tytler," *Bibliotheck* 6 (1971): 1–16.
42. James Boswell, *Register of Letters*, March 9, 1789. The original letter has not survived.
43. Pottle, *Literary Career*, 121–23.
44. Ibid.
45. Tobias Smollett to John Wilkes, March 16, 1759, Letter 39, in *The Letters of Tobias Smollett, M.D.*, ed. Edward S. Noyes (Cambridge, MA: Harvard University Press, 1926), 56
46. *Life* 3:209, reporting conversation of September 24, 1777; cf. Journal September 24, 1777.
47. Peter Pindar [John Wolcot], *A Poetical, Supplicating, Modest, and Affecting Epistle to Those Literary Colossuses The Reviewers* (London, 1778), lines 117–18.
48. Charles Churchill, *The Ghost*, books 1 and 2 (London, 1762; 1762; 1763); book 3 (London, 1762; 1763); and book 4 (London, 1763); James Gillray, "Apollo and the Muses, Inflicting Penance on Dr. Pomposo, round Parnassus" (London, 1783).
49. James Boswell, *Boswell: The Applause of the Jury, 1782–1785*, ed. Irma S. Lustig and Frederick A. Pottle (New York: McGraw-Hill, 1981), 144n8; and his *Boswelliana: The Commonplace Book of James Boswell*, ed. Charles Rogers (London, 1874), 318.
50. See Philip Smallwood, "The Johnsonian Monster and the *Lives of the Poets*: James Gillray, Critical History, and the Eighteenth-Century Satirical Cartoon," *British Journal for Eighteenth-Century Studies* 25 (2002): 217–24; Edward A. Bloom, "'As Fly Stings to a Stately Horse': Johnson under Satiric Attack," *Modern Language Studies* 9, no. 3, (Autumn 1979): 137–49; William Kenney, "Parodies and Imitations of Johnson in the Eighteenth Century," *Studies in Eighteenth-Century Culture* 7 (1978): 463–73.
51. For the view of Boswell as mere stenographer, see *Johnsoniana*, ed. Croker, 416 (anecdote 640); Frances Burney, Diary, October 15, 1782, in *Diary and Letters of Madame D'Arblay*, ed. Charlotte Barrett (London 1842–1846), 2:155–56. The "stenographical heresy" was declared demolished by John Everett Butt, *James Boswell*, University of Edinburgh Inaugural Lecture 3 (Edinburgh: Oliver and Boyd, 1959), 7–8. For the praise of Boswell's memory, see F. A. Pottle, "The Power of Memory in Boswell and Scott," in *Essays on the Eighteenth Century: Presented to David Nichol Smith in Honour of His Seventieth Birthday* (Oxford, Clarendon Press, 1945), 168–89; Frank Brady, *James Boswell: The Later Years, 1769–1795* (New York: McGraw-Hill, 1984), 329–33; Baldwin, "Conversation," 492–506; William R. Siebenschuh, "Boswell's Second Crop of Memory: A New Look at the

Role of Memory in the Making of the Life," in *Boswell's Life of Johnson: New Questions, New Answers*, ed. John A. Vance (Athens: University of Georgia Press, 1985), 94–109. For Boswell as liar, or at best, fabulist, see Murray G. H. Pittock, "Boswell's Li(f)e? Making Johnson Up," chap. 6 of his *James Boswell* (Aberdeen: AHRC Centre for Irish and Scottish Studies, 2007), 95–112; and Robert H. Bell, "Boswell's Notes Toward a Supreme Fiction: From *London Journal* to *Life of Johnson*," *Modern Language Quarterly* 38, no. 2 (June 1977): 132–48. The general debate on the accuracy of the life as biography is examined in Schwartz, "Epilogue," and John J. Burke, Jr., "But Boswell's Johnson Is Not Boswell's Johnson," both in *Boswell's Life of Johnson: New Questions, New Answers*, ed. John A. Vance (Athens: University of Georgia Press, 1985), 172–203, 248–59.
52. The ancestor of this line of argument is Ralph Rader, "Literary Form in Factual Narrative," in *Boswell's Life of Johnson: New Questions, New Answers*, ed. John A. Vance (Athens: University of Georgia Press, 1985), 25–52. Rader and his successors are discussed in Clingham, *New Light on Boswell*, 207–30. See also Irma S. Lustig, "Fact into Art: James Boswell's Notes, Journals, and the *Life of Johnson*," in *Biography in the 18th Century*, ed. John D. Browning (New York: Garland, 1980), 128–46.
53. See Caudle, "O Rare Sam Jonson," 23–71.
54. Geoffrey Scott, "The First Records," in *Private Papers of James Boswell From Malahide Castle*, ed. Geoffrey Scott and Frederick A. Pottle (privately printed, 1928–34), 6:15–27; Scott, "The Making of the Life of Johnson as Shown in Boswell's First Notes," in *Twentieth Century Interpretations of Boswell's Life of Johnson*, ed. James L. Clifford (Englewood Cliffs, NJ: Prentice-Hall, 1970), 27–39; James Boswell, *The Correspondence and Other Papers of James Boswell Relating to the Making of the Life of Johnson*, ed. Marshall Waingrow, 2nd ed. (New Haven, CT: Yale University Press, 2001), Brady, "Introduction," in *James Boswell: The Later Years*, 329–33.
55. Frederick A. Pottle, "The Adequacy as Biography of Boswell's *Life of Johnson*," originally in *Transactions of the Johnson Society*, Lichfield, 1974; repr. in *Boswell's Life of Johnson: New Questions, New Answers*, ed. John A. Vance (Athens, GA: University of Georgia Press, 1985), 147–60.
56. The text first appeared in Boswell, *Journal of a Tour to the Hebrides*, 2nd ed. (1785), 532; *Life*, 5:419.
57. Beinecke Library, Yale, Boswell MSS A24.
58. John Strawhorn, "Master of Ulubrae: Boswell as Enlightened Laird," in *Boswell: Citizen of the World, Man of Letters*, ed. Irma S. Lustig (Lexington: University Press of Kentucky, 1995), 117–34, 126–27.
59. James Boswell, *Boswell: The Great Biographer, 1789-1795*, ed. Marlies K. Danziger and Frank Brady (New York: McGraw-Hill, 1989), 189.
60. *Boswell's Journal of a Tour to the Hebrides with Samuel Johnson, LL. D*, ed. Pottle and Bennett (1936; 1961); Ronald Black, *To the Hebrides: Samuel Johnson's Journey to the Western Islands of Scotland and James Boswell's Journal of a Tour to the Hebrides* (Edinburgh: Birlinn, 2007), 584.

Part Two

LITERARY RELATIONSHIPS

Major Texts and Topics

4
OLIVER GOLDSMITH'S REVISIONS TO *THE TRAVELLER*

JAMES E. MAY

We think of Oliver Goldsmith as the author of imaginative works such as *The Traveller*, *The Deserted Village*, *The Vicar of Wakefield*, and *She Stoops to Conquer*, but he was a second Joseph Addison to his contemporaries, a master of prose. Before the publication of those major works, but after *The Citizen of the World* in 1762, William Rider, when surveying the best authors of his age, defines Goldsmith as a stylist: "While he is surpassed by few of his Contemporaries with Regard to the Matter which his Writings contain, he is superior to most of them in Style, having happily found out the Secret to unite Elevation with Ease, a Perfection in Language, which few Writers of our Nation have attained to."[1] Within a network of publishers, editors, and fellow writers, Goldsmith supported himself by recasting what others said into his own words. During most of his seventeen years as an author, he was a professional reviser, much like a modern copyeditor. After years of straightening out others' sentences, he brought considerable skill to late revisions of his own earlier works.

GOLDSMITH AS A RE-WRITE MAN

Even Goldsmith's translations were exercises in rewriting, much akin to recasting knowledge for John Newbery's juvenile readers, forging the clear, plain style praised by Rider and others. His first substantial publication was a translation of Jean Marteilhe's *The Memoirs of a Protestant Condemned to the Galleys of France, for his Religion . . . Translated . . . By James Willington* (1758), which Ralph Wardle describes as "never literal" and rewritten to make the account "more vivid and moving" than the original.[2] Goldsmith's journalism and historical writings are full of plagiarized translations, identified in Arthur Friedman's edition *Collected Works of Oliver*

Goldsmith and in Ralph Wardle's biography.[3] The first number of *The Bee* has acknowledged and unacknowledged translations from Boccaccio, the *Encyclopédie*, Justus Van Effen, and Voltaire; the second number, from the last two; and the third, from all but Boccaccio. On occasion in *The Bee* Goldsmith rewrote what he had written for *An Enquiry into the State of Polite Learning*.[4] Translation with revision was the foundation of many of the Chinese letters in *Public Ledger* (1760–1761), reprinted as *The Citizen of the World* (1762), and also enabled Goldsmith to produce historical works like *A History of England, in a Series of Letters from a Nobleman to his Son* (1764); *The Roman History* (1769); *The Grecian History* (1774); and *A History of the Earth and Animated Nature* (1774).[5] The popular English and Roman histories were subsequently abridged by Goldsmith. More relevant to his developing editorial skills were his abridgment of *Plutarch's Lives* to fill the first four volumes of *A Compendium of Biography* (1762), and a number of incidental tasks for Newbery that are conjectured, such as revising *The Martial Review; Or, A General History of the late Wars* (1763), which, says Temple Scott, he "licked into shape."[6] Newbery's ledger for Goldsmith as updated October 11, 1763, credits him for "Brookes' History," that is, *A New and Accurate System of Natural History*, by Richard Brookes, MD (1763-[1764]).[7] Wardle remarks that "Goldsmith seems to have revised the text and to have written a general preface for the entire work and introductions for the separate volumes."[8] Another rewriting project prior to *The Deserted Village* was the translation of Jean Henri Samuel Formey's *Histoire Abrégée de la Philosophie*, published as *A Concise History of Philosophy and Philosophers* (F. Newbery, 1766), for which John Newbery credited Goldsmith £20.[9] Goldsmith revised the sentences of *The Vicar of Wakefield* for its second edition (1766), making over twice as many alterations as Samuel Johnson did to *Rasselas*. Perhaps the finest application of Goldsmith's well-honed skills was to *An Enquiry into the Present State of Polite Learning* (1759), in which he improved phrasing and syntax on nearly every page. Of its second edition (1774), Friedman remarks, "So much of the material of 59 is omitted, rearranged, or modified in 74 that it is not possible to print a single text that will clearly present both forms of the work."[10]

A quick characterization of Goldsmith's revisions to prose is offered by *Essays by Mr. Goldsmith* (1765).[11] The first edition has a short preface and twenty-seven items, the final two of which are poems. The revised second edition for Griffin in the following year was entirely reset, with two added items, numbered 26–27, followed by the two poems completing the 1765 edition.[12] As the title page's motto "Collecta revirescunt" suggests, all the items were reprinted after earlier periodical publication except perhaps the poem "A New Simile in the Manner of Swift."[13] Unless they have revised accidentals, eleven of the essays were not revised for the second edition in 1766 (nos. 2–3, 5–6, 10, 12–13, 16, 18,

22, and 25). However, seventeen were revised, as were the preface and the two poems. Six were lightly revised (nos. 1, 4, 6, 17, 19–21), but others were closely revised, such as nos. 5 and 7–9 and the first poem (no. 28 in 1766). Furthermore, of the twenty-eight items in the first edition all but a translation of rules for assemblies in Russia (no. 22) had been revised for inclusion in *Essays* (1765). In addition, nine items that are from *The Citizen of the World* (essays nos. 10–14, 18, 20, 23, and 24), had been revised for *The Citizen* (1762) after prior publication in periodicals. Then all nine essays were further revised before inclusion in *Essays* (1765), and then five of these were additionally revised for the second edition of *Essays* (1766) (nos. 11, 14, 20, 23, and 24). Goldsmith was often hard on himself, parting with many sentences and even paragraphs. A convincing case can be made that Goldsmith's revisions of the *Essays* included punctuation and some other accidentals, certainly paragraphing. One sort of variant speaks tellingly of his obsession with getting it right: he sometimes alters a word from X to Y and then later returns it to X. To give two instances, when in essay no. 18 from letter 108 of *Citizen of the World*, he denies that a foreigner's entry into Asiatic societies is impossible, he wrote in the *Public Ledger* (February 27, 1761) that merchants "found admission into regions the most suspicious"; in 1762 for *Citizen*, he revised this to "most suspecting"; then in 1765 he returned the reading to "most suspicious."[14] Similarly, when letter 119 was first published as an essay in *British Magazine* of June 1760, in its narrative a distressed former soldier recalls, "I gave a very good account"; for *The Citizen* 1762 this was changed to "long account"; then in 1765 it reverted to "good account" and in 1766 it became "true account."[15]

Friedman's Clarendon edition of Goldsmith in 1966, with its careful record of textual variants,[16] reveals for scholarly analysis Goldsmith's extensive revisions, yet, to judge from annual bibliographies like the *Modern Language Association's International Bibliography*, few have put to use its textual record—perhaps because of the complexity of the revisions and the strangeness of the notational system. (Roger Lonsdale's treatment of variants in Goldsmith's poems is much easier to grasp.)[17] Even the rare Goldsmith scholar who employs the Friedman edition's variants can be stumped. In discussing Goldsmith's uncertainty about there being an audience for poetry, Ricardo Quintana quotes two sentences from the dedication to *The Traveller* and remarks that Goldsmith "allowed the first sentence . . . to stand . . . after the success of *The Deserted Village* [when he revised the sixth edition in 1770]. . . . The sentence which followed he properly enough cut out." But no edition of the poem has the two sentences quoted by Quintana: he offers a misrepresentation of the first edition reconstructed presumably from Friedman's notes. The first sentence quoted is not in the first edition but is the sixth edition's revision that subordinates what is of value from the sentence following (that cut).[18] Quintana does not realize that the sentence deleted in the sixth could be cut because its essential information had been subordinated in the earlier sentence. Another rare use of Goldsmith's revisions occurs when Robert H. Hopkins responds to F. L. Lucas's criticism that *The Traveller* "rambles too much." Hopkins denies that it rambles "if we read the first edition (416 lines) rather than the sixth edition (438 lines). Seventeen [*sic*] of the additional 22 lines in the later editions occur in one verse paragraph attacking freedom (lines 363–80)."[19] Hopkins accordingly chooses to direct his ingenious examination at the first edition. But he should have noted that the lengthy addition he discusses occurred in the second edition, where, as discussed below, two lines were replaced with twenty lines and two of these were cut from the sixth edition—a detail suggesting that Goldsmith countenanced Hopkins's complaint about the length of the addition.

My hope is that this essay provides a thorough examination of Goldsmith's revision to one major work, *The Traveller; Or, A Prospect of Society* (1765 [1764]), which directly represents a solitary author confronting society while pursuing happiness, and which was revised with the aid of society. Of Goldsmith's two major poems, *The Traveller* reveals more about his practice and his craft. Although he made revisions throughout two revised editions of each, *The Traveller* was overhauled more intensively than was *The Deserted Village*, written after Goldsmith had gained assurance as well as reputation. In addition, we have a prepublication printed draft of *The Traveller*.[20] We also know a good deal about its composition. In the dedication to his brother Henry, Goldsmith indicates that "a part of this Poem was formerly written to you from Switzerland," in 1755, and, as Friedman indicates, that portion then completed is believed to be about 200 lines, an estimate based on William Cooke's anecdotes of Goldsmith published in *The European Magazine* in 1793.[21] Thomas Percy in his memoir of Goldsmith stressed that "nothing could exceed the patient and incessant revisal, which he bestowed upon" his major poems, and he notes that Goldsmith wrote drafts with "very wide" spaces between lines filled up "with reiterated corrections, that scarcely a word of his first effusions was left unaltered."[22] For Goldsmith, writing and revising were inseparable, and even his last revision reached beyond mere correction.

REPEATEDLY REVISING *THE TRAVELLER* AND *THE DESERTED VILLAGE*—EVEN ACCIDENTALS

After the sale of *The Traveller* to John Newbery in October or November 1764, Goldsmith continued to revise the poem. We know how aggressively he revised from the prepublication proof-sheets that have survived, entitled "A Prospect of

Society," the subtitle of the finished poem.[23] This incomplete draft, presumably impressed to assist revision, has five half-sheets signed B-E with roughly 20 lines per page for a total of 310 lines. Half-sheets B-D have leading (spacing), running titles, and pagination ([1] 2–12). The E half-sheet, without head-line and pagination, lacks the spacing that would aid in correcting the text. This proof contains an early version of Goldsmith's text incorrectly reproduced in nine blocks, with the last section coming first and the first, last. The non-extant F half-sheet, if it was set, would have held the initial lines of the poem (whatever came before line 73 of the first edition). The last lines of the first edition found in the draft are 385–400 (on B2/3 of "Prospect), and they could not conclude the poem; so we might assume the introduction was as yet unfinished.

After an earlier hypothesis by A. T. Quiller-Couch that the press simply composed Goldsmith's written sheets backwards, the now standard explanation was offered by A. E. Case and R. S. Crane and argued by William B. Todd: Goldsmith's draft was first typeset in eleven galleys with thirty-six lines in most but others with twenty-eight, thirty-eight, and forty-two lines, and, after galley proofs were produced for Goldsmith, these stored galleys were mistakenly set into formes for page-proofs in reverse order, such that the galley with the end of the poem ended up in the half-sheet B.[24] Between the jumbled imposition of "A Prospect of Society" and the first edition, the poem underwent extensive revision and considerable expansion as it grew to 416 lines. Friedman recognizes that "revisions and additions" occurred at this stage, but he understates the authorial effort separating *The Traveller* from the earlier draft, particularly when he describes changes as due to a "press-corrector,"[25] a claim that suited his choice of "A Prospect of Society" as a copy-text. There were at least two proofs of the title and dedication dated 1764, one with a single-sentence dedication and one with the published four-page dedication.[26] During these revisions, through inter-related changes in title and dedication, the poem was re-envisioned as "The Traveller." At this stage Samuel Johnson contributed lines to the poem.[27] Goldsmith's penchant for revision is especially apparent when one compares the first edition to the "Prospect" draft. At least 94 of the 310 lines of "A Prospect" have substantive alterations in the first edition (including those cut entirely): thirty-one lines in half-sheet B, twenty-one in C, seventeen in D, and twenty-five lines in E. Although half-sheet E in "A Prospect" is unleaded, it is not apparent from the overall changes that it held some earlier state of the poem that had received less authorial review than had text in leaded half-sheets. Besides the final sixteen lines of the poem, "A Prospect" is missing lines 93–102, containing part of the thesis and important lines setting up the prospect structure ("let us view these truths . . . through the prospect as it lies . . ." [lines 97–98]). Lines were added, cut and replaced in all but half-sheet C. For instance, the first and third couplets were never used in the published text, and the employed second couplet has a substantive variant. Plus, ten punctuation changes occur on nine lines, and two paragraph indentations are added.

 The Traveller, first published December 19, 1764, was considerably revised in the second edition, published March 14, 1765 without acknowledgment of its being revised, and later reissued as a "third" with corrections to three substantive errors and perhaps some accidentals in a cancellans F2/19–20. Two unrevised editions followed, the "fourth" on August 6, 1765 and the "fifth" on February 25, 1768, and then "The Sixth Edition Corrected," appeared on June 29, 1770. Seventh and eighth editions sharing an engraved 1770 title page with the imprint of "T. Carnan and F. Newbery junr." followed on December 8, 1770 and in late February 1772.[28] All these editions took the preceding edition for printer's copy, thus admitting some uncorrected errors into the sixth edition, which Goldsmith revised probably by marking up a copy of the fifth. The second edition has revisions on all but four pages fully set with type: Goldsmith added twenty-four lines, replaced four, reversed the order of lines in two passages, and cut a couplet and a four-line sentence from the dedication.[29] He rephrased substantives in twenty-one additional lines and altered all but one word in two lines (lines 141 and 337). Yet, surprisingly, more pages are revised in the sixth edition: all but one page with a full text contains a likely revision. In the dedication, Goldsmith cut a sentence, added an independent clause, and made seven other substantive changes; in the poem, he added four lines (lines 91–92 and 143–44 [lines 143–44 cut by the second edition], inserted after lines 90 and 138 of first edition), cut four others (lines 151–52 of the first edition, cut after line 154 of the sixth; and the lines 13–14 of the eighteen-line second edition insertion after line 358 of the first edition), and made fifteen phrasing changes involving multiple words and over thirty involving single substantives. That Goldsmith is responsible for almost all the single word changes is evident from there being few if any substantive variants in unrevised reprints and those usually being variant forms of the same word (noted below).

 Goldsmith's improvements to *The Traveller* can be sampled from changes in the second edition of *The Traveller* to lines quoted with approval by the *London Chronicle* (December 18–20, 1764). The sons of Holland

   Lift the tall rampire's artificial pride,
   That spreads its arms amidst the watry roar,
   Scoops out an empire, and usurps the shore.
   Onward methinks, and diligently slow
   The firm connected bulwark seems to go;
   While ocean pent, and rising o'er the pile,
   Sees an amphibious world beneath him smile. (lines 282–88, 1st ed.)

The first and final lines are not altered aside from final punctuation, but the movement of one couplet ahead of another and two phrasing changes make the second edition's image clearer, more dynamic, and more memorable:

> Lift the tall rampire's artificial pride,
> Onward methinks, and diligently slow
> The firm connected bulwark seems to go;
> Spreads its long arms amidst the watry roar,
> Scoops out an empire, and usurps the shore.
> While the pent ocean rising o'er the pile. (lines 284–89, 2nd ed.)

In the first edition, despite "Onward" earlier, the line "The firm connected bulwark seems to go" vaguely raises the question "go where?" In the second edition, "go" is followed by the moved line 283 ("That spreads. . . .") and rephrased initially so that the bulwark acts aggressively and its length is emphasized: "Spreads its long arms . . . Scoops out an empire. . . ." (The sixth edition will change "go" to "grow," which is the reading in the *London Chronicle*.) The second phrasing change uncouples the adjectives "pent, and rising," which conflict, and eliminates "and," already used twice in the third foot of several lines. Two pages later, Goldsmith reversed the order of lines in the couplet "I see the lords of human kind pass by / Pride in their port, defiance in their eye" (lines 323–24, 1st ed.), in a passage that brought a tear to Johnson when he recited it to Boswell in Scotland (Lonsdale, *Poems*, 649n). A passage more heavily revised in the second edition (lines 75–82, reduced to lines 75–80, 2nd ed.) further demonstrates the value of Goldsmith's revisions—it is discussed below as a potential impact of Johnson's review of the poem.

Of course, all Goldsmith's alterations in *The Traveller* will not be improvements for some readers—they were not for Goldsmith himself. In revisions for the sixth edition, Goldsmith removed or reversed a number of changes that he had introduced in the second edition, sometimes returning to a reading in "A Prospect." I am not referring to corrections of obvious blunders, such as in the fifth edition: "Gardian," "uncreasing," and "slooping" with "guardian," "unceasing," and "sloping" (lines 12, 25, and 105 of 1st ed; line 107 of 6th ed.), which the compositor might have corrected without an authorial tip, but changed readings repeated in the fourth and fifth editions. These re-revisions include (line numbers of first/sixth are given where they differ):

line 7: returning "realm" (2nd-5th eds.) to "realms" (the 1st ed. reading)
line 10: returning "Or" (2nd-5th eds.) to "And"
line 31: new paragraph added, returning the indentation cut in 2nd-5th eds.
line 50: returning "tenant, all" (2nd-5th eds.) to "heir, the world"

line 68: returning "night (2nd-5th eds.) to "nights"
line 69: replacing "Savage" (2nd-5th eds.; lowercase in 5th ed.) with "negroe" ("negro" in 1st ed.)
lines 122/124: replacing "this" (1st-5th eds.) with "the," the reading in "A Prospect"
lines 139–40 / lines 143–44: a couplet cut in the second is returned with a word change: "And late the nation found with fruitless skill / Its ["Their" in 1st ed.] former strength was but plethoric ill."
lines 351/357: returning "claim" (2nd-5th eds., including the cancellans F2 of 3rd ed.) to "flame"

With three months between the first and second editions, it seems unlikely that second-edition changes were hastily made. Also, the return in the sixth to earlier readings suggests that Goldsmith may have critically compared readings in earlier editions. Certainly he seems to have looked closely at the fifth edition. One of two substantive variants in the fifth is the sort of compositorial error that is long repeated in later editions due to its making sense. In the second edition he added the couplet "And even those ills, that round his mansion rise, / Enhance the bliss his scanty fund supplies" (inserted after line 98 of 1st ed.; lines 201–2 of 6th ed.). The fifth edition changed "ills" to "hills," which might well "rise" over a mansion, but Goldsmith returned the reading to "ills" in the sixth.[30] One curious oddity is that all but one of the nine instances of reversion are from the B and C half-sheets (C2v ends with line 145), but authorial changes in substantives and accidentals are frequent in the later half-sheets, some altering readings new in the second edition. For instance, in a couplet added to the second edition after line 336 of the first (line 340 of the 6th ed.), Goldsmith replaced "kindred claims that soften life" with "claims that bind and sweeten" (now there are two consequences of the claims not shared by "self-dependent lordlings"). Other changes in the sixth edition to readings late in the text and new in the second edition include "proud" replacing "cold" and "Hence" replacing "While" in line 368 and line 375. This same vacillation can be found in revisions of the second edition where readings not in "A Prospect" but introduced by the first edition are altered, as when the second removes lines 81–82.

Accidental changes that seem authorial occur throughout the sixth edition, and these deserve further scrutiny given the general inattention to accidental changes in Friedman's edition. The most frequent alteration in the sixth edition that fits a consistent pattern is the removal of contractions for "even." The spelling within "A Prospect" and the first and second editions of *The Traveller* show the same preference for "even." The compositor of the fourth edition, who contracted diverse other words, changed "even" to "ev'n" eight times (lines 130, 175, 201, 260, 306, 333, 338, and 413 of 6th ed.), and the compositor in the fifth converted seven of those "ev'n" readings to "e'en" (all but line 130), and changed one reading "Even" not changed in the fourth to "E'en" (line 31). In eight of nine of these cases (all but line 130), the sixth edition returned the reading to the full spelling. Although a couple contractions of "even" are not expanded in the sixth edition, we can suspect that these are authorial changes because the same change occurs to standing type revised for the fourth edition of *The Deserted Village* (in D2v/12.12 [line 212 of 4th ed.]). The authority of the change was sufficiently evident to Friedman that it is a rare case of his admitting a sixth-edition accidental variant into his copy-text. Two lines earlier, "even" was used, and apparently Goldsmith desired repetition. Critics have recognized Goldsmith's reliance upon the reiteration of words—if you seek repetition, you will not want an alternation of "even" with "ev'n" and "e'en." Generally compositors add contractions when resetting poetic texts, and certainly many uncontracted words (like "even") in the first editions of the two major poems (and in "A Prospect") become contracted in reprints. Yet, when single words that could be contracted replaced others in standing type of the fourth edition of *The Deserted Village*, "Unpractised" and "skilled" at line 147 and line 150, these are not contracted. While not a sure guide to what he wished in print, generally in his manuscripts Goldsmith wrote words out in full, employing few contractions, as is apparent from Katharine C. Balderston's exact transcription of spelling in her edition of his letters (which includes verse as in the letter to Mrs. Bunbury December 25, 1773) and Friedman's transcription of such autographs as the "Dodsley" version of *The Captivity: An Oratorio*.[31]

There is also evidence in standing type reimpressed in revised editions of *The Deserted Village* that Goldsmith made punctuation changes. Five authorized editions of *The Deserted Village* were published "for W. Griffin" in 1770, all quartos in half-sheets with the same layout: a half-sheet with a half-title and title page ("[A]"), a second unsigned half-sheet with the dedication to Joshua Reynolds ([a]), half-sheets B-G with the text, initially of 432 lines (with G2v blank). The first edition appeared May 25, 1770; the revised second on June 7; the "third," in fact but a variant-title reissue of the second, on June 13; the revised "fourth" on June 28; and the unrevised "fifth" and "sixth" on August 9 and October 4.[32] Not surprisingly given the speed of reprinting, the second through fifth quartos were reprinted with some pages, usually both formes of the half-sheet, set from standing type. The second/third edition was set with standing type of half-sheets [a], B and G and page E2r/16. In the 296 lines newly reset, eight words in the first edition were replaced with seven words, and fifteen accidentals were changed, ten involving punctuation. The shared typesettings have four accidental changes, all punctuation variants in half-sheet B: in line 47 (B2/3.17) a comma is added inside the line after "bowers"; in line 52 (B2v/4.4) the semi-colon after "decay" is changed to a colon; and in line 54 (B2v.6) and line 60 (B2v.12) the periods after "made" and "more" are changed to a semicolon and a colon, the last three all occurring at the line ends. Although the end-line changes might have involved accidents during the storage of type, the internal change argues for their authority as does the fact that the end-line variants are not in the longest lines on the page and are distributed down the page. Furthermore, the change to a colon after "made" and the period after "more" are clearly for the better, yoking contrasting elements in the first case ("A breath can make them, as a breath has made. / But a bold peasantry, . . . can never be supplied" (lines 54–56) and in the second preventing lines 61–62 with noun clusters from being a fragment. In the next edition of *The Deserted Village*, the "fourth," there are substantive and accidental revisions in the standing type of half-sheets C-D and the outer forme of F (F1r-F2v), 196 lines, and, on reset pages, authorial substantive changes on F2/19 and G1/21 as well as a number of accidental changes, some of which are probably authorial. Eight of ten pages with stored type have variants. Besides the change to "even" on D2v, there are four punctuation variants in the typesettings shared with the second edition: At the ends of line 120 and line 122 (line 16 and line 18 of C2/17) the semi-colons after "young" and "school" are replaced with commas, and within line 305 "ah, where" is changed to "ah where," (line 3 of F1/17). The lines ending "young" and "school" have longer lines above and below them, and there are good syntactical and logical reasons for the changes (lines 119–24 give a sequence of coordinate details, and the semicolons, coming at the end of couplets, break up the coordinate pattern). Friedman retains the first edition's punctuation in all eight instances, but editions through the seventh (1772) follow the revised readings.

Some of the punctuation changes in the sixth and, especially, the second editions of *The Traveller* are likely to be authorial because they are much more numerous than in the unauthoritative reprints of *The Traveller* and *The Deserted Village*. There are twenty-severn punctuation changes in the second edition and fifteen in the sixth edition of *The Traveller*, which work out to roughly 6.5 and 3.5 per 100 lines. The fifth, seventh, and eighth editions introduce into the 438 poetic lines, respectively, only 5, 2, and 9 punctuation variants, for an average of but 1.2 punctuation variants per 100 lines. (They introduce only two, zero, and one substantive variants.) The fourth edition of *The Traveller*, though it has no substantive variants, is more problematic, introducing fifteen punctuation variants (which excludes hyphenating three words), but the rate, at 3.4 per 100 lines, is still far lower than the revised second edition.

Although there are surely compositorial blunders in the punctuation changes of the second edition of *The Traveller*, many seem to be corrections that are likely authorial, not only by virtue of their frequency but by their position (as near substantive changes). One example is in line 74 where commas are added in the second edition after "first" and "is" in remarking that for the patriot "His first best country ever is at home." In line 97, where "view" is changed to "try," the comma after "eyes" is cut in "But let us view these truths with closer eyes, / And trace them through the prospect as it lies." Later in the paragraph the second cuts the comma after "shrub" in "Like yon neglected shrub, at random cast" (line 101). And it cuts the commas in "Woods over woods, in gay theatric pride" (line 106, 1st ed.; line 108, 2nd ed.) and "These here disporting, own the kindred soil" (line 117, line 119). Commas inside the line are rarely cut in unrevised reprints. Another sort of change in the second that should be suspected to be authorial is the return of punctuation in the first edition to a reading in "A Prospect": these changes fit vacillating ambivalence noted above. One such alteration occurs in the return of a comma after "partner" in "While his lov'd partner boastful of her hoard, / Displays . . ." (line 193 and line 195); another is the removal of the comma in "while around, the wave-subjected soil" (line 293 and line 297), occurring two lines before a phrasing change. Similarly, in a heavily revised passage, a corrective comma is added after "right" in "True to imagin'd right above controul" (line 328 and line 332) in a line following one with a substantive change (Friedman does not accept or note this revision). Goldsmith liked long descriptive sentences, yoking many details into a period; thus, I suspect his hand when a semicolon replaces the period after "smile" (line 288 and line 292) before a four-line fragment of noun phrases (moreover, Goldsmith rephrased the adjacent line 287 and line 291). Goldsmith's verse paragraphs, where couplets are not often end-stopped, have a syntactic complexity in which punctuation often is essential for sorting out syntax and sense. For instance, in the first verse paragraph on Britain, where general lines on the place are followed by a portrait of noble Britains, the line "Stern o'er each bosom reason holds her state" (line 321 and line 325) ends with a period in the first edition, making it part of the preliminary section. But in the second edition where the lines following are rephrased and two reversed in order, the period is changed to a comma (as it also is in Johnson's review in the *Critical Review*). With the comma, the line beginning "Stern"—as does the second line of the couplet—modifies "the lords of human kind" in line 324 and line 328.[33]

The cancellation of leaf F2 of the third edition to correct errors in the second edition indicates that Goldsmith did not read proofs (spelling blunders in other leaves went uncorrected), but the cancel does show he was attentive to the second edition after it was printed. The cancellans (with lines 345–68, 1st ed.; lines 349–90, 6th ed.), corrects three of the new substantives in the second edition: "Paint" with "pant," "Freedom's" with "Freedoms," and "fictious" with "factious" (line 352 and line 356; line 355 and line 361; and line 383, a line added 2nd ed.), and it introduces four punctuation variants, a relatively high number. All four punctuation changes can be justified grammatically, and one places a comma after "toil" between two independent clauses in a line with a substantive correction (line 355 and line 361), but none significantly impact meaning. When punctuation in the cancellans repeats a punctuation change in the second edition (as the removal of the comma after "freedom" in "To call it freedom when themselves are free," line 362 and line 384), it strengthens the case for accepting the change as authorial (Friedman keeps the comma). Cancellans F2 raises the possibility that some of many corrections in the fourth edition were requested when errors in the second were pointed out, corrections not justifying a cancellation but later made, like correcting "disply'd" with "display'd" (line 299 and line 303).

It is instructive to hypothesize why Goldsmith revised certain phrases, especially those altered after having already been changed. For instance, in line 69, the return of the reading to "negro" was helpful because there is a contrast in the passage between this individual "at the line" and the resident of the "frigid zone" that is lost with "Savage." With dozens of alterations in the two revised editions, the variants in *The Traveller* offer a literature class a good exercise for debating why a poet changed X to Y and whether Y is superior. Students will be divided over such comparable phrasings as "Soon Commerce turn'd on other shores her sail" and its replacement in the sixth edition, "Commerce on other shores display'd her sail" (line 138 and line 140) or "sleeps beneath" replaced by "slumber in" within "Dull as their lakes that sleeps beneath the storm" (line 308 and line 312). One can also take several revisions at once into consideration, such as the change of "expanded to the skies" and "extended wide" to present participles, "expanding" and "extending" (lines 6 and 35). And, taken together, the revisions to *The Traveller* and *The Deserted Village* offer great insight into Goldsmith's intentions in the poems and his values as a poet, his beliefs and his tastes, particularly when addressed historically, mindful of the reviews and the succeeding editions.

Writing and then revising *The Deserted Village* probably led Goldsmith to re-examine *The Traveller*. Of course, *The Traveller* (and reviews of it) provided inspiration for *The Deserted Village* as well as specific materials and language for treating luxury and depopulation and for modeling similar rhetorical appeals and persona affectively. Much is shared by the retired pastoral personae of both poems, both circumstantially outsiders but, as spectators, both with heightened sensibilities, thus not loners: he in the first poem wistfully envies his brother rooted in a community, and that in the second mourns his loss of a comparable rural community in which he had wished to make a home. One could read an isolated couplet or two about a careworn poet ("Here for a while my proper cares resign'd") wishing to "sit in sorrow for mankind, / Like yon neglected shrub" (lines 99–101) and mistakenly think it came from *The Deserted Village*. But the author of *The Traveller* might well have learned from the revision of *The Deserted Village*, or been reminded of practices involving diction, syntax, assonance, contractions, and punctuation that he liked or disliked, such as that involving participial forms noted above, for Goldsmith could have made changes in the sixth edition of *The Traveller* after twice revising *The Deserted Village* (the sixth edition of *The Traveller* appeared a day after the revised fourth of the other). Parenthetically, another instance of the new influencing the older poem is the publisher's decision to add an illustrative vignette like that on the title-pages of *The Deserted Village* to the title page of the seventh edition of *The Traveller* (1770), designed by Samuel Wale (1721–1786) and cut by Charles Grignion the elder (1721–1810).

The consensus in the best criticism on *The Traveller*, as by Hopkins, Lonsdale, and Quintana, is that the poem should be approached as neoclassical, that is, a rhetorical construct with not only logical arguments but appeals employing ethos and pathos and governing the persona. The poet reflecting on the world and his travels is a fictional construct even though Goldsmith in the dedication makes it clear that there is a personal expression in the part drafted long ago in Switzerland. As we would expect, the strongest non-logical appeals are in the introduction and conclusion. *The Traveller* has the speaker present himself as a "solitary" wanderer from the start, beginning with a contrast between himself, a "houseless stranger," and his brother engaged by "the ruddy family," which stresses the "ceaseless pain" felt by his heart at this separation from his brother, who invites in strangers, while the poet is sometimes shut out (lines 3–4). In paragraph 3 the speaker calls on our sympathy: "My prime of life in wand'ring spent and care.... My fortune leads me to traverse realms alone, / And find no spot of all the world my own" (lines 24–30). Then in paragraph 4: "where Alpine solitudes ascend, / I sit me down a pensive hour to spend" (lines 31–32), and this initiates the poem's prospect structure, where reflections on happiness shift from the personal to the national. The image is that of the title-page vignette for the seventh edition. Looking "downward where an hundred realms appear" (line 35), the melancholic traveller is pressed to find relief, but also, as part of his philosophical quest, a society most conducive to happiness, and he is pained further to survey a world where "the sum of human bliss" is "small" (line 58). Personal and universal happiness are linked, for people are social creatures: where the first edition speaks of "social bonds, / As duty, love, and honour," the sixth edition replaces "social bonds" with "nature's ties" (lines 349–50, 6th ed.). The poem then logically develops its theses about nature supplying man with a sufficient if uneven bounty and man creating cultural goods and values that bring happiness but, as the dedication puts it, "may be carried to a mischievous excess." The contrasting survey through Italy, Switzerland, France, Holland, and England will end with a critique of England, peaking in a satire on reckless wealth and modulating into sympathy for those forced off the land and then for the poet (there is a transition as the "exile . . . bids his bosom sympathize with mine"). In closing, the traveler reflects on his "vain . . . weary search to find / That bliss which only centers in the mind" and sums up his political survey treating happiness as a social product: "Each government" bestows it (lines 401–4—a point also made at the end of the dedication).

I dwell on the traveler's expression of his emotional experience because the reviewers passed over the non-argumentative dimension of *The Traveller* with quick praise of the poetical merit before summarizing and analyzing the logical argument. This is also largely true of the reviews of *The Deserted Village* in the *Critical Review* (anonymous) and by John Hawkesworth in the *Monthly*, which spend much time denying Goldsmith's social critique—in the words of the former, "Whatever is, must be ultimately right."[34] Yet what Quintana said of *The Deserted Village* is true of *The Traveller*: "It is indeed a kind of argument, [but] it is always a poem."[35] Lines portraying the speaker or making non-logical rhetorical appeals received the fewest of Goldsmith's revisions. The reviewers' focus on the political within the poem apparently encouraged Goldsmith to focus his revisions on the political and philosophical contents of the poem. All the new lines added to the second and sixth editions develop the theme of comparative happiness; none focus on the traveler. Deletions of a few lines can be related to reviews, but most cuts seem intended to eliminate poorly phrased or somewhat redundant couplets. Only a few phrasing changes are related to the persona.[36] Looking at Goldsmith's major revisions in the light of the reviews directs attention to his (and others') understanding of his central theses about happiness and its foundations.

REVISING IN RESPONSE TO JOHNSON'S AND OTHERS' PUFFS AND REVIEWS

Immediately upon publication several newspapers supported Goldsmith by announcing the poem with favorable reviews and excerpts. *The Traveller* was puffed with two paragraphs and a lengthy excerpt in both the *London Chronicle* of December 18–20, 1764, and *Lloyd's Evening Post* of December 19–21.[37] The *London Chronicle* begins by noting poets have failed to "solicit the attention of the Public in any extraordinary degree, without leaning on party for support," thus echoing a critique in Goldsmith's dedication.[38] This writer "builds upon a nobler and more extensive plan." Then comes greater praise: "It were injustice to this ingenious gentleman not to allow him a degree of poetical merit beyond what we have seen for several years, and we must acknowledge him possessed of a strength and connexion of thought which we little expected to see." There follows a specimen involving a "description of England and Holland" (lines 277–330). This puff gives no attention to the thematic argument, perhaps thus further stressing the poem's freedom from politics or ideology. *Lloyd's Evening Post* has a longer introduction summing up more of the dedication and poem before quoting lines 162–234.[39] The review begins by noting the poem "was written when the author was in Switzerland, [and] is addressed to his brother, a Clergyman [retired on £40]," and then plagiarizes Goldsmith's thesis statement at the end of the dedication: "This poem was written with an intent to show, that the happiness of most countries is nearly equal; that each country has some one peculiar principle of happiness; and that this principle may be carried in every country (and in our own in particular) to a mischievous excess." It concludes with fulsome praise, employing the word "connexion" found in the previous review: "All that harmony of numbers, or admirable connexion can give to render this doctrine pleasing, is here exhibited, and whether we consider this ingenious writer as a Philosopher, or a Poet, we shall find him excellent in either capacity." Choosing what to quote bewilders ("we know not where to fix"); so, "we shall select an example from the prospect of Switzerland, not because it is the best, but because it has been hitherto unobserved" (lines 162–234 inclusive, reprinted with few variants). The reason for the selection indicates the knowledge that other papers have reprinted other lines. This suggests a coordinated media blitz involving periodicals to which Goldsmith contributed as well as friends like Samuel Johnson and Tobias Smollett. Johnson's contribution to the first edition and the promotion of the poem will be discussed below, but in the context of this free publicity I would stress that Goldsmith's creative life was not that solitary; probably some revisions were suggested privately by colleagues and the reviews themselves offer suggestions for revisions, perhaps even inadvertently when making an error in transcription, like "grow" for "go" in the *London Chronicle* review, a reading inserted in the sixth edition's revisions (line 288).

The laudatory notice in the *Gentleman's Magazine* of December (1764) offers another two-paragraph review.[40] It begins, "We congratulate our poetical readers," a remark with which Johnson's review ends, but here the flattery is explained as owed the public for recognizing good poetry, as opposed to those "virulent rhapsodies" formerly approved that in "future time will disgrace the present."[41] As in the *Lloyd's* review, the *Gentleman Magazine*'s second paragraph sums up the poem's thesis by plagiarizing the dedication: "*there may be happiness in other states* equal to our own, *though differently governed*, and *that each state has a peculiar principle of happiness*, which, however, *may be carried to a mischievous excess.*" The italicized words are Goldsmith's. In the original Goldsmith's first proposition has more modification: "other states, though differently governed from our own." Goldsmith, who revised the dedication twice, later also became impatient with the often-quoted phrasing and tightened the sentence in the sixth edition to "states that are differently governed,"[42] but it continued to call attention to the poem's questioning of patriotic ethnocentrism. Deleted from the second assertion in the *Gentleman's Magazine*, but present in *Lloyd's*, are words critical of Britain: "That this principle [of happiness] in each state, and in our own in particular, may be carried to a mischievous excess."[43] In the sixth edition, Goldsmith cut "state, and in our own in particular," perhaps encouraged not to single out criticism of England by the patriotism in this review. The reviewer goes on to indicate that the thesis is shown by "comparison [later called "contrast"] of *Italy* with *Switzerland*, and *France* with *Holland*." Then he inaccurately notes the poem "concludes with an apostrophe to *England*, in which the author has shewn a warm love for his country, without deviating into either bigotry or enthusiasm,"[44] apparently playing up the patriotic angle for sales.

The reviewer would like to "exhibit as a specimen the prospect of *Italy* and *Switzerland*" but that would be "too long" and so "selects only that of *Britain*." Four verse paragraphs are quoted (lines 313–70): the first praises Britain's landscape and its independent "lords of human kind"; the second decries the "independence Britons prize too high" for breaking "the social tie" (line 336); the third satirizes how "wealth and law . . . force unwilling awe" and "merit weeps unknown; / Till Time may come, when . . . kings unhonor'd die"; and the fourth, also severe in tone, insists that, "when contending chiefs blockade the throne, . . . I fly from petty tyrants to the throne" (lines 358–70). What is quoted seems remarkably Tory, ironically demonstrating the "enthusiasm" that the reviewer denies to be in the poem; however, the *unquoted* next paragraph is more strident: it refers to that "baleful hour / When first ambition struck at regal power," probably alluding to the regicide of Charles the first, though Norma Clarke asserts the reference is to the Glorious Revolution.[45] Given the media blitz, the similarity to Johnson's review, and the quotation of all the lines that Johnson quoted (including lines that later made Johnson shed a tear on reciting them), one cannot but wonder if Johnson orchestrated the review.

Some of Goldsmith's revisions appear to be responses to John Langhorne's lengthy account in the *Monthly Review* for January 1765, which could be called "favorable with reservations" and quotes 226 lines.[46] Langhorne repeatedly questions the precision of Goldsmith's remarks, thus maintaining a contentious tone. At the start he criticizes as vain Goldsmith's claim in the dedication to being "not much solicitous to know what reception it [the poem] may find," especially as the poem is delightful on three counts: beautiful "scenery, a refined elegance of sentiment, and a correspondent happiness of expression."[47] Curiously, in the sixth edition Goldsmith cut "much" before "solicitous,"[48] as if doubling down. After defining the poem as a prospect poem, quoting lines 37–50, he takes issue with Goldsmith's slighting of "patriotic boasting" of one's native home (lines 81–82), for, although "Nature has, in general, observed an equality in the distribution of her bounties," this boast "is amongst those pleasing errors that contribute to our happiness."[49] As discussed more below, Goldsmith will cut lines 81–82 in the second edition. Langhorne then doubts Goldsmith's essential proposition that "there is in every state a peculiar principle of happiness" since states are composed of individuals whose principles vary among themselves.[50] Langhorne's central point seems summed up by a long introduction to verses on Italy (lines 103–62): "our Author makes no great figure in political Philosophy, [but] he does not fail to entertain us with his poetical descriptions."[51] Though Langhorne thinks the portrait of Italians "just," for comment, he quotes a second time lines 153–56: "When struggling Virtue sinks by long controul, / She leaves at last, or feebly mans the soul; / While low delights . . . In happier meanness occupy the mind." Then he asks whether Goldsmith has not "laid open a redoubt which the Moralist ought never to give up, when he represents the Italians as a happier people [by virtue of "low delights"] when fallen from their virtue?"[52] Of those two couplets, Goldsmith in the second edition revised the first, softening the characterization of Italy as a land without virtue: "When noble aims have suffer'd long controul, / They sink at last, or feebly man the soul." In the sixth edition, he cut the preceding couplet that claimed Italy's passivity left it vulnerable ("At sports like these, while foreign arms advance, / In passive ease they leave the world to chance" [lines 151–52]), cut the indentation of the new paragraph at line 153, and rephrased lines 153–54 again: "Each nobler aim represt by long controul, / Now sinks at last, or feebly mans. . . ."

Dissatisfaction with the Italian section led Goldsmith in the second edition to replace a couplet earlier quoted by Langhorne that also treats the aftermath of commerce's decline in Italy: "And late the nation found, with fruitless skill, / Their former strength was now plethoric ill" (lines 139–40). The replacement was not evidently due to dissatisfaction with the unpoetical, pretentious word "plethoric," for the couplet (with "Its" replacing "Their") was returned to the text in the sixth edition after that replacing it. The new lines 139–40 are more concrete and clear and add another instance of depopulation, looking forward to that theme in the English section: "While nought remain'd of all that riches gave, / But towns unman'd, and lords without a slave." None of the reviews of *The Traveller* discuss the depiction of depopulation; however, reviews of *The Deserted Village* did, and

Goldsmith had presumably already heard from friends the disbelief mentioned in the dedication of *The Deserted Village*.

Langhorne proceeds to a very lengthy quotation on Switzerland (lines 163–234), which he praises as "beautiful—but the simile of the babe is something more; there is a grandeur as well as beauty" (referring to "And as a babe, when scaring sounds molest . . . ," lines 201–4, in which Goldsmith will substitute "child" in the sixth edition). Goldsmith will make very few revisions to lines characterizing the Swiss, but within the paragraph highly praised he adds a couplet after line 198 in the second edition that balances the opening couplet: "Thus every good his native wilds impart, / Imprints the patriot passion on his heart" is now followed with darker notes: "And even those ills, that round his mansion rise, / Enhance the bliss his scanty fund supplies." The addition develops at least three points: that nature's bounty is uneven, that adverse circumstances make us happier with our lot (a paradox relevant to the attack on luxury), and that Switzerland is a rocky, "barren" state (line 205), helping set up the ensuing contrast with lush Italy. Langhorne makes a transition to his final quotation on the French by summing up Goldsmith's own transition and echoing the distinction between differing qualities of pleasure, remarking that "moral and intellectual refinements" augmenting the "happiness of life in cultivated societies" are not expected of the Swiss but are beheld in "people almost of a different species," the French.[53] After quoting Goldsmith's lines on France, including those on his playing the flute for dancers (lines 235–76), Langhorne remarks that, whether it be "fact or fancy" that the "Author" led the dancers, the image is "just."[54] The only substantive change in the French section quoted is "We" to "I" in line 236, noted above. Langhorne closes by insisting that the portraits of nations are not "full, or perfect" but from "a single point of view; such an one, indeed, as they are generally beheld: but the lights are much strengthened by the powers of poetic genius." Although he concludes by recommending *The Traveller* as "a work of very considerable merit,"[55] Langhorne throughout, while pointing out beauties, mainly examines the solidity of generalizations.

In his review for the *Critical Review* of December (1764), Johnson has almost nothing to say about the poetic elements of the poem, focusing on the "sentiments," meaning *sententiae*, developing the argument.[56] Other than an opening reference to the dedication to Goldsmith's brother, Johnson's commentary ignores most personal expressions in the poem. Like Langhorne, Johnson alternates quotations with comments, quoting 110 lines without noting omitted couplets within those quoted. Johnson begins by drawing the theme, or intention, from the close of the dedication, just as the reviewers in *Lloyd's* and the *Gentleman's Magazine* do, a practice directing attention to the "Prospect of Society," not to "The Traveller." Then Johnson quotes lines 1–10 and lines 31–44, which set up the Alpine perspective and the "sympathetic" mind's exaltation at "all the good of all mankind" (lines 43–44). From this quotation, Johnson affirms that "The author already appears, by his numbers, to be a versifier; and by his scenery [Langhorne's word, too], to be a poet," thus giving over any critique of the poetical qualities of the performance; what "remains" to be seen, for Johnson, is whether "his sentiments discover him to be a just estimator of comparative happiness."

After leaping over the traveler's subjective lines describing his alternating responses to human life (lines 51–62), Johnson advances to Goldsmith's big question ("where to find that happiest spot below," line 63) and a summary of Goldsmith's arguments: "Nature has distributed her gifts in very different proportions, yet all her children are content; but the acquisitions of art are such as terminate in good or evil, as they are differently regulated or combined."[57] Johnson accurately reflects the first proposition about nature, unlike Langhorne, who thought Goldsmith claimed nature's bounty was equal to all, but Johnson will overlook the role of this first assertion in the structure of the poem when he later surveys the sections on Italy and Switzerland. The second proposition about cultural products will be the focus of Johnson's review. This comment is followed by lines 63–72 and lines 83–96. These lines describe the "tenant of the frigid zone" (line 65) and "The naked Negro, panting at the line," thanking "his Gods for all the good they gave" (lines 71–72), and then jump to an account of the unequal but sufficient distribution of nature's gifts: "Nature, a mother kind alike to all, / Still grants her bliss at Labour's earnest call" (lines 83–84). Perhaps recognizing from reviews like Langhorne's a misperception at least in emphasis, Goldsmith strengthened his point about uneven natural resources by adding in the second edition, after line 84, the couplet "With food as well the peasant is supply'd / On Idra's cliff as Arno's shelvy side"—playing on the Italian word "selva" (forest) in "shelvy."

The last section of Johnson's quotation develops the second "proposition," involving cultural disparities:

> From Art more various are the blessings sent;
> Wealth, splendours, honour, liberty, content;
> Yet these each other's power so strong contest,
> That either seems destructive of the rest.
> Hence every state, to one loved blessing prone,
> Conforms and models life to that alone. . . .
> 'Till, carried to excess in each domain,
> This favourite good begets peculiar pain.[58]

For Johnson, this is the thematic core, more complex than that offered in the dedication. Despite Johnson's satisfaction with these lines, Goldsmith in the second edition changed "splendours" (which I take to mean arts and artifacts) to "commerce" (line 88). In the sixth edition, after line 90, he added a couplet developing the "contest" between these social goods: "Where wealth and freedom reign contentment fails, / And honour sinks where commerce long prevails." The dangers from excessive wealth and freedom look forward to the later accounts of Holland and England; the remark about commerce's destruction of honor looks toward the account of Italy. Johnson notes that this "position" Goldsmith "conducts through Italy, Swisserland, France, Holland, and England; and which he endeavours to confirm by remarking the manners of every country."[59]

Johnson skips over the section on Italy, only noting he "censured the degeneracy of the modern Italians,"[60] and then quotes twenty lines on the contentment of the Swiss (lines 163–82). Readers, however, might wish Johnson had commented on the Italian section's relation to the second proposition, that "favourite" goods are carried to excess. For Goldsmith, Italy is the place where nature is most bountiful, but culture now contributes less to happiness ("small the bliss that sense alone bestows, / And sensual bliss is all this nation knows," lines 121–22). Italy is sketched as living with the "degeneracy" (Johnson's word) that follow the splendors of luxury and collapse of commerce (lines 129–40). Now, writes Goldsmith, the people "An easy compensation . . . find . . . in bloodless pomp," in "Processions" and "sports of children" (lines 141–52). Unless it is happiness ("content"), the poem does not present a cultural "good" or blessing that is overdeveloped into excess and becomes an ill in the way that it later shows "wealth," "honour," and "liberty" to have become evils, respectively, in Holland, France, and England. The motivation for the Italian section is best understood in conjunction with Goldsmith's lines on Switzerland following, excerpted by Johnson: Goldsmith contrasts the bountiful nature in Italy with cold, stony nature of Switzerland, "Where the bleak Swiss their stormy mansions tread, / And force a churlish soil for scanty bread" (lines 165–66). Italy and Switzerland are not developed to exemplify the second proposition about cultural goods but the first about people's being capable of contentment with whatever natures bestows. The poem also displays the unevenness of nature's bounty in references to harsh or easy environments in descriptions of those in polar and equatorial lands (lines 65–72), of France's and England's pleasant landscapes (lines 240–42 and lines 315–19), and of America's "swamps" and "tangled forests" full of dangerous beasts (lines 389–93). Nonetheless, Goldsmith wished to advocate a posture of contented acceptance, a principal theme of the author according to Wardle,[61] and developed in such passages as "Creation's charms around combine, / Amidst the store, 'twere thankless to repine" [revised in the second edition to "should thankless pride repine?"] and in the exclamation "Creation's heir, the world, the world is mine" [revised in the second to "Creation's tenant, all" but then revised back] (lines 37–38 and line 50). The *Gentleman's Magazine* should not have stressed the poet's "warm love" for England but his love for creation—that wider appreciation dampened nationalistic ethnocentrism.

This cosmopolitan theme is most explicit in a verse paragraph (lines 75–82) that Johnson passed over in quoting lines 63–96. It follows the observation that the "patriot's boast" is that "His first best country ever is at home" (lines 73–74), also skipped by Johnson. This paragraph is more heavily revised than any in the second edition, and perhaps Johnson's omission of it, implying dissatisfaction, led Goldsmith to revise it:

> And yet, perhaps, if states with states we scan,
> Or estimate their bliss on Reason's plan,
> Though patriots flatter, and though fools contend,
> We still shall find uncertainty suspend,
> Find that each good, by Art or Nature given,
> To these or those, but makes the balance even:
> Find that the bliss of all is much the same,
> And patrioric [sic] boasting reason's shame. (lines 75–82)

In his revision, Goldsmith cut the wordy repetition of "find" and the vague abstractions "Reason's plan," "uncertainty suspend," and "makes the balance even"; and he twice replaced the word "bliss" with "blessing," thus maintaining the repetition of a key word. The revised paragraph is shorter, with simpler syntax and language, and without the troublesome claim that patriotism is "reason's shame":

> And yet, perhaps, if countries we compare,
> And estimate the blessings which they share;
> Tho' patriots flatter, still shall wisdom find
> An equal portion dealt to all mankind,
> As different good, by Art or Nature given,
> To different nations makes their blessings even. (lines 75–80, 2nd ed.)

The deleted attack on patriotism was at odds with some sentiments in the poem, as the Swisser's love of home (lines 197–204), but Goldsmith's revision might have been a response to Langhorne's criticism noted above.

After characterizing the lines on Switzerland as showing "the rural life of a Swiss has its evils as well as comforts" ("evils" moralizes the theme but seems incongruous with the presentation), Johnson briefly notes that the poet "turns to France." He selectively quotes five couplets from two paragraphs with lines 235–62, ignoring lines 239–52 on the villagers' dancing to the poet's "tuneless pipe" and 255–58 on honor's sources (repeating the point of line 254 by saying honor "passes current; paid from hand to hand"). The first omission leaves out Goldsmith's self-reference, presenting the poem as more choric or impersonal than it is. But the sketch of old and young dancing, even the village's "praise [of] my wond'rous power," illustrates the enthusiasm for art and society in France, for "arts that mind to mind endear" (line 253). The second omission (lines 255–58) suggests impatience at redundancy. Then, keeping the focus on the thesis stipulated earlier, Johnson remarks, "Yet France has its evils" and quotes two couplets, skips over six lines on "ostentation" in dress and dining, and then quotes another couplet. The six lines offered assert the undermining of character when "praise [is] too dearly lov'd . . . And the weak soul . . . Leans for all pleasure on another's breast. . . . Nor weighs the solid worth of self applause" (lines 265–68, and line 276). One wonders if in private Johnson roasted Goldsmith on the wisdom of the six lines *not* quoted, which detail how vain "ostentation" "defrauds" "daily cheer / To boast one splendid banquet once a year" (lines 269–74), for Goldsmith ran up large debts with his tailor and caterer—moreover, Boswell and Johnson thought Goldsmith shared the fundamental flaw imputed to the French, straining after recognition.[62]

Then, only noting the section on Holland to say that it precedes, Johnson quotes from the treatment of England six lines envisioning the parade of noble Britains, "lord of human kind": "Stern o'er each bosom reason holds her state . . . fresh from Nature's hand" (lines 321–26), the lines Johnson quoted for Boswell in Scotland. This panegyric he balances with his final quotation of successive lines from two paragraphs on freedom (lines 331–54), England's main cultural "blessing." Johnson's selection begins after four lines apostrophize freedom to attribute to it "blessings pictur'd here," with the caveat that "without alloy" freedom can foster "ills" (lines 331–34). One might chuckle at Johnson's characterization of the "ills" flowing from England's peculiar excess, not as "evils" (used for other societies' excesses) but as "inconveniences that harrass the sons of freedom"[63]—"inconveniences" could not have been used if Johnson had summarized or quoted the next verse paragraphs. The twenty consecutive lines quoted begin, "That independence Britons prize too high, / Keeps man from man, and breaks the social tie" (lines 335–36) and end with a prophecy that, "As social bonds" are replaced by those of "wealth and law," there may come a time when "One sink of level avarice shall lie, / And scholars, soldiers, kings unhonor'd die" (lines 343–54). The final couplet was recently written, for it is not in "A Prospect of Society." As elsewhere, Goldsmith tried to improve the passage Johnson quoted. In the second edition he added after the first couplet quoted another stressing the identification of happiness with social ties: "The self dependent lordlings stand alone, / All kindred claims that soften life unknown." In the sixth edition he rewrote the second line (line 342) as "All claims that bind and sweeten life unknown." To the second couplet quoted by Johnson, "See, though by circling deeps together held, / Minds combat minds, repelling and repell'd," Goldsmith in the second edition replaced the first line with "Here by the bonds of nature feebly held." Whatever the vortex image "circling deeps" means, it is not as clear as what replaces it.

Following his quotation, Johnson offers no final comment about the thematic content, though that is the review's focus (there is no expansion of how excessive zeal for freedom leads to injustice or political fracturing); rather, he "congratulate[s] the public, . . . on a production to which, since the death of Pope, it will not be easy to find any thing equal."[64] Johnson need not refer to the final four paragraphs to complete the argument through contrast regarding the relative contentment of mankind. However, these paragraphs (lines 355–416) greatly expand the critique of contemporary England, raising the thesis of *The Deserted Village*, and they contain many self-references, first as the speaker adopts an authoritative posture as a virtuous poet full of Juvenalian indignation at injustice and then as the speaker, as traveler, reflects on his quest. They contain lines heavily revised from "A Prospect" or written after it.

Perhaps Johnson found the continuation via "kings" strained. Goldsmith concluded the paragraph quoted with the prospect that "kings unhonor'd [may] die" (line 354) and began the next with his persona defending himself and decrying what was happening in England:

> Yet think not thus, when Freedom's ills I state,
> I mean to flatter Kings, or court the great;
> Perish the wish; for, inly satisfy'd,
> Above their pomps I hold my ragged pride.
> But when contending chiefs blockade the throne,
> Contracting regal power to stretch their own,
> When I behold a factious band agree
> To call it freedom, when themselves are free;
> Each wanton judge new penal statutes draw,
> Laws grind the poor, and rich men rule the law;
> The wealth of climes, where savage nations roam,
> Pillag'd from slaves, to purchase slaves at home;
> Fear, pity, justice, indignation start,
> Tear off reserve, and bare my swelling heart;
> 'Till half a patriot, half a coward grown,
> I fly from petty tyrants to the throne. (lines 355–70).

The paragraph rings true to readers today and must have seemed impassioned at the end of 1764, when the *Gentleman's Magazine* quoted it. But Johnson may have found this posturing too affected and conventional, or he may have felt the lines undermined the dedication's claim not to espouse "the cause of any party."[65] The paragraph risked the label "bombast" in insisting "my swelling heart" is bursting with emotions. The invocation at the start of the next paragraph ("Yes, brother, curse with me") testifies to how personal these feeling are. There is a strong shift in tone, but it seems natural that the poet would drop the earlier posture of a philosophical spectator when confronting the excesses of his own country. It suits an Englishman to have intense feelings about freedom. Furthermore, the "Freedom's ills" that he attacks actually involve the aftermath of too much freedom or its false charade, for now freedom is waning, as commerce waned in Italy.

Goldsmith was dissatisfied with the second couplet ("Perish . . . ragged pride"), and in the second edition replaced it while adding twenty didactic lines of political theory prefacing the attack on oligarchy. The long addition begins rhetorically as a prayer invoking "Ye powers of truth" to free the poet of "low desire" and then "fair freedom" to continue to bloom despite "The rabble's rage, and tyrant's angry steel" (lines 363–69 of Friedman). The speaker would only "repress" freedoms "to secure" them, for, according to the social model offered, freedom requires a hierarchy with "proportion'd loads" on each rank of society, wherein "those who think must govern those that toil" (lines 371–74 of Friedman). Here follows a couplet in the second edition that was mercifully cut in the sixth edition: "Much on the low, the rest, as rank supplies, / Should in columnar diminution rise." It is a poor couplet in several respects. For one, there are contradictory connotations in saying "much" will be put on the bottom and then "rise" in "diminution," for rising implies growing. "Columnar diminution" brings to mind Wardle's complaint that in the *Enquiry into the Present State of Polite Learning* Goldsmith at times "tried to sound impressive" or Boswell's, that he tried "to shine in conversation."[66] As earlier noted, several other pretentious words were cut in Goldsmith's revisions, and, here as in *The Deserted Village*, the usual consequence of his revisions is increased clarity, often through greater simplicity. Perhaps, too, Goldsmith was conscious of a contradiction in claiming that freedom calls for putting "Much on the low" while also complaining that the chiefs "grind the poor." And the couplet conflicted with the next: "While, [changed to "Hence" in the sixth edition] should one order disproportion'd grow, / Its double weight must ruin all below." The addition ends with a warning of a "fast approaching danger" (lines 380 of Friedman) from the aspiration of that class today called "the one percent."

The two following paragraphs, also overlooked by Johnson, maintain the emotional intensity and offer a preview of *The Deserted Village*. The first attributes the ascendancy of wealth to the decline of monarchy and the rise of unchecked commerce, before modulating to sympathy over the plight of the underclass, whose villages "fall" at the pleasure of lords. The poet asks, "brother, . . . Have we not seen . . . opulence, her grandeur to maintain, / Lead stern depopulation in her train, . . . Beheld . . . The modest matron, and the blushing maid, / Forc'd from their homes" (lines 371–90). Then the penultimate paragraph conjures up a vision of the frightened and pathetic exiles, preyed on by "the brown Indian" in the "tangled forests" (lines 391–400). Prior to publication, Johnson contributed to this paragraph the line that the exiles were "To stop too fearful, and too faint to go" (lines 398). Johnson's collaboration on the final paragraph certainly prevented him from discussing or quoting it. While scholars believe Johnson contributed more than the nine lines that he could mark out for Boswell years later, eight in the closing paragraph, we can presume that none of the 110 lines quoted were written by Johnson.[67] The reviewer in *Lloyd's Evening Post* suggests that he was not free to quote any line in the poem, but Johnson seems to have quoted freely, and he chose to quote lines allowing him to sketch the tragically ironic theme involving "comparative happiness," that, "in each domain" the "favourite good begets peculiar pain" (lines 95–96). Furthermore, we know Johnson quoted lines on Britain that touched his heartstrings and can assume he only quoted lines he thought well written, something that David Fong might have considered in his essay exploring why Johnson liked the poem as much as he did, preferring it to *The Deserted Village*.[68]

The final three paragraphs were not quoted in the reviews and, perhaps in consequence, Goldsmith left them largely untouched: he made only two substantive changes in the last forty-six lines. In the sixth edition, "Indian takes a deadly aim" is replaced with "Indian marks with murderous aim" (line 392) and the "fond look" cast by the exile is changed to a "long look" (line 399). Satisfaction with the final paragraphs fits the general pattern: Goldsmith's revisions tend to occur in those areas of the dedication and poem on which reviews directed their spotlights through comment and quotation. In so far as reviews were mostly positive, they did not offer a checklist of corrections. In some cases, Goldsmith would not yield to correction, as when John Hawkesworth complained in the *Monthly Review* of June 1770 that a simile in *The Deserted Village* required a change from "As" to "So."[69] But the reviews offered perceptions of theme and structure and also quotations that surely directed the inveterate reviser's attention, for as Langhorne said, "No Writer was ever yet indifferent to the reputation of his works."[70]

NOTES

1. William Rider, *An Historical and Critical Account of the Lives and Writings of the Living Authors of Great-Britain* (London: For the Author, 1762), 14.
2. Jean Marteilhe, *The Memoirs of a Protestant Condemned to the Galleys of France, for his Religion . . . Translated . . . By James Willington*, ed. Oliver Goldsmith, trans. James Willington (London: R. Griffiths et al., 1758), in 2 vols.; Ralph Wardle, *Oliver Goldsmith* (Lawrence: University of Kansas Press, 1957), 81. On the publication, see Temple Scott (a pseudonym), *Oliver Goldsmith Bibliographically and Biographically Considered: Based on the Collection of Material in the Library of W. M. Elkin, Esq.* (New York: Bowling Green Press, 1928), 30–34.
3. Oliver Goldsmith, *Collected Works of Oliver Goldsmith*, ed. Arthur Friedman (Oxford: Clarendon, 1966), in 5 vols.
4. Goldsmith, *Works*, ed. Friedman, 1:423n.
5. Oliver Goldsmith, *The Citizen of the World; Or Letters from a Chinese Philosopher* (London: J. Newbery, 1762), in 2 vols.; and his *A History of England, in a Series of Letters from a Nobleman to His Son* (London: J. Newbery, 1764), in 2 vols.; *The Roman History* (London: S. Baker et al., 1769), in 2 vols.; *The Grecian History* (London: J. and F. Rivington, 1774); and *A History of the Earth and Animated Nature* (London: J. Nourse, 1774), in 8 vols.
6. Oliver Goldsmith, *A Compendium of Biography* (London: J. Newbery, 1762), vols. 1–4; and *The Martial Review; Or, A General History of the late Wars* (London: J. Newbery 1763); Temple Scott, *Oliver Goldsmith*, 77. Scott remarks that Goldsmith revised *The History of Mecklenburgh from the First Settlement . . . to the Present Time* and *A Description of Millenium Hall* (*Oliver Goldsmith*, 77), both written by Sarah Scott and published by Newbery, 1762, but Wardle walks this back, noting that Goldsmith "may have revised the *History of Mecklenburgh*" (Wardle, *Oliver Goldsmith*, 131), and indicating that he has seen no evidence for the claim (308n34).
7. Richard Brookes, MD., *A New and Accurate System of Natural History* (London: J. Newbery, 1763-[1764]), in 6 vols.
8. Wardle, *Oliver Goldsmith*, 148–49. Iolo A. Williams' bibliographical description of the work has the note "Goldsmith revised it for the press, and wrote the general Preface [and five introductions]. . . . Goldsmith certainly received sums of £11 11s, £6 6s, and £30 for his work on this compilation, but possibly the two smaller amounts were included in the largest one" (*Seven XVIIIth Century Bibliographies* [London: Dulau, 1924], 129).
9. Williams, *Seven XVIIIth Century*, 138–39. Wardle, *Oliver Goldsmith* 168, dates Goldsmith's translating to the winter of 1765–1766. Jean-Henri-Samuel Formey, *Histoire Abrégée de la Philosophie* [*A Concise History of Philosophy and Philosophers*] trans. Oliver Goldsmith, (London: F. Newbery, 1766).
10. Goldsmith, *Works*, ed. Friedman, 250.
11. Oliver Goldsmith, *Essays. By Mr. Goldsmith. Collecta Revirescunt* (London: Printed for W. Griffin, 1765), 12mo, pp. [2], vi, 248, [2].
12. Oliver Goldsmith, *Essays. By Oliver Goldsmith. Collecta Revirescunt*, 2nd ed. (London, 1766).
13. Goldsmith, *Works*, ed. Friedman, 4:372n.
14. Ibid., 2:421, line 10.
15. Ibid., 2:461, line 14.
16. After collating Goldsmith's major poems and *Essays* in pursuit of oversights and errors by Friedman, I found very few substantives in first and revised editions that were not recorded. He did not record substantive variants that he considered "obvious" errors, and he neglected substantive variants in non-authoritative editions and most accidental

changes in authoritative editions (Goldsmith, *Works*, ed. Friedman, 4:240); however, he recorded nearly all paragraphing and some punctuation variants in authoritative editions.
17. *The Poems of Thomas Gray, William Collins, and Oliver Goldsmith*, ed. Roger Lonsdale (London: Longmans, 1969, 1976).
18. Ricardo Quintana, *Oliver Goldsmith: A Georgian Study* (New York: Macmillan, 1967), 118. All editions before the sixth have two sentences that the sixth conflates into one: "But of all kinds of ambition, as things are now circumstanced, perhaps that which pursues poetical fame, is the wildest. What from the encreased refinement of the times, from the diversity of judgments produced by opposing systems of criticism, and from the more prevalent divisions of opinion influenced by party, the strongest and happiest efforts can expect to please but in a very narrow circle" (ii). The first sentence quoted by Quintana is the sixth edition's more economical expression of both these sentences.
19. Robert H. Hopkins, *The True Genius of Oliver Goldsmith* (Baltimore: Johns Hopkins University Press, 1969), 67–68.
20. Oliver Goldsmith, *The Traveller, Or A Prospect of Society. A Poem* (London, 1765 [1764]); *The Traveller 1765 and The Deserted Village 1770 with "A Prospect of Society" (1764)*, facsimile (Menston, UK: Scolar Press, 1970), *Eighteenth Century Collections Online* (*ECCO*), https://www.gale.com/primary-sources/eighteenth-century-collections-online; and *The Deserted Village, A Poem* (London, 1770).
21. William Cooke, *European Magazine* 24 (1793): 93, cited in Goldsmith, *Works*, ed. Friedman, 4:235.
22. Thomas Percy, quoted in Goldsmith, *Works*, ed. Friedman, 4:235–36.
23. The proof, found by the bookseller Bertram Dobell in 1902, is shelved in the British Library as C.58.g.7, reproduced in facsimile in Goldsmith, *Traveller* (1970), and available on *ECCO*.
24. William B. Todd, "Quadruple Imposition: An Account of Goldsmith's *The Traveller*," *Studies in Bibliography* 7 (1955), 103–11. Some problems in Todd's hypothesis were noted in a review of the volume of *Studies in Bibliography*, by L. W. Hanson (*Library*, 5th ser. 10 [1955]: 297–98), and Todd in correspondence to *The Library* accepted a few of these reservations (11 [1956], 123–24). In his rejoinder, to Hanson's argument that sheets B-D are too imperfect to be a "suppressed issue," Todd asserts without evidence that William Griffin probably printed the poem and was an error-prone printer. However, as shown below, many of the reprints are very accurate, and the printer is not known for certain. There is only one work explicitly printed "by W. Griffin" for J. Newbery, Isaac Bickerstaffe's *Love in a Village*, in multiple editions during 1762–1763, and the *English Short Title Catalogue* (ESTC), http://estc.bl.uk, has no records with both Griffin as printer and Goldsmith as author.
25. Goldsmith, *Works*, ed. Friedman, 4:239.
26. On the two 1764 settings of the title-page, in states apparently lacking the first edition's half-title and advertisement leaf, see Temple Scott, *Oliver Goldsmith*, 140–42; and Todd, "Quadruple Imposition," 110–11.
27. Goldsmith, *Works*, ed. Friedman, 4:236.
28. The *Gazetteer and New Daily Advertiser*, March 13, 1765, listed the second edition as published "To-morrow"; "this day" publication announcements for the fourth through sixth editions appeared, respectively, in the *Public Advertiser*, August 7, 1765; the *Gazetteer*, February 25, 1768; and the *Middlesex Journal*, June 28–30, 1770. The *Public Advertiser*, Thursday, December 6, 1770 announced the seventh edition as coming "On Saturday"; it announced the eighth edition as "this day" published on February 29, 1772.
29. Relative to the first edition, these second-edition changes are: lines added: two after lines 84, two after line 198, two after line 336, and eighteen after replacing lines 357–58; lines replaced: lines 139–40 (later returned in the sixth edition) and lines 357–58; lines reversed:

lines 283–84 moved after lines 285–86; and lines 323 and 324 reversed); and lines cut: lines 81–82 of 1; the final sentence of the second paragraph of the first edition is cut. Note that Friedman's edition of *The Traveller* has the line numbers of the sixth edition.

30. The other substantive variant in the fifth edition is "were" for "are" in line 111 (line 113 in Friedman), left as "were" in the seventh and eighth editions.
31. Oliver Goldsmith, *The Collected Letters of Oliver Goldsmith*, ed. Katharine C. Balderston (Cambridge: Cambridge University Press, 1928), 128–36, for the letter to Bunbury (which, on checking, I find an accurate transcription). For *The Captivity* transcription, see Goldsmith, *Works*, ed. Friedman, 4:209–31. These texts also show that Goldsmith frequently neglected punctuation at the ends of lines, rarely using colon and semi-colon there (Balderston notes Goldsmith often "used commas in place of periods," in *Collected Letters*, li).
32. Goldsmith, *Works*, ed. Friedman, 4:278.
33. Although punctuation changes are not frequent enough in the revised sixth edition of *The Traveller* to suspect Goldsmith changed many, paragraphing changes are unusually frequent, with three added (at line 31, returning the indentation cut in the second, and at line 175 and line 377 of the sixth, the latter in lines added by the second edition) and two cut (at line 75, two lines after a substantive change, and at line 153 first/155 sixth edition, after two lines were cut).
34. *Goldsmith: The Critical Heritage*, ed. G. S. Rousseau (London: Routledge & Kegan Paul, 1974), 77.
35. Ricardo Quintana, "*The Deserted Village*: Its Logical and Rhetorical Elements," *College English* 26, no. 3 (1964), 211.
36. One of the few changes involving self-presentation is the replacement of "We turn" [to France] in the first edition with "I turn" in line 234 and line 240, returning the focus to the solitary poet. The previous self-reference at a transition uses both singular and plural: "My soul turn from them, turn we to survey" the Swiss. But the next two transitions, to Holland and England, have first-person references (in lines 277 and 313–14 of the first edition)
37. The *London Chronicle*'s account, repr: in *Critical Heritage*, ed. G. S. Rousseau, 34.
38. Goldsmith, dedication in *The Traveller*, iii; quoted in ibid.
39. *Lloyd's Evening Post*, p. 595.
40. Notice in *Gentleman's Magazine*, December 34 (1764): 594.
41. *Critical Heritage*, ed. G. S. Rousseau, 33.
42. Goldsmith, dedication in *The Traveller*, iv, quoted in ibid.
43. Ibid.
44. *Critical Heritage*, ed. G. S. Rousseau, 33–34.
45. Norma Clarke writes, "The reference [of "baleful hour"] is to the events of 1688–1689, the so-called Glorious Revolution," "the beginning of faction-driven politics" (*Brothers of the Quill: Oliver Goldsmith in Grub Street* [Cambridge, MA: Harvard University Press, 2016], 99). She further supposes "Goldsmith's imagery [of depopulation] belongs to Ireland, for the 'baleful hour' had especially baleful consequences there" to the Catholic majority (100), and this view is repeated for *The Deserted Village* (334).
46. *Monthly Review* 32 (January 1765): 47–55; repr. *Critical Heritage*, ed. G. S. Rousseau, 35–43, from which my quotations are taken. In the March 1760 *Critical Review*, Goldsmith had found some virtues in *The Death of Adonis: A Pastoral Elegy. From the Greek of Bion* (R. Griffiths, 1759), by Reverend Langhorne (1735–1779), who later began reviewing for the *Monthly* (Richard C. Taylor, *Goldsmith as Journalist* [Rutherford, NJ: Fairleigh Dickinson University Press, 1993], 32, 70). Langhorne had published six other volumes of poetry (three with R. Griffiths) before reviewing *The Traveller*.
47. *Critical Heritage*, ed. G. S. Rousseau, 35.

48. Goldsmith, dedication in *The Traveller*, iv, quoted in ibid., 33.
49. Ibid., 36–37.
50. Ibid., 37.
51. Ibid., 38.
52. Ibid., 39.
53. Langhorne, quoted in ibid., 43.
54. Ibid.
55. Ibid.
56. Samuel Johnson, quoted in *Critical Review* 18 (December 1764): 458–62; repr. in ibid., 29–33.
57. Ibid., 30.
58. Ibid., 31, quoting lines 87–92, 95–96.
59. Ibid., 31.
60. Ibid., 32.
61. With reference to the philosophical tale "Asem, the Man-Hater" (1759), Wardle writes, "Experience had convinced him [Goldsmith] that the doctrine of contented acceptance was the best guide to a satisfying life," and he notes that in his serial essay "A Comparative View of Happiness," which shares many ideas with *The Traveller*, Goldsmith linked making "one individual more happy in himself" with making that "man who now boasts his patriotism, a citizen of the world" (Wardle, *Oliver Goldsmith*, 107, 116).
62. Wardle, *Oliver Goldsmith*, 146, 252.
63. Johnson, quoted in *Critical Heritage*, ed. G. S. Rousseau, 32.
64. Ibid., 33.
65. Goldsmith, dedication in *The Traveller*, iv, quoted in *Critical Heritage*, ed. G. S. Rousseau, 33.
66. Wardle, *Oliver Goldsmith*, 95, 252.
67. Friedman notes, "Johnson told Reynolds that 'the utmost that I have wrote in that poem . . . is not more than eighteen lines'; but in 1783 when he marked his contribution for Boswell, nine lines were all of which he could be sure" (Goldsmith, *Works*, ed. Friedman, 4:236, quoting from Boswell's *Life*). In Friedman's edition, these are line 420 (i.e., line 398, 1st ed.), lines 429–34 (lines 406–12: "How small, . . . domestic joy"), and lines 437–38, the final couplet (lines 415–16: "To men remote . . . | Leave reason, faith and conscience all our own"). Johnson's lines are only altered by the removal of the comma after "How small" in line 429 of the second edition and the insertion of commas in the final line after "faith" and "conscience" of the fourth edition.
68. David Fong, "Johnson, Goldsmith, and *The Traveller*," *New Rambler* (Autumn 1971): 22–30. I thank Michael Bundock for providing access to this article and Susan Stravinski for checking details in early editions of *The Traveller*.
69. *Critical Heritage*, ed. G. S. Rousseau, 86, regarding lines 191–94; Goldsmith, *Works*, ed. Friedman, 4:294, where lines 189–93.
70. Langhorne, in *Critical Heritage*, ed. G. S. Rousseau, 35

5

"DOWN WITH HER, BURNEY!"

Johnson, Burney, and the Politics of Literary Celebrity

MARILYN FRANCUS

IN SEPTEMBER 1778, Hester Thrale invited Elizabeth Montagu, queen of the Bluestockings, to come to Streatham to meet Frances Burney, whose first novel *Evelina* was the literary sensation of the year. When Samuel Johnson heard that Montagu had accepted the invitation, he

> Began to see-saw, with a Countenance strongly expressive of *inward fun*,—&, after enjoying it some Time in silence, he suddenly, & with great animation, turned to me, & cried "*Down* with her, Burney!—*down* with her! spare her not! attack her, fight her, & *down* with her at once!—*You* are a *rising* Wit,—*she* is at the *Top*,—& when *I* was beginning the World, & was nothing & nobody, the Joy of my Life was to fire at all established Wits!—& then, every body loved to hallow me on;—but there is no Game *now*, & *now*, every body would be glad to see me *conquered*: but *then*, when I was *new*,—to vanquish the Great ones was all the delight of my poor little dear soul!—So at her, Burney!—at her, & *down* with her!"
> O how we all hollow'd! By the way, I must tell you that Mrs. Montagu is in very great estimation here, even with Dr. Johnson himself, when others do not praise her *improperly*: Mrs. Thrale ranks her as the *first of Women*, in the Literary way.[1]

The laughter that Burney recorded, and the respect for Montagu, did not dispel Johnson's vision of Burney engaging Montagu in literary combat: "Some Time after,—when we had all been a few minutes wholly silent, he [Johnson] turned to me, & said 'Come, Burney,—shall you & I *study our parts* against Mrs. Montagu comes?'" (*EJL*, 3:153). The next day, as Henry Thrale urged Burney to attack Dorothea Gregory, Montagu's companion (as a prelude to attacking Montagu), Johnson cried out, "No, no,—fly at the *Eagle*!—*down* with Mrs. Montagu herself!—I hope she will come *full* of Evelina!" (*EJL*, 3:153).

These exchanges are more than Samuel Johnson acknowledging (and attempting to control) his uneasy relationship with Elizabeth Montagu, and they differ from his efforts to mentor women writers, which usually centered on promoting their works through prefaces, subscriptions, and dealings with publishers.[2] Rather, Burney captured a shifting cultural paradigm, as Johnson spoke of the contrast between his early career with his literary eminence in 1778, when "there is no Game now." Johnson's comments reflect a hierarchical literary world in which recognition and celebrity were in limited supply—a literary world that required aggression for the writer to survive and thrive.[3] Johnson's nostalgia for literary warfare was at once a jest, an effort to draw out Burney, and a commentary on literary power and prestige. But as much as Burney was gratified by Johnson's partisanship, she refused to engage in literary aggression or competition. Unlike Johnson, Burney looked to shield her public persona from criticism and controversy, and hesitated to wield her cultural power.

Burney and Johnson's differing responses to literary warfare are not surprising, given that they were separated by age, character, gender, and experience. But they reflect upon cultural capital at the end of the eighteenth century—cultural capital that was not only a product of literary merit, but increasingly enmeshed with celebrity. In September 1778, mere months after her authorship of *Evelina* became public—and not long after meeting Johnson (*EJL*, 3:73–74)—Burney was struggling with her newfound literary celebrity. What Burney probably did not realize was that Johnson, in the midst of writing *Lives of the Poets*, was also grappling with literary power and celebrity as metrics that contributed to the canonization of authorship, and in light of his own legacy. By analyzing the key terms of Johnson's speech—"now/then," "rising wit," "nothing & nobody," "attack," and "game"—I will bring Johnson and Burney's concerns with celebrity into focus. Their struggles reveal that the new, evolving culture of literary celebrity, while largely free from the problems of literary patronage, raised significant problems of its own.

NOW AND THEN

As Johnson's use of "now" and "then" indicates, the literary world of 1778 was quite different from the one he confronted in the 1730s and 1740s. Norma Clarke observes, "Johnson lived through a major cultural transition in a century which saw a commercial nation emerging into immense power and confidence. The expansion of print and the rise of the reading public contributed to the weakening of an old social order based on rank and privilege of which patronage (not literary patronage alone) had been an essential part."[4] Catherine Gallagher goes further, emphasizing Johnson's role in changing the literary landscape: "The rude combative days of the 1730s and 1740s (when Johnson was "nobody") had given way to the genteel civility he had himself... done so much to promote by attacking the patronage mentality that had encouraged scandal. Perhaps one could still make a living writing scandal and personal satire, but powerful people would no longer pay much for it, and it was certainly not a respectable occupation."[5] While the history of the changing literary marketplace of eighteenth-century Britain is well known,[6] I want to recall three points of that history that are relevant for this discussion regarding literary status, cultural capital, and celebrity.

First, earning a living through writing, while difficult in the eighteenth century, was more economically feasible than it had been previously. As the patronage system began to erode, copyright laws changed and the economy expanded—and literary works were subject to marketing and cross-marketing, which increased authorial profit and/or cultural capital. In the wake of Gay's 1727 *Beggar's Opera*, there was not only a published version of the text and a sequel (*Polly*), but fans, screens, and playing cards with scenes and quotes from the play. Daniel Defoe took advantage of the phenomenal success of *Robinson Crusoe* by writing two sequels, and Robinsonades abounded in the wake of his novel; the name "Gulliver" appeared in poems and miscellanea, appealing to readers' knowledge of Swift's work; the cultural explosion surrounding the publication of Richardson's first novel *Pamela* included parodies, satires, and paraphernalia of all sorts.[7] Second, the development of public criticism in periodicals like the *Tatler* and the *Spectator*, and later the *Monthly Review* and the *Critical Review*, recognized the need for, and perpetuated, a public discourse about culture, aesthetics, and literary value.[8] Third, the rise of celebrity culture in the arts—initially a function of the professionalization of actors, artists, and musicians—reconfigured authorship, and writers became celebrities like other culture producers. The cultural capital of authorship (and celebrity in its wake) provided authors with access to political and social power, as authors increasingly socialized with politicians, aristocrats, and cultural celebrities, and various forms of social, political, and cultural capital reinforced each other.[9]

Johnson's path to literary celebrity was long and hard-won; the narrative of Johnson's career is well known, from his early difficult days in journalism to the triumph of the *Dictionary* in 1755, which he marked with his scathing letter to his erstwhile patron Lord Chesterfield. While his career after the *Dictionary* was not without its share of detractors and challenges—including problems completing the Shakespeare edition, the animosity of Charles Churchill, and satirical caricatures of him in the press—Johnson had achieved financial and professional success. He was awarded a royal pension, and his reputation and celebrity continued to grow through his writings and social and professional networks. In 1777, Johnson was commissioned "to write little Lives, and little Prefaces, to a little edition of the English Poets."[10] Johnson expanded the project, often providing not-so-little biographies and extensive literary analyses of each author's works. (Johnson also made suggestions regarding the selection of authors in the collection.) When *The Lives of the Poets* appeared in 1779–1781, it canonized Johnson as the literary arbiter for the age. That the aging Johnson felt that there was no game for him in 1778 makes sense, for as a venerated author adjudicating literary history, his position in the literary world had put him largely beyond its reach.

Burney's path to literary success and celebrity could not have been more different.[11] Unlike Johnson, she did not have to struggle to earn a living; Burney wrote *Evelina* while living in her father's home and serving as his copyist. Initially Burney did not associate with writers—unlike Johnson, who from the beginning helped authors with prefaces, dedications, publishers, and marketing.[12] She had some knowledge of the publishing industry as her father's amanuensis for his *History of Music*, and Burney understood cultural capital, the mechanisms of reputation, and professionalism in the arts, because she socialized with opera and theatre practitioners known through her father. (And Frances Burney was well aware that Charles Burney's career exemplified the power of cultural capital to achieve upward mobility.[13]) But Burney was not functioning in the milieu of professional authorship.[14] Everything changed, however, with the publication of *Evelina* in January 1778. Although Burney published anonymously, her identity was revealed within months; readers devoured her novel and recommended it to others, and she became an instant celebrity. That Burney achieved success so quickly not only signifies the public recognition of the quality of her work, but a cultural shift, for by 1778, the public had become practiced in fandom, and was looking for celebrities in the arts.

So when Johnson encouraged Burney to attack Montagu, their reactions not only reflect their radically different cultural experiences, but their different assumptions about celebrity and authorship. Johnson, like many of the authors in his *Lives of the Poets*, sought attention and celebrity in order to succeed; Burney did not, for attention and celebrity came to her. Burney neither wanted nor needed to attack Elizabeth Montagu to become famous. (When Montagu visited Streatham, Burney ran out of the room, needing to calm herself before facing Montagu, who she barely spoke with during her stay.)[15] Burney did not want "now" to be like "then," where literary warfare was seemingly inevitable; as she wrote to her sister in October 1779, "All *Authorship Contention* I shudder to think of!" (*EJL*, 3:399). But by projecting his professional history onto Burney—even as a joke—Johnson makes claims about authorship, literary value, and celebrity that Burney respects, resents, and resists.

MARILYN FRANCUS

A RISING WIT

Burney was stunned as she was thrust into the spotlight as the author of *Evelina*. Aside from the loss of her anonymity and privacy, Burney was confounded by the experience of celebrity, starting with the public's insistence upon identifying her wholly and solely with her work. The conflation of Burney with her novel was reasonable, given that the public had no other knowledge of her—arguably, that reaction should have been expected. But for Burney, *Evelina* was her creation and separate from her identity. Burney was delighted by the accolades that *Evelina* received from cultural luminaries, by the cultural capital, and she danced a jig when she heard of Johnson's praise (*EJL*, 3:61). But she was uncomfortable when attention focused on her rather than her book. In her letters she made the distinction between her self and her text: "Let them Criticise, cut, slash, without mercy my *Book*,—& and let them *neglect me,*—but may God [two illegible words] avert my becoming a public Theme of Ridicule."[16] Burney envisioned authorship as a literary version of the king's two bodies, in which the products of a public self were recognized as related to, but separate from, the private experience of the individual.

But the public made no such distinction, and people made assumptions about Burney based on *Evelina*. Some readers assumed that Burney *was* Evelina, because they could not account for her depiction of a young woman's responses to the world otherwise. (A more charming version occurred when readers thought Burney's *narrative* was historical truth, and they wanted news about Evelina, Lord Orville, the Branghtons, and Madame Duval.)[17] Some people called Burney Evelina, much to her annoyance; she was not a seventeen-year-old country girl coming to London, but a twenty-five-year-old native of the capital when she published her novel.[18] She was equally annoyed in 1782 when people started referring to her as Cecilia, the protagonist of her second novel: "I hate mightily this method of naming me from my Heroines, of whose Honour I think I am more jealous than of my own" (*EJL*, 5:133). The conflation of a celebrated woman with her work was not unusual: actresses had been identified with their roles—and some cultivated that identification to enhance their celebrity and cultural capital—from the Restoration onward.[19] Such readers resisted recognizing Burney's craft as an author, and her identity as an individual, by collapsing author and text.

Other readers believed that Burney ought to be feared, based on the sharp social commentary in *Evelina*. Miss Palmer remarked, "But though we all want so much to know the Author, both Mrs. Cholmondeley, & my uncle himself, say they should be frightened to Death to be in her Company, because she must be such a very nice observer, that there would be no escaping her with safety" (*EJL*, 3:141). Burney was flabbergasted, as she wrote her sister: "Good God, my dear

Susy,—what strange ideas are taken from mere *Book-reading*!" (*EJL*, 3:141) Some readers, like Anna Williams, wanted to meet Burney but feared that they would be written into Burney's next book as satiric targets (*EJL*, 3:224; cf. 154, 205, 286).[20] Still other readers simply wanted to see her, like pilgrims seeking a shrine—as if seeing Burney would satisfy their desire about *Evelina*. Frances Reynolds told Burney, "what would not Mrs. Horneck & Mrs. Bunbury give to see the Writer of—*that* Book! Lord! they say they would walk 100 & 60 miles only to *see* her, if that would do!" (*EJL*, 3:195) (Burney's response was characteristic: "I would walk just as far to *avoid* them!") Much to her chagrin, but to no one else's surprise, the public response to *Evelina* was beyond Burney's control, and it shaped her identity and social interactions in ways that Burney found embarrassing, exasperating, and daunting.

It was particularly difficult for Burney to be present as others praised her work. Johnson sympathized: "Why it is true, said he, kindly, that such things are disagreeable to sit,—nor do I wonder you were distressed, yet, sometimes, they are *necessary*" (*EJL*, 3:161). Johnson had his moments of frustration with flattery, as when he admonished Hannah More: "Madam, before you flatter a man so grossly to his Face, you should consider whether or not your flattery is worth his having."[21] More than two years after the publication of *Evelina*—having published nothing subsequently—Burney was still encountering waves of adulation for her novel. In summer 1780, she met a Mrs. Dobson who praised *Evelina* at such length that Burney wrote, "I had almost thrown myself out of the window in my eagerness to get out of the way of this gross & noisy applause."[22] Burney would deflect praise when she could see it coming: when Dr. Finch remarked, "I met with a Book,—a certain Book of 3 volumes—in that shop Yesterday which I propose myself great pleasure in perusing," Burney "pretended not to hear him, & asked an abrupt question concerning Mrs. Dellingham" (*EJL*, 4:164) and avoided the subject afterwards. Codes of politeness forced Burney to listen to praise, however much she resented doing so—but she avoided indulging it whenever possible.

While Johnson could not help Burney escape public praise, he did provide Burney with a rubric to decide whose comments were worth paying attention to: "There are 3 distinct kind of Judges upon all new Authors or productions;—the first, are those who know no rules, but pronounce entirely from their natural Taste & feelings; The 2d are those who *know*, & *judge* by *rules*; & the 3d are those who *know*, but are *above* the rules. These last are those you should wish to satisfy: *next* to them, rate the *natural* judges,—but ever despise those opinions that are formed by the *rules*" (*EJL*, 3:222). Johnson's rubric reminded Burney that there were readers that she could ignore; her judgment, like the judgment of the best readers, was not to be bound by rules. Literary culture is a series of exchanges and negotiations—in production, reception, circulation, and judgment—in which neither the author nor reader has absolute power, but to Burney's chagrin, both hold sway. So while Burney needed to acknowledge (intellectually, if not socially) the variety of her readership, she was not obligated by their judgments or behaviors.

For Johnson, it was perfectly reasonable that readers associated authors with their texts, and that readers wanted to know more about the writers whose works appealed to them. As he told Burney, "do you suppose your Book is so much talked of, & not yourself?—do you think your Readers will not ask questions, & inform themselves whether you are short or Tall, young or old?"[23] Johnson was not dismayed by the sobriquet "Dictionary Johnson," which, according to Boswell, was in common usage when he met Johnson in 1763, eight years after the publication of the *Dictionary* (*Life*, 1:383–84). Admittedly, readers' expectations of non-fiction are different from those of fiction; writing an authoritative text—particularly a text without a narrative, like a dictionary—carries a different cultural valence than writing a novel.[24] Johnson's identity was not likely to be appropriated or reconfigured based on his essays or criticism either; Johnson's critical voice emanated from his texts, and he could shape his public image as he wished.[25] So Johnson did not feel the need for the writerly equivalent of the king's two bodies as Burney did: Johnson was more publicly exposed, yet ironically more in control of his identity, than she was. This is not to say that Johnson had control over his celebrity; he had more than his fair share of bad press in the later phases of his career.[26] But Johnson's temperament enabled his interactions with the public, for Johnson was "clubbable" rather than shy; he thrived on professional and social networks that sustained cultural capital and celebrity. He did not balk at attention, and given Johnson's tics and behaviors, it would have been difficult for him *not* to be noticed.

That knowledge of an author was of interest to readers, if not a primary means for understanding literature, was a major premise of Johnson's *The Lives of the Poets*. Biography merged with literary criticism in *The Lives*, helping to contextualize and explain literary texts. The authors featured in *The Lives of the Poets* were dead, so there were no personal ramifications in relating their life stories, no concern of exposure, or of Johnson's judgments of their behavior. As a living author, Burney was very concerned about her readers' desire for public intimacy: the reader's (or fan's) sense of a personal connection with a celebrity, and wanting to pursue that connection.[27] Some eighteenth-century authors cultivated public intimacy to market their work: Laurence Sterne signed his private letters as Yorick, and referred to himself by that name.[28] But Burney, whose first novel became famous through word of mouth, was not invested in self-promotion or public intimacy; having acquired cultural capital on her own terms—quietly, privately—that's the way she wanted things to remain. Yet as more people read *Evelina*, and as her cultural capital generated celebrity (which generated more cultural capital), Burney spent more time striving to retain her privacy and identity.

Although Burney resented the conflation of herself with her work, she engaged in this biographical practice with other authors. She wrote of a conversation with Sir Joshua Reynolds, in which "Our subject was chiefly Dr. Johnson's *Lives of the Poets*;—we had both Read the same, & *therefore* could discuss them with equal pleasure,—& we both were charmed with them, & *therefore* could praise them with equal warmth,—& we both love & reverence the writer, & *therefore could mix observations on the Book with the Author with equal readiness*" (*EJL* 3:201; emphasis mine). The repeated "therefore" gains power and force, so that by its third iteration, Burney can "mix observations on the Book and the Author" and justify her biographical reading of Johnson's *Lives of the Poets* as causal and inevitable. Burney also had expectations of authors she did not know personally. In Brighton she encountered the playwright Richard Cumberland, and she was astonished that he snubbed her because of her success: "And are you not *surprised*, Susy, that the Author of the *West Indian* can be so pitifully jealous, & meanly spiteful?"[29] When Burney met Christopher Anstey, the author of *New Bath Guide* (1766) she wondered whether he would be witty like his book, and was disappointed when he was not (*EJL*, 4:87; see also 114). Burney's speculation about authors seems contradictory given that she bristled when others had expectations of her. But it is less a contradiction than a reflection of Burney's comfort as a reader and her discomfort with her celebrity. Other people's celebrity was not problematic, but Burney had difficulties being the subject of attention, and she resisted being a celebrity. This is not to say that Burney lacked professional ambitions—just that celebrity was not among them. Anonymity appealed to Burney because it did not leave her open to expectation, appropriation, misprision—or, as Johnson's sally about Montagu suggests, attack.

WHEN *I* WAS BEGINNING THE WORLD, & WAS NOTHING & NOBODY

Johnson's statement, "when *I* was beginning the World, & was nothing & nobody" resonates with Burney's early journals, which she started by writing to "Nobody," the only audience that the sixteen-year-old Burney could then claim.[30] For Burney, "Nobody" was a confidante for her thoughts, ideas, opinions—an addressee that was a figuration of herself and a cipher that could stand in for an audience. "Nobody" was safe but also pragmatic, as Burney practiced writing for herself, to herself. "Nobody" had other resonances as well, as Gallagher writes, "in eighteenth-century England Nobody was not a complete cipher, for the name had come to signify a common person, a person of no social consequence. Henry Fielding, for example, defined "No Body" as "All the People in Great Britain, except about 1200." So while "Nobody" could be juxtaposed with "somebody" (a person, a body) or "everybody" (the crowd) sometimes "nobody" *was* "somebody"—or "everybody."[31]

"Nobody" has considerable traction in Burney studies and eighteenth-century women's studies in general, where Nobody-ness has been construed as a sign of eighteenth-century women's lack of social, legal, or political consequence.[32] For Johnson, being "nobody" did not reflect a gendered invisibility so much as it signaled a lack of cultural and professional power, the failure to be recognized as a talent: it signaled cultural capital that did not generate celebrity. Perhaps Nobody and Nobody-ness belong to beginnings, as they did for Burney in her journal and Johnson at the start of his career; like divine creation in Genesis, beginnings seem to be generated from the void. But as Johnson described the arc of his career—from nobody, to struggling writer, to professional success—he traced one celebrity narrative without acknowledging the alternatives, even though he was writing and assessing those narratives in *The Lives of the Poets*. Some achieved cultural capital and celebrity early in their careers, like Cowley, Milton, and Pope; some were one-hit wonders, like Pomfret, Denham, and Garth; others achieved celebrity late, like West; some attained celebrity with mediocre talent, like Stepney. Still others, like Burney, achieved success through Nobody-ness. It's far from clear that Burney's "Nobody"—an alter ego that facilitated success—existed for Johnson, or that he would want it if it did.

Burney was comfortable writing for, and being, nobody—and based on her journals and letters, Burney became somebody even though she had not intended to do so.[33] Burney struggled to keep her authorship of *Evelina* secret, even as others made a hullabaloo about her work: "*Snugship*, however, is now, I fear, all over!—for the fear of *accident* betraying me, since the affair is in so many Hands, has occasioned still *further* spreading even with my *Consent*, which *now* I know not how to withhold, lest I *disoblige* my Friends, merely to gain a *few Weeks* privacy,—for longer I know not how to *hope*, as things are now situated, & as all quarters are blabbing away" (*EJL*, 3:135). Each person who knew her secret wanted to tell just one more person, and it became impossible to keep control of her anonymity. Part of Burney's anxiety centered on the stereotypes of female authors, which did not suit her taste: "Thus it is, that an *Authoress* must always be supposed to be flippant, assuming & loquacious!" (*EJL*, 3:135). And part of Burney's anxiety was meeting the expectations of others—professional and social expectations that she could not avoid because she was no longer anonymous.[34]

Burney mourned "the loss of my dear old obscurity" (*EJL*, 3:143) for anonymity proffered safety and freedom, even if it did not offer social or cultural power in any typical sense. In December 1778, Burney became incredibly upset when "little Burney" was mentioned in a pamphlet entitled *Warley: A Satire Addressed to the First Artist in Europe*. Although she was not the satiric target (which was Sir Joshua Reynolds) nor was the reference offensive, Burney was anxious, fearful, and frustrated that her name was in print (*EJL*, 3:193). Her response seems over-sensitive and exaggerated to a modern reader (as it did to Hester Thrale) but that dread was real to Burney (*EJL*, 3:205–07, 211; cf. 115–18). Her dismay elicited a surprisingly sympathetic response from Johnson: "On Friday, *I* had a visit from Dr. Johnson! he came on *purpose* to reason with me about this pamphlet, which he had heard from my *Father* had so greatly disturbed me.... He repeatedly charged me not to *fret*; & bid me not repine at my story, but think of Floretta, *in the Fairy Tale*, who found sweetness & consolation in hers sufficient to counter-ballance her scoffers & Libellers!! Indeed he was all good humour & kindness, & seemed quite bent upon giving me comfort" (*EJL*, 3:196). Johnson's advice—not to worry, to remember her own value—recalls earlier comments that she should "Never let them [the papers, the public] know *which* way you shall most mind them, & then they will stick to the *Book*,—but you must never acknowledge how tender you are for the *Author*."[35] That Johnson's advice about *Warley* was couched in the language of a fairy tale reminds Burney that she was already living a fantasy of success. But while Burney was flattered by Johnson's attention, she may have realized that her name may have appeared in print because of Johnson—for he was the one who had nicknamed her "little Burney" (*EJL*, 3:205).

A single woman's name in the press had a very different valence than a man's, and Johnson's effort to placate Burney may reflect his guilt over Burney's anguish. As a recognized cultural authority, Johnson was subject to frequent appearances in the media, and if they were not positive (and many were not) Johnson did not get upset every time. Burney watched Johnson listening to published verses against him and claimed, "I believe he wishes his abusers no other Thing than a *good Dinner* [like Pope]" (*EJL*, 3:112). Before the *Warley* episode, Thrale had encouraged Burney to accustom herself to appearing in the media, and harden herself against attack. Thrale remarked, "is not *every* body abused that meets with success? You must prepare yourself not to mind a few squibs. How is Mr. Johnson abused!—& who thinks the worse of him?" (*EJL*, 3:163). Burney delighted at the comparison with Johnson, but she found it difficult to internalize the advice. Burney never achieved Johnson's equanimity about public attention, nor, as we shall see, did she exhibit his towering rages about it either.

Burney was no longer "nobody," and she rarely knew when her name would appear in print, or what to expect when it did. In March 1782, her name appeared in a poem extolling literary ladies, in a group that was the female equivalent of Johnson's *Lives of the Poets*. Burney acknowledged the compliment when she wrote to her sister Susan, yet she felt awkward about the attention: "Do you know they have put me again into the newspapers in a Copy of verses made upon Literary Ladies?—where are introduced Mrs. Carter—Chapone—Cowley—Hannah More—Mrs. Greville, Mrs. Boscawen, Mrs. Thrale, Mrs. Crewe, Sophy Streatfield, & Mrs. Montagu. In such honourable Company, to repine at being placed, would perhaps be impertinent; so I take it quietly enough, but I would to Heaven I could keep clear of the whole!" (*EJL*, 5:36). Six years later, in 1788, she dreaded the publication of Hester Thrale Piozzi's correspondence with Johnson, fearing how the Burneys would be represented.[36] That the same year, the *Literary Chronicle* commented that Burney had not published anything recently, and she wrote, "the original repugnance to being known returns with every panic." (*CJ*, 4:478–79; see also *CJ*, 3:231–32).

Burney never reclaimed her Nobody-ness, although as many scholars have noted, being nobody, particularly a female nobody, resonates throughout her fiction. With her anonymity gone, it was difficult to hide—and to hide what she was doing. (In a letter to Susan in May 1780, Burney wrote, "I am perpetually discovering that I am well known here [in Bath] by people that I am unconscious of having ever seen, & quite certain I have never spoken to" [*EJL*, 4:123]). People asked if she was writing, what she was writing, and made suggestions to her about what to write—starting with Hester Thrale, who urged Burney to write a play (*EJL*, 3:64). Her works immediately after *Evelina*—*The Witlings* and *Cecilia*—were written under conditions of heightened public expectation.[37] Although *The Witlings* was not produced because of objections by Charles Burney and Samuel Crisp—objections that Burney was attacking the eagle, Elizabeth Montagu—Arthur Murphy read the first acts of the play, Sheridan was waiting to read and produce it, and others begged to see the manuscript. Seemingly everyone was anxious for her next publication, and Burney knew it. When Burney returned to novel writing, as her father recommended, Hester Thrale and Samuel Crisp devoured the manuscript chapters of *Cecilia* as Burney produced them.

Tellingly, Johnson did not read *Cecilia* in manuscript, and it seems unlikely that he read *The Witlings*. Johnson admired and respected Burney's talent, and trusted her literary instincts. Burney asked Johnson for advice while writing *The Witlings*: "He gave me advice which just accorded with my wishes,—viz—not to make known that I had any such intention;—to keep my own Counsel,—not to *whisper* even the *Name* of it to my *Bedfellow*,—to raise no expectations of it, which were *always* prejudicial, &, finally to have it *performed* while the Town knew nothing of whose it was." (*EJL*, 3:250) Perhaps by acknowledging the high stakes of authorship and urging Burney toward privacy, Johnson gave Burney a bit of her Nobody-ness back.

ATTACK HER, FIGHT HER, DOWN WITH HER AT ONCE!

Soon after Burney became famous, Hester Thrale told her, "now you are *in for it!*—but if you *will* be an Author & a Wit—you must take the Consequence!" and Johnson concurred (*EJL*, 3:116; cf. *EJL*, 3:172–73). Literary battles presented authors in performance, as a form of public entertainment.[38] Authorial celebrity was not only based on the writer exercising his or her craft (and the expectation of continuous, quality production), but in justifying one's opinions, taste, and work in public. Johnson was famous for his pronouncements and his verbal aggression, and in no instance was this more evident to Burney than in Johnson's response to criticism of his "Life of Lyttelton," one of the last entries in *The Lives of the Poets*.

Johnson had been working on this life in August 1780, and it was published in May 1781.[39] Roger H. Lonsdale's notes to "The Life of Lyttelton" summarize Johnson's struggle to find materials, his concern about offending Lyttelton's relatives, and his efforts to avoid doing so.[40] Elizabeth Montagu read the "Life" before publication, and disliked it intensely; according to Horace Walpole, in January 1781, "she 'and all her Maenades intend to tear [Johnson] limb from limb for despising their muppet Lyttelton.'"[41] Burney wrote in her journal in June 1781: "The long War which has been proclaimed among the Wits concerning Lord Lyttelton's life by Dr. Johnson, & which a whole tribe of *Blues*, with Mrs. Montagu at their Head, have Vowed to execrate & revenge, now broke out with all the fury of actual hostilities, stimulated by long concerted schemes & much spiteful information: Mr. Pepys, Dr. Johnson well knew was one of Mrs. Montagu's steadiest Abettors, & therefore, as he had some Time determined to defend himself with the first of them he met, this Day he fell sacrifice to his Wrath" (*EJL*, 4:366). The elevated military rhetoric is mocking—recalling Swift's *Battle of the Books*—and like Walpole's reference to the classical Maenads, genuine in capturing the emotional volatility of the participants. Johnson was furious with Montagu and her crowd, and he attacked William Weller Pepys when he visited Streatham: "Never before have I seen Dr. Johnson speak with so much passion; 'Mr. Pepys,' he cried, in a voice the most enraged, 'I understand you are offended by my Life of Lord Lyttelton, what is it you have to say against it? come forth, Man! Here am I! ready to answer any charge you can bring'" (*EJL*, 4:367). Johnson's words echo the calling out of an honored adversary, but his tone was bullying, taking advantage of the immediate circumstance to vent his concerns and protect his reputation.

Pepys was not looking for a fight; in fact, he spoke with Burney before this meeting, asking her to intervene so that he could avoid an argument with Johnson. When Pepys equivocated, Johnson "repeated his attack & his Challenge, & a violent disputation ensued, in which this great, but *mortal* man did, to own the truth, appear unreasonably furious & grossly severe: I never saw him so before, & I heartily hope I never shall again" (*EJL*, 4:367–68). That Johnson refused to relinquish the argument signals his fury: as the author, Johnson felt that he was the victim, the one whose cultural capital and reputation were at risk. It is significant that Burney italicized the word "mortal" in her recounting of the scene; as much as she admired Johnson and appreciated his friendship, Burney needed to remind herself that he was human and flawed. But that did not excuse Johnson's behavior, as she acknowledged that the argument brought out the worst in his character.

Burney tried to sympathize with Johnson's position, but his behavior perpetually worked against him: "He [Johnson] has been long provoked, & justly enough, at the *sneaking* complaints & murmurs of the angry Lytteltonians, & therefore his long excited wrath, which hitherto had met no Object, now burst forth with a vehemence & bitterness almost incredible. Mr. Pepys mean time never appeared to so much advantage; he preserved his Temper, uttered all that belonged merely to himself with modesty, & all that more immediately related to Lord Lyttelton with spirit" (*EJL*, 4:368). Burney's rhetoric is evocative: that Johnson had been "provoked" (as if he did not start the argument with his criticism of Lyttelton); the "*sneaking* complaints & murmurs" suggesting that Montagu and her adherents were not as forthright or honest as Johnson; the "angry Lytteltonians" recall Swift's similarly named Lilliputians, icons of pettiness and meanness; Johnson's "long excited wrath," is nearly divine in his displeasure and desire for justice. But it was Pepys who garnered Burney's admiration. Although Burney did not recount the specifics of his answers, Pepys' calm, polite behavior makes him appear "to so much advantage."

This encounter between Johnson and Pepys highlights issues that shaped Burney's early perceptions of the celebrity experience. First, while the conflation of author and text was expected, as Johnson told Burney, here it exacerbated the situation. If Johnson had separated himself from his work, he would not have been as vehement in his response to criticism—and it is likely that he could have conducted his defense in a more effective manner. Or differently: the public merging of author and text did not mandate that authors conflate themselves with their texts; an author's self could be private if an author so chose. So, Burney's notion of separating herself from her work had some merit after all. Second, when confronted with a real literary battle with Elizabeth Montagu—not a manufactured one, as he had laughingly suggested to Burney—Johnson did not fly directly at the eagle either. It is difficult to imagine Montagu tolerating Johnson's rudeness or listening to him on a rampage as Pepys did, much less being persuaded to concede to Johnson. Perhaps Johnson was mistaken or misremembered his youth: it was not so easy to go after the great ones after all. Insofar as there was still a game afoot for Johnson, it seems that there was little joy in being a player, and for Burney, little amusement in being a witness. Which leads to a third point: Johnson's argument with Pepys justified Burney's opinion that literary aggression was to be avoided at all costs. This fight only diminished Johnson, and did not resolve anything about the "Life of Lyttelton."

Johnson's argument with Pepys resonated for some time afterwards. After being admonished for his behavior by Hester Thrale, Johnson and Pepys reconciled in August 1781, much to Burney's satisfaction (*EJL*, 4:371; 429–30). But their détente only lasted a year, for when Johnson and Pepys met in Brighton in November 1782, they got into an argument about Thomas Gray and Alexander Pope:

> [Pepys] joined Dr. Johnson, with whom he entered into an argument upon some lines of Gray, & upon Pope's definition of Wit, in which he was so roughly confuted, & so severely ridiculed, that he was hurt & piqued beyond all power of disguise, & in the midst of the discourse, suddenly turned from him, & wishing Mrs. Thrale good night, very abruptly withdrew. Dr. Johnson was certainly right & *most* right with respect to the argument, & to reason, but his opposition was so warm, & his wit so satirical & exulting, that I was really quite grieved to see how unamiable he appeared, & how greatly he made himself dreaded by all, & by many abhorred. What pity that he will not curb the *vehemence* of his love of victory & superiority! (*EJL*, 5:139; see also 140)

It did not matter that Johnson was right. Not only did this argument end the friendship between Johnson and Pepys, but it turned Johnson into a social pariah in Brighton. Johnson was excluded from Lady Rothes' subsequent invitation to the Thrales (Pepys was her brother-in-law) and Johnson was omitted from other social invitations as well: "He [Johnson] is almost constantly omitted, either from too much *respect*, or too much *fear*. I am sorry for it, as he hates being alone, & as, though he scolds the others, he is well enough satisfied himself, &, having given vent to all his *own* occasional anger or ill-humour, he is ready to *begin again*, & is never aware that those who have so been 'downed' by him, never can much covet so triumphant a visitor!" (*EJL*, 5:145; see also 162–63). People were not obligated to socialize with Johnson, and by insisting on his intellectual supremacy, Johnson alienated his audience. Burney had not been subjected to Johnson's moodiness or his anger; if she had, given her sensitivities, Burney likely would not have spoken to Johnson again either. Burney was correct about Johnson's self-satisfaction and his misreading of people: it was as if he were playing the game according to the literary rules of Swift and Pope, and no one else was following those rules. A year later, in December 1783, when Burney recounted the story of Johnson's argument with Pepys to George Owen Cambridge, whose father was an admirer of Montagu, she still cringed at Johnson's vehement behavior.[42]

Johnson's conduct was surprising given his comments on literary aggression, reputation, and fame in his "Life of Pope," which he published in 1781, the same year as his "Life of Lyttelton." As Johnson traced the events that led Pope to enshrine Colley Cibber as the king of the dunces in the revised *Dunciad*, he observed,

> Pope had now been enough acquainted with human life to know, if his passion had not been too powerful for his understanding, that, from a contention like his with Cibber, the world seeks nothing but diversion, which is given at the expence of the higher character. When Cibber lampooned Pope, curiosity was excited; what Pope would say of Cibber nobody enquired, but in hope that Pope's asperity might betray his pain and lessen his dignity.
> He should therefore have suffered the pamphlet to flutter and die, without confessing that it stung him. The dishonor of being shewn as Cibber's antagonist could never be compensated by the victory. Cibber had nothing to lose; when Pope had exhausted all his malignity upon him, he would rise in the esteem both of his friends and his enemies. Silence only could have made him despicable; the blow which did not appear to be felt, would have been struck in vain. (*Lives*, 4:50)

If Johnson felt that Pope should have been silent in the face of Cibber's pamphlet, surely Johnson should have ignored Pepys's and Montagu's objections to the "Life of Lyttelton"—objections that were not even published. And why argue vehemently with Pepys about Pope's poetry? Johnson did not need to attack Pepys or Montagu to safeguard his reputation or his celebrity. But Johnson, like Pope, could not resist a fight, or resist an opportunity to triumph, even when it was in his interest to do so. Pepys, like Cibber, lacked the cultural capital of his opponent, and "had nothing to lose"; by pursuing the argument, Johnson—the eminent wit—could only "lessen his dignity," much as Pope had. (Johnson would have lost against Montagu too, for even though she had far more cultural authority than Pepys, she could not approach Johnson's literary or critical power.) It is ironic, and very human, that Johnson could see the problems of authorial ego and literary aggression in Pope's life, but not his own. But Burney learned the lesson: "In contests of Wit, the Victor is as ill off in future consequences, as the Vanquished in present ridicule" (*EJL*, 5:145).

Literary celebrity had changed since Johnson's youth, even though hierarchies of literary status remained, and authors continued to run through a gauntlet of commentary and criticism. The public performance of literary debate could be entertaining, but there were expectations of fair play and courtesy that changed the rules of the game, the perception of the participants, and the response of the audience. It is not news that British culture increasingly invoked conduct codes in the eighteenth century, even if those codes were not necessarily followed—and celebrities, including authors, were subject to them. Burney was particularly sensitized to the culture of politeness, which she documented extensively in *Evelina*, a conduct novel that interpreted the nuances and violations of civility. Burney could be as censorious as Johnson, but her public criticism was fashioned to fit a culture of courtesy: her second novel *Cecilia*, which she began while Johnson was finishing his *Lives of the Poets*, dissected the evils of social manipulation, expectation, and obligation—with decorum and an unflinching eye. As her journals and her letters make clear, Burney did not hesitate to express criticism fully in private. But Johnson, a critic by profession, wanted the freedom to speak his mind without circumlocution—and literary honesty often ran counter to courtesy. So Johnson's judgments and pronouncements, no matter how accurate, always ran the risk of offense. With the persistent conflation of author and text, and the rise of authorial celebrity, there was no way to prevent literary debate from becoming personal, painful, and public.

"THERE IS NO GAME NOW"

Although Johnson proclaimed "there is no Game now," he was mistaken; the game to achieve literary eminence was still afoot. But an author's status did not rely upon attacking other authors so much as it depended on cultural critics and the public. Burney recognized this when she appealed to the authors of the *Monthly Review* and the *Critical Review* in her preface to *Evelina*; she knew the cultural power that the reviewers wielded, and she could hope but not compel them to review her work kindly. The desire to define literary value was evident in the increase in canon-forming anthologies in the last quarter of the eighteenth century.[43] And the desire to be the authority to set literary criteria was strong, as

Johnson's arguments with Pepys make clear. But even as a literary critic, Johnson knew that literary value had changed and would change: his comments throughout *The Lives of the Poets* about older styles of poetry (most pointedly about metaphysical poetry in "The Life of Cowley") make that evident. Johnson also knew, as he told Burney, that readers who only followed the rules in their evaluation of literature were the readers least worth listening to. Identifying literary value was a matter of judgment, context, and taste—so much so that literary value and an author's value were moving targets more than authors (and perhaps their readers) cared to admit.

The rise of celebrity exacerbated the situation, for it granted the public a cultural power that was unregulated and eccentric, capable of recognizing or ignoring literary value at whim. (Johnson always questioned the value of quirky, popular works, as he famously and incorrectly said of Laurence Sterne: "Nothing odd will do long. *Tristram Shandy* did not last.")[44] Celebrity was both a cause and an effect of literary status: as the mechanisms of celebrity helped authors acquire cultural capital in new ways, so too celebrity put authors and their conduct under scrutiny previously unheard of, precisely because they had cultural power. Johnson and Burney both struggled with this new celebrity: the fickleness and intensity of public attention, the expectations of celebrity behavior, and the ways that celebrity affected the perception of literature and literary value. Their experiences between 1778 and 1782 shaped their critiques of the evolving culture of literary celebrity in different, and arguably complementary, ways. Burney's anxieties about public intimacy were generally not shared by Johnson, while Johnson's concerns about celebrity and literary status were generally not shared by Burney. This is not to say that Burney did not care about literary status (because she did), or that Johnson did not care about privacy and the perceptions of his character (because he did)— only that their experiences highlight different challenges of emergent literary celebrity.

The Johnson of the late 1770s and early 1780s was more comfortable with the mechanisms of celebrity than Burney—having sought, and been subject to, public attention for far longer than Burney had. But Johnson's manners were not calibrated for the social exchanges that public intimacy often required of celebrities. Johnson was a very social person, but even his friends had difficulties with his brusque behavior and eccentric habits. It is not surprising then that his fame did not fit the evolving model of celebrity: Johnson's literary celebrity centered on veneration for his accomplishments, his cultural capital—not on his efforts to establish or maintain public intimacy. (While Johnson's essayistic voice generated a kind of public intimacy with his readers, arguably Johnson truly achieved public intimacy most fully after his death in Boswell's *Life of Johnson*.) Although

Johnson had less at stake at the end of his career than Burney did at the beginning of hers, in the early 1780s he, too, was affected by the expectations of the new culture of celebrity. Johnson had as little patience for fans as Burney did, and he was more likely to express his impatience with them, and his critics, than she was. After the "Life of Lyttelton," Johnson could not reclaim his relationship with Elizabeth Montagu and the Bluestockings—nor could he prevent others from knowing about their argument, and passing judgment on his behavior and his work. It was publicly available for scrutiny and comment, as Burney's conversation with George Cambridge about the Johnson-Bluestocking debate suggests.

Burney's manners equipped her to navigate the nexus of cultural, social, and political power better than Johnson: Johnson received a government stipend in recognition of his work on the *Dictionary*, but it was Burney who was invited to become a member of the royal court. Yet Burney resented the invasive politics of public intimacy, and she disliked the politics of literary competition and the court. Celebrity put Burney in the position to wield cultural power—to become a cultural arbiter beyond the social critique in her novels—but she chose not to do so. By making that choice, Burney resisted her status as a celebrity author, and the cultural responsibilities of literary celebrity, unlike Johnson, who desired cultural authority. Famed for his literary discernment—even if people did not always agree with him—Johnson believed that literary celebrity not only had the power but the responsibility to shape culture wisely. The ability to identify and promote literary value and talent mattered, not only to the individual author but to society and the nation. Burney clearly benefitted from the discernment of critics and cultural celebrities: it worked to her advantage when the word spread that Burke and Reynolds could not put her novels down, or when Johnson declared that her novels were better than Fielding's, and would have made Richardson jealous (*EJL*, 3:149, 157; 109–10). Certainly Burney had the knowledge and taste to be a cultural arbiter; she recognized canons of literary value as she invoked a hierarchy of novelists in the preface to *Evelina*: Johnson, Marivaux, Fielding, Smollett, Rousseau and Richardson. But the work of shaping public sentiment and forming literary canons would tie Burney closely to the aspects of celebrity that dismayed her: public attention, criticism, and competition. By cherishing her privacy, Burney missed the opportunity to shape the terms of the cultural discussion and to promote literature that fit her criteria of value.

Not long after Johnson died in 1784, his celebrity gained a new dimension as Piozzi, Hawkins, Murphy, and Boswell were busy with their biographies of Johnson, writing him into literary and cultural history.[45] The game was not over for Johnson—merely changed—and he would have been pleased. But Burney did not enter the fray, nor did she feed the Johnson celebrity machine.[46] She continued to write, refusing to fly at the eagle nor interested in becoming the eagle.[47] Her later works—the novels *Camilla* and *The Wanderer,* her produced play *Edwy and Elgiva,* and *The Memoirs of Dr. Burney*—did not garner the universal praise that her earlier novels received, and while Burney retained her cultural capital, her celebrity dimmed as literary style changed. After her death in 1840, an edition of Burney's journals and diaries was published—and ironically, for nearly a century, Burney was far better known for her private writings than her public ones. As a chronicler of her age, Burney gained cultural capital and celebrity through revealing her private self, through public intimacy—precisely what she wished to avoid while living. Burney's literary afterlife changed yet again at the end of the twentieth century, as she was reinscribed into literary history as a novelist. Burney, unlike Johnson, did not seek the literary game or celebrity. She didn't have to. In death, as in life, they sought her.

NOTES

1. Frances Burney. *The Early Journals and Letters of Fanny Burney,* ed. Lars E. Troide et al. (Montreal and Kingston, ON: McGill-Queen's University Press, 1988–2012), 3:150–51 (hereafter cited *EJL,* by volume:page). All italics appear in the original unless otherwise noted.
2. See Isobel Grundy, "Samuel Johnson as Patron of Women," *Age of Johnson: A Scholarly Annual* 1 (1987): 59–77; Norma Clarke, *Dr. Johnson's Women* (London: Hambledon, 2000); Kate Chisholm, *Wits and Wives: Dr. Johnson in the Company of Women* (London: Chatto and Windus, 2011). For Johnson as a mentor of Burney, see Clarke's chapter on Burney, 183–246; See also John Glendenning, "Young Fanny Burney and the Mentor," *Age of Johnson: A Scholarly Annual* 4 (1991): 281–312; and Anthony W. Lee, "Allegories of Mentoring: Johnson and Frances Burney's *Cecilia,*" *Eighteenth-Century Novel* 5 (2006): 249–76.
3. I concur with Clarke, who argues that the "fly at the eagle" passage reveals Johnson's opinion that literature needs aggression to thrive: "Thus the life cycle was perpetuated; the individual was toppled but the institution survived. . . . Some flying at the eagle was desirable, so Johnson understood, if the institutional structure was to strengthen and grow" (*Dr. Johnson's Women,* 204).
4. Ibid., 218. Patronage did not disappear, but it was no longer the primary or preferred means of support for writers in the new literary marketplace. As Clarke notes, "By the early 1780s, when Montagu fell out with Woodhouse, when Hannah More got into difficulties with Ann Yearsley, when Mrs. Thrale was pained by Fanny Burney, and when Dorothea Gregory jumped ship, the very idea of patronage carried unacceptable meanings of servility on the one hand and tyranny on the other" (ibid., 201). While Johnson disdained patronage, he achieved financial independence after the *Dictionary* because of his government pension—arguably a form of patronage. See ibid., 218–19.
5. Catherine Gallagher, *Nobody's Story: Vanishing Acts in the Marketplace, 1670–1820* (Berkeley: University of California Press, 1995), 229.
6. See John Feather, *The Provincial Book Trade in Eighteenth-Century England* (Cambridge: Cambridge University Press, 1985); Clifford Siskin, *The Work of Writing: Literature and Social Change in Britain, 1700–1830* (Baltimore: Johns Hopkins University Press, 1999);

Jody Greene, *The Trouble with Ownership: Literary Property and Authorial Liability in England, 1660–1730* (Philadelphia: University of Pennsylvania Press, 2005); Thomas F. Bonnell, *The Most Disreputable Trade: Publishing the Classics of English Poetry, 1765–1810* (Oxford: Oxford University Press, 2008); *The Cambridge History of the Book in Britain, Volume 5 1695–1830*, ed. Michael F. Suarez and Michael L. Turner (Cambridge: Cambridge University Press, 2009), and James Raven, *Publishing Business in Eighteenth-Century England* (Woodbridge: Boydell, 2014).

7. See Johnson's "Life of Gay," which cites Alexander Pope on the reception of *Beggar's Opera*: "Besides being acted in London sixty-three days without interruption, and renewed the next season with equal applause, it spread into all the great towns of England.... The ladies carried about with them the favourite songs of it in fans, and houses were furnished with it in screens." In Samuel Johnson, *The Lives of the English Poets: With Critical Observations on Their Works*, ed. Roger H. Lonsdale (Oxford: Clarendon Press, 2006), 3:99 (hereafter cited as *Lives*, by volume:page). See Melissa Free, "Un-Erasing *Crusoe*: Farther Adventures in the Nineteenth Century," *Book History* 9 (2006): 89–130 for a discussion of the *Crusoe* sequels and Robinsonades. See David Brewer's discussion of Gulliveriana in *The Afterlife of Character, 1726–1825* (Philadelphia: University of Pennsylvania Press, 2005), 32–42, and *Pamela in the Marketplace: Literary Controversy and Print Culture in Eighteenth-Century Britain and Ireland*, ed. Tom Keymer and Peter Sabor (Cambridge: Cambridge University Press, 2005) for the considerable marketing and cultural impact of Richardson's novel.

8. See Frank Donoghue's *The Fame Machine: Book Reviewing and Eighteenth-Century Literary Careers* (Stanford, CA: Stanford University Press, 1996).

9. Literary celebrity coincided with political and social power through Bluestocking meetings and the Literary Club; friendships (Pope with Bolingbroke, Bathurst, Cobham, and Burlington; Richardson with Lady Bradshaigh; Fielding and Ralph Allen, etc.); and professional appointments (like Burney's position as the Queen's Keeper of the Robes). The rise of celebrity in the late eighteenth century has been most fully analyzed in terms of the theatre: see Joseph Roach, *It* (Ann Arbor: University of Michigan Press, 2007); Felicity Nussbaum, *Rival Queens: Actresses, Performance, and Eighteenth-Century British Theater* (Philadelphia: University of Pennsylvania Press, 2010); and Laura Engel, *Fashioning Celebrity: Eighteenth-Century British Actresses and Strategies for Image Making* (Columbus: Ohio State University Press, 2011).

10. Samuel Johnson, Letter to James Boswell, May 3, 1777, in *Letters*, 3:20.

11. The one point of commonality is that Johnson and Burney both exemplify what Chris Rojek calls "achieved celebrity"—celebrity that is based on individual accomplishment, rather than "ascribed celebrity" (based on lineage) or "attributed celebrity" (as an individual is deemed noteworthy by others). See Rojek, *Celebrity* (London: Reaktion Books, 2001), 17–18.

12. See, for example, Anthony W. Lee, *Mentoring Relationships in the Life and Writings of Samuel Johnson: A Study in the Dynamics of Eighteenth-Century Literary Mentoring* (Lewiston, NY: Edwin Mellen Press, 2005), 55–58.

13. See Frances Burney D'Arblay's biography of her father, *The Memoirs of Dr. Burney* (London, 1832). For commentary on Charles Burney's obsequious character and his scramble for success, see Margaret Anne Doody, *Frances Burney: A Life in the Works* (New Brunswick: Rutgers University Press, 1988), 12–13, 14–15, 18.

14. Clarke argues that Burney behaved like a professional novelist in her dealings with her publisher (*Dr. Johnson's Women*, 186–87). Generally, I agree, although it was somewhat cloak and dagger to enlist her brother Charles, in costume, to serve as currier for the manuscript (Doody, *Frances Burney*, 38). Rather, I am suggesting that Burney was removed from the common experience of authorship. As Gallagher observes in *Nobody's Story*, "in his

self-characterizations and his numerous literary biographies, Johnson created the writer's life as one long heroic struggle against almost impossible economic odds" (152). Burney's career does not fit that narrative of authorial experience.

15. *EJL*, 3:158–60. Burney's reaction was shaped by her perception of Montagu as a celebrity: "I determined, . . . [to] keep myself as much out of the way as I could. Indeed, at *any* rate, a woman of such celebrity in the Literary world, would be the *last* I should covet to converse with, though one of the *first* I would wish to listen to." (*EJL*, 3:144–45)

16. *EJL*, 3:163; cf. 3:212. This is not to say that Burney wanted to be attacked as an author: "for the truth is, I am frightened out of my wits from the terror of being attacked *as an author*, & therefore *shirk*, instead of *seeking*, all occasion of being drawn into notice." (*EJL*, 3:143) Rather, she made a distinction between her private and professional selves, although they were related.

17. In June 1780, Burney was accosted by ten-year-old Miss Miller, who wanted to know where Evelina was: "'And pray, Ma'am, is Madame Duval with her now?' And several other Questions she asked me, with a childish simplicity that was very diverting. She took the whole for a true story, & was quite eager to know what was become of all the people. And when I said I would enquire, & *tell* her when we next met, 'O but, Ma'am, she said, had not you better write it down because then there would be more of it, you know'" (*EJL*, 4:172; see also 171).

18. Johnson and Dr. Parker referred to Burney as Evelina (*EJL*, 3:95, 301); Hester Thrale called Burney "the great Evelina" (*EJL*, 3:205), and Edmund Phipps, anticipating meeting Burney, hoped that she would be like Evelina (*EJL*, 3:335). See also *EJL*, 3:186, 4:125, 168, and 446.

19. See Nussbaum, *Rival Queens*:
> Audiences of both sexes recognized that the woman player acting on stage joined the virtual body of the character she represented with her actual body as a person. These dual bodies were not easily separated. Creating this simulation of intimacy involved performing within the public realm with the express intent to expose private matters and to generate affect around one's own person in order to kindle celebrity. Early actresses, sometimes seeming to perform a stylized version of their personal lives on stage, manipulated privacy into the construction of a partially fictive offstage personality that became a theatricalized substitute for authentic knowledge about the actress's life. (44)

20. Johnson probably would have appreciated this attribution of social power. He certainly recognized this critical mean streak in *Evelina*—as his delight in Mr. Smith and the Branghtons make clear (*EJL*, 3:61, 70, 89–90, 92–93, 108)—which may have been part of his motivation to goad Burney to attack Montagu.

21. *EJL*, 3:120. Cf. Boswell's *Life*: "Sir, you have but two topicks, yourself and me. I am sick of both" (*Life*, 3:57). Nevertheless, Johnson praised Burney extravagantly: he claimed that Burney was better than Richardson and Fielding (*EJL*, 3:90, 109–10); he told Hester Thrale that Burney was a wonder, because no man had ever written a book like *Evelina* so young (*EJL*, 3:329); he complained when people discussed Siddons "till, at last, wearied out, I [Johnson] went yonder, into a corner, & repeated to myself Burney! Burney! Burney! Burney!'" (*EJL*, 5:195–96).

22. *EJL*, 4:102–06. Cf. Burney's initial response to Augusta Byron (*EJL*, 3:424) and her troubled response to Miss White (*EJL*, 4:144–46). While Burney disliked dealing with her fans, Burney enjoyed fangirling over Johnson.

23. *EJL*, 3:221. Cf. Burney's mentor, Samuel Crisp: "Would You wish Your Book to die such a Death? There is no Alternative—if it lives, it's fate & yours are inseparable, & the Names

of Evelina & Burney must & will go together, so that your discontent at what has happen'd, to me seems, strangely ill-founded" (*EJL*, 3:238).
24. See Robert DeMaria Jr. and Gwin J. Kolb, "Johnson's *Dictionary* and Dictionary Johnson," *Yearbook of English Studies* 28 (1998): 19–43, for a discussion of Johnson's authorship—and perceptions of his authorship—of the *Dictionary*.
25. Manushag N. Powell's discussion of the eidolon, the projected persona of the periodical author, astutely analyzes periodical authorship and readership, and many of her remarks can be applied to non-fiction generally. See *Performing Authorship in Eighteenth-Century English Periodicals* (Lewisburg, PA: Bucknell University Press, 2012), 23–34.
26. See, for example, Helen Louise McGuffie, *Samuel Johnson in the British Press, 1749–1784: A Chronological Checklist* (New York and London: Garland, 1976).
27. See Roach's discussion of "public intimacy": "Images circulate widely in the absence of their persons—a necessary condition of modern celebrity—but the very tension between their widespread visibility and their actual remoteness creates an unfulfilled need in the hearts of the public. One aspect of this need manifests itself as a craving to communicate with the privately embodied source of the aura" (*It*, 17). Books serve the same function as images in generating desire for (and accessibility to) authors, while signaling their remoteness.
28. See Peter Briggs, "Laurence Sterne and Literary Celebrity in 1760," *Age of Johnson: A Scholarly Annual* 4 (1991): 251–80.
29. *EJL*, 3:400. Hester Thrale secured Cumberland's ire by praising *Evelina* (*EJL*, 3:387, 398–99, 407). Thrale, like Johnson, was invested in literary aggression, whether for her own amusement or to shore up her cultural capital as a social patron of Burney. Burney thought Cumberland's behavior was uncalled for and ineffective: Cumberland's snubs did not stop the sales of *Evelina* or diminish her success (*EJL*, 3:410).
30. "To whom, then, *must* I dedicate my wonderful, surprising & interesting adventures?—to *whom* da[re] I reveal my private opinion of my nearest Relations? the secret thoughts of my dearest friends? my own hopes, fears, reflections & dislikes?—Nobody!
To Nobody, then, will I write my Journal! Since To Nobody can I be wholly unreserved—to Nobody can I reveal every thought, every wish of my Heart, with the most unlimited confidence, the most unremitting sincerity to the end of my Life!" (*EJL*, 1:2).
31. Gallagher, *Nobody's Story*, 206–7. I am indebted to Gallagher's comments on "nobody," "somebody," and "everybody" in her chapter on Burney, particularly 203–14.
32. While women participated in the public sphere more than Jürgen Habermas suggests in *The Structural Transformation of the Public Sphere: An Inquiry into a Category of Bourgeois Society*, trans. Thomas Burger, with Frederick Lawrence (1962) (Cambridge, MA: MIT Press, 1991), eighteenth-century women faced considerable pressure to be domestic; as wives and daughters they lacked legal status, and they were excluded from university education, political office, and in most denominations, clerical office. The scholarship on this subject is considerable; key texts include Margaret Ezell, *The Patriarch's Wife: Literary Evidence and the History of the Family* (Chapel Hill: University North Carolina Press, 1987); Bridget Hill, *Women, Work, and Sexual Politics in Eighteenth-Century England* (London: Blackwell, 1989); Amanda Vickery, *The Gentleman's Daughter: Women's Lives in Georgian England* (New Haven, CT: Yale University Press, 1998); Naomi Tadmor, *Family & Friends in Eighteenth-Century England: Household, Kinship, Patronage* (Cambridge: Cambridge University Press, 2001); and Michael McKeon, *The Secret History of Domesticity* (Baltimore: Johns Hopkins University Press, 2005). Since the 1980s, feminist scholarship has addressed female "nobodiness" by recuperating and analyzing women's experience and writing. Recent efforts include Deborah Kennedy, *Poetic Sisters: Early Eighteenth-Century Women Poets* (Lewisburg, PA: Bucknell University Press, 2012); Chloe Wigston Smith,

Women, Work, and Clothes in the Eighteenth-Century Novel (Cambridge: Cambridge University Press, 2013); *Stage Mothers: Women, Work, and the Theater, 1660–1830*, ed. Laura Engel and Elaine M. McGirr (Lewisburg, PA: Bucknell University Press, 2014); and Melissa Sodeman, *Sentimental Memorials: Women and the Novel in Literary History* (Stanford, CA: Stanford University Press, 2014). The ur-text on Burney and nobody-ness is Joanne Cutting-Gray's *Woman as Nobody and the Novels of Fanny Burney* (Gainesville: University Press of Florida, 1992).

33. *EJL*, 3:116; also 115, 117, 118. Claire Brock finds Burney to be disingenuous; in *The Feminization of Fame, 1750–1830* (Basingstoke: Palgrave Macmillan, 2006), she argues that Burney was an ambitious, adroit manager of her public relations. I think that Burney could be professionally ambitious *and* uncomfortable with certain types of attention.

34. See Kate Hamilton's dissertation, "Frances Burney and Celebrity," (PhD diss., Carnegie Mellon University, 2016), especially chap. 1, for Burney's ambivalence toward celebrity (particularly the ways that public intimacy could make women vulnerable) and chap. 2, on the challenges Burney faced in shaping and maintaining her reputation once she achieved fame.

35. *EJL*, 3:173; cf. *EJL*, 3:161. Despite this advice, when Burney wrote to Samuel Crisp about *Warley*, she could not shake her anxiety about publicity and celebrity: "Yet, after all, I feel very forcibly that I *am* not—that I *have* not been—& that I never *shall* be formed or fitted for any business with the *Public*—yet, now, my best friends, & my Father at their Head, absolutely *prohibit* a retreat;—otherwise, I should be strongly tempted to empty the whole contents of my Bureau into the Fire, & to vow never again to fill it.—But, had my *Name* never got abroad with my *Book*,—ere this, I question not, I should again have tried *how the World stood affected to me*" (*EJL*, 3:211).

36. Frances Burney, *The Court Journals and Letters of Frances Burney*, Gen. Ed. Peter Sabor (Oxford: Clarendon Press, 2011-), 3:35–36, 44 (hereafter cited *CJ*, by volume:page). All italics emphasis appear in the original unless otherwise noted.

37. *EJL*, 3:234–36, 245–46, 267–68, 278, and 287; *EJL*, 5:16–21, 28, 30–32, 34, 40, 47–48, and 67; see also *EJL*, 4:7. The pressure of the expectation continued for most of Burney's career. In December 1798, Burney visited Princess Amelia, who asked, "Are you writing any thing?" "This was too hard an interrogatory for evasion—& I was forced to say,—the truth,—That I was about nothing I had yet fixed if or not I should ever finish, but that I was rarely without some project" (*The Journals and Letters of Fanny Burney (1791–1840)*, ed. Joyce Hemlow et al. [Oxford Clarendon Press, 1972–1984], 4:233). At the time, Burney had completed a play, *Love and Fashion*, while working on two plays ("A Busy Day" and "The Woman Hater") and a second edition of her novel *Camilla*.

38. See Johnson's *Rambler* 176 (November 23, 1751): "The diversion of baiting an author has the sanction of all ages and nations, and is more lawful than the sport of teizing other animals, because for the most part he comes voluntarily to the stake" (Yale *Works*, 5:165).

39. See William McCarthy's "The Composition of Johnson's *Lives*: A Calendar," *Philological Quarterly* 60 (1981): 60–62.

40. *Lives*, 4:502–4. Johnson wrote to Lord Westcote, Lyttelton's brother, suggesting that he find someone else to write Lyttelton's biography, while Johnson would focus on the literary criticism of Lyttelton's work. Westcote did not recommend another author.

41. Horace Walpole, quoted in *Lives*, 4:505. Walpole described a gathering at Lady Lucan's in February 1781, at which Montagu refused to engage Johnson: "There she told me as a mark of her high displeasure that she would never ask him to dinner again. I took her side and fomented the quarrel" (*Lives*, 4:505). Walpole's reaction—to foment the quarrel—may have been his version of flying at the eagle (i.e., Johnson); in any case, Walpole's vision of an aggressive literary world appears to have been cognate with Johnson's. See chap. 2

("The Poetics of Gloom") of Anthony W. Lee's *Dead Masters: Mentoring and Intertextuality in Samuel Johnson* (Bethlehem, PA: Lehigh University Press, 2011), esp. 58–65.

42. *EJL*, 5:437–40. In 1783, Johnson claimed that he had mellowed, yet he was still primed to fight Montagu: "Why I am now, said he, come to that Time when I wish all bitterness & animosity to be at an end. I have never done her [Montagu] any serious harm,—nor would I;—though I *could* give her a *bite*!—but she must provoke me much first. In volatile talk, indeed, I may have spoken of her not much to her mind; for in the tumult of Conversation, malice is apt to grow sprightly; & *there*, I hope, I am not yet decrepid!" (*EJL*, 5:439).

    In December 1782/January 1783, Johnson was still teasing beginners to fly at the eagle, as he encouraged Susan Thrale to attack Burney (*EJL*, 5:226–27).

43. For anthologies and canon-formation at the end of the period, see Richard C. Taylor, "James Harrison, *The Novelist's Magazine*, and the Early Canonizing of the English Novel," *Studies in English Literature* 33, no. 3 (Summer 1993): 629–43; and Claudia Johnson, "'Let Me Make the Novels of a Country': Barbauld's 'The British Novelists' (1810/1820)," *Novel: A Forum on Fiction* 34, no. 2 (Spring 2001): 163–79; Barbara M. Benedict, *Making the Modern Reader: Cultural Mediation in Restoration and Eighteenth-Century Literary Anthologies* (Princeton, NJ: Princeton University Press, 1996).

44. *Life*, 2:449. See also *Rambler* 106 (March 23, 1751): "Of the innumerable authors whose performances are thus treasured up in magnificent obscurity [in a library], most are forgotten, because they never deserved to be remembered, and owed the honours which they once obtained, not to judgment or to genius, to labour or to art, but to the prejudice of faction, the stratagem of intrigue, or the servility of adulation. Nothing is more common than to find men, whose works are now totally neglected, mentioned with praises by their contemporaries as the oracles of their age, and the legislators of science" (Yale *Works*, 4:201).

45. Some of the unseemliness of the Johnson industry was captured by Hannah More in a letter to her sister in 1788: "Burke said to me the other day in allusion to the innumerable lives, anecdotes, remains, &c which have been published of Johnson,—"How many maggots have crawled out of that great body!" There are some good sprightly letters from Mrs. Thrale herself; but it is odd to print one's own letters while one is alive and merry" (William Roberts, *Memoirs of the Life and Correspondence of Mrs. Hannah More*, 3rd ed. [London, 1835]: 2:101).

46. When Boswell asked Burney for her correspondence with Johnson, she refused (Doody, *Frances Burney*, 31). That she was appalled by the private images of Johnson that Piozzi and Boswell published was predictable.

47. In the Dedication of *The Wanderer* (1814) to her father, Burney significantly recasts the meaning of "fly at the eagle" to suggest individual striving for excellence, rather than literary competition: "He [Charles Burney] will recollect, also, how often their so mutually honoured Dr. Johnson has said to her, "Always aim at the eagle!—even though you expect but to reach the sparrow!" (Frances Burney, *The Wanderer*, ed. Margaret Anne Doody et al. [Oxford: Oxford University Press, 2001], 8).

6
IN THE FIRST CIRCLE
The Four Narrators of the *Life of Savage*

LANCE WILCOX

WHEN WE SPEAK OF THE "JOHNSON CIRCLE," we are speaking of the people Johnson drew about him in the later decades of his life. We think of the aging literary lion surrounded by writers, artists, and politicians in meetings of the Club, or ringed by Thrales and Burneys in the drawing room at Streatham. The most consistent feature of such imagery, in fact, is Johnson's centrality; Johnson does not orbit others, they orbit him. His situation earlier in the century, however, was different. The circles of the early eighteenth century were dominated by Pope, Swift, and the Scriblerians, by Addison and Steele, by Aaron Hill and the Hillarians, to none of whom was Johnson known personally. For knowledge of the Johnson Circle of the 1760s to 1780s, we have James Boswell's, John Hawkins's, and Hester Piozzi's biographies. For the 1720s to 1740s, what we have is *An Account of the Life of Mr Richard Savage*, Johnson's scalding indictment of such circles written during his time as a Grub Street hack.[1] Through the *Life of Savage*, Johnson traces the ascent, impoverishment, and death of a beloved fellow writer and the failures of the circle obliged to support him. Decades later, the lessons learned from the experience were to be seen in the composition of the Johnson Circle itself.

As Savage charms, alienates, and attacks the "Savage Circle," and the Circle adopts, wearies of, and rejects Savage, the reactions of the narrator of the *Life of Savage* range from judicious detachment to grief, vexation, and outrage. When we try to focus on the narrator directly, however, what we find is an elusive, fluctuating figure whose relationship to the moody young journalist for the *Gentleman's Magazine* is far from clear. Critics who have looked at the narrator have tended to treat him as a single unified character, though this creates serious interpretive problems.[2] Richard Holmes, for instance, finds the attitude of the narrator difficult to pin down: "Though intensely personal and partial, its narrative voice appears distanced and carefully withdrawn. This makes Johnson's attitude, and the level of his irony, peculiarly difficult to judge."[3] Virginia Spencer Davidson suggests one escape from the problem when she writes that we should "recognize Johnson as a choric voice . . . accommodating to himself typical choric patterns of omniscience, severity, compassion, caution, and regret."[4] Timothy Erwin, also aware of the narrator's fluctuating attitude, suggests that it is "a feature that may reflect the unreliable narrator of fiction."[5]

Rather than consider the narrator a puzzling unified entity, however, it may be more helpful to think in terms of multiple narrators, each with its own perspective, attitude, and rhetorical habits, and each related to the others in strategic ways. In examining how the language of the text functions, the decision whether to speak in terms of one narrator with multiple "voices" or of multiple distinct "narrators" is purely pragmatic, the goal being to cast the greatest possible light on the language of the *Life of Savage*. As used in such an analysis, the terms "voices" and "narrators" are equally figurative. If the former usage is more common and more intuitive, it also runs a greater risk of conflating the narrator of the text with the author, though Sarah R. Morrison warns us of "the need to distinguish carefully between Johnson and the narrator of the *Life of Savage* and thereby to keep the focus on Johnson's strategy and tactics."[6] If we maintain the distinction between the author and the narrator or narrators, we can more meaningfully raise the question of how the former deploys the latter. To think in terms of multiple narrators also saves us from paradoxes such at that with which Holmes struggles, of a single narrative voice that is both "intensely personal" and "distanced." It may be more informative to start by positing two narrators, one "intensely personal" and one "distanced," and see what else we can observe about their respective language and functions. Once we are free of the need to construct a single coherent narrator, we are in a better position to highlight the variety of rhetorical strategies Johnson adopts.

It appears to me that the narrator of *Savage* is, in fact, a composite figure, and that it can best be understood in terms of four separate personae, which I label the Sage, the Historian, the Memoirist, and the Friend.[7] In this essay, I describe the styles and attitudes of these narrators, then trace them through Johnson's account of the conflict between Savage and his Circle, examining what each narrator contributes to our sense of it. The results suggest why for Johnson the patronage system died, not in Lord Chesterfield's waiting room, but in a prison cell in Bristol, and what effect his friendship with Richard Savage had on the constitution of the Johnson Circle decades later.

A QUARTET OF NARRATORS

The Sage

The first voice we hear in *The Life of Savage* is that of the Sage: "It has been observed in all Ages, that . . ." (*LRS* 49). The voice is immediately recognizable, speaking in the grandiloquent diction, elaborate syntax, and stately cadences of the *Rambler*. The comments of the Sage reflect the sort of general truth that constantly drives Johnson's thinking. W. Jackson Bate, in a discussion of the genres found in *Savage*, suggests that one is the "moral essay" of the kind Johnson would be writing in the 1750s: "It is wrapped around, in and through the narrative; and it appears at its best when Johnson—like the chorus in a Greek drama—stops to comment on human life."[8] Such passages are voiced exclusively by the Sage.

The Sage's pronouncements are characterized in part by their logical independence, their ability to make sense when cited in isolation. Other narrators, especially the Historian, draw conclusions from the events, but the Historian's remain tied to the details of the narrative. If the passages by the Sage sound like moral essays, it is because they are so readily detachable from their context. Following a description of the treatment Savage suffered after he was banished from Lord Tyrconnel's house, the Sage rises to a general truth: "So much more certain are the Effects of Resentment than of Gratitude: it is not only to many more pleasing to recollect those Faults which place others below them, than those Virtues by which they are themselves comparatively depressed; but it is likewise more easy to neglect, than to recompense; and though there are few who will practise a laborious Virtue, there will never be wanting Multitudes that will indulge an easy Vice" (*LRS*, 90). While the comment serves to illuminate the specific event, it is perfectly intelligible apart from its narrative surroundings. We would not be surprised to find it in one of the *Ramblers*.

The characteristic tone of the Sage is a resonant melancholy. He opens the biography with a hopeful proposition which experience unfortunately refutes: "It seems rational to hope, that . . . Minds qualified for great Attainments should first endeavour their own Benefit, and that they who are most able to teach others the Way to Happiness, should with most Certainty follow it themselves. But this Expectation, however plausible, has been very frequently disappointed" (*LRS*, 49). Having pronounced this dismal truth, the Sage declares it his intention to add to the "mournful Narratives" illuminating it, though he has, we sense, already revealed his deepest conviction, that "the general Lot of Mankind is Misery" (*LRS*, 49). While the Historian laments the sufferings of Richard Savage, the Sage laments the sufferings of humanity.

The Historian

The Historian is by far the dominant voice in the *Life of Savage*, responsible for perhaps two-thirds of it. He is the factual chronicler of the major events. We hear the Historian first in a graceful segue from the Sage, then in pure form when the story actually begins: "In the Year 1697, *Anne* Countess of *Macclesfield*, having lived for some time upon very uneasy Terms with her Husband, thought a public Confession of Adultery the most obvious and expeditious Method of obtaining her Liberty, and therefore declared, that the Child, with which she was then great, was begotten by the Earl *Rivers*" (*LRS*, 49–50).

The prose is formal without being as elaborate syntactically as that of the Sage. The diction is moderately abstract—"uneasy terms" is almost a euphemism—and the tone is dry and detached. Throughout the *Life of Savage*, the Historian freely assigns motives, however speculative or demeaning, to characters' actions, here indicting Lady Macclesfield as an adulteress willing to publicize her sin for personal gain. Despite the controversial, even libelous, nature of the claim, the Historian provides no documentation. In the case of the Memoirist and the Friend, who base their accounts on information received straight from Savage, footnotes would be superfluous, but the Historian is working from a variety of public documents.[9] Whenever he can, he explicitly draws on these sources, though most of his text is presented, as here, in the guise of unimpeachable fact in no need of empirical support.

Wayne Booth long ago taught us to discriminate dramatized and undramatized narrators. In the *Life of Savage*, all but the Sage are dramatized, though in different ways. The Memoirist is at least peripherally part of Savage's story, while the Friend is visibly involved. The Historian, by contrast, plays no part in the events, though we watch him actively selecting and arranging his material in the construction of the text. He is, paradoxically, the only narrator who slips readily into first person; the Sage and Memoirist do so rarely, and the Friend never. The Historian makes himself vividly present to us as he tells about his questions, doubts, and hesitancies with respect to his material. When uncertain, he hedges a claim with an *I believe* and fills several gaps with a frank *I know not*. In other places, he evokes a sort of authorial code, partly aesthetic and partly ethical, to explain his decisions about the text he is creating: "Mr *Savage* related another Fact equally uncommon, which, though it has no Relation to his Life, ought to be preserved" (57). "It is proper that I observe the Impartiality which I recommend, by declaring . . ." (79). "As no other Person ought to prosecute that Revenge from which the Person who was injured desisted, I shall not preserve what Mr *Savage* suppressed" (113). When George Justice argues that Johnson's goal in writing *Sav-*

age was in part to create a positive image of the professional author, the Historian is the narrator who fulfills that role.

By dramatizing the Historian in the act of selecting and arranging his material, Johnson leads us to accept such manipulation as a convention of biography. This, in turn, safeguards the Historian's credibility when he carries out the most aggressive manipulation in the book. In the aftermath of Savage's conviction, while Hill, Tyrconnel, and others were seeking to secure him a royal pardon, the Historian tells us that the attempt was almost foiled by the opposition of Lady Macclesfield. He then announces a remarkable displacement he has made in the chronology: "To prejudice the Queen against him, she made use of an Incident, which was omitted in the order of Time, that it might be mentioned together with the Purpose which it was made to serve" (*LRS*, 71). The "Incident" was that several years earlier, Savage had found the door of Lady Macclesfield's house open, entered it, and gone up to her room hoping "to salute her." She, not surprisingly, panicked, called others to throw him out, and claimed he tried to murder her. While Savage's friends were attempting to persuade the Queen to support their petition for a royal pardon, Lady Macclesfield managed to inform her of the incident, nearly dissuading her from saving Savage's life. Lady Macclesfield's use of this "atrocious Calumny," her accusation of attempted murder, goads the Historian into one of his most acidic comments: "Thus had *Savage* perished by the Evidence of a Bawd, a Strumpet, and his Mother" (*LRS*, 72). Had the Historian presented the incident "in the order of Time," Savage's sudden appearance in Lady Macclesfield's bedroom would have made him appear the aggressor. Moving it to after the trial allows the Historian to present Savage instead as the victim of his mother's persecution. We accept the rearrangement of the events without much demur because Johnson has already made us so aware of the Historian as the hand shaping the narrative.

The Historian usually attempts to treat the characters with a calm, even-handed fairness. In narrating the conflicts between Savage and Richard Steele or, later, between Savage and Lord Tyrconnel, the Historian presents the dispute from both sides, a task made easier by his freedom to speculate about motivations. But this fairness breaks down spectacularly whenever he turns his attention to Lady Macclesfield. At such times, the Historian becomes the most passionately partisan of the narrators. He does not present himself as a man upset at the treatment of a friend, but as the voice of humanity outraged by the evils visited upon an innocent victim. This moral stance, along with the grounding of his charges in documentary sources, authorizes the Historian to make the most incendiary comments: "If they deserve Death who destroy a Child in its Birth, what Pains can be severe enough for her who forbears to destroy him only to inflict sharper Miseries upon him?" (*LRS*, 62). The Sage would never express such fury, and it would seem too blatantly partisan coming from the Memoirist or the Friend, but the Historian, armed with his documentary sources and his stance of outraged humanity, can all but advocate burning Lady Macclesfield at the stake.

The Historian is also, finally, the narrator responsible for the literary criticism in the *Life of Savage*. The Historian treats Savage's writings with ostentatious fairness, pointing out their strengths and weaknesses, and overrating their quality. As Edward Tomarken writes, "The voice that we hear here is that of the judicious literary critic, Johnson as literary biographer."[10] Compared to the Preface to Shakespeare or the discussion of the Metaphysical Poets in the "Life of Cowley," the criticism is rudimentary. The Historian sketchily assesses each work's imagery, language, and structure, then quickly returns to his narrative.

The Memoirist

In the advertisement for his biography of Savage published in the *Gentleman's Magazine*, August 1743, Johnson presented himself as "a Person who was favoured with his Confidence, and received from himself an Account of most of the Transactions which he proposes to mention."[11] While Johnson did receive much of his information from Savage, he had no plans to write his biography when he knew him. Unlike Boswell, he neither interviewed his subject nor kept a record of their interactions. What he knew of Savage when he was writing the *Life of Savage* was thus limited to whatever he could recall four years after the end of a year-long friendship—the material, that is, less for a biography than a memoir. His sense of the conventions of biography, however, required him to focus sharply on Savage and to keep himself as much as possible out of the picture. The result was the Memoirist, a sort of hybrid narrator of a hybridic text. In discussing how the friendship between Johnson and Savage affected the *Life of Savage*, Clarence Tracy highlights the role of this narrator: "This intimacy is reflected in the biography, even though Johnson chose to conceal himself under the disguises of 'a Friend' and 'the Author of this Narrative.' . . . In the early pages, for example, he told us that Savage 'always spoke with Respect' of his schoolmaster, a remark reminiscent of long evenings of good talk, and a few pages later, rather irrelevantly, he repeated two of Savage's yarns about Steele. He implied also that Savage must have frequently talked about his trial for murder."[12]

Any time we are told of a comment that Savage made with regularity, we are generally hearing from the Memoirist: "As Mr *Savage* used to relate it," "*Savage* always declared," "Mr *Savage* made no Scruple of asserting," and so on. He was evidently a tireless retailer of his complaints, opinions, and misadventures, and

Johnson a tireless listener. The other common sign that we are hearing from the Memoirist is the content. As David Ellis writes, "Once one begins to look closely at the 'Life' all kinds of details emerge which Johnson must either have learned directly from Savage, or very probably did."[13] Most of these are reported by the Memoirist.

We begin to hear from the Memoirist about a third of the way through the *Life of Savage*, his contributions increasing in frequency until they almost, but never quite, match those of the Historian. But whatever they lack in quantity, they more than make up for in color. Most of the anecdotes we remember from *Savage* are told by this narrator. In the account of Savage's trial, for instance, the Memoirist adds only one paragraph, but it is certainly the most memorable of the episode, the "eloquent Harangue" Judge Page delivers to the jury: "'Gentlemen of the Jury, you are to consider, that Mr *Savage* is a very great Man, a much greater Man than you or I, Gentlemen of the Jury; that he wears very fine Clothes, much finer Clothes than you or I, Gentlemen of the Jury; that he has abundance of Money in his Pocket, much more Money than you or I, Gentlemen of the Jury; but, Gentlemen of the Jury, is it not a very hard Case, Gentlemen of the Jury, that Mr *Savage* should therefore kill you or me, Gentlemen of the Jury?'" (*LRS*, 70). Though Page did give instructions to the jury clarifying the relevant points of law, there is no evidence outside the *Life of Savage* that he ever actually gave such a "Harangue." It is simply too good to be true, and in introducing it, the Memoirist tips his hand. This is not, he admits, *Page*'s actual speech; it is the speech "as Mr *Savage* used to relate it," a bit of shtick that Johnson heard often enough to reproduce years later.[14]

The Historian records events that occur only once—Lady Macclesfield's divorce, the brawl in Robinson's coffee house, the cancellation of Savage's pension—presenting them as things that *happened to* Savage, misfortunes of which he was the passive victim. The Memoirist, as we have seen, records what Savage said or did repeatedly, thereby revealing the behaviors and attitudes by which he drew his disasters on his own head. This shift in focus affects the tone of their respective observations. While the Historian oscillates between cool detachment and partisan rage, the Memoirist swings between affection for Savage and irritation with him.[15]

The Memoirist finds Savage's approach to the profession of writing especially vexing. He presents Savage as undisciplined at best and at worst a poseur, playing the role of writer rather than actually producing marketable texts. While the Historian critiques the works, the Memoirist critiques the work habits, and the list of charges he draws up is formidable. The Memoirist repeatedly accuses Savage of hypocrisy, criticizing him for "living in an Appearance of Friendship with some whom he satirised" (*LRS*, 77) and for publishing "a Panegyric on Sir *Robert Walpole*," at the command of Lord Tyrconnel, though "he was far from approving

[Walpole's] Conduct" (*LRS*, 80–81). The Memoirist icily concludes that Savage "had not Resolution sufficient to sacrifice the Pleasure of Affluence to that of Integrity" (*LRS*, 81), as if for Savage integrity was merely one pleasure among others.

At other times, he complains of Savage's laziness. In revising *Sir Thomas Overbury*, he tells us, Savage "proceeded but slowly, and probably only employed himself upon it when he could find no other Amusement" (*LRS*, 117). He similarly notes Savage's failure to develop promising ideas for new works. He is disappointed, for instance, that Savage never wrote his projected *Progress of a Free-Thinker*: "This Plan was, like others, formed and laid aside . . . and soon gave Way to some other Design, which pleased by its Novelty for a while, and then was neglected like the former" (*LRS*, 104). Even when Savage does produce a text, he allows himself to be crippled by typographical scruples in his attempts to publish it: "A superstitious Regard to the Correction of his Sheets was one of Mr *Savage's* Peculiarities; he often altered, revised, recurred to his first Reading or Punctuation, and again adopted the Alteration; he was dubious and irresolute without End, as on a Question of the last Importance, and at last was seldom satisfied" (*LRS*, 83–84). When it comes time to sell his work, Savage again manages to abdicate his professional responsibilities. The Memoirist admits to "some Degree of Indignation" in reporting that Savage sold his 2,000-line masterpiece, *The Wanderer*, for ten guineas. Savage, he tells us, was not driven to accept such a paltry sum by the avarice of the booksellers or even his own pressing needs, but by his "intemperate Desire of Pleasure, and habitual Slavery to his Passions. . . . He happened at that Time to be engaged in the Pursuit of some trifling Gratification, and being without Money for the present Occasion, sold his Poem to the first Bidder, perhaps for the first Price that was proposed, and would probably have been content with less, if less had been offered him" (*LRS*, 84). By selling his wares so cheaply, Savage undercuts the bargaining power of every writer.

Once his works are published, Savage's vanity prevents his accepting their occasional failures with his readers. The Memoirist describes Savage's gift for explaining away poor sales. They were the result of bad timing, a distracted public, weak marketing. "The Blame was laid rather on any other Person than the Author" (*LRS*, 94). Extending this habit to his personal life, Savage "accustomed himself to impute all Deviations from the right to foreign Causes" (*LRS*, 95). In describing the inevitable results, the Memoirist sounds like a weary Virgil describing, in Robert Folkenflik's words, "a minor denizen of Dante's Inferno."[16]

> By imputing none of his Miseries to himself, he continued to act upon the same Principles, and follow the same Path; was never made wiser by his Sufferings, nor preserved by one Misfortune from falling into

> another. He proceeded throughout his Life to tread the same Steps on the same Circle; always applauding his past Conduct, or at least forgetting it, to amuse himself with Phantoms of Happiness, which were dancing before him; and willingly turned his Eyes from the Light of Reason, when it would have discovered the Illusion, and shewn him, what he never wished to see, his real State. (*LRS*, 94–95)

The Memoirist can love Savage and pity his sufferings, but he finds it difficult to defend him. He knows too much.

The Friend

While the Memoirist reveals his personal familiarity with Savage by the nature of his material, the Friend appears as part of the narrative itself. The Memoirist stands outside the events, the Friend inside. The Memoirist's knowledge of Savage appears something he has long possessed, while we watch the Friend in the process of acquiring his. It may be, in fact, the time that elapses between the moment each narrator acquires his information and when he reports it that results in the tonal differences between them. The Memoirist has had time to brood over his experiences and realize the seriousness of the character flaws they reveal. The Friend, observing Savage's actions in something like "real time," responds with quiet amazement, his pointed silences often eloquently satiric.

As a narrator, the Friend is as furtive as the Historian is intrusive. While the Historian discusses his efforts in first person, the Friend requires us to infer his presence from his account: "Mr *Savage* was likewise very far from believing, that the Letters annexed to each Species of bad Poets in the *Bathos*, were, as he was directed to assert, *set down at Random*; for when he was charged by one of his Friends with putting his Name to such an Improbability, he had no other Answer to make, than that *he did not think of it*, and his Friend had too much Tenderness to reply, that next to the Crime of writing contrary to what he thought, was that of writing without thinking" (*LRS*, 79). The narrator I am calling the Friend and the "Friend" in the paragraph are, obviously, the same. If the narrator can tell us what Savage's friend is thinking despite the friend's having "too much Tenderness to reply," it can only mean that the narrator is the friend himself. If we imagine the paragraph written in first person—"when I charged him with . . . I had too much Tenderness to reply"—the somewhat labored third person appears a deliberate rhetorical policy, maintained here at some cost.

Sometimes the Friend presents himself as one of a number of people in Savage's company, witnessing some telling bit of behavior by the poet. We hear of

Savage being so ashamed of having acted in *Sir Thomas Overbury* that "he always blotted out his Name from the List, when a Copy of his Tragedy was to be shown to his Friends," and of his "snatching the Play out of their hands" if they were about to read the Dedication (*LRS*, 64–65). We see the Friend again with others observing that Savage "could not easily leave off when he had once began to mention himself or his Works, nor ever read his Verses without stealing his Eyes from the Page, to discover in the Faces of his Audience, how they were affected with any favourite Passage" (*LRS*, 142). The same ghostly presence—and the same sardonic amusement—appear in the account of one of Savage's pet fantasies: "To form Schemes for the Publication [of his works] was one of his favourite Amusements, nor was he ever more at Ease than when with any Friend who readily fell in with his Schemes, he was adjusting the Print, forming the Advertisements, and regulating the Dispersion of his new Edition" (*LRS*, 115). The phrasing suggests that Savage entirely monopolizes the activity, amusing himself in his friend's company, while for the friend it is purely a spectator sport. In the hands of the Memoirist, such incidents might have prompted an attack on Savage's lack of professionalism, his preference for imaginary success over the hard work of writing, but the Friend is content merely to narrate what happened and let the behavior speak for itself.

It is left to the Friend to narrate two of the most memorable incidents in the *Life of Savage*, one perhaps the funniest, the other perhaps the most touching. Alarmed at the shabby state of his clothes, Savage's friends commissioned a tailor to take his measurements and make what he needed, though without bothering to consult with Savage on the matter. This was, the narrator admits, "not very delicate," though he could never have predicted Savage's response: "Upon hearing the Design that was formed, he came to the Lodging of a Friend with the most violent Agonies of Rage; and being asked what it could be that gave him such Disturbance, he replied, with the utmost Vehemence of Indignation, 'That they had sent for a Taylor to measure him'" (*LRS*, 121). Once again, the Friend declines to comment. "How the Affair ended," he archly informs us, "was never enquired, for fear of renewing his Uneasiness." Though he sympathizes with Savage's indignation, the Friend is left speechless by the form it takes. Only a couple of pages later, we reach the emotional climax of the biography: "[Savage] left *London* in *July* 1739, having taken Leave with great Tenderness of his Friends, and parted from the Author of this Narrative with Tears in his Eyes" (*LRS*, 123). In this, his one explicit appearance in the story, the Friend moves as close to Savage as he ever will, while holding himself at arm's length from the reader. The effect of the sentence would be quite different if Johnson had written "me" instead of "the Author of this Narrative." For Johnson the difference in self-reference marks the generic difference between memoir and biography. While the narrator of a memoir would be "I" within the events, the narrator of a biography can only be "I" in his role of Historian grappling with his sources.

SAVAGE, THE CIRCLE, AND THE NARRATORS

Compared to the Johnson Circle, what I am calling the "Savage Circle" is a shifting, nebulous entity at best, comprising all those who at one time or another sought to stand between Savage and the actions of others or between Savage and the consequences of his own. It was in reality a series of groups through whose hands Savage passed, following a pattern of depressing regularity. A particular group would adopt Savage as a *cause célèbre*, a sort of communal charity case. Over time, he would become demanding, belligerent, and self-destructive, alienating those who were trying to help him. They, in turn, would cut off his support and abandon him, leaving him on the street, until he would drift into the protection of the next group and it would all begin again.[17]

Savage's story is thus in large part that of the groups he was adopted by, and ejected from, over the course of his life. He was, he claimed, born into the aristocratic families of Macclesfield and Rivers, from which he was ejected by Lady Macclesfield and an act of Parliament. Kept at arm's length by his purported mother, he was picked up by the London theatre community. They led him to Richard Steele, who tried to make him a member of his family by marrying him to an illegitimate daughter. After Steele broke with him, Savage was adopted by Aaron Hill and the Hillarians, a group of writers and artists that included, among others, Eliza Haywood. Savage and Haywood were quickly close, then violently at odds, while the rest disentangled themselves from Savage as they could. In the meantime, Hill introduced him to Pope, whom Savage served as a "spy" for *The Dunciad*, thereby making inveterate enemies of the writers of Grub Street, the community to which he most naturally belonged. As if to render their hostility permanent, he published at about the same time *An Author to be Let*, an excoriating attack on writers for pay. For several years, Savage associated himself with the royal family by setting up as Queen Charlotte's "volunteer laureate." After her death, however, he was struck from the government pension rolls and abandoned to poverty. Pope and some of his friends, in a last ditch effort to save him, offered Savage a pension if he would leave London for Wales. Ending up in Bristol, his continued intransigence cost him the support of Pope's friends and, finally, of Pope himself. Even while being dropped by his old supporters, however, Savage managed to draw new ones about him, only to antagonize them in turn. Near the end, Johnson presents Savage in Bristol's Newgate Prison, incarcerated for debt, where he "diverted himself in the Kitchen with the Conversation of the Criminals" (*LRS*, 138)—the last Savage Circle of all. From the aristocracy through the literati to the felons of Newgate, the Circle shows a continual change of elements while maintaining a remarkable continuity of form.

As Johnson carries us through the conflicts between Savage and his Circle, he shifts among the four narrators depending on the meaning or color he wishes to give to his account. The Historian begins the narrative with a thesis he will argue consistently: Savage is a man "whose Misfortunes claim a Degree of Compassion, not always due to the Unhappy, as they were often the Consequences of the Crimes of others, rather than his own" (*LRS*, 49). The Historian carries us from Savage's birth through his trial for murder, conviction, and pardon, culminating with an outburst of rage directed, as always, at Lady Macclesfield: "This Mother is still alive, and may perhaps even yet, though her Malice was so often defeated, enjoy the Pleasure of reflecting, that the Life which she often endeavoured to destroy, was at least shortened by her maternal Offices; that though she could not transport her Son to the Plantations, bury him in the Shop of a Mechanick, or hasten the Hand of the publick Executioner, she has yet had the Satisfaction of imbittering all his Hours, and forcing him into Exigences, that hurried on his Death" (*LRS*, 73). This is the story as the Historian has it from his sources, supported by all the authority of print and entirely one-sided.

The tone of the narrative changes, however, when the Memoirist starts to enter the text. He sides with Savage in his conflicts with the Circle, but is forced to reckon with his firsthand knowledge of Savage's character. David E. Schwalm writes that "Johnson seems to be trying to elicit from his readers a sympathetic response toward Savage which he does not always share and which most of the evidence he supplies tends to contravene."[18] This describes precisely the plight of the Memoirist. One of his earliest passages reflects the tension between his desire to blame the Circle and his awareness of Savage's faults. Savage, he tells us, "spent his Life between . . . Beggary and Extravagance; for as whatever he received was the Gift of Chance, . . . he was tempted to squander what he had, because he always hoped to be immediately supplied" (*LRS*, 75–76). But having admitted this about Savage, the Memoirist fires a broadside at the Circle in turn: "Another Cause of his Profusion was the absurd Kindness of his Friends, who at once rewarded and enjoyed his Abilities, by treating him at Taverns, and habituated him to Pleasures which he could not afford to enjoy, and which he was not able to deny himself, though he purchased the Luxury of a single Night by the Anguish of Cold and Hunger for a Week" (*LRS*, 76).

The Memoirist blames the Circle for not tailoring their care to Savage's weaknesses; instead, they are, in effect, buying drinks for an alcoholic. A few pages later, the Memoirist accuses Savage of hypocrisy for writing in praise of Walpole, then mitigates the charge by considering his situation: it is "just to impute much of the Inconstancy of his Conduct" to "the Misery of living at the Tables of other Men," for he was "sometimes obliged to . . . submit his own Judgment and even his Virtue to the Government of those by whom he was supported" (*LRS*, 81). If Savage is guilty of hypocrisy, it is because he is forced into it by his supporters' abuse of the power they obtained over him by their money.

As if against his will, the Memoirist admits that Savage is a signal failure as an object of charity. However slack his work habits, he was remarkably diligent as a sponger, and though he never expressed the slightest gratitude for a loan, he was incensed by a refusal to lend him what he requested or by any suggestion that he should repay what he had borrowed. Once he received any money, he immediately squandered it in a tavern, so that a loan or gift that should have kept him in food and lodging for a month would be gone overnight. Inviting him into one's home, furthermore, was only asking for trouble, since he would stay up requiring attention far into the night and then refuse to come down to breakfast the next morning. The Memoirist's account, in fact, offers a strong argument in the Circle's defense: "It was not always by the Negligence or Coldness of his Friends that *Savage* was distressed, but because it was in reality very difficult to preserve him long in a State of Ease" (*LRS*, 112). The members of the Circle could plausibly justify withdrawing their charity on the grounds that any attempt to help Savage was pouring water into a sieve. This is not an admission the Memoirist finds it easy to make, but honesty compels him.

The conflict between Savage and the Circle—and between the Memoirist and both of them—reaches a crescendo in the run-up to Savage's Welsh exile. The pages describing "the Scheme proposed for this happy and independent Subsistence" (*LRS*, 119) are the most consistently ironic in the biography. The plan, orchestrated by Pope, was for Savage to be given £50 a year "on which he was to live privately in a cheap Place, without aspiring any more to Affluence, or having any farther Care of Reputation" (*LRS*, 120). The Memoirist presents the plan less as a favor than a brush-off, and he takes a grim pleasure in informing us that Savage accepted the offer "with Intentions very different from those of his Friends" (*LRS*, 120). Rather than "continue an Exile from *London* for ever," as the Circle intended, Savage planned to revise his play *Sir Thomas Overbury*, prepare his collected works for publication, and return to London in glory. But though the Memoirist would be delighted to see the Circle foiled in this fashion, he knows that Savage's plans are rooted in fantasy: "With regard to his Works, he proposed very great Improvements, which would have required much Time, or great Application" (*LRS*, 120), neither of which, of course, did he have. Even more preposterous was Savage's "Scheme of Life for the Country, of which he had no Knowledge but from Pastorals and Songs." The Memoirist materializes as the Friend long enough to tell of a showdown between the hardworking realist Johnson and the supine fantasist Savage:

> With these Expectations he was so enchanted, that when he was once gently reproach'd by a Friend for submitting to live upon a Subscription, and advised rather by a resolute Exertion of his Abilities to support himself, he could not bear to debar himself from the Happiness which was to be found in the Calm of a Cottage, or lose the Opportunity of listening, without Intermission, to the Melody of a Nightingale, which he believ'd was to be heard from every Bramble, and which he did not fail to mention as a very important Part of the Happiness of a Country Life. (*LRS*, 120)

As always, the Friend coyly refers to himself in third person, tells his damning anecdote, and moves on without comment.

The Memoirist continues in the same vein of wry amusement and vinegary frustration. The Circle begins "to prescribe to [Savage] with an Air of Authority, which he knew not how decently to resent, nor patiently to bear" (*LRS*, 121), culminating in the episode of their sending the tailor. Savage repeatedly quarrels with his supporters over their plans for him, though without making any effort to help himself. In time, what Holmes calls the "Savage Relief Fund" is able to raise the money needed to send him packing. The Memoirist informs us that Savage was satisfied with the arrangement, having determined "to commence a rigid Oeconomist" and live within his means, "for nothing was in his Opinion more contemptible than a Man, who, when he knew his Income, exceeded it; and yet he confessed that Instances of such Folly were too common" (*LRS*, 123). The next sentence contains the moving scene of the narrator's parting from Savage, yet even it begins with the barbed phrase, "Full of these salutary Resolutions, . . ." The Memoirist is still vexed at Savage's self-deception even as he is grieved to part with him.[19]

The rest of the *Life of Savage*, from Savage's exile onward, is narrated by the Historian, who tells of the widening breach between the poet and his supporters leading to Savage's arrest and death. Compared to his earlier sections, however, his attitude has shifted. No longer supported by his documentary sources, and with Lady Macclesfield out of the picture, he tries to be fair to both Savage and the Circle. He records in his cool, matter-of-fact register the evidence of Savage's ingratitude, emotional violence, and unfairness, and his squandering of the resources placed in his hands. It is as if the Historian has acknowledged the truths revealed by the Memoirist but without the latter's anger. In the end, the Historian concludes that no matter how badly Savage behaved, his treatment by the Circle was indefensible:

> It may be alleged, and, perhaps, justly, that he was petulant and contemptuous, that he more frequently reproached his Subscribers for not giving him more, than thanked them for what he had received; but it is to be remembred, that this Conduct, and this is the worst Charge that can be drawn up against him, did them no real Injury; and that it, therefore, ought rather to have been pitied than resented, at least, the Resentment that it might provoke ought to have been generous and manly; Epithets which his Conduct will hardly deserve, that starves the Man whom he has persuaded to put himself into his Power. (*LRS*, 125)

Less strident than in his attacks on Lady Macclesfield and eschewing the irony of the Memoirist, the Historian delivers his calm, plain-spoken verdict with considerable authority.[20] Shortly thereafter, the Historian conducts his summary of Savage's character with scrupulous fairness, weighing his virtues and vices frankly and without rancor.

It is difficult at first to say which narrator speaks the famous conclusion of the *Life of Savage*.[21] Insofar as it concerns Savage specifically, it would suggest the Historian, but the stately cadences and loftiness of perspective are ultimately the Sage's: "Those are no proper Judges of his Conduct who have slumber'd away their Time on the Down of Abundance, nor will a wise Man easily presume to say, 'Had I been in *Savage*'s Condition, I should have lived, or written, better than *Savage*'" (*LRS*, 143).[22] The perspective is so lofty, in fact, that Savage barely figures as the topic of the comment, which is really the impossibility of any person fairly judging another. Savage himself is sublimated to a figure in a parable. The conclusion complements, furthermore, the claim made throughout the *Life of Savage* that the unworthiness of a recipient does not cancel the obligation of charity. Savage was ungrateful, vindictive, and impossible to help; nonetheless, those who supported and then abandoned him "will find it no easy Task to vindicate their Conduct" (*LRS*, 125). The Sage, having begun the *Life of Savage* in broadly Stoic terms, concludes it from a perspective firmly grounded in the New Testament.

FROM MARGIN TO CENTER

Though we hear of the conflict between Savage and his Circle from four distinct narrators, standing behind them all is the disillusioned young journalist Samuel

Johnson, outraged by the Circle's behavior and tormented by his knowledge of how Savage, whom he loved, contributed to his own downfall. Though Johnson condemns Savage's supporters, he cannot forgive Savage's refusal to help himself: "He appeared to think himself born to be supported by others, and dispensed with all Necessity of providing for himself; he therefore never prosecuted any Scheme of Advantage, nor endeavoured even to secure the Profits which his Writings might have afforded him" (*LRS*, 141). The system of patronage, as Johnson saw it, seduced Savage into a life of dependence that wasted his talents, compromised his integrity, and left him starving in the streets, while Savage, for his part, was only too willing to be seduced.[23]

By the time of Savage's death, Johnson had come to see the options of a writer in starkly dichotomous terms: he could be either the slave of patronage, first mouthed to be last swallowed, or the self-reliant professional. In *Rambler* 145, Johnson offers a heartfelt defense of the hacks of Grub Street, "who have been long exposed to insult without a defender, and to censure without an apologist."[24] Among these censurers was Savage himself, who viciously satirized Grub Street in *An Author to be Let*. Johnson does not claim that the hacks deserve great honor, but that they should at least be granted the respect due to "the husbandman, the labourer, the miner, or the smith."[25] Savage's rejection of this humble status does not raise him in Johnson's eyes. In the *Life of Savage*, Johnson notes that the young Savage, "having no Profession, became, by Necessity, an Author" (*LRS*, 55). His motivation for taking up the pen was thus no more (or less) honorable than that of any other denizen of Grub Street, Johnson included, though he would have done better to embrace the trade and support himself by it than to become the dependent plaything of the Savage Circle.

The moral characters of the protégé and the professional take on yet deeper meaning in the Celebrated Letter. Johnson had dedicated the *Plan of a Dictionary* to Chesterfield in 1747. In 1748, he published the second edition of *The Life of Savage*, which included hundreds of minor improvements in punctuation and wording. Johnson was thus seeking Chesterfield's patronage at the same time that he was meticulously revising his account of how the patronage system had failed, if not destroyed, his early friend. After seven years of work, during which Chesterfield proved fully as negligent and irresponsible as the Savage Circle, Johnson was in no mood to forgive. The Letter suggests a catalogue of the responsibilities of a patron, all of which Lord Chesterfield shirked, while Johnson had been "pushing on my work through difficulties of which it is useless to complain."[26] But though Chesterfield failed him, Johnson had not been without help of another kind. He declares himself "unwilling that the Public should consider me as owing that to a Patron, which Providence has enabled me to do for myself."²⁷ He is, in effect, deposing Chesterfield in favor of a more exalted patron.

By placing his literary work under the patronage of Providence, Johnson invests it with an intensified ethical and religious significance. It is not that God requires him to write—his motive is always pecuniary—but by accepting God's patronage he is required to write to God's standards. Providence entails judgment. Johnson prays that the *Rambler* essays "may promote [God's] glory, and the Salvation both of myself and others,"²⁸ and in the final issue consoles himself for their lack of popularity by declaring them "exactly conformable to the precepts of Christianity."²⁹ The writer dependent on an earthly patron can be bribed or coerced into writing in violation of his conscience, as Savage was by Lord Tyrconnel. The independent professional can choose his project, negotiate payment with the bookseller, and write what he thinks. While he can still prostitute his talents in the manner of Iscariot Hackney, Savage's fictional "author to be let," he can also choose to stand by his principles and take his chances with the reading public. Unlike a patron, the public does not order one to write in praise of a corrupt Prime Minister, though it may decline to buy one's work. It is the frankly commercial character of a professional's work, its not being written but for money, that, paradoxically, allows the writer to maintain his integrity.

The same principle applies across a wide range of enterprises. Johnson's respect goes to the hard-working, self-reliant professional in any field. If a genius is, as he famously defines it, "a mind of large general powers, accidentally determined to some particular direction," a professional is a person of disciplined work habits and hard-won competence succeeding in some particular employment. True professionals are defined not by their line of work but by their approach to it, their willingness and ability to support themselves, and thus preserve their integrity, by the diligence and skill they bring to bear on a marketable service or product. As a maker and seller of texts, Johnson had, to his own mind, earned at least the respect due to "the husbandman, the labourer, the miner, or the smith." The satisfaction he takes in identifying his own efforts with such forms of employment comes through in his cheerful use of "low" verbs to describe high cultural achievements, as when he describes the sculptor Joseph Nollekens as "able to chop out a head with any of them,"³⁰ or when he asks Reynolds, "How much do you think you and I could get in a week, if we were to *work as hard* as we could?—as if," Boswell notes, "they had been common mechanicks."³¹ Johnson is so far from seeking to distance his trade from that of "common mechanicks" that he honors them in highlighting the disciplined skill and effort their jobs require. And it is precisely the lack of such professional discipline that Johnson as the Memoirist condemns in the *Life of Savage*.

The people Johnson draws about him from the 1760s through the 1780s are, as a result, almost all distinguished by their hard-earned professional success, especially the members of his clubs: the Ivy Lane, Turk's Head, and Essex Head. It is also true of the many women whose literary careers Johnson championed, such as Frances Burney, Charlotte Lennox, Elizabeth Carter, and, for that matter, Hester Thrale. The broader, more loosely defined Johnson Circle is dominated, not surprisingly, by members of what we might call the text industry—writers (Goldsmith, Hawkesworth, Murphy), scholars (Charles Burney, Baretti, the Whartons), and booksellers (Davies, Strahan, Payne)—though it also includes legal professionals (Chambers, Boswell, Hawkins), political figures (most notably, Burke), physicians (Lawrence, Brocklesby), and artists (Joshua and Frances Reynolds, James Barry, and Joseph Nollekens).[32] Categories of persons who are missing or underrepresented in the Circle include clergymen, aristocrats, and actors. (As friends of Johnson's youth, Taylor and Garrick are special cases.) Given Johnson's support of "subordination," it is striking that the only actual aristocrat among his friends is Topham Beauclerk and that, despite his piety, Johnson rarely makes friends of the clergy. The absence of actors and musicians would surprise no one, though Johnson's contempt might have been softened if he had been more familiar with the preparation and effort that goes into a professional performance. Garrick, perhaps, made it look too easy.

There is, most importantly, not a single member of the Johnson Circle primarily reliant on aristocratic patronage. They may, like Johnson, accept a pension from the king, but they pay their bills by the sale of their wares and services on the open market. They do not depend on the caprice of patrons nor compromise their standards to satisfy a demanding lord. They do not sleep on a bulk in summer or the ashes of a glass house in winter because they were thrown out of a home where they were merely a guest. They do not work only when they can find no other amusement or indulge a ruinous perfectionism. They do not borrow money and refuse to repay it or squander in one night an amount that would sustain them for a month. And they do not end by dying miserable and alone in prison. Johnson is always willing to befriend a "young dog"—a rake like Beauclerk or a whoremonger like Boswell—but after 1744 he never befriends anyone who squanders the talents he could use to support himself the way Richard Savage did. In his attempt to produce an objective account of his early friend, Johnson created multiple narrators, each unique in style and attitude, to capture different aspects of Savage's fragmented personality and kaleidoscopic fate. The narrative stresses in the *Life of Savage* reflect stresses in Johnson provoked by his attempt to maintain a friendship with the dependent, vengeful, and doomed poet. In coming to grips with the character and fate of Richard Savage, Johnson learned both what sort of writer he himself wished to be and the kind of people he wished to have about him. What we see in the Johnson Circle is a professional surrounded by professionals.

NOTES

1. Samuel Johnson, *The Life of Mr Richard Savage*, ed. Nicholas Seager and Lance Wilcox (Peterborough, ON: Broadview Press, 2016) (hereafter cited as *LRS*).
2. Wilson Snipes, for instance, argues that a biographer selects one of several available personae, which then controls the rhetoric of the text: "These would include the *chronicler* who offers a *record* of a life, the *historian* who offers a *reconstruction*, the *narrator* who offers a *story*, the *critic* who offers an *interpretation*, and the *psychologist* who offers an *analysis*." Snipes, "Authorial Typology in Literary Biography," *Biography* 13, no. 3 (Summer 1990), 236. Others have tried to describe the personality of the *LRS*'s narrator per se. Blakey Vermeule claims that "The narrator's voice is that of a moralist" in *The Party of Humanity: Writing Moral Psychology in Eighteenth-Century Britain* (Baltimore: Johns Hopkins University Press, 2000), 122. When George Justice writes that "Johnson the author is the hero of the *Account*," his argument requires that the hero be not the failed Midlands schoolteacher, but the narrator Johnson creates in answer to Pope's *Dunciad* and Savage's *Author to be Let*. Justice, *The Manufacturers of Literature: Writing and the Literary Marketplace in Eighteenth-Century England* (Newark: University of Delaware Press, 2002), 98.
3. Richard Holmes, *Dr. Johnson & Mr. Savage* (New York: Pantheon Books, 1993), 56.
4. Virginia Spencer Davidson, "Johnson's *Life of Savage*: The Transformation of a Genre," in *Studies in Biography*, ed. Daniel Aaron (Cambridge, MA: Harvard University Press, 1978), 64.
5. Timothy Erwin, *Textual Vision: Augustan Design and the Invention of Eighteenth-Century British Culture* (Lewisburg, PA: Bucknell University Press, 2015), 66.
6. Sarah R. Morrison, "Toil, Envy, Want, the Reader, and the Jail: Reader Entrapment in Johnson's *Life of Savage*," *Age of Johnson: A Scholarly Annual* 9 (1998): 146.
7. Anthony W. Lee writes, "*Life of Savage*'s narrative possesses no monolithic consistency: Savage receives both praise and reproach, defense and judgment. These two perspectives might be usefully considered metaphorically as opposing fields of energy that inhabit the narrative and vie for its aesthetic focus and moral authority" (Lee, *Mentoring Relationships in the Life and Writings of Samuel Johnson: A Study in the Dynamics of Eighteenth-Century Literary Mentoring*, [Lewiston, NY: Edwin Mellen Press, 2005], 97). What Lee describes as "opposing fields of energy" I discuss as separate narrators. When he personifies the energy fields with the verbs *inhabit* and *vie*, our metaphors become very similar. As will be seen, I attribute the functions of praise and defense to one narrator, reproach and judgment to another.
8. W. Jackson Bate, *Samuel Johnson* (New York: Harcourt Brace Jovanovich, 1975), 222.
9. The documents Johnson drew on include the 1727 "Newgate Biography," published while Savage was in prison awaiting execution; the *Plain Dealer* essays of Aaron Hill; and pieces by and about Savage, many of them in the *Gentleman's Magazine*. All, be it noted, were written by Savage or his partisans and are completely one-sided.
10. Edward Tomarken, *Genre and Ethics: The Education of an Eighteenth-Century Critic* (Newark: University of Delaware Press, 2002), 166.
11. Reprinted in *LRS*, 23.
12. Clarence Tracy, "Introduction," in *Life of Savage*, by Samuel Johnson, ed. Tracy (Oxford: Clarendon Press, 1971), xii.

13. David Ellis, "Biography and Friendship: Johnson's *Life of Savage,*" in *Imitating Art: Essays in Biography,* ed. David Ellis (London: Pluto Press, 1993), 20.
14. Holmes describes it as "a favourite performance of Savage's in later years: how Judge Page condemned him to the gallows" (*Dr. Johnson & Mr. Savage*, 118).
15. Lee makes a similar observation: "Both of Johnson's narrative strategies—the modes of extenuative defense and of satiric reproach—are useful to his biographical project.... More significant, though, is the difference between the two narrative practices. Very simply, the former focuses upon the external and environmental, the latter on the internal and psychological, sources of Savage's misfortunes" (*Mentoring Relationships*, 108).
16. Robert Folkenflik, *Samuel Johnson, Biographer* (Ithaca, NY: Cornell University Press, 1978), 203.
17. According to Steven D. Scherwatzky, Johnson implies that the instability of Savage's life reflects in part the instability of the social order resulting from the ascendancy of the Whigs: "the narrative ... implies that, had a more natural order been preserved, Savage would have stood a greater chance to become a more virtuous citizen." Scherwatzky, "'Complicated Virtue': The Politics of Samuel Johnson's *Life of Savage,*" *Eighteenth-Century Life* 25, no. 3 (2001): 90.
18. David E. Schwalm, "Johnson's *Life of Savage*: Biography as Argument," *Biography* 8, no. 2 (Spring 1985): 130.
19. Peter Martin captures the Memoirist's disgust with all parties in his summary of this sequence: "The Welsh idyll that seduced Savage destroyed him, but so did insensitive and clumsy efforts to alleviate his poverty. Johnson was enraged by society's obtuse, clumsy, ill-conceived philanthropy that organised Savage's 'miseries of dependence' and coerced him to go west." P. Martin, *Samuel Johnson: A Biography* (Cambridge, MA: Harvard University Press, 2008), 169.
20. Lawrence Lipking's summary of the Historian's verdict is pithy and precise: "The pride of a hack, however deluded, deserves more consideration. A pittance that costs the patron very little may turn out to decide the poor author's life or death." Lipking, *Samuel Johnson: The Life of an Author* (Cambridge, MA: Harvard University Press, 1998), 81.
21. By "conclusion" I mean the penultimate paragraph. The last paragraph is so at odds with the rest of the biography as to render its relationship to it problematic. In his own copy, now at the University of Glasgow, Johnson wrote "Added" next to it, as if attempting to distance himself from its heavy-handed moralizing.
22. In the 1744 first edition, the down is the "Down of Affluence." For the 1748 second edition, on which the edition cited here is based, Johnson revised it to the "Down of Abundance." For the 1781 *Lives of the Poets*, he made one of his very few further alterations, changing it to the "Down of Plenty." A remarkable thirty-seven-year search on Johnson's part for the *mot juste*!
23. Robert DeMaria describes Johnson as "chastising Savage when he fails to live up to the ideal of a print-world writer, allowing himself to sink back into the soft oppression of patronage." DeMaria, Jr., *The Life of Samuel Johnson: A Critical Biography* (Cambridge, MA: Blackwell Publishers, 1993), 85.
24. Samuel Johnson, *The Rambler*, eds. W. J. Bate and Albrecht B. Strauss (1969), in Yale *Works*, 5:10.
25. Ibid., 5:10.
26. *Letters*, 1:95.
27. Ibid., 1:96. According to James H. Sledd and Gwin J. Kolb, Johnson felt that Chesterfield's puffs in *The World* gave the impression that he had helped Johnson more than he had: "His complaint, therefore, was not merely that Chesterfield had done next to nothing for him but that now, at last, Chesterfield was acting as he might properly have acted if he

had done something for him." The letter, they argue, was specifically intended to forestall this conclusion. Sledd and Kolb, *Dr. Johnson's Dictionary: Essays in the Biography of a Book* (Chicago: University of Chicago Press, 1955), 101.
28. Samuel Johnson, *Diaries, Prayers, and Annals*, ed. E. L. McAdams Jr. et al., in Yale *Works*, 1:43.
29. Johnson, *Rambler*, in Yale *Works*, 5:320.
30. John Thomas Smith, *Nollekens and His Times: A Life of that Celebrated Sculptor and Memoirs of Several Contemporary Artists, from the Time of Roubiliac, Hogarth and Reynolds to that of Fuseli, Flaxman and Blake*, 2nd ed. (London, 1829), 50n.
31. Boswell, *Life*, 1:246.
32. Categorizing Boswell and Hawkins as legal professionals, of course, hardly does full justice to either, but it is, I think, the way Johnson prefers to think of them, especially Boswell. Johnson treats Boswell's legal work with great respect but scolds him when he is swanning about London as "Corsican Boswell"—like Savage, playing the role of writer rather than actually writing.

7

"UNDER THE SHADE OF EXALTED MERIT"

Arthur Murphy's *A Poetical Epistle to Mr. Samuel Johnson, A.M.*

ANTHONY W. LEE

ARTHUR MURPHY WAS A TALENTED AUTHOR of the mid to late eighteenth century who excelled in writing plays, periodical essays, and classical translations. He is perhaps best remembered today for his comedies and farces.[1] Yet he was also a biographer, writing important lives of his friends Henry Fielding, David Garrick, and Samuel Johnson. Arthur Sherbo has written of Murphy: "It is, I think, almost equally undeniable, that he is one of the major-minor writers of the eighteenth century whose work, meritorious per se, has been too much neglected.... He ranks high indeed in the roll of the dramatists and periodical essayists of the second half of the century."[2] Murphy is significant today, both because of the intrinsic aesthetic merit of his authorial achievement and because of his unique value as historical witness. He sauntered with easy grace—and at times with vituperative antagonism—through his age, befriending and provoking a cast of literary luminaries that included Samuel Foote, Christopher Smart, Charles Churchill, Oliver Goldsmith, Owen Ruffhead, Tobias Smollett, and George Steevens, to name but a few. In addition, he was granted entrée into the heart of the Johnsonian inner circle, alongside such memorable literary celebrities as James Boswell, Oliver Goldsmith, Frances Burney, and Hester Thrale.

Murphy played a persistently important role in the life of Samuel Johnson. It was Murphy who introduced him to Hester and Henry Thrale, and it was Murphy who helped arrange the annual government pension of £300—the two events that perhaps most profoundly shaped the day-to-day texture of the last two decades of Johnson's life. Earlier, in the 1750s, Murphy assisted with the production of Johnson's periodical, the *Literary Magazine, or Universal Review*. At Johnson's death, Murphy served as one of his executors, and after the death Murphy wrote extensively about him in the *Monthly Review*. Later, he joined Boswell,

Hester Piozzi, and Sir John Hawkins by producing one of the four key biographies written by close associates of Johnson.

On a personal level, Johnson liked Murphy—or "Mur," as he affectionately called him.[3] Over time, the friendship between these two proved unusually deep—according to the report of Johnsonian acquaintance Dr. William Maxwell, Murphy was a man "whom he [Johnson] very much loved" (*Life*, 2:127). And Johnson respected him: in a letter to Charles Burney of March 8, 1758, Johnson recalled of his *Shakespeare* proposals that Murphy "introduced them with a splendid encomium"; in a note to *King Lear* in the Shakespeare edition, Johnson denominated Murphy "a very judicious critic," later remarking, "at present I doubt much whether we have any thing superiour to Arthur."[4] When the second major edition of Johnson's *Works* was published in 1792, Murphy was asked to write the introduction that became *An Essay on the Life and Genius of Samuel Johnson, LL. D.* Most of the editions of Johnson's works printed or reprinted in the nineteenth century included Murphy's effort. As the latest of the four major biographies, Murphy's is, literally, the last biographical word on Johnson to come from the quill of a trusted friend. Simultaneously it is also a penetrating account written by the biographer who personally knew Johnson longer than any other, save Hawkins.[5]

Murphy consciously crafted a work that was "short, yet full, faithful, yet temperate"—likely meant that, over the one hundred years following Johnson's death, the number of people who read the *Essay on Johnson* was likely far greater those who made their way through the entirety of Boswell's sprawling epic.[6] The influence it thus enjoyed and the way in which it worked to shape the reception and perceptions of its subject lend Murphy's biography a distinguished status within field of Johnson studies. But there are numerous additional intrinsic qualities that recommend it as well. Murphy's piece provides details absent from other contemporary accounts, such as the famous moment when, decades after the fact, Johnson dramatically revealed his authorship of the *Parliamentary Debates* to a group of dinner companions. Moreover, those scenes and anecdotes that we also find related by other contemporary biographers are shown in the *Essay on Johnson* with a different point of emphasis—one often critical of Murphy's rivals (especially of Sir John Hawkins and, to a lesser extent, of Boswell). Murphy himself was a direct participant in many of these contested scenes—one salient example being the above-mentioned affair of Johnson's pension—and thus provides a more historically and biographically valid perspective, in many respects, than do Boswell, Hawkins, or Piozzi. Furthermore, the *Essay on Johnson* provides significant documentary evidence absent from his biographical rivals, such as the initial English "paraphrastic translation" of Johnson's morbid Latin poem, *Gnōthi Seauton* ["Know Thyself"] and the letter that he wrote to Samuel Richardson in 1756 when arrested for debt.[7] In the words of a recent scholar, Murphy's work, "the last great biography of Johnson," is "a mature and balanced assessment" offering "a thoughtful, refined, and dispassionate" characterization of Johnson.[8]

The present chapter looks at the poetry that Murphy produced while standing "under the shade of [Johnson's] exalted merit."[9] Successful protégés of major authors endeavor to flourish under their mentor's large shadow in various ways: deviation from the master's path, as in the case of Oliver Goldsmith; surface homage laced with carefully disguised resistance, as in the case of Boswell; furiously open defiance, as with the irascible Percival Stockwell; or devoted dedication to honoring and extending the *manes* of the great precursor—the way chosen by Murphy. If his ardent—but not slavish—devotion betrays his status as a minor talent, it nonetheless offers an interesting perspective into some of the ways in which contemporaries assimilated and redeployed the Johnsonian influence, an influence well-nigh irresistible, as another initially receptive and eventually hostile protégé concluded with a bitter surliness: "Johnson, Johnson, it is he that has been at you with his terrible words, and I myself feel his austere voice lording over my own mind and sense."[10] Murphy's Johnsonian poetry reveals how he productively responded to the immense weight of Johnson's "exalted merit."

Amongst the number of poems by Murphy that might be considered Johnsonian, we here examine only one, *A Poetical Epistle to Mr. Samuel Johnson, A.M.*[11] Murphy apostrophizes his hero in the opening and the concluding lines; in between, he scarifies a host of personal literary foes, principally classicist, clergyman, and writer Thomas Francklin.[12] Some contextualization is in order. Francklin published a translation of Voltaire's *L'Orphelin de la Chine* in 1756, the same year Murphy staged his own immensely successful version, *The Orphan of China*.[13] Tension over the credit of introducing Voltaire's work to an English audience possibly led to the dispute. The exact chronology is uncertain; however, we do know that the two traded verbal blows in the periodical wars of 1757.[14] Later, in early March 1759, they met at a London tavern, where a violent quarrel nearly led to physical blows. Francklin sought legal action against his opponent days later, "swearing the Peace against him."[15] In 1760, he published *A Dissertation on Antient Tragedy*, which dismissed Murphy's *Orphan of China* and characterized Murphy himself as "formerly a wretched actor."[16] Murphy then retaliated with the *Poetical Epistle*, which, despite its title, is more about Francklin (and Murphy's other enemies) than Johnson himself.

Nonetheless, the poem begins and ends with its titular addressee. Here are portions from those sections:

> Transcendant genius, whose prolific vein
> Ne'er knew the frigid poet's toil and pain;
> To whom Apollo opens all his store,
> And ev'ry Muse presents her sacred lore;
> Say, pow'rful Johnson, whence thy verse is fraught
> With so much grace, such energy of thought,
> Whether thy *Juvenal* instructs the age
> In chaster numbers, and new-points his rage.
>
> Teach me to sep'rate talents from desire,
> From genuine rapture ineffectual fire;
> And, since I ne'er can learn thy classic lore,
> Instruct me *Johnson*, how to write no more.[17]

Murphy in these lines offers unambiguous praise for Johnson: Boswell printed some of them to extol his subject (*Life*, 1:355–56). In these verses we discern the aspect of Murphy's relationship to Johnson that reflects subservient homage to his esteemed mentor. However, in addition to the polarity between the admired Johnson and despised Francklin, other writers latently inform the *Poetical Epistle*, most importantly, Boileau and Pope and their respective "interlocutors," Molière and Arbuthnot. Analysis of the pressures exerted by these intertextual voices will help map out more precisely the dimensions of Johnson's presence within, as well as absence from the poem, while also illuminating the dynamic structure of what actually turns out to be a complex, sophisticated, and compelling, if neglected, text.

BOILEAU, POPE, AND MURPHY

Murphy published two versions of the *Poetical Epistle*. In his Advertisement to the earlier 1760 edition, he observes: "The reader, if he will turn to the second satire of BOILEAU addressed to MOLIERE, will perceive that the ensuing piece is formed after his model; and, besides that general resemblance, will see many occasional traces of imitation."[18] The reference is to Nicolas Boileau-Despréaux's *Second Satire*, also known as *La rime et la raison*, or *Épître à Molière* (1664).[19] This poem turns on the conceit of Molière as the greater poet, or at least the more prolific one. While Molière's quill exudes an easy fluency, Boileau's spurts with agonizingly sporadic effort, by dribbles and drips—and often poorly (by his own ironic account). This clever fit of rhyming against rhyme is also a defense of Molière against his detractors and critics, particularly those attacking the 1662 *L'École des femmes* [*The School for Wives*].[20] While Murphy's version considerably expands its source (it is more than 200 lines long, in comparison to the 100 lines forming the original), he follows Boileau's model fairly closely, at times directly echoing the French neoclassic poet and critic.[21] For example, we read in Boileau's original,

> La raison dit Virgile, et la rime Quinault,[22]

which may be more literally rendered,

> My reason dictates Virgil, Rhyme suggests Quinaut.[23]

Murphy's version runs thus,

> Reason says WHITEHEAD, Rhyme will have it FRANKLIN.[24]

In his adaptation Murphy is here working within a tradition of earlier imitators of Boileau; see, for example this rendering from a 1712 work supervised by Joseph Addison and Nicholas Rowe: "Reason's for Dryden, but the Rhyme for Lee."[25] Comparison of these passages reveals the relative freedom exercised by Murphy. Instead of naming authors worthy of praise, Murphy instead inserts two objects of his satirical scorn. The rebuke is heightened by the deployment of feminine rhyme—a satiric technique mastered in the seventeenth century by Samuel Butler—and the simultaneous off-rhyme and pointed rhyme of "rankling / Franklin": "Who know no malice, feels no envy rankling; / Reason says WHITEHEAD, Rhyme will have it FRANKLIN." These three prosodic features cleverly cohere to lash Franklin for his fumbling and impotent malice.

Boileau's *Second Satire* was appropriated by a number of other British writers. For example, Samuel Butler closely followed it under the title *A Satire to a Bad Poet*, while John Oldham's *Letter from the Country to a Friend in Town* owes its general conception to the *Second Satire*. An anonymous "An Imitation of the Second Satire of Boileau, inscribed to Pylades" appeared in 1723.[26] This list constitutes but a fraction of the influences Boileau exerted upon English literature during the Restoration and the eighteenth century.[27] Murphy's *Poetical Epistle* thus has a rich Boleviant textual prehistory in both French and English letters.

While Boileau is an important ancestor for Murphy, he is by no means the *Poetical Epistle*'s only influence. Boileau was much admired by eighteenth-century English authors such as Dryden, Pope, and Johnson.[28] Most students of eighteenth-century literature know that Alexander Pope regarded and considered his *Essay on Criticism* to be the British version of the *Art poétique*. And his masterful apologia, the *Epistle to Arbuthnot*, operates in many respects as a reworking of the *Second Satire*.[29] Given these intertextual relationships, Murphy's *Poetical Epistle* may be profitably contextualized within Pope's oeuvre as well as Boileau's.[30]

In 1979, Robert D. Spector noted of the *Poetical Epistle*, "the form—mixing styles, varying panegyric with satire—recalls the *Epistle to Arbuthnot*."[31] Spector singled out this passage from the *Poetical Epistle*:

> Here, bring me paper, boy—bring, bring a quire:
> The God!—the God!—what bright ideas rife!
> What wit, what fancy sparkles in my eyes![32]

This clearly corresponds to Pope's opening of *Arbuthnot*:

> The Dog-star rages! nay, 'tis past a doubt,
> All *Bedlam*, or *Parnassus*, is let out:
> Fire in each eye, and Papers in each hand,
> They rave, recite, and madden, round the land.[33]

The points of resemblance between the two imitations include the dialogic form (the conversational diction, the presence of an interlocutor) and the coincidence of images: "*Fire* in each *eye*, and *papers* in each hand"; "bring me *paper*, boy," "*fancy* sparkles in my *eyes*." Later in the poem, Murphy recurs to this intertext, when he writes:

> But from that moment, when the scribling strain,
> The rage poetic seiz'd my troubled brain;
> I rave by night, of some new plan I think;
> Wit, plot, and character ne'er yield a wink.[34]

Also noteworthy here is Murphy's witty turning of Pope's lines on their head. Instead of describing the fops and dunces that assail Pope, Murphy directs the satire toward himself, complaining that he is a frenzied, frustrated writer who would be better off pursuing more innocent, less dangerous occupations. In this effort, he has support from elsewhere in Pope, when at lines 15–16 the former writes:

> Me, whom my angry stars have dipt in ink,
> Who for my sins am doom'd these Rhymes to link

which of course is lifted directly from Pope's *Arbuthnot*:

> Why did I write? what sin to me unknown
> Dipt me in Ink, my Parents', or my own?[35]

Pope's lines in turn take their cue from lines 11–12 of Boileau's *Second Satire*,

> Mais moi, qu'un vain caprice, une bizarre humeur,
> Pour mes péchés, je crois, fit devenir Rimeur.[36]

Murphy's "dipt in ink" clearly derives from Pope; the image is not to be found in the French original. The obviousness of this repetition suggests that Murphy intends the reader to recognize the phrase and note his clever incorporation of *Arbuthnot* in his own imitation. The fact that Murphy collapses both of his models within a single couplet suggests something of the intertextual and poetic strength that the *Poetical Epistle* possesses.

Another passage in Murphy's poem invites closer scrutiny, one that seems to depart entirely from Boileau and take its cue directly from Pope:

> As when the sun withholds his genial ray
> Foster'd by warmth, which dirt and dung convey,
> The forc'd production vegetates its way.
> Spur-gall'd to write, all genius they oppose,
> Sworn at some *Grub-street* altar learning's foes!
> What tho their Muse no long excursions tries,
> But feeble born, just sees the light and dies!
> Yet, insect-like, it darts th' envenom'd sting,
> And buzzes for a day on scandal's wing.[37]

This is one of the most powerful moments in the poem. The principal image throughout is that of insects, particularly those (following the influential *locus classicus* from Ovid),[38] generated not by biological interaction but spawned from mud by the sun. The direct analogue in *Arbuthnot* is the infamous satiric takedown of Lord Hervey, in the guise of Sporus:

> Let *Sporus* tremble—"What? That Thing of silk,
> *Sporus*, that mere white Curd of Ass's milk?
> Satire or Sense, alas! can *Sporus* feel?
> Who breaks a Butterfly upon a Wheel?"
> Yet let me flap this Bug with gilded wings,
> This painted Child of Dirt, that stinks and stings;
> Whose Buzz the Witty and the Fair annoys,
> Yet Wit ne'er tastes, and Beauty ne'er enjoys.[39]

The similitudes are striking. "Foster'd by warmth, which dirt and dung convey" modulates easily from "this painted child of dirt, that stinks and stings," while "spur-gall'd to write, all genius they oppose" derives cogent animation from "whose Buzz the Witty and the Fair annoys, / Yet Wit ne'er tastes, and Beauty ne'er enjoys." The image of insignificant writers as insects is a common one, especially with respect to the eighteenth century's derogatory image of Grub Street. However, the real urgency of Murphy's lines would seem to issue from an earlier work of Pope's, the *Essay on Criticism*:

> Those half-learned Witlings, num'rous in our Isle,
> As half-form'd Insects on the Banks of *Nile*;
> Unfinished Things, one knows not what to call,
> Their Generation's so *equivocal*.[40]

This intersection locates Murphy's abortive witlings within a context of physical deformity, one that intimates their moral impairment. Such moments reveal the force of Pope's influence as much as, if not more than Boileau's. The former's pressure upon the *Periodic Epistle* is also manifest elsewhere in Murphy's contributions to Christopher Smart's *Hilliad*—among other pieces—suggesting a resurrection of the war against the Dunces amidst the heated periodical literature culture of 1750s England, a topic deserving closer future critical scrutiny. Pope's original context—unlike the Sporus episode—attacks the proto-dunces and would-be wits that populate Murphy's own satirical universe in the *Periodic Epistle* and other of his writings.

JOHNSON'S LATENT PRESENCE IN *A POETICAL EPISTLE*

In light of this background, it is not surprising that Murphy's poem departs significantly from Boileau's, as it also responds to and forms itself out of Popean influences. Where Boileau's "original" is relatively sparing in its attacks upon its literary foes, Pope's is rife with them. And Murphy, adapting Pope more in spirit than in the letter, populates his own version with savage attacks upon his own personal enemies. By thus following Pope, Murphy diverges considerably not only from Boileau but also his putative inspiration, Samuel Johnson. For example, a key difference between Murphy and Boileau's poems consists in the realization that the latter was an authentic defense of Molière, who faced credible threats, while the former defends Johnson from no threats: (1) Johnson could take care of himself and needed no help; (2) Johnson tended to ignore his critics; and

(3) Murphy attacks not Johnson's critics but rather his own, some of whom might, in some instances, be said to be hostile to Johnson, but not active foes.[41]

Teasing out the intertextual implications at play here, we see that the *Poetical Epistle* furtively positions Murphy as Pope to Johnson's John Arbuthnot, even as it positions Murphy as Boileau to Johnson's Molière.[42] Put another way, the poem's intertextual apparatus elevates Murphy's status, suggesting his rough equivalence to Johnson, paralleling that found between Pope and Arbuthnot, Boileau and Molière. This maneuver runs counter to Murphy's self-abasement found in the surface tone of the poem we noticed earlier. Murphy surely secured beforehand Johnson's permission to name him so prominently, and the act of acknowledging this implicit permission and thus indirectly promoting his association with Johnson in so public a fashion suggests Murphy's capitalizing upon his friend's literary celebrity. The situation is analogous to Oliver Goldsmith's more naked admission in the 1773 dedication of his final play, *She Stoops to Conquer*, to Johnson: "By inscribing this slight performance to you, I do not mean so much to compliment you as myself. It may do me some honour to inform the public, that I have lived many years in intimacy with you. It may serve the interests of mankind also to inform them, that the greatest wit may be found in a character, without impairing the most unaffected piety."[43] Thus, the generous praise of Johnson that bookends the *Poetical Epistle* may be seen, on the one hand, as genuine, yet on the other, as a kind of disingenuous and self-promoting literary hyperbole in the manner of Boileau's *Second Satire*, one that disingenuously downplays Boileau's own talent in comparison to the older Molière.[44] Johnson, who despised flattery, was doubtless aware of these machinations; yet, he probably countenanced the poem in order to support the literary aspirations of his younger protégé.

Given the complexities elucidated here, how are we to evaluate *A Poetical Epistle*? Compared to the inexhaustible depth and richness of Pope and Johnson's poetry, Murphy's verses read as rather thin. Yet, if Murphy is not a great poet, he is a good one. All members of the eighteenth-century cultural and political elite (including actors such as David Garrick, politicians such as Lord Chesterfield, and dilettantes such as Horace Walpole) were expected to be polished versifiers, and Murphy successfully achieves competence in this vein. If at other times he fell beneath this level (see, e.g., *Ode to the Naiads of Fleet Ditch*), we see him rising above it in the *Poetical Epistle*. It illustrates Donald Davie's contention that a culture of poetic diction allows minor poets to achieve fine results.[45] Writers such as Murphy, Charles Churchill, and John Wolcot occupied a place within a stable system of conventions and modalities enabling them to creatively flourish safely inside the parameters of their literary culture. The *Poetical Epistle* manages to capitalize upon these conditions and—fueled by personal satirical fury and energized by a complex intertextual fabric—is easily Murphy's greatest accomplishment in verse.

If Murphy was a fervent admirer of Johnson who sought to follow in the *cursus honorum* of the latter's literary path—dramatist, periodical essayist, public poet, scholar, biographer, translator, literary critic, and urbane man-of-letters—he was distinctly different from Johnson in character and personality. Johnson, as Murphy himself acknowledges, writes "in chaster numbers": that is to say, he doesn't resort to the scatology found in Pope and Swift (and Juvenal) and replicated by Murphy in couplets such as "Thus phosphorus, resplendent in the night, / Owes to stale urine its deceitful light."[46] While Johnson maintained a public and private persona of eminent probity, Murphy was willing to take ethical shortcuts (as in his not infrequent plagiaristic pillaging);[47] if Johnson refused to lower himself to answer criticisms of other writers (save one notable exception),[48] Murphy's moody sensitivity rendered him unable to resist engaging in very public and at times unsavory polemical battles. If they are very different, yet they both drank deep from the font of what might be called late or midcentury Augustanism. This culture, based upon the one inaugurated by Dryden and codified by Swift and Pope, deeply informed Johnson's literary and critical authority. He sought to sustain it during a period when a very different literary sensibility was emerging, that which would eventually come to be called Romanticism. Murphy was a Johnsonian protégé who sought to continue Johnson's memory and the last phase of the Augustan moment for more than a decade after Johnson's death, until this effort was intercepted by his own demise. He is worth further attention because of this, but also because, as I hope to have shown here, he possesses a compelling intrinsic interest paradoxically apart from and yet attributable to his association with Johnson. At least in the *Poetical Epistle*, Murphy emerged a few steps out of "the shade of exalted merit" to enjoy his own moment in the sun.

NOTES

1. In addition to his authorial activities, Arthur Murphy also successfully pursued a brief acting career and, later in life, a more extensive legal career, as well as demonstrating interest in and an active involvement with public affairs, such as the abolition movement. In 1803, he was awarded a £200 annual pension by George III for his contributions "to the entertainment and instruction of the public," John Pike Emery, *Arthur Murphy: An Eminent English Dramatist of the Eighteenth Century*, (Philadelphia: University of Pennsylvania Press, 1946), 162.
2. Arthur Murphy, *New Essays by Murphy*, ed. Arthur Sherbo (East Lansing: Michigan State University, 1963), 185. The works Sherbo refers to include: Emery, *Arthur Murphy*; Howard H. Dunbar, *The Dramatic Career of Murphy* (New York: Modern Language Associa-

tion of America, 1946); and Ronald B. Botting, "The Textual History of Murphy's *Gray's-Inn Journal*," *Research Studies of the State University of Washington* 25 (1957): 33–48.
3. For the "Mur" nickname, see Hester Lynch Piozzi, *Anecdotes of Samuel Johnson, LL.D.*, in *Memoirs and Anecdotes of Dr. Johnson*, ed. Arthur Sherbo (London and New York: Oxford University Press, 1974), 138.
4. *Letters*, 1:160; Yale *Works*; Samuel Johnson, *Johnson on Shakespeare*, ed. Arthur Sherbo (New Haven, CT: Yale University Press, 1968), in Yale *Works* 7:705; *Life*, 2:127.
5. For the length of the Hawkins-Johnson friendship, see Sir John Hawkins, *The Life of Samuel Johnson, LL.D.*, ed. O M Brack, Jr. (London and Athens, GA: University of Georgia Press, 2009): 379n129, 384n167.
6. For the quotation, see Arthur Murphy, *An Essay on the Life and Genius of Samuel Johnson, LL.D.* (London, 1792), 6 (hereafter *Essay on Johnson*); for the work's popularity, see David Fleeman, *A Bibliography of the Works of Samuel Johnson*, ed. James McLaverty (Oxford: Clarendon Press, 2000), 2:1641–712.
7. For the poem, see Murphy, *Essay on Johnson*, 84–87; the phrase "paraphrastic translation" comes from Samuel Johnson, *The Poems of Samuel Johnson*, ed. David Nichol Smith and Edward L. McAdam, rev. David Fleeman, 2nd ed. (Oxford: Clarendon Press, 1974), 188 (hereafter cited *Poems*). For the Richardson letter, March 16, 1756, see Murphy, *Essay on Johnson*, 88–89; and *Letters*, 1:132.
8. Thomas Kinsella, "The Pride of Literature: Arthur Murphy's *Essay on Johnson*," *Age of Johnson: A Scholarly Annual* 16 (2005), 133.
9. "He that succeeds a celebrated writer, has the same difficulties to encounter; he stands under the shade of exalted merit, and is hindered from rising to his natural height, by the interception of those beams which should invigorate and quicken him" (Yale *Works*, 4:87).
10. Giuseppe Baretti, "Ode to Charlotte Lennox," quoted in Miriam Small, *Charlotte Ramsay Lennox: An Eighteenth Century Lady of Letters* (London and New Haven, CT: Oxford University Press and Yale University Press, 1935), 159. For fuller discussions of the dynamics of literary mentoring, see Anthony W. Lee, *Mentoring Relationships in the Life and Writings of Samuel Johnson: A Study in the Dynamics of Eighteenth-Century Literary Mentoring* (Lewiston, NY: Edwin Mellen Press, 2005); and his *Dead Masters: Mentoring and Intertextuality in Samuel Johnson* (Bethlehem, PA: Lehigh University Press, 2011).
11. Other Johnsonian poems would include, for example, *Seventeen Hundred and Ninety-One*.
12. As well as a number of other Grub Street "dunces," such as John Hill, Charles Churchill, George Colman, and John Lockman.
13. See Dunbar, *Dramatic Career of Murphy*, 75: "The play was a success because of its novelty, its patriotic appeal, its affecting situations, its excellent cast, and its scenic effects. . . . It *was* good theatre."
14. In 1757, Murphy probably wrote two reviews of Thomas Gray's Odes for the *Literary Magazine* (September 15–October 15, 2:422–26; and October 15–November 15, 2:466–68) which contain a thinly veiled sneer at Francklin's error regarding the Greek Aeolian Lyre, a charge made more explicit in *A Poetical Epistle to Mr. Samuel Johnson, A.M.* (London: Vaillant, 1760), 5, line 31) and note (see Dunbar, *Dramatic Career of Murphy*, 40n33, 75n133). Dunbar (75–76n135) mentions a possible attack by Francklin upon Murphy in 1756 or 1757. Murphy's *Poetical Epistle* seems to have settled the fray; when he revised it in 1773, in true Popean fashion, he replaced Francklin and Hill with George Steevens and William Kenrick (Dunbar, 249–50).
15. "To the Author of *The Orphan of China*," quoted in Arthur Murphy, *The Life of David Garrick* (London, 1801), 2:42.

16. Thomas Francklin, *A Dissertation on Antient Tragedy* (London, 1760), 24n. Murphy was an actor for about two years.
17. Murphy, *Poetical Epistle*, 1, lines 1–8; 15 lines 228–31.
18. Murphy, *Poetical Epistle*, 2. Later, when he included the poem in his *The Works of Arthur Murphy*, he revised the poem considerably, changing the title to *To Dr. Johnson, A Poetic Epistle*: See Arthur Murphy, *The Works of Arthur Murphy* (London, 1786), 7:3–12.
19. "The difficulty of finding rhymes and of associating them with reason," Nicolas Boileau-Despréaux, *The Satires of Boileau Despréaux and his Address to the King*, trans. Hayward Porter and illustrated by James Magnus (Glasgow: James MacLehose and Sons, 1904), 20. The second translates, "Epistle to Moliere."
20. Such as Abbé Pure, or Michel, Abbé de Pure. See lines 17–18 of Boileau's French original. Older scholars have blamed the preciouses for the negative reaction to *École*: See Charles H. C. Wright, *French Classicism* (Cambridge, MA: Harvard University Press, 1920), 65–67. More recent critics have suggested that the reaction seems to have stemmed from conservative religious and aristocratic camps, worried about the subversive elements in Molière's satirical presentation of these two *estates*: See Hallam Walker, *Molière* (Boston: Twayne, 1971), 72.
21. Boileau's text may be fairly characterized as probing "the societal status of the poet in relation to his personal happiness," Robert T. Corum, Jr., *Reading Boileau: An Integrative Study of the Early Satires* (West Lafayette, IN: Purdue University Press, 1998), 33; Murphy's has a less noble or generalized theme and may be said to be more of a personal apologia, along the lines, as we shall soon see, of that found in Pope's *Epistle to Arbuthnot* (see note 33).
22. Nicolas Boileau-Despréaux, *Œuvres Complètes*, ed. Françoise Escal (Paris: Pléiade, 1966), 17, line 20.
23. Boileau, *Satires*, 20.
24. Murphy, *Poetical Epistle*, 5, line 28.
25. Nicolas Boileau-Despréaux, *The Works of Monsieur Boileau* (London, 1712–1714), 1:150. The translator was possibly either John Ozell or Samuel Cobb.
26. A. F. B. Clark, *Boileau and the French Classical Critics in England (1660–1830)* (New York: Burt Franklin, 1970), 115, 119.
27. See ibid., 1–79, passim.
28. For Johnson's familiarity with Boileau, see Fred Springer-Miller, "Johnson and Boileau," *Notes & Queries* 196 (November 10, 1951): 497. Dryden was the first to comment upon the emergence of Boileau as an important force in English poetry. In a 1673 letter to John Wilmot, he writes about a lost imitation by George Etherege of Boileau's *First Satire*, one which "changing the French names for English, [he] read it so often that it came to their eares who were concernd; and forc'd him to leave off the design e're it was half finish'd," *The Letters of John Dryden*, ed. Charles E. Ward (Durham, NC: Duke University Press, 1942; reprinted New York: AMS Press, 1965), 10.
29. Elias F. Mengel, "Pope's Imitation of Boileau in *Arbuthnot*," *Essays in Criticism* 38, no. 4 (October 1988): 295–307; see also Niall Rudd, "Variation and Inversion in Pope's *Epistle to Dr. Arbuthnot*," *Essays in Criticism* 34, no. 3 (July 1984): 216–28.
30. Other Murphy poems influenced by Pope include: *Ode to the Naiads of Fleet Ditch* (1761), *The Examiner* (1761)—also drawing upon Boileau's *Ninth Satire*—and *Seventeen Hundred and Ninety-One* (1791).
31. Robert D. Spector, *Arthur Murphy* (Boston: Twayne, 1979), 51–52.
32. Murphy, *Poetical Epistle*, 6, lines 45–47.
33. Pope, *Arbuthnot*, lines 3–6. See Alexander Pope, *The Twickenham Edition of the Poems of Alexander Pope*, ed. John Everett Butt et al. (New Haven, CT: Yale University Press, 1939–1969), 4:96.

34. Pope, *Arbuthnot*, lines 148–51, in *Twickenham Edition*, 4:106–107.
35. Ibid., lines 125–26, in *Twickenham Edition*, 4:104.
36. Boileau-Despréaux, *Œuvres Complètes*. ed. Escal (1966), 17; cf. the 1904 translation, Boileau, *Satires*, trans. Porter, 20: "But I by Fate, Caprice, or possibly by crimes / Condemned, against my will, to turn out endless rhymes"; and cf. the 1714 translation Boileau, *Works*, 1:150; lines 13–14: "While I, who only by Caprice and Whim, / I doubt, am for my Sins condemn'd to Rhyme."
37. Pope, *Arbuthnot*, lines 83–91, in *Twickenham Edition*, 4:101–102.
38. See *Metamorphosis*, 1:422–31; also see Dryden's rendering, which may have influenced Pope's passage, quoted below:
    Thus when the *Nile* from *Pharian* Fields is fled,
    And seeks, with Ebbing Tides, his ancient Bed,
    The fat Manure with heav'nly Fire is warm'd;
    And crusted Creatures, as in Wombs, are form'd:
    These, when they turn the Glebe, the Peasants find
    Some rude, and yet unfinish'd in their Kind;
    Short of their Limbs, a lame imperfect Birth;
    One half alive; and one of lifeless Earth. (*The Works of John Dryden*, ed. Edward Niles Hooker et al. [Berkeley and Los Angeles: University of California Press, 1956–2000], 4:392)
39. Pope, *Arbuthnot*, lines 305–12, in *Twickenham Edition*, 4:117–18.
40. Pope, *Essay on Criticism*, lines 40–44; in *Twickenham Edition*, 1:243.
41. For example, in the "Life of Pope" Johnson describes Whitehead sneeringly as "a small poet," in *Lives*, 4:47; on the other hand, in 1780 Francklin dedicated his translation of Lucian's biography of the Greek Cynic philosopher *Demonax* with this inscription: "To Dr. Samuel Johnson, the Demonax of the present age" (*Life*, 4:34). Francklin was also was amongst the company who drafted the Round Robin urging emendations to Johnson's epitaph of Oliver Goldsmith (*Life*, 3:83n3 and Appendix F, 482–83).
42. The allusion to Arbuthnot is a happy one. Johnson expressed his admiring opinion of Arbuthnot in the "Life of Pope," where he called him "a man estimable for his learning, amiable for his life, and venerable for his piety" (*Lives*, 4:46); Boswell's records Johnson as saying: "Talking of the eminent writers in Queen Anne's reign, he observed, 'I think Dr. Arbuthnot the first man among them. He was the most universal genius, being an excellent physician, a man of deep learning, and a man of much humour'" (*Life*, 1:425).
43. Oliver Goldsmith, *Collected Works of Oliver Goldsmith*, ed. Arthur Friedman (Oxford: Clarendon Press, 1966), 5:102.
44. In *Boileau and the Nature of Neo-Classicism* (Cambridge: Cambridge University Press, 1980), Gordon Pocock briefly outlines (while not entirely agreeing with) this ironic reading: "A traditional comment . . . is that in fact Boileau is a more accomplished rhymer than Molière, so that there is an element of jokiness in Boileau's attitude in this poem. This comment is linked with the assumption that in 1663 Boileau and Molière were close friends and regarded each other as equals, and that Boileau is at least in part assuming an unwonted modesty for the purposes of the poem" (32).
45. See Donald Davie, *Purity of Diction in English Verse and Articulate Energy* (Manchester: Carcanet, 2006), 6–7.
46. Cf. Johnson's remark about Pope's *Dunciad* in his "Life of Pope": "The beauties of this poem are well known; its chief fault is the grossness of its images. Pope and Swift had an unnatural delight in ideas physically impure, such as every other tongue utters with unwillingness, and of which every ear shrinks from the mention" (*Lives*, 4:75).

47. Murphy's contemporary reputation as a "potted author" was common knowledge to his contemporaries; cf. Cuthbert Shaw's remark, in Murphy's voice "For whose [Virtue] dear sake I've scratch'd my drowzy head, / And robb'd alike the living and the dead" (Mercurious Spur [Cuthbert Shaw], *The Race* [London, 1765], 17).
48. Johnson's restraint in the face of a heavy and nearly continuous onslaught of attacks is impressive: See Helen Louise McGuffie, *Samuel Johnson in the British Press, 1749-1784: A Chronological Checklist*, New York: Garland, 1976, passim.

8

JOHNSON, BURKE, BOSWELL, AND THE SLAVERY DEBATE

Elizabeth Lambert

IN ITS JULY 1976 *ATLANTIC MONTHLY* advertisement Christie's auction house used the words of two clients to sum up British feelings about the American colonists' revolt. The two were Samuel Johnson and Edmund Burke, and they had very different opinions. Johnson: "They are a race of convicts and ought to be content with anything we may allow them short of hanging." Burke: "An Englishman is the unfittest person on earth to argue another Englishman into slavery." Johnson would have scorned Burke's use of the word "slavery" in the context of the American colonists for he vigorously defended Britain's right to tax them; Burke, on the other hand, argued that concessions were needed in order to keep the American colonies within the emerging empire. While they never agreed on the legitimacy of the colonists' rebellion, they were in accord on the evils of slavery and the slave trade. Conversely, James Boswell, Johnson's biographer and Burke's sometimes friend, differed from them in his unabashedly pro-slavery views. From this position he took it upon himself to criticize in print both Johnson and Burke for their opposition to slavery. The attitudes of Johnson, Burke, and Boswell toward slavery mirror, in varying degrees, the temper of the time, and their attitudes reflect each man's character as well as his life's experiences.

JOHNSON'S VIEW AS BOSWELL RECORDED AND INTERPRETED IT

Johnson had a lifelong visceral reaction to injustice anywhere: witness his castigation of both French and English treatment of Native Americans. This attitude was reflected in many of his earliest writings.[1] Slavery in the abstract became real to him in 1752 when the young Jamaican slave Francis Barber came to live with him. In his ten years of life, Barber had experienced all the horrors and humiliations of slavery, and his description of them most certainly fueled Johnson's hatred of the institution. To recount the history of Johnson's lifetime devotion to Francis is beyond the scope of this essay.[2] Suffice it to say that he gave Barber a home, an education, and emotional support. He also made him residual heir in his will. In Boswell's words: "Having no nearer relations, it had been for some time in Johnson's intention to make a liberal provision for his faithful servant, Mr. Francis Barber, whom he looked upon as particularly under his protection, and whom he had all along treated truly as an humble friend." When his friend Dr. Brocklesby told Johnson that fifty pounds a year "was considered as an adequate reward for many years of faithful service, Johnson responded: "Then shall I be *nobilissimus* for I mean to leave Frank seventy pounds a year."[3] Admittedly there were times when Johnson acted in an overly paternalistic manner, such as when he took an unwilling Francis away from a career in the navy, but such measures were not considered unusual in a father figure. Through the years Barber reciprocated Johnson's devotion, particularly when he and his wife Elizabeth took Johnson under their care in the last year of his life, and when Francis was at his death bed. While Boswell gives Barber a place in his *Life of Johnson*, it is a minor one relative to the extent of his role.

The ink was hardly dry on the first edition of Boswell's *The Life of Johnson* when critics took aim at it, frequently citing Boswell's lack of discretion in detailing Johnson's foibles and weaknesses. This criticism was not new to Boswell. After the 1785 publication of *A Tour to the Hebrides*, the *English Review* speculated as to whether it was "right or justifiable in Mr. Boswell to record and to publish [Johnson's] prejudices, his follies and whims, his weaknesses, his vices."[4] Furthermore, Hester Thrale, now Mrs. Piozzi, recorded Michael Lort's report that Edmund Burke had "come down hard on Boswell "for the absurdities" in the *Tour*.[5] Another set of criticisms, very much alive today, has to do with the extent to which Johnson's biography becomes Boswell's autobiography.[6] Critics charge that Boswell the biographer so obtrudes himself into the *Life* that he corrects Johnson's opinions by injecting his own.[7] This purported weakness proves valid when we look closely into Boswell's handling of Johnson's opinions on the subject of slavery.

A case in point is his account of Johnson's toast given at an Oxford dinner in 1769: "Here's to the next insurrection of the negroes in the West Indies" (*Life*, 3:200). Boswell prefaces Johnson's comment with his own observation that Johnson "discovered a zeal without knowledge" on the subject of slavery in every form. As an example of this zeal, Boswell records Johnson's comment and notes "it was given in company with some very grave men at Oxford." A reader is given the impression that Johnson's toast was thoughtless as well as inappropriate given, as it was, in the company of "grave men." James Basker has written a critical evaluation of this incident, filling in significant details that Boswell has left out. Among such details is Johnson's extensive knowledge of slave insurrections throughout the world that the *Gentleman's Magazine* regularly reported. Basker notes "no one in the room could have been unaware or indifferent to the frequency and bloodiness of slave insurrections," least of all Johnson.[8] In effect, his zeal was the result of the vast knowledge Basker tracks. If Boswell was aware of the articles and reports, there is no mention of it in his journals or letters.

A second, more extensive example in the *Life*, is found when Boswell used Johnson's remarks to state his own pro-slavery position in September 1777. At the time Johnson was staying at the home of his long-time friend Dr. Taylor in Ashbourne, and he invited Boswell to visit him there. After dinner on the 23rd, Boswell asked Johnson to dictate an argument in favor of "the Negro who was then claiming his liberty in an action in the Court of Session in Scotland" (*Life*, 2:174). The unnamed "Negro" was Joseph Knight, a Jamaican slave brought to Scotland in 1769 who filed for his freedom against John Wedderburn.[9] When the justices of the peace in Perth found in favor of Wedderburn, Knight appealed. At this point Wedderburn took his case to the Court of Session in Edinburgh. Knight won his freedom, but this is where the case stood when Boswell asked Johnson to dictate an argument in favor of Knight.

Boswell frames their conversation in the context of Johnson's anti-slavery position: "He had always been against slavery in any form." This statement is immediately counterbalanced by Boswell's own judgment, given "with all deference," that in his opposition to slavery Johnson "discovered 'a zeal without knowledge,'" and he instances the Oxford toast discussed above. Continuing the theme of Johnson's zealousness with respect to slavery, he editorializes: "His *violent prejudice* [emphasis mine] against our West Indian and American settlers appeared whenever there was an opportunity." As an example, Boswell uses the accusation with which Johnson concludes *Taxation No Tyranny*: "How is it we hear the loudest yelps for liberty among the drivers of negroes?"[10] Boswell brings the reader's attention to these two instances of Johnson's antipathy to slavery as preface to the complete text of the argument Johnson composed for him.

Johnson begins the brief he dictated for Boswell by acknowledging that, while slavery has always been a part of human history it "can never be the natural condition of man." In fact, Johnson continues "it is impossible not to conceive that men in their original state were equal; and very difficult to imagine how one would be subjected to another but by violent compulsion." A criminal, he argues, can forfeit his liberty, but his children cannot be made to suffer the same punishment by virtue of the fact they are a criminal's offspring. The same condition, Johnson argues, applies to slavery; a man cannot entail servitude on his descendants. Turning to the specifics of the case Boswell presented, Johnson states that the Negro in question is not subject to any law that enslaved him but to the violence by which he was obtained. He concludes his remarks with a reference to English liberty: "Inhabitants of this island can neither gain riches nor power by taking away the liberty of any part of the human species. The sum of the argument is this:—No man is by nature the property of another" (*Life*, 3:200–204). Presenting himself as the fairest of commentators, Boswell assures his readers: "I record Dr. Johnson's argument fairly upon this particular case; where, perhaps, he was in the right." Note "perhaps."

Up to this point Johnson, with only a few editorial asides, has center stage, but now Boswell steps in with an extended argument against abolition. He calls slavery "a very important and necessary branch of commercial interest" and says that it is a "*status*, which in all ages God has sanctioned, and man has continued." Although Boswell begins the September 23, 1777 account by pointing up Johnson's too zealous and intemperate remarks on slavery, he seems to overcome such reservations regarding Johnson's rhetoric when he indulges in a bit of his own. For Boswell, the efforts of abolitionists are "wild and dangerous" attempts made by a pack of "insignificant zealots." While admitting that there are some men of "superior abilities" who encourage the abolitionists, he questions their motives and asserts they are led by "a love of temporary popularity, when prosperous or a love of general mischief when desperate." These men of superior abilities who advance the cause of abolition excite his "wonder and indignation." Unlike such individuals whose questionable motives lead them to support abolition, Boswell's clear-sightedness leads him in another direction. He rhapsodies: "It would be extreme cruelty to the African Savages, a portion of whom it saves from massacre, or intolerable bondage in their own country, and introduces into a much happier state of life, especially now when their passage to the East-Indies and their treatment there is humanely regulated. To abolish that trade would be to "shut the gates of mercy on mankind" (*Life*, 3:204). At the conclusion of his argument Boswell assures the reader that he "has read, conversed, and thought much upon the subject." The evening goes downhill from there with Boswell "unluckily" bringing up the subject of Parliament's right to tax America and Johnson responding with heat and agitation in favor of Parliament. At the conclusion of it all, Boswell acknowledges that they "were very willing to separate and go to bed."[11]

At least two notable things are present here. The way Boswell characterizes Johnson's anti-slavery stance as simply emotional in nature denigrates the strength of Johnson's argument and does not give a full picture of his beliefs. In addition, the fact that it is missing from the first edition of the *Life* gives rise to some scholarly controversy. While James Basker questions Boswell's assertion that he "mislaid" the brief,[12] Michael Bundock argues that "Boswell took some pains to ensure that Johnson's argument became public knowledge"[13] by drawing attention to it in a footnote in the first edition, and publishing it in the second edition. Added to the mix is the fact that Boswell was one of Knight's counsels and served gratis, but there is no mention of this fact in the *Life*.[14] This latter issue does not affect the charge that Boswell used Johnson's brief to set out his own pro-slavery position. Furthermore, his blatant insertions undermining Johnson's argument undercuts what he claims was the "scrupulous authenticity" of his biography, and provides evidence to those critics who charge that the *Life* is a portrait of Boswell's Johnson rather than an objective account of his subject. Admittedly Samuel Johnson was larger than life, and attempts to capture his essence always seemed to elude a perfect replica even in the hands of the most scrupulous biographers. But the fact is, Boswell's handling of this section of the *Life* tells us more about Boswell than it does about Johnson.

BOSWELL'S OPPOSITION TO ABOLITION

James Boswell is a study in contradictions. He had a reputation for actively aiding the oppressed, and he took on the most desperate cases in his legal practice. One of the most familiar instances of the latter is his 1774 unsuccessful defense of the accused sheep-stealer John Reid in Edinburgh's High Court of Justiciary. Boswell's efforts to gain a reprieve for Reid impelled him to consider extralegal attempts, even devising a plan to retrieve Reid's body immediately after the hanging and try to revive it.[15] In more ordinary ways, he often provided money and assistance to those in need.[16] Yet, with few exceptions, such as the case of Joseph Knight cited above, this ability to identify, to sympathize, and to imagine the plight of the destitute and less fortunate, did not extend to black slaves.

The term "slave" here might be significant. Boswell always treated Frances Barber with respect, gave him a copy of *Tour to the Hebrides*, and in the pages of the *Life* refers to him as "Mr. Barber," or "good Mr. Francis." Could it be that Boswell made a distinction between a slave and a freed black? If so, he would not have been alone. Bundock speaks of the ways slavery added complexity to beliefs about race and color: "The links between the two were not at all straightforward. There were pro-slavery figures who were on friendly terms with individual blacks, and there were opponents of slavery who believed that blacks constituted a race which was inferior to whites."[17] All the evidence puts Boswell in the first category: a pro-slavery figure who was on friendly terms with individual blacks.

Boswell claimed that he had done much reading, conversing, and thinking upon the subject of slavery; he was also personally acquainted with a former slave, yet his pro-slavery stance was fixed. A few examples suffice. In March of 1787, he accepted an invitation from Bennet Langton to a dinner at his home where the other guests included Thomas Clarkson and William Wilberforce. The purpose of the dinner was to convince Wilberforce to act as leader in bringing the abolition of the slave trade bill to Parliament. After dinner Clarkson discussed the slave trade at length and detailed his account by citing the number of seamen lost in the trade. His listeners responded: "Sir Joshua Reynolds gave his unqualified approbation of the abolition of this cruel traffic. . . . Mr. Boswell, after saying the planters would urge that the Africans were made happier by being carried from their own country to the West Indies, observed, '"Be it so. But we have no right to make people happy against their will.'" As a postscript to the account Clarkson noted: "I do not know upon what grounds, after such strong expressions, Mr. Boswell, in the next year, and Mr. Windham, after having supported the cause for three or four years, became inimical to it."[18]

Clarkson's query as to what changed Boswell's mind about abolition quite possibly has a simple answer in that Boswell was caught up in the sentiment of the moment and by Clarkson's display of knowledge. But later, upon cooler reflection, he felt that he indulged in the fault for which he accused Johnson: an unreflective zeal. At any rate, it appears that Boswell rather quickly reverted to his unyielding position against abolition. Four years later, in 1791, as the bill reached a vote in Parliament, Boswell published a panegyric on the slave trade titled "No Abolition of Slavery, or The Universal Empire of Love." The poem, 298 lines in length, is dedicated to "The Respectable Body of West India Planters and Merchants" and is addressed to an unnamed Miss—.[19]

The poem is a bizarre performance, both in its contradictory title that links the enslavement of human beings with universal love, and in the vicious, unlovely way Boswell attacks supporters of abolition. He first takes on various Members of Parliament whom he does not identify other than by the first letter of their names. Thus: "Go, W[ilberforce]—with narrow scull, / Go home, and preach away at Hull."[20] However, beginning at line 47, Boswell attacks by name Sir William Dolben, author of the bill to regulate the slave trade, as well as Prime Minister William Pitt and Edward Thurlow, Lord Chancellor.

After a brief aside decrying a regency, Boswell abandons the attack on members of Parliament and introduces his next theme:

> Where have I wander'd? do I dream?
> Sure slaves of power are not my theme;
> But honest slaves, the sons of toil,
> Who cultivate the Planter's soil.[21]

The remaining 120 lines enlarge upon the themes Boswell put forth in the *Life* when he amended Johnson's brief against slavery with observations of his own: slavery always has existed as part of "subordination's plan"; London's poor live in the same destitute state as do slaves; blacks on West Indian plantations live in a sort of paradise and are happy there—"no human beings are more gay."[22] Boswell's notes accompanying the poem enlarge upon these themes, asserting, "The Africans are in a state of savage wretchedness,"[23] a state that can be changed by "well-regulated restraint."[24] The poem concludes with a paean to Miss X connecting slavery to that which lovers feel for the beloved: "For, Slavery there must ever be, / While we have Mistresses like thee!"[25]

Boswell's attack on Pitt and members of Parliament who supported abolition echoes the same charges in the popular press, but when he turns to intimate friends, Boswell's critique becomes personal. He puts William Windham[26] in the "whining tribe" of abolitionists and warns him against descending to a "blue stocking" type of thinking that will "emasculate" his mind. He then accuses John Courtney, one of "The Gang,"[27] of wildly raving; however, Courtney, with a sharp wit that got him into trouble more than once, may have contributed these reflections on his own conduct.[28] These snipes at his friends, John Courtney and William Windham, are mild when compared with the vitriolic attack on Edmund Burke that follows. Boswell first refers to Burke's assault on Thomas Paine's *Rights of Man*: "Pray, by what logic are those rights / Allow'd to *Blacks*— deny'd to *Whites*?" In the next ten lines Boswell stoops to the ad hominem attacks:

> Of talents vast, but with a mind
> Unaw'd, ungovern'd, unconfin'd
> Best humour'd man, worst politician,
> Most dangerous, desp'rate state physician;
> Thy manly character why stain
> By canting, when 'tis all in vain?
> For thy tumultuous reign is o'er;
> THE PEOPLE'S MAN thou art no more.[29]

This is a strange way to describe a man Boswell had repeatedly wished to be. Much has been written about Boswell's relationship with Johnson, yet Edmund Burke had been a star in Boswell's firmament for some twenty-two years.

BURKE AND BOSWELL'S CONFLICTED RELATIONSHIP

Boswell and Burke met in 1772, and within a short time Burke had fixed himself in Boswell's mind as a man with whom to identify and to imitate. Readers of Boswell's journals know of his propensity to invoke the names of the famous as an inspiration for his own conduct. However, he identified with Burke more than any other figure: "I was in such a frame as to think myself an Edmund Burke"; "I thought myself a kind of Burke today," and after one morning in Burke's company, "I told Burke he was the only man I could wish to be, and this not until I had seen his domestic happiness."[30] The Burke/Boswell relationship was more nuanced than the following indicates; however, in the context of their disagreement about abolition, the dynamics of their connection described below typify the whole.[31]

Through the years Boswell cultivated a friendship with Burke, calling on him at his London home, taking meals with the family when Burke was delayed in the House of Commons, asking his advice on professional matters, and confiding in him. When Boswell was in Scotland, he tried—without much success—to establish an on-going correspondence. Despite the fact that Burke's busy life left little or no time for casual correspondence, he reciprocated the younger man's overtures of friendship by lengthy conversations on matters ranging from politics to literature to sexuality. He dropped in on him of an evening, and entertained Boswell at his country estate in Beaconsfield.

In reading about the relationship in Boswell's journals, his letters to Burke, and Burke's to him, one has the impression that the latter's responses to Boswell were warm but never confidential. Here we can turn to Johnson for a relevant distinction between friends, companions, and intimate friends.[32] Johnson described an "intimate friend" as one "with whom to compare minds," and in *Idler* 23 he lists "opposition of interest," and "suspicion" as elements that work against intimate friendship (Yale *Works*, 2:73). All of these elements played out in the Burke/Boswell relationship.

Burke's statement that Boswell "had so much good nature it was scarce a virtue" characterizes his initial assessment of the man and never seems to have moved beyond it. For instance, in 1782 the position of Judge Advocate became open, and Boswell asked Burke to write a letter of recommendation to Henry Seymour Conway. In that letter Burke emphasizes Boswell's personality rather than his services: "He is a Lawyer of Ability and of general Erudition, and the pleasantest and best tempered man in the <World.>." Burke goes on to assure Conway that "when he has an opportunity of coming to thank you for your protection you will have no cause to repent of having attached to you so agreeable a

Man as Mr. Boswell."[33] The only mention in the letter of Boswell's qualifications is the phrase, "He is a Lawyer of Ability and general Erudition."

There was also the matter of their political differences with Boswell boasting to Burke of his "Tory zeal" in opposition to Burke's Whig alliances. Until 1783 essential political differences did not seem to affect the cordiality between the two men. However, in that year Boswell published his opposition to Fox's East India Bill in a pamphlet, *Letter to the People of Scotland* arguing the Bill violated the property rights of the East India Company.[34] Burke played an important role in writing and promoting the East India Bill in the House of Commons; not only had it been defeated in the House of Lords, but also Burke lost his position as Paymaster of the Forces when the King dismissed the coalition ministry. Furthermore, in the months that followed Burke had suffered attacks in the press (which he dismissed as vexatious) and from younger Members of Parliament (which he did not). In Scotland Boswell, curiously insensitive to the change in Burke's political fortunes, took great pride in the fact that his *Letter to the People* was widely popular. He assumed it would enhance his chances for obtaining a position in a Tory Ministry and sent copies to Johnson, Reynolds, Wilkes, and Burke, among others. Initially he assured himself that Burke was of "too liberal a mind" to be angry, and, even if he were, Boswell journalized, "I was fully conscious I was in the right."[35]

Such assurances were significantly dulled when Boswell learned that Burke had come to Scotland to be installed as Lord Rector of the University of Glasgow and had not notified him of his coming. At some level, Boswell knew he had to face Burke after the publication of his *Letter to the People*, but when that occasion became imminent, he was more than a little uneasy. He set off for Glasgow, and upon arriving in the city, wrote to Burke announcing his visit. The draft of that letter is full of revisions and second thoughts such as: "I cannot easily believe <scarcely allow myself to believe> that <Mr.> Edmund Burke is <deficient>." However, the letter that Burke received shows none of Boswell's trepidation. The tone is that of an equal: Boswell is the Laird who is somewhat offended by Burke's not advising him of his coming to Scotland, and he hopes their differences will not cause a break in the relationship; if it did, both would suffer. According to Boswell's journal, when Burke received the note, "he came quickly into the parlor and approached me with all the good humor he had ever showed at our meetings."[36] Boswell was relieved, although Burke's comment, "What has made you go so mad of late?" should have given him pause. This incident is a microcosm of what eventually ended the relationship: Boswell's feelings of inadequacy when it came to Burke, coupled with a fear of offending him, and yet forging ahead with something he knew would endanger their relationship—Johnson's "opposition of interests" and "suspicion." The first, a sense of inadequacy, was sharpened by the perception that Burke was his rival for Johnson's esteem, a perception that had its beginnings when he and Johnson toured the Hebrides in the fall of 1773.

During those months Johnson frequently spoke of Burke's intellectual talents, detailing them to anyone who asked. He told Dr. Robertson[37] of Burke's "great variety of knowledge, store of imagery, copiousness of language," and stated that "if you met him for the first time in a street where you were stopped by a drove of oxen, and you and he stepped aside to take shelter but for five minutes, he'd talk to you in such a manner that when you parted you would say, 'This is an extraordinary man.'"[38] On another occasion he described the excellence of Burke's eloquence as consisting in "copiousness and fertility of allusion . . . great knowledge and great command of language."[39] Johnson also told Boswell that he did not grudge Burke being the first man in the House of Commons, "he was the first man everywhere." All of this high praise would not have stung, had not Johnson, at the beginning of the trip, told Boswell that several members of the Literary Club had wished to keep him out: "Burke told me he doubted you were fit for it, but now you are in, none of them are sorry. Burke says you have so much good humor naturally, it is scarce a virtue."[40] Thus, at the same time Johnson detailed Burke's powers of mind he informed Boswell that Burke doubted he was intellectually fit for the Club. And he probably made matters worse by attempting to ease the harshness of Burke's initial estimation of Boswell's abilities by telling him Burke admired his good nature—it sounded condescending. Moreover, it struck at an essential element in Boswell's personality: the need to be considered as a man of consequence, even by Johnson. A few months after their first meeting he gleefully recorded Johnson's opinion that he "was very forward in knowledge for my age; that . . . perhaps I had not six above me. Perhaps not one."[41] However these moments of assurance were undercut by other thoughts. Thus, his self-judgment: "There is an imperfection, a superficialness [sic], in all my notions. I understand nothing clearly, nothing to the bottom."[42] In essence, Burke's evaluation of his intellectual abilities may have confirmed Boswell's sense of inadequacy, i.e., "he is right."

With this background of Johnson's high praise of Burke's intellectual powers set against Burke's initial judgment that Boswell was "unfit" for the Club, Boswell's attack on Burke in "No Abolition of Slavery" takes on added significance. He attacks Burke's mental prowess in several ways. First, by questioning his logic and quality of mind: "Pray, by what logick are those rights / Allow'd to *Blacks*—deny'd to *Whites* . . . with a mind / Unaw'd, ungovern'd, unconfin'd." And then, using Burke's own words describing Boswell's primary attribute as "so much good humor it is scarce a virtue," he taunts: "Best *humour'd* man, worst politician." The last two lines relating to Burke have the impact of a grand finale: "For thy tumultuous reign is o'er; / THE PEOPLE'S MAN thou art no more."[43] Whether Burke ever read or even knew of the poem is immaterial; the harsh lines were there for anyone to see. Besides, Boswell's use of the phrase "no more," sets the stamp on what he has contended for some time—that the relationship between the two men had turned sour in a way that precluded any resolution.

In June 1786 Boswell ran into Burke in Pall Mall and recorded in his journal: "I lamented that politics made a cold separation between us which never could be got over."[44] He said as much to Edmond Malone who set him straight. "The true cause I perceive, of B's coldness, is that he thinks your habit of recording throws a restraint on convivial ease and negligence."[45] Malone was referring, among other things, to Burke's portrait in the *Tour to the Hebrides*, published in 1785. There, Burke found Johnson's judgment: "Burke never once made a good joke" and faulted his humor as: "'Tis low; 'tis conceit."[46] Even Malone's lengthy clarification attached to Boswell's note contradicting Johnson's opinion did not mollify Burke. The tone of the letter Burke wrote thanking Boswell for sending "the second Edition of your very entertaining Book" is at once condescending and styled in a way that contradicts the judgment that he lacked wit.[47] In the last letter exchanged between the two men Burke sounded a note of finality, telling Boswell: "I wish you all happiness, whenever you retire to Auchinleck, from the entertainment of your friends and the applauses of the public. We shall, I trust, find ourselves hereafter as much obliged to your invention as hitherto we have been to your recollection.... Whether, in the present possession of the favourable opinion of the world as you are, it will be prudent for you to resque the further publication of anecdotes, you are infinitely more competent to judge than I am."[48] Malone was correct: political differences put into print may have irritated Burke, but nothing could make him so angry as making public the opinions, sentiments, and casual observations rendered in private conversation. Why this was so can be traced to Burke's childhood experiences in Ireland, experiences that gave him a particularly keen sense of oppression that, in later life, made him an active participant in the abolition movement.

BURKE AND OPPRESSION IN IRELAND AND ENGLAND

Burke had first experienced the effects of social injustice when, as a child suffering from ill health, his parents sent him to live with his maternal Catholic relatives, the Nagles, in the Blackwater country outside of Cork. There he witnessed the restrictions Penal Laws placed on Catholics affecting the practice of their religion, their possibilities for education and entry into the professions, and, significantly, their right to property. A sensitive, intelligent child quickly picks up the nuances of behavior in those surrounding him. Observing, loving, and respecting his Uncle Patrick, and hearing the discontented, angry, rebellious murmurs of his cousins, the young boy absorbed the indignities and fears imposed by the penal laws.

A further important and profound influence on Burke was his schooling under the tutelage of the Quaker Abraham Shackleton in the village of Ballitore. As early as the 1680s the Quakers had taken a collective stand against slavery and the slave trade. While there is nothing in Burke's early correspondence to indicate the issue of slavery ever came up in the Ballitore school, Shackleton's moral qualities inspired in Burke a deep veneration for the schoolmaster. In a youthful poem he described Shackleton as one in "Whose breast all virtues long have made their home."[49] These childhood experiences in Ireland with outlawed Catholics, among them his maternal relations, and dissident Quakers made real the situation of oppressed or minority peoples.[50] African slaves did not become a part of that equation until 1750 when he began law studies at Middle Temple in London. From that point on, his perspective shifted, and slaves and slavery became part of his everyday landscape.

According to the work of Julie Flavell, when Burke began his political career in 1760 there were 15,000 blacks living in London.[51] Many were the slaves of American colonists who had come to the mother country as tourists or who owned homes in London and lived there part of the year. Burke would have encountered both enslaved and freed blacks, such as Francis Barber, among London's servant population. In addition, when he was at Middle Temple there were many students from the American colonies, particularly Virginia, Maryland, and South Carolina. We know Burke discussed at some length life in the colonies because at one point he anticipated immigrating to America.[52] While that particular plan never worked out, his fellow students from the colonies taught him much about the slave system there. Such facts and figures appear in a 1756 work he wrote, with William Burke, *An Account of the European Settlements in America*. In the *Account* he is severely critical of the West Indian slave trade and the treatment of slaves on the plantations: "The negroes in our colonies endure a slavery more complete, and attended with far worse circumstances, that what any people in their condition suffer in any other part of the world, or have suffered in any other period of time. Proofs of this are not wanting."[53] Eighteen years later his election to Parliament in 1774 as MP from Bristol brought the issue of slavery and the slave trade to his front door.

BURKE AS MEMBER OF PARLIAMENT FOR BRISTOL

Bristol was the so-called second city in the kingdom, and it was one of the three largest centers of the slave trade in England, the other two being Liverpool and London. By 1774 when Burke was elected for Bristol, Liverpool had superseded it as Britain's most important slaving port. However, slave ships still were a feature of Bristol's docks where they were refitted and supplied, and trading in slaves remained a major area of investment by the port's merchants. In the records of the Merchant Venture's company Thomas Clarkson found that the mortality rates of Bristol slave ship crews were heavy in comparison to other cities involved in the triangular trade. Given all of this, it is curious, as Bristol's MP Burke's record on opposing the slave trade seems to evaporate.

In 1777, as Member for Bristol, he defended the African Company against Parliamentary intervention, and again, in 1779 he fought against replacing the Company of Merchants trading to Africa with a joint stock company.[54] In his correspondence and in various reports of the proceedings, Burke defended free trade against monopolies. He argued that a monopoly would permit slave traders to set their own price and raise "whatever sums they please upon your planters."[55] With respect to the African Company the morality of the slave trade did not appear to be an issue.

But two years earlier Burke had turned to the issue of slavery with respect to the American colonies. In his 1775 *Speech on Conciliation with the Colonies* he spoke against a plan to free slaves as a way of bringing the rebellious colonists to heel. That plan, he opined, had "moral difficulties" and declared that the slaves themselves would look upon a general enfranchisement of Virginia's slaves with suspicion. "Slaves as these unfortunate black people are, and dull as all men are from slavery, must they not a little suspect the offer of freedom from that very nation which has sold them to their present masters. . . . An offer of freedom from England would come rather oddly, shipped to them in an African vessel . . . with a cargo of three hundred Angola negroes." There is more than a slight touch of sarcasm in this statement. Moreover, when he characterizes the particular spirit of individual colonies, he refers specifically to the southern slave-owning colonists: "Freedom to them is not only an enjoyment, but also a kind of rank and privilege."[56]

In addition to African Company matters, Burke's relationship with his Bristol constituents was certainly not a love match, and it began to unravel from the first when, on the occasion of his election, he gave a now-familiar portrait of what he felt to be his duty: "It ought to be the happiness and glory of a representative to live in the strictest unions, the closest correspondence and the most unreserved communication with his constituents. . . . But his unbiased opinion, his mature judgment, his enlightened conscience, he ought not to sacrifice to you or to any set of men living. . . . You choose a member, indeed; but when you have chosen him, he is not a member of Bristol, but he is a member of Parliament."[57] During the following years, the American war with its effect upon trade did nothing to engender a positive mood in Bristol voters, and they were infuriated by Burke's support of relaxations upon Irish trade with England and the empire. Adding insult to injury, his support of measures for Catholic relief further alienated them. Nor did Burke visit Bristol to explain his positions or even to assess the mood of the people. In August 1776 he answered a request to visit the city with a somewhat lame reply: "It is certainly very inconvenient for me to go to Bristol at this particular time, though no other, in this summer is perfectly easy. Nothing could give me such sincere pleasure as often to see the faces of such uncommon friends and men of such excellent principles, publick and private. . . . But I really am so engaged that I cannot be positive, so of course you will not expect me; though if I can, I will come."[58] By the time of the 1780 election, Burke knew he had lost Bristol, and he went there to resign his seat. Interestingly enough, he did not leave immediately, but, as he wrote to Lady Rockingham:[59] "[I stayed] a considerable time . . . and saw, as from a bold shore, my companions tossing in the storm of the Election. I felt a serenity which I never before experienced. . . . My election was a matter of meer accident; and I never had an Inch of firm Ground under me whilst I sat for that place.[60] The objectifying phrase, "that place," signals an almost visceral distaste for Bristol. It was then, after declining election Burke set to paper his thoughts on the slave trade: *Sketch for a Negro Code*. In composing his own document Burke may have known about the French *Code Noir* that regulated the status of slaves and free blacks, as well as relations between masters and slaves in the French Caribbean colonies. Compiled in 1685 and applied to Louisiana in 1724, the *Code Noir* gave extensive rights to slaves but forced them to practice only the Roman Catholic faith and expelled the Jews from Louisiana. However, Burke makes no mention of the French *Code*, and the two documents are different in significant ways.

DOLBEN, DUNDAS, AND BURKE

The abolitionist movement in England had been gaining momentum since it achieved a legal victory with the 1772 Mansfield decision in the Somerset case. The fugitive slave James Somerset forced a decision by the courts after his master,

Charles Stewart, had him captured and imprisoned on board a ship, intending to ship him to Jamaica to be resold into slavery. While in London, Somerset had been baptized as a Christian, and his three godparents made an application for a writ of *habeas corpus*. In January 1772, Lord Mansfield, Chief Justice of the Court of the King's Bench, heard both sides of the arguments, and in June gave his judgment that Somerset's abduction was unlawful because chattel slavery was unsupported by English common law. The case received national attention because, at the time, the judgment was generally taken to mean slavery had never been authorized by statute in England and was unsupported by common law.

That was the situation in 1788 when the Abolitionist movement was given a voice in Parliament. Sir William Dolben, one of the two members for Oxford University, detailed the horrendous conditions of the passage from Africa to the West Indian plantations, the infamous Middle Passage. Dolben asked Parliament to take action that session to end the slave trade. In July Dolben's efforts led to the passage of a bill called the Slave Trade Regulation Act. That act placed limitations on the number of people British slave ships could transport, related to tonnage. It was the first official act to end the trade, but before other efforts could materialize, the Regency crisis, the impeachment trial of Warren Hastings, Governor General of India, and the events in revolutionary France absorbed Parliament's attention.

Four years later, in 1792, the House of Commons again considered measures to end the slave trade and asked Henry Dundas, Home Secretary, to produce a plan. Somehow he knew Burke had written a document titled *Sketch for a Negro Code* and asked him for a copy. In the lengthy letter to Dundas accompanying his *Code*, Burke speaks to the complexity of the issue as the difference between regulating the slave trade and the total abolition of slavery. In moral terms, Burke allowed, the trade was tied to total abolition; in practical terms, it was not. At this juncture, there were too many financial ramifications in terms of trading competition from other nations to make total abolition of slavery an uncomplicated process. Burke describes the climate in which he wrote the document twelve years before: "At the time when I formed the plan . . . an abolition of the slave trade would have appeared a very chimerical project. My plan, therefore, supposes the continued existence of that commerce. Taking for my basis, that I had an incurable evil to deal with, I cast about how I should make it as small an evil as possible, and draw out of it some collateral good."[61] Hence, in the *Sketch*, Burke focuses on a series of regulations which would have the force of law and which, in his words to Dundas, would "provide against the manifold abuses to which a Trade of that nature is liable, but that the same may be accompanied, as far as possible, with such advantages to the natives, as may tend to the civilizing them, and enabling them to enrich themselves by means more desirable, and to carry on hereafter a Trade, more advantageous and honorable to all parties."

BURKE'S *SKETCH FOR A NEGRO CODE*

Burke's *Sketch for a Negro Code* has two aspects: the practical administrative element and the personal, psychological.[62] The administrative regulations come under four headings: the qualifications for ships engaged in the traffic; the mode and conditions of permitting the said trade to be carried on upon the coast of Africa; rules providing for the treatment of the Negroes in their passage from Africa to the West Indies, and lastly, rules for the government of the Negroes employed in the colonies and plantations in the West Indies.

Essentially the first section deals with legislation requiring slave ships to qualify under the same law as any ship trading to the West Indies with further provisions relative to the number of Negroes to be taken on ship and the size of the interior space allotted to each person. This section also includes such details as the kind of clothing and bedding provided to each slave as well as a list of "sufficient and sound provisions."[63] The ship and its provisions are to be certified by an inspector with authority to let ships leave port.

The second set of regulations applies to the way the trade is to be controlled on the coast of Africa by providing for a specific number of named stations or marts. Each of the stations will have a governor and three counselors overseeing it; these individuals will have no share in the trade and will "keep a journal of all their proceedings."[64] This section also stipulates for one church, one schoolhouse, and one hospital. The numerous specific details in this section establish laws as to who may trade and where, as well as those Africans who can and cannot be sold, such as those above the age of thirty-five, those stolen or carried away by surprise, any person who is able to read, or any woman advanced three months in pregnancy.

The third set of regulations addresses the abuses of the middle passage—that from Africa to the West Indies—and stipulates measures to eliminate them. To this end Burke provides for a certain order on the ship with the appointment of one Negro man for each twenty slaves who will have authority over a group and who will receive compensation in the form of "extraordinary diet or presents."[65] This section also details penalties for raping a woman slave; her accusation and the testimony of a witness are needed.

The final section is the longest and addresses the subject of governing the Negroes employed in the colonies and plantations in the West Indies. In this section Burke states that family members should not be sold separately at the initial sale or at any other time. The attorney general is charged with being the protector of the Negroes and, as such, is empowered to bring to trail those who commit any offences against the provisions provided in the *Code* and/or those persons who commit wrongs against the Negroes. In view of the size of the islands and the number of slaves used on these islands, each island is divided into districts with a governor and protector appointed for each district. There are also requirements for written records of births, marriages, and burials of all Negroes. The kind and duration of punishments are set out for public offences. Burke also provides a series of regulations for the life of the slaves on the plantations: their education, their instruction in the catechism of the Church of England or one of the Dissenting churches, their family life, and their housing.

The parts of the *Code* just described are, in the main, impersonal and general. However, when Burke turns to the treatment and the life of an enslaved individual, he becomes quite specific. Musical instruments "according to the fashion of the country" are to be given to slaves; on the islands, young Negroes shall be taught three days a week for four hours; extraordinary abilities are to be encouraged and those who excel are to be sent to London for further education.[66] When such an individual returns to the islands, he is "to be there as a free negro."[67] Other stipulations require that no pregnant woman is obliged to field work for one month before her delivery and for six weeks afterward, and no field negro shall be compelled to work from eleven o'clock on Saturday forenoon until Monday morning. Stable and permanent housing are to be provided to each Negro and shall remain in his possession for his natural life or during his bondage; his other property is also secured under the law.

Given the well-known abuses of the slave trade and the horror of an enslaved individual's life, one can wonder how Burke realistically thought those who had a commercial interest in the trade would implement such a plan. Moreover, given the nature of some of these details, one could charge Burke with paternalism and with a misplaced urge to "civilize" those who already had a civilization of their own. It is useful here to remember Burke's words to Henry Dundas when he gave him a copy of the *Code* twelve years after he wrote it: "If the African trade could be considered with regard to itself only, and as a single object, I should think the utter abolition to be, on the whole more advisable than any scheme of regulation and reform." Burke then refers to his document as an attempt to draw some "collateral good" out of an "incurable evil." The collateral good is found in the strictures meant to keep families together, in the importance given to education in general, and in measures to foster native talents and abilities. In essence, the document is shot through with moral principles as background for practical measures.

Interestingly enough, we find some of the demand for adherence to universal moral principles here that is apparent in Burke's impeachment charges against Warren Hastings, Governor General of India. In the thousands of pages that constitute the documents of Hasting's Impeachment trial, Burke repeatedly speaks against the concept of geographical morality, that spirit of exclusion that justifies departing from ordinary moral codes of conduct when dealing with marginal and vulnerable societies. In 1786 Mary Palmer, Sir Joshua Reynolds' niece, wrote to Burke questioning his motives in trying Hastings for high crimes and misdemeanors as Governor General of India. She told Burke that she had friends in India who charged him with acting from self-interest in prosecuting Hastings. In his reply, Burke assured her that the proofs for his accusations were solid and could be found in the records of Parliament. He continues: "I have no party in this Business, my dear Miss Palmer, but among a set of people who have none of your Lilies and Roses in their faces; but who are the images of the great Pattern as well as you and I. I know what I am doing; whether the white people like it or not."[68] Here, as well as in his *Sketch for a Negro Code*, the voice of Burke the political realist and the voice of Burke the moralist combined. His assertion: "I know what I am doing; whether the white people like it or not" brooks no argument.

PARTICULAR INFLUENCES ON BURKE'S ABOLITIONIST THINKING

Significantly, those closest to him lacked such sensitivity. His kinsman William Burke once commented to Edmund's son Richard that he could not "for the soul of me" feel as Edmund did about "the black primates."[69] Like so many of William's sentiments, he probably did not dare voice this one aloud. And in William Burke we have another piece to the pattern of Burke and abolition.

Burke's cousin William and his younger brother Richard had known slavery in the West Indies from personal experience. In 1759 when William became Secretary and Registrar of the Island of Guadeloupe, both he and Richard went out to the island intending to make their fortunes. Four years later, in 1763, Richard was appointed Collector of Customs in Grenada and lived there from 1763–1765 and again in 1769–1771. We can presume that many of the details in Burke's *Sketch for a Negro Code* came from information supplied by William and Richard. His brother's experiences were particularly pertinent because he owned slaves during his tenure as Collector of Customs.

The whole account of Richard's escapades in the West Indies is a long and complicated one. The significant fact is that in 1770 he illegally purchased a considerable tract of land on the island of St. Vincent, which purchase the Board of Trade later nullified. Even more to the point is a document from Richard addressed to the Lords of the Treasury and charges his successor as Collector of Customs in Grenada, one John Menzies, with taking his property. According to Richard's deposition, this property included "Eleven Negroes all employed in and about the Custom House . . . which Negroes Mr. Burke most truly assured the Board were worth and would have sold for £770 sterling. He had also two Negroes who were coopers and moderately valued at £200."[70] Clearly Richard looked upon his slaves as valuable property from whose sale he would have received significant profit. Did Burke ever question his brother's sentiments? We have no way of knowing. But the story of the Burke's close acquaintance with slavery and slaves does not end with Richard.

In 1774 Mrs. Thrale, Bluestocking friend of Samuel Johnson, visited the Burke's at their countryseat in Beaconsfield. She recorded her impressions of his domestic life in her diary, *Thraliana*: "In 1774 I lived with him and his Lady at Beaconsfield among Dirt, Cobwebs, Pictures and Statues that would not have disgraced the City of Paris itself. . . . That Mrs. Burke drinks as well as her Husband, and that their Black a moor carries Tea about with a cut finger wrapt in Rags, must help to apologize for the Severity with which I have treated so very distinguished a Character."[71] Mrs. Thrale's reference to the "Black a moor," buried in her diatribe against Burke's housekeeping and casual way of life catches our attention. The only other possible reference to such an individual comes from the Duke of Portland, who wrote to Burke in 1788 concerning Dolben's bill for regulating the slave trade. Portland commented: "So you see you cannot be sure of keeping Douglas." Unfortunately, the tale of Burke's black servant stops here. Had Richard brought him back from St. Vincent's, or had Burke met him in Bristol? Moreover, can we assume from Portland's use of the word "keeping," that Burke did not free "Douglas"? We may speculate as to where he came from and the conditions of his servitude in the household, but there are no answers as to the identity of Burke's "Black a moor."

Bristol brings us full circle back to Burke's composition of the *Sketch for a Negro Code* that he wrote in 1780, the year he witnessed the "storm of the election" that he had declined. "I felt a serenity which I never before experienced." Is it a coincidence that in that same year he wrote the *Code*? In a 1976 article, *Edmund Burke's Negro Code*, Robert W. Smith says it is not: "It suggests that [Burke] had been chafing under the obligations to family and constituents and now he was free."[72] By "obligations to family" Smith is referring William's and Richard's investments in the West Indies. He also argues that Burke's defense of the African Company was a reflection of the family situation at the time.

In his book *Moral Capital: Foundations of British Abolitionism* Christopher Brown claims that all of the men and women who became part of the abolitionist movement "did not begin life as abolitionists. . . . Instead, over the course of their lives they became abolitionists. Something in their experience of the world led them into active opposition to slavery."[73] I think this is what happened to Burke—the experiences of his kinsman William and brother Richard, with their acceptance and endorsement of slavery, made the experience of owning and trading in human flesh very real to him. Moreover, we know that Burke's relationship with the servants in his house was an amiable one, and he was in the habit of talking with them about their lives and their experiences. It is very likely that he would have had such conversations with Douglas, if indeed, that is the name of Mrs. Thrale's "Black-a-moor." Finally, Bristol, with its slave ships in the harbor and its merchants insisting on their ways of doing things—a way that clearly rubbed against Burke's own perceptions of what should be done—may have given the final impetus to Burke's thoughts on abolition which resulted in his *Code*. In 1788 he spoke against the trade in Parliamentary debate and a year later, in 1789, sided with Wilberforce. The last record of Burke's official stance against slavery is in April 1791 when he supported immediate abolition over regulation.

FATE OF BURKE'S *CODE* AND JOHNSON

The fate of Burke's *Code* as a document is a mixed one, in that some used it to delay abolition in favor of regulation. When he retired from Parliament in 1794, he entrusted the document to his protégé William Windham. Two years later it appears that others, such as Philip Francis, approached Windham asking for bits and pieces of Burke's *Code* to use in constructing one of their own. Burke told Windham to keep the document intact, "Otherwise the whole will be blown up by every ones running and snatching a piece here and there."[74] After Burke's death in 1797, *Sketch for a Negro Code* became part of his published works and remains so today.

Given their various positions on the subject of slavery and abolition, it is interesting to consider that James Boswell and William Windham were together that evening at Bennet Langton's when Thomas Clarkson spoke. According to Clarkson, the two men supported the abolition movement, but they later withdrew that support. It appears he was mistaken about Windham, for he was one of those abolitionists Boswell attacked in his 1791 poem, "No Abolition of Slavery"; furthermore, Burke entrusted the manuscript of his *Sketch for a Negro Code* to Windham. Most tellingly, several days before he died, Johnson asked Windham to be Barber's "friend, adviser, and protector," asking him to repeat that promise in Barber's presence.[75] Burke and Johnson were astute students of human nature; they would not have trusted Windham in the ways that they did had he been an anti-abolitionist like his friend Boswell.

We know that Samuel Johnson and Edmund Burke had their quiet evenings together when neither "talked for victory." One of those times was in October 1783 after which Johnson wrote to Mrs. Thrale telling her: "Two nights ago Mr. Burke sat with me a long time, he seems much pleased with his journey. We had both seen Stonehenge this summer for the first time."[76] Their talk during that long evening quite likely ranged beyond a discussion of Stonehenge. The Peace of Paris ending the American Revolution had been signed the month before; one suspects they did not discuss that still volatile subject. However, they may have talked about the end of the slave trade and the abolition of slavery—an issue that was very much in the news. It was one topic upon which both of them were in complete agreement.

NOTES

1. Samuel Johnson, *Observations on the Present State of Affairs*, in *The Works of Samuel Johnson* (Oxford: Talboys and Wheeler, 1825), 6:113–23. See also Donald J. Greene, *The Politics of Samuel Johnson* 2nd ed. (Athens: University of Georgia Press: 1900), 154–72.
2. See Michael Bundock, *The Fortunes of Francis Barber: The True Story of the Jamaican Slave Who Became Samuel Johnson's Heir* (New Haven, CT: Yale University Press, 2013).
3. *Life*, 4:401.
4. James Boswell, *Boswell: The Applause of the Jury 1782–1785*, ed. Irma S. Lustig and Frederick A. Pottle (New York: McGraw-Hill, 1981), 348.
5. Michael Lort to Hester Thrale Piozzi, December 31, 1785 (Manchester: John Rylands University Library, English MS 544, no. 5).
6. See *Modern Critical Interpretations: James Boswell's* Life of Samuel Johnson, ed. Harold Bloom (New Haven, CT: Chelsea House Publishers, 1986); Greg Clingham, ed., *New Light on Boswell: Critical and Historical Essays on the Occasion of the Bicentenary of the Life of Johnson*, ed. Greg Clingham (Cambridge: Cambridge University Press, 1991); and *Boswell's Life of Johnson: New Questions, New Answers*, ed. John A. Vance (Athens: University of Georgia Press, 1985).
7. For the complexity of Boswell's voice in *The Life of Johnson*, and the question of the rivalry between Boswell and Johnson, see Anthony W. Lee, *Dead Masters: Mentoring and Intertextuality in Samuel Johnson* (Bethlehem, PA: Lehigh University Press, 2011), 183–98; and John Radner, *Johnson and Boswell: A Biography of Friendship* (New Haven, CT: Yale University Press, 2012).
8. James Basker, "Johnson and Slavery," in *Johnson After Three Centuries: New Light on Texts and Contexts*, ed. Thomas Horrocks and Harold D. Weinbrot (Cambridge, MA: Harvard University Press, 2011), *Harvard Library Bulletin* 20, nos. 3–4 (Fall–Winter 2009): 29–50.

9. John Wedderburn (1729–1803) was a Scottish landowner who made his fortune in the West Indian sugar trade. He was the largest landowner in Jamaica.
10. Yale *Works*, 10:454.
11. Yale *Works*, 3:212–14. See also James Boswell, *Boswell in Extremes: 1776–1778*, ed. Charles M. Weis and Frederick A. Pottle (New York: McGraw-Hill, 1970), 182–84.
12. Basker, "Johnson and Slavery," 35.
13. Bundock, *Fortunes of Francis Barber*, 142.
14. Boswell, *Boswell in Extremes*, 183n7.
15. Gordon Turnbull, "Boswell and Sympathy: The Trial and Execution of John Reid," in *New Light on Boswell: Critical and Historical Essays on the Occasion of the Bicentenary of the Life of Johnson*, ed. Greg Clingham (Cambridge: Cambridge University Press, 1991), 104–15.
16. See Frank Brady, *James Boswell: The Later Years, 1769–1795* (New York: McGraw-Hill, 1984), 464–66.
17. Bundock, *Fortunes of Francis Barber*, 109.
18. Thomas Clarkson, *The History of the Rise, Progress, and Accomplishment of the Abolition of the Slave-Trade, by the British Parliament* (New York, 1836), 1:193–94.
19. James Boswell, *No Abolition of Slavery or the Universal Empire of Love, A Poem* (London, 1791), 5, http://www.gutenberg.org/ebooks/20360.
20. Ibid., 8, lines 25–26.
21. Ibid., 17, lines 175–78.
22. Ibid., 21, line 248.
23. Ibid., n.p., n4.
24. Ibid.
25. Ibid., 24, line 296–97.
26. William Windham (1750–1810) was MP and Secretary at War. He was a protégé of Edmund Burke.
27. Philip Metcalfe (1733–1818) MP for Horsham and wealthy brewer called John Courtney, James Boswell, Edmond Malone, and Sir Joshua Reynolds "the Gang."
28. Brady writes that Courtney "obligingly supplied some lines himself" (*James Boswell: The Later Years*, 422). John Courtney (1738–1816) was an Irish MP known for his political skill and caustic wit. He became one of Boswell's closest friends.
29. Boswell, *No Abolition of Slavery*, 12, line 99–108.
30. James Boswell, *Boswell for the Defence, 1769–1774*, ed. William K. Wimsatt Jr. and Frederick A. Pottle (London: William Heinemann, 1959), 264. If numbers mean anything, according to his journals, Boswell identifies with Burke more than with anyone else (*Boswell in Extremes*, 267–72).
31. See Elizabeth Lambert, "Boswell's Burke: The Literary Consequences of Ambivalence," in *The Age of Johnson: A Scholarly Annual* 9 (1998): 201–35.
32. See Elizabeth Lambert, "Johnson on Friendship: The Example of Burke," in *Johnson After Two Hundred Years*, ed. Paul J. Korshin (Philadelphia: University of Pennsylvania Press, 1986), 111–23.
33. Edmund Burke, *The Correspondence of Edmund Burke*, ed. Thomas W. Copeland et al. (Cambridge: Cambridge University Press, 1958–78), 4:444.
34. Frederick A. Pottle, *The Literary Career of James Boswell, Esq: Being the Bibliographical Materials for A Life of Boswell* (Oxford: Clarendon Press, 1929), 108.
35. Boswell, *Applause of the Jury*, 177.
36. Ibid., 204–5.
37. Dr. William Robertson (1721–1793) was a Church of Scotland minister and historian. His *History of Scotland* was published in 1758.

38. James Boswell, *Journal of a Tour to the Hebrides with Samuel Johnson, LL.D. 1773*, ed. Frederick A. Pottle and Charles H. Bennett, 2nd ed. (New York: McGraw-Hill, 1961), 19. See also 409, "Corrections," 19n15, where Pottle notes R. W. Chapman's discussion of the metaphor "stopped by a drove of oxen" and the ways "Boswell criss-crossed remarks which Johnson made on two different occasions." See Chapman, "Mrs. Piozzi's Omissions from Johnson's Letters to Thrales." *Review of English Studies* 22, no. 85 (1946): 17–28.
39. Ibid., 172.
40. Ibid., 19.
41. James Boswell, *London Journal: 1762–63*, ed. Frederick A Pottle (New York: McGraw-Hill, 1950), 326.
42. James Boswell, *Boswell: The Ominous Years: 1774–1776*, ed. Charles Ryskamp and Frederick A. Pottle (New York: McGraw-Hill, 1963), 203.
43. Boswell, *No Abolition of Slavery*, 12, line 99–108; emphasis mine.
44. James Boswell, *Boswell: The English Experiment 1785–1789*, ed. Irma S. Lustig, Frederick A. Pottle (New York: McGraw-Hill, 1986), 71.
45. James Boswell, *The Correspondence of James Boswell With David Garrick, Edmund Burke, and Edmond Malone*, ed. James M. Osborn and Peter S. Baker (London: Heinemann, 1986), 329–30.
46. Boswell, *Tour to the Hebrides*, 19n14.
47. Boswell, *Correspondence with . . . Burke*, 149.
48. Ibid., 161–62.
49. Edmund Burke, *The Early Life, Correspondence and Writings of the Rt. Hon. Edmund Burke*, ed. Arthur Purefoy Irwin Samuels and Arthur Warren Samuels (Cambridge: Cambridge University Press, 1923), 17.
50. Moreover, by the time Burke was a noted figure in political circles, some of his cousins in Ireland were running afoul of the law. One was a member of the outlawed group the so-called "Whiteboys," an illegal agrarian protest movement, and another, in defiance of the penal laws outlawing religious orders and education, formed a congregation of nuns to teach the poor children of Cork.
51. Julie Flavell, *When London Was Capital of America* (New Haven, CT: Yale University Press, 2010), 34.
52. Burke, *Correspondence*, 1:123.
53. Ibid.
54. Ibid., 3:345–46, 4:60–62.
55. Robert W. Smith, "Edmund Burke's Negro Code," *History Today* 26, no. 11 (November 1976): 716.
56. Edmund Burke, *The Writings and Speeches of Edmund Burke*, gen. ed. Paul Langford and William Todd (Oxford: Oxford University Press, 1981–2016), 3:122–23.
57. Ibid., 3:68–69.
58. Burke, *Correspondence*, 3:289.
59. Lady Rockingham (bap. 1735, d. 1804) [née Mary Bright] was active in her husband's career. When Lord Rockingham died suddenly in 1782, Burke wrote to her: "Your names indeed ought to go down together; for it is no mean part you have had in the great services which that great and good man has done to his country" (Burke, *Correspondence*, 5:46).
60. Burke, *Correspondence*, 4:300.
61. Ibid., 7:123.
62. Burke, *Writings and Speeches*, 3:562–81.
63. Ibid., 3:564.
64. Ibid., 3:568.

65. Ibid., 3:571.
66. Ibid.
67. Ibid., 3:577.
68. Burke, *Correspondence*, 5:255.
69. Burke, *Writings and Speeches*, 5:11.
70. Northamptonshire Archives, Northamptonshire County Council Record Office, Fitzwilliam Milton Estates, Northampton, United Kimgdom, A.v.48.
71. Hester Lynch Piozzi [Mrs. Thrale], *Thraliana: The Diary of Mrs. Hester Lynch Thrale (Later Mrs. Piozzi), 1776–1809*, ed. Katherine C. Balderston, 2nd ed. (Oxford: Oxford University Press, 1951), 1:475.
72. R. W. Smith, "Edmund Burke's Negro Code," 717.
73. Christopher Leslie Brown, *Moral Capital: Foundations of British Abolitionism* (Chapel Hill: University of Carolina Press, 2006), 25.
74. Burke, *Correspondence*, 8:451.
75. Bundock, *Fortunes of Francis Barber*, 167.
76. *Letters*, 4:221.

9

SAMUEL JOHNSON AND ANNA SEWARD

Solitude and Sensibility

CLAUDIA THOMAS KAIROFF

WHY DID SAMUEL JOHNSON LOOK at a mountain range and see "a dreariness of solitude," while Anna Seward was enraptured by a similar vista? Any attempt to define the contrasting opinions of Seward and Johnson must begin with the admission that the two writers were, in many ways, quite similar in beliefs and personality despite their different generations and political philosophies. Both extended the literary fame of their birthplace, Lichfield, and were outspoken Anglicans as well as patriotic Britons. Both enjoyed surrounding themselves with friends and engaging in sometimes vehement exchanges of opinion. Both admired past British writers including Shakespeare, Dryden, Milton, and Pope. Both devoured current publications and, besides literature, were intrigued by current science. Both enjoyed cultural influence during their lifetimes. Writers since Seward's first biographer have pondered her dislike of Johnson, her senior by thirty-three years, who dined at her parents' home whenever he visited Lichfield. Was this dislike based on snobbery due to his humble origins, since her mother's father had been Johnson's boyhood teacher? Was it based upon failure to appreciate his literary superiority? In fact, there were many reasons for Seward's reaction to Johnson. Among these were her belief that Johnson's robust criticism of English poets, living and dead, tarnished their reputations. Another was her resentment of Johnson's near-canonization by admirers shortly after his death, despite wide knowledge of his character flaws. Finally, she resented James Boswell's proprietary, and in her view, sycophantic, control of his mentor's biographic record. The latter's idealization of Johnson led Seward to insist on a counter-record of Johnson's apparent envy and hypocrisy.[1] While all of these provoked Seward's antipathy, a chief underlying cause was their contrasting views of sensibility, manifested in their respective correspondence, literature, and criticism. Johnson's and Seward's representations of solitude, prominent in their responses to landscape, exemplify both their temperamental differences and the generational chasm between their estimates of sentiment.

Samuel Johnson was born in 1709, during what is still called the "Augustan Age of British literature," due to its fascination with Roman precedents, some of which were construed as flattering and others as admonitory.[2] Dryden had recently died, Swift was prominent, and Pope would soon dominate the cultural landscape. While in his maturity sometimes critical of these writers and their contemporaries, Johnson had been deeply influenced by them in his youth. He valued precise diction and conservative wit. From Pope—himself informed by the new science—he learned that the purpose of studying the natural world was to "[look] thro' Nature, up to Nature's God."[3] Although Johnson later mocked Pope's *Essay on Man* ("Never were penury of knowledge and vulgarity of sentiment so happily disguised"), his references to landscape often resemble the Royal Society's antiquarianism and its propensity to read nature as the record of its creator, the purpose defined in Pope's philosophical poem.[4] Seward, on the other hand, was born in 1742, during what some scholars describe as the Age of Sensibility.[5] Johnson had recently published *London* (1738), the Juvenalian imitation through which he gained the attention of the Opposition literary establishment led by Pope, and which extended the Augustan tradition of Swift and Pope. But Seward was most influenced in her youth by poets Akenside, Gray, Collins, the Wartons, and Macpherson, and by the English translation of Jean-Jacques Rousseau's *Julie; ou, la nouvelle Heloïse* (1761). Each of these writers exemplified the prevailing theory that sense perceptions were carried by the nerves to the brain, and that those whose sensations were most swift, pronounced, and sympathetic were superior.

Johnson and Seward, then, lived in the same century, and their lifetimes overlapped, but their respective births into distinct generations made different perceptions and values inevitable. Johnson valued "wit," in the sense of cleverness, intelligence, and apt expression. In his scathing remarks on Pope's *Essay on Man*, for example, he complained that the poem contained "more harshness of diction, more thoughts imperfectly expressed, more levity without elegance, and more heaviness without strength, than will easily be found in all his other works" (Yale *Works*, 23:1221). In Johnson's opinion, Pope's poem failed to exhibit "wit" at every level and was consequently his worst composition. Seward, on the other hand, valued sentiment, declaring herself an "enthusiast"—a word still reserved for dangerous fanatics during Johnson's youth. Louisa, eponymous heroine of Seward's verse novel, exemplifies the link between sense perception, most often visual, and emotional response. As she surveys her garden while recollecting her fiancé's betrayal, Louisa exclaims,

> O ye known objects!—how ye strike [m]y heart!
> And keen regrets, with keener force, impart!
> Slow, thro' the faded Grove, past Pleasures glide,
> Or sadly linger by the fountain's side.[6]

Louisa has only to view her surroundings to be stricken, as by a blow, with anguish caused by Eugenio's desertion. Present objects instantly recall memories, or rather, vividly recreate experiences, simultaneously accompanied by emotions as fresh as when they first occurred, if not "keener." Her capacity for such instant and vivid response distinguish Louisa as the heroine of sensibility *par excellence*. Similar expressions of what Wordsworth would later call "emotion recollected in tranquility"—which, he felt, were the essence of poetry—occur often in Seward's writings, especially when she describes lone encounters with landscape. Her emotional response to geographical features marks Seward as a poet of sensibility, while the rarity of such evocations in Johnson's writings marks him as the product of a different era.

JOHNSON AND THE LONELINESS OF SOLITUDE

Any generalization about Johnson must be made with great caution. Because, as Boswell described his friend's conversations, Johnson often "talked for victory" rather than to express his sincere beliefs, evidence can easily be found to support contradictory impressions of his opinions.[7] Seward refused to countenance Johnson's competitive argumentation, accusing him of insincerity, for which she was in turn reproached by Boswell for failing to appreciate his "wonderful dexterity in retort."[8] Whatever his motives, Johnson's verbal dexterity resulted in a potentially confusing record of his beliefs. In addition to his recorded conversations, Johnson's personality was often conveyed as interpreted by acquaintances. Boswell, for example, recalled Johnson responding emotionally to a piece of literature: "Such was his sensibility, and so much was he affected by pathetick poetry, that, when he was reading Dr. Beattie's 'Hermit' . . . it brought tears into his eyes" (*Life*, 4:180). Boswell, a near-contemporary of Seward's, perhaps wished his hero to exemplify a cherished trait.[9] Johnson's letters suggest he distrusted apparently spontaneous displays of emotion. Writing to Hester Thrale in November 1779, for example, he admonished, "You shall not hide Mrs. Byron from me, for if she be a feeler, I can bear a feeler as well as You, and hope that in tenderness for what she feels from nature, I am able to forgive or neglect what she feels by affectation."[10] A week later, he repeated his impression: "Poor Mrs. Byron is a feeler" (*Letters*, 3:216).

Although he disparaged Henry Fielding, Johnson shared with the novelist and many other contemporaries the suspicion that emotional displays could be, and often were, feigned for selfish purposes. This skepticism was not, of course, confined to their generation. Among older writers, Daniel Defoe had portrayed Moll Flanders as a woman apt to deceive or manipulate with tears.[11] Hester Thrale and Frances Burney also distrusted people whose tears flowed too readily. Burney recorded an incident at Streatham in June 1779 where a group of visitors mocked the young Greek scholar Sophia Streatfeild for her consciousness of "how beautiful she looked in Tears."[12] On a second occasion, Mrs. Thrale entreated Streatfeild until "two Crystal Tears came into the soft Eyes of the S. S.,—& rolled gently down her Cheeks! . . . . She offered not to conceal, or dissipate them,—on the contrary, she really *contrived* to have them seen by every body."[13] Such incidents convinced Burney and Thrale, like Fielding and Johnson, that ulterior motives such as vanity often lurked behind emotional responses. Seward had no such misgivings. In a letter of 1787 to George Hardinge, she described her response while reading a mutual friend's letter in terms that define sensibility: "With the *heart*, sweetly shining out in his last epistle, I am so intemperately charmed, that his idea often fills my eyes with those delicious tears, which, beneath the contemplation of virtues . . . instantaneous spring to the lids, without falling from them; tears, which are at once prompted, and exhaled by pleasurable sensations."[14] While Burney cynically mocked an acquaintance's ready tears, implying they rose from the desire to create an attractive appearance, Seward conveys without irony her customary tears while simply thinking about a person's goodheartedness. Her self-characterization as "intemperately charmed" implies that she was swept away by enthusiasm—typical of Seward—but also her capacity to be enraptured by benevolence. Seward does not present her reaction for congratulation, but as a simple account of her response. Her description would most likely place her among Johnson's mistrusted "feelers."

SEWARD AND THE SUBLIMITY OF NATURAL SOLITUDE

A final observation before comparing Johnson's and Seward's responses to solitude is that neither of them coveted, or even liked, being alone. In a literal sense, genteel people were rarely alone in the eighteenth century. Both Johnson and Seward would have had at least one servant attending them. Johnson usually had Frank Barber on hand, while Seward described her daily walks, supported by one of her maids. Johnson was married from 1735 until his wife's death in 1752, and afterward housed several tenants, such as Robert Levett and Anna Williams.[15] Seward managed her father's household until and after his death in 1790, and late in her life engaged a young unmarried woman, Elizabeth Fern, as her companion.[16] But in addition to relations and dependents, both Johnson and Seward relished companionship. Johnson's aversion to solitude and concomitant love of society is a principal theme in this volume. Johnson's definition of "solitary" in his *Dictionary* is notably pejorative. "Solitary," as an adjective, denotes "1. Living alone; not having company. 2. Retired; remote from company. 3. Gloomy; dismal. 4. Single." The third and only non-neutral meaning suggests Johnson's opinion of the state represented by the other three. Defined as a noun, a "Solitary" is "One that lives alone; an hermit" (*Dictionary*, s.v. "solitary"). Johnson's definition of "solitude" confirms his distaste: "1. Lonely life; state of being alone. 2. A lonely place; a desert." To illustrate this meaning, Johnson includes Bacon's quotation, in his essay on friendship, of the remark "whosoever is delighted with *solitude*, is either a wild beast or a god," and Dryden's observation that "Such only can enjoy the country who are capable of thinking when they are there: Then they are prepared for *solitude*, and in that *solitude* is prepared for them" (*Dictionary*, s.v. "solitary"). To borrow a phrase from the sage Imlac in *Rasselas*, solitude, for Johnson, was "a state in which much is to be endured, and little to be enjoyed."[17]

Seward wrote several poems after visits by, or to the homes of, friends and relatives. These compositions invariably contrast her enjoyment of companionship and hospitality with her anticipated loneliness. The "Epistle to William Hayley, Esq." commemorates the latter's return home after a visit to Lichfield in 1781: "Silence and vacancy around me rise! / Wrap my chill'd spirit in their icy vest, / And chace each dear illusion from my breast."[18] Disappointed when his visit is cut short, Seward confesses that even her beloved Lichfield landscape has no charm for her, bereft of Hayley's companionship. With only her aged father for company, when "the clamorous bell's unwelcome peal / Calls me, reluctant, to the cheerless meal . . . [I] turn my head, and hide the starting tear."[19] Preparing to leave Hayley's estate after a visit the following year, Seward anticipates her return home: "Thy bowers, Lichfield, lovely scenes afford, / But ah! What keen regrets must wake my sighs, / To miss the pleasures of the Haylean board!"[20] Seward's verse often recalls places associated with departed companions. En route to a Sheffield music-meeting in 1788, for example, she detoured to Eyam, where her father was rector during her early childhood. Comparing the current "Scenes paternal" with those past, she finds a "deserted Rectory" and church with "vacant Pulpit," flooding her eyes with tears as she compares her father's present feeble state to his decayed parish (Seward, "Elegiac Ode, written during a Journey through Derbyshire").[21] In a late poem to a long-absent friend, Seward recalls three visits with her and her brother. She longs to see them again but knows a reunion is unlikely:

> Yet, friends esteem'd, to memory oft ye rise,
> Bright from the past, as refluent pleasures cheer,
> Though ye no more may glad these mortal eyes.[22]

Like Johnson, Seward was happiest with companions; her descriptions of familiar scenes almost always express pleasure in shared activities or regret for those missing.

Despite these resemblances, however, Johnson and Seward held contrasting opinions of solitude's value. Their respective evocations of solitude differ most when they describe landscapes. As in his definition, Johnson associates solitude with deserted places best suited for hermits or beasts. Seward overlays current landscapes with bittersweet memories. These habits lead to contrasting descriptions, once again reflecting temperamental and generational differences between the two writers. Johnson's depictions of landscapes are exemplified in *A Journey to the Western Islands of Scotland*, published after his tour with Boswell in 1773. In her introduction to the Yale edition of the *Journey*, Mary Lascelles notes Johnson's awareness of predecessors Martin Martin and George Pennant, whose accounts were published in 1703 and 1771, respectively, and also mentions Defoe, whose *Tour Thro' the Whole Island of Great Britain* (1724) Johnson likely would have known. Lascelles observes Johnson's and Pennant's opposed political perspectives, which would of course apply as well to Johnson's and Defoe's.[23] But beyond these differences, there is a strong congruence among all four authors' purposes for writing, which influences how and where they direct their readers' attention. Martin, for example, provides measurements of the western islands.[24] He describes the climate, soil, crops, and products of each and the situation of its harbors. After these categories, he describes an island's buildings, such as castles and forts, which he measures. He narrates ancient legends and the tales associated with various ruins. His descriptions of the islands' inhabitants might today be described as anthropological or sociological. Since Johnson told Boswell that reading Martin had piqued his curiosity as a boy (Yale *Works*, 9:xiv), Martin's descriptions of the western islands as a kind of *terra incognita*, almost as foreign to the English as Tahiti, probably influenced Johnson's later attitude toward Scotland as well as his conception of the role of the travel writer.

Defoe shared with Martin the assumption that Scotland was nearly unknown to English readers. His *Tour* approached Scotland with the aim of introducing to the British the northern part of their now united kingdom. Defoe acknowledged the current state of Scotland as one too frequently marred by neglect and poverty, but he emphasized at every opportunity its rich potential. As in his accounts of all the English counties, he overlooked what we would consider glorious landscapes, hurrying toward villages, towns, and cities, which he valued according to their population and productivity. Entering Scottish territory, for example, he describes vividly the hilly country's bone-chilling wind.[25] He deplores having to traverse "a most frightful Moor for Travellers . . . upon which, for about eight Miles, you see hardly a Hedge, or a Tree . . . nor do you meet with but one House in all the Way."[26] Readers sense Defoe's palpable relief upon "Having pass'd this Desart, which indeed, makes a Stranger think Scotland a terrible Place."[27] Defoe's avowed purpose, to promote Scotland, leads him to assess many landscape features in terms of their potential commercial development. In keeping with his practical interest, perhaps, is his concern to explain the facts behind many Scottish legends, particularly regarding their fabled clan warfare, from a modern Whig perspective. Since Defoe lacked the entrée into the noble families and homes he describes, he certainly left an opening for Johnson to exploit from his competing political point of view. But both writers shared a lack of interest in picturesque landscapes for their own sake, preferring comfortable accommodations and the pursuit of the facts behind myths—whether Bonnie Dundee's exploits, in Defoe's case, or the writings of Ossian, in Johnson's.

Closer to Johnson's venture was Thomas Pennant's *A Tour in Scotland*, which, as Lascelles observes, shares Defoe's Whig point of view. Visiting in 1771, Pennant is pleased by recent cultivation along the border, but still finds remnants of the "old negligence left amidst the recent improvements, which look like the works of a new colony in a wretched impoverished country."[28] Soon afterward, the landscape lapses back into a "black joyless heathy moor."[29] Johnson disputes Pennant's account in some places, emphasizing the advantage given him and Boswell by the hospitality of Donald Maclean, heir to the Laird of Col, who conducted them through various islands (Yale *Works*, 9:128). But he shared the interest of Pennant and all his predecessors in measuring and describing, in estimating populations and describing commercial and agricultural production.

Johnson rarely describes a landscape for its own sake and does not find the desolate islands appealing. Reflecting on the numbers of tacksmen (large leaseholders) being driven to emigrate by high rents, he remarks: "He who lives in Col, and finds himself condemned to solitary meals, and incommunicable reflection, will find the usefulness of that middle order of tacksmen. . . . Without intelligence man is not social, he is only gregarious; and little intelligence will there be, where all are constrained to daily labour, and every mind must wait upon the hand" (Yale *Works*, 9:136). Johnson deplores the loss of a middle rank between lairds and laborers, especially because the rulers will be left alone on their barren islands. Departing from Col, Johnson travels across Mull en route to Iona, riding "many hours through a tract, black and barren," enduring "this gloom of desolation" while contemplating "whether something may not be done to give nature a more cheerful face, and whether those hills and moors that afford heath cannot with a little care and labour bear something better?" (Yale *Works*, 9:139). Trees might be planted, but the profit of such an effort would not help the present generation of inhabitants. Wishing for a practical solution to the surrounding poverty, Johnson finds the landscape frustrating: "We were always struggling with some obstruction or other, and our vexation was not balanced by any gratification of the eye or mind. We were now long enough acquainted with hills and heath to have lost the emotion that they once raised, whether pleasant or painful, and had our minds employed only on our own fatigue" (Yale *Works*, 9:140).

Johnson's reaction to the Scottish landscape consistently reflects his dislike of solitude. Before embarking for the islands, he describes the Highlands as "a dreariness of solitude," due principally to its lack of agriculture (Yale *Works*, 9:35). Curiously, however, Johnson here finds the mountains' loneliness inspiring: "I sat down on a bank, such as a writer of romance might have delighted to feign. I had indeed no trees to whisper over my head, but a clear rivulet streamed at my feet. The day was calm, the air soft, and all was rudeness, silence, and solitude. Before me, on either side, were high hills, which by hindering the eye from ranging, forced the mind to find entertainment for itself. Whether I spent the hour well I know not; for here I first conceived the thought of this narrative" (Yale *Works*, 9:40). Johnson's solitude drives him to occupy his mind, leading to a practical and perhaps profitable outcome. Much like his later wish for a profitable solution to the barrenness of Mull, Johnson redeems this "desert" by imagining a successful commercial outcome for his travels. The author of *Rambler* 4, which questions how romance fictions were ever credited, Johnson did not compliment his surroundings when he compared them with a romance writer's feigned landscape. A mountain stream is not a place where one might expect to encounter adventure or even pastoral lovers, but merely the site of "rudeness, silence, and solitude." The eye is not captivated by the surrounding mountains but feels imprisoned within their narrow bounds. Johnson explains that this was not the kind of place to induce "a placid indulgence of voluntary delusions, a secure expansion of the fancy, or a cool concentration of the mental powers." Instead, he is reminded of "want, misery, and danger" and the terrors awaiting unprepared travelers. "Whoever had been in the place where I then sat, unprovided with provisions and ignorant of the country, might . . . have . . . perished with hardship" (Yale *Works*, 9:41).

The thought of privation, not the inspiration of an unspoiled pastoral scene, leads Johnson to envision a potentially lucrative outcome for his Scottish adventure.

Besides such practical observations, Johnson's *Journey* records at least one deeply emotional reaction to his surroundings. J. D. Fleeman, David Fairer, and Anthony W. Lee have all discussed the powerful episode in which Johnson visits Iona as epitomizing an important quest for glimpses of eternal life and his devotion to language, and as what Lee calls the "Johnsonian sublime."[30] During their tour, Johnson and Boswell's acquaintance with young Col begins when Maclean discovers their desire to visit Iona, also called "Icolmkill," site of an important medieval monastery that had preserved learning and promoted Scottish Christianity. Arriving with Col on the island, Johnson experiences a sensation of wonder comparable to descriptions of encounters with the sublime: "To abstract the mind from all local emotion would be impossible, if it were endeavoured, and would be foolish, if it were possible. Whatever withdraws us from the power of our senses; whatever makes the past, the distant, or the future predominate over the present, advances us in the dignity of thinking beings. Far from me and from my friends, be such frigid philosophy as may conduct us indifferent and unmoved over any ground which has been dignified by wisdom, bravery, or virtue" (Yale *Works*, 9:148). Johnson confesses himself swept up in a rush of feelings inspired by consciousness of Iona's significance. This lonely island, over a millennium before, brought "savage clans and roving barbarians . . . the benefits of knowledge, and the blessings of religion" (Yale *Works*, 9:148). For a man to whom Christianity and knowledge were of paramount importance, Iona induces irresistible sensations. Johnson's emotions derive from consciousness of the island's past as a great monastic center, creating a state in which he is "withdraw[n] from the power of [his] senses," that is, from the perception of his present surroundings, and rapt in contemplation of the place as it once was: a center of religion and learning rising, improbably, amid these inhospitable islands.

Others might define the sensation of being "withdraw[n] from the power of his senses" as one of sensibility, the spontaneous response to an encounter with the sublime. Boswell and Seward both quoted this passage as their favorite in the *Journey*.[31] It is significant, however, that Johnson's feelings are not aroused by the island as it is—by the barren, windswept landscape dotted with ruins—but by contemplation of what it has been; by what is no longer there. Johnson's few admissions of sensibility are usually related to piety. Pope looked through nature in order to discern nature's God; Johnson looked beyond Iona's ruins and glimpsed its inspired heritage. Predictably, perhaps, the rest of Johnson's visit to Iona is far more mundane. He describes the travelers' accommodation by the island's friendly but rustic headman and gives a detailed account of the various monastic ruins. His chief impression is ironic: in this place, "once the metropolis of learning and piety," there is no church or school; the local people are illiterate (Yale *Works*, 9:152). The visit to Iona, occurring near the end of his journey and perhaps its emotional climax, could have been among the examples in Johnson's *The Vanity of Human Wishes*. The place reminds him that even this most pious and inspired human endeavor was doomed to end in oblivion. Such a characteristic reflection does not extricate Johnson from the tradition of travel narratives he inherited. Like Martin, Defoe, Pennant, and other travel writers mentioned by Lascelles in her notes to the Yale *Works*, Johnson is eager to report facts to his readers, to replace myths with accurate history and vague descriptions with solid information. But he also follows his predecessors in conveying his information for a purpose, whether, like Defoe, encouraging British investment in Scottish commerce and agriculture, or like Pennant, refuting Jacobite legends. Johnson's *Journey* supports his philosophical vision of ceaseless human endeavors toward improvement; efforts that invariably conclude in ruins such as he discovers at Iona.

However, Johnson's intimations of human vanity are subtle; his *Journey* chiefly supports his belief in travel's practical usefulness. "If the passenger visits better countries, he may learn to improve his own, and if fortune carries him to worse, he may learn to enjoy it" (Yale *Works*, 9:138). This apothegm, uttered on the particularly uncomfortable island of Mull, echoes Johnson's own earlier discourse on travel writing in *Idler* 97 (February 23, 1760). There, Johnson had disparaged travelers who describe landscape features but not local history and customs. Such are writers who travel through "savage countries," somewhat as he describes the Highlands and islands of Scotland, and "range through solitude and desolation; who pass a desert, and tell that it is sandy; who cross a valley, and find that it is green."[32] Johnson abhors such pointless description. For him, "the great object of remark is human life." If a writer describes nothing but empty landscapes, or even urban buildings and art, his or her writing is futile. "He only is a useful traveler who brings home something by which his country may be benefited; who procures some supply of want or some mitigation of evil, which may enable his readers to compare their condition with that of others, to improve it whenever it is worse, and whenever it is better to enjoy it" (Yale *Works*, 2:300). For Johnson, a solitary encounter with natural solitude was by this definition worthless. As we have seen, Johnson derived a practical benefit from his personal experience by a stream in the Highlands; he conceived the publication that justified his adventure by conveying what he learned about Scotland. His mystical experience on Iona was induced by thoughts of the past rather than by the ruins before him which, in any case, would have been difficult to discern due to the lateness of his party's arrival on the island. For Johnson, the opportunity to inculcate piety was as valuable a contribution as was the description of an effective school for the deaf—knowledge which might benefit his country—with which he ends his narrative.

Johnson's and Seward's differing responses to natural solitude illustrate what Susan Lamb has discussed as a shift in touristic practices during their lifetimes: "The sentimental and the picturesque modes of tourism that developed after midcentury treated the site, whether human or natural, as in some sense artificial, as a picture, and suppressed the shaping forces of economic and political conditions and history."[33] Johnson, we have seen, represented a tradition that was precisely interested in economic and political conditions, and in history. Seward expressed little interest in economics unless, as at Eyam and Coalbrookdale, industry has ravaged a once beautiful landscape. Hers was the generation taught by Addison and Burke to relish the sublime, and by Rousseau to seek it in rugged, forbidding landscapes.[34] Thomson's *The Seasons* (1726–1730) taught readers to derive moral, philosophical, and political reflections from attentive rambles, while poems like Gray's *The Bard* (1757) associated sublime scenery with lofty declamations.

During Johnson's last months, while sharing with correspondents her impressions of his final visit to Lichfield, Seward was also devouring the Reverand T. S. Whalley's epistolary descriptions of his tour, from 1784 to 1786, through Switzerland, France, and Italy. She copied passages into letters to friends such as the poets William Hayley and Helen Maria Williams, savoring in turn the excerpts from Whalley's letters they shared with her. Neither Whalley, Seward, nor their correspondents expressed interest in the commercial or political aspects of his tour. Instead, they perfectly illustrate Lamb's comment about the mid-century turn to the picturesque and the literary, as a result of which, for example, "Rousseau and his works became integral to tourism around Geneva."[35] Seward indeed thanked Whalley for his "*living* descriptions of the Alpine scenery" and sites such as Vevay and Clarens associated with *Julie*.[36] Even more intriguing to Seward were Whalley's descriptions of the Fountain of Vaucluse, the laurel-shaded site where Petrarch mourned his unrequited love. She quoted Whalley's admission that "While I sat and leaned on a rock, what a soft melancholy did the striking scene of tender poetic consecration breathe over my soul!"—even though the laurels have disappeared and "The scenery is in reality that of bare and broken rocks."[37]

It is not hard to imagine what Johnson would have said of the spectacle of a man sitting among barren rocks but rapt in pleasurable melancholy due to their association with a legendary infatuation. Throughout her life, though, Seward sought precisely the kinds of scenery Johnson either shunned or considered how to cultivate. Her comments often illustrate Lamb's observation that before midcentury, travelers learned to appreciate landscapes and other sites by immersing themselves in the cultures they visited; after mid-century, travelers were encouraged to admire landscapes in visual terms that excluded consideration of "human content." By late century, they were "reading" sites including "the human in aesthetic terms or for its bearing on the self."[38] Seward's letters frequently record her devotion to natural vistas composed, through description, into pictures. She boasted to her friend Sophia Weston, on September 6, 1783, of her courage during a visit to Eyam with her father, when she explored "the heights of those near mountains, which high as it stands itself, yet towers above our village, and shew us from their summits, beyond the lesser hills, the rich vale of Chastsworth [sic], and immediately look upon the more romantic beauties of Stoke."[39] She especially admires "a steep, narrow, romantic, and grassy dell . . . that scene where the awful and terrible Graces only dwell;—though the barren rocks and desert cliffs, their residence, are picturesque and grand."[40] Of recent industrial rock quarrying, she notes only that it makes the scene even more rugged; the Peak District is still a "sublime country."[41] In her determination to compose her native scenery into a landscape, Seward deplores but then looks past the ugly signs of human intervention, and even past the magnificent Chatsworth estate, to the naturally "barren rocks and desert cliffs" that make it the dwelling of poetic Graces.

Seward's letters often sound as if she were making notes before painting a scene. Unlike Johnson, who found that surrounding mountains, "by hindering the eye from ranging, forced the mind to find entertainment for itself," Seward rejoiced in such vistas. "Are you not fond of the bounded horizon of a mountainous country," she asked Weston, "where the situation, whether high or low, looks up to grand elevations in several points of view?"[42] She teased correspondents who regaled her with particularly luscious descriptions by calling them "Claude [Lorrain]" or "Salvatore [Rosa]," names indicative of her models for scenic description both picturesque and sublime. Like Johnson, Seward was rarely alone amid such places. During the visit to Eyam in 1783, for example, she was too constrained by social obligations "to permit the wish of that sequestration dear to me in scenes like those, silent, vast, and awful."[43] Also like Johnson, she was capable of abstracting herself from her entourage and forming reflections that in turn reinforced her pleasure in literature and the visual arts. Writing of Eyam to Christopher Smith in April 1792, Seward reflected that "The first scenic objects that met my infant glance, and impressed me with their lonely and romantic grandeur, were the mountains, and rocks, and the vales of Derbyshire . . . poetic descriptions and penciled resemblances please me best when they take the Salvatorial style. This early acquired predilection steeps my eyes in the dews of pensive transport, when they stray over the pages of Ossian."[44] Seward's explanation leaves it unclear whether she loves Ossian because its scenic descriptions remind her of Derbyshire, or because they remind her of Salvatore Rosa's depictions of mountainous scenery. For Seward, as for many in her generation, literal, literary, and painted sites each enhanced the viewer's or reader's experience of the others, and each piqued the imagination. By contrast, during his Scottish journey Johnson had reminded Hester Thrale that "The use of traveling is to regulate imagination by reality," and that although he was no longer able to climb steep hills, he was content to know "that by a Scrambling up a rock, I shall only see other rocks, and a wider circle of barren desolation."[45]

Johnson's letters, even more than his published memoir, narrate a disillusioned review of the rigors, alternating with periods of boredom, incident to his Scottish journey. Seward, on the other hand, longed to encounter the sublime, even when it required a hike. While visiting the Whalley's hilltop estate in 1791, she described her daily regimen: "I climb, by seven o'clock in a morning, the highest terrace, and 'drink the spirit of the mountain gale,' which seems to invigorate my whole frame."[46] In a letter to John Saville, she narrated an astonishing experience at Scarborough on July 28, 1793, in which she risked physical danger to experience the fury of an ocean storm. At eight in the evening, she "saw the waves of a sublimely agitated sea dashing and bounding up the sides of the fort" situated on a nearby promontory, site of the local mineral springs. Told it was possible to view the storm from the fort, Seward determined "to taste, amidst the incumbent gloom of a very lowering night, a scene congenial to my taste for the terrible graces." Unsurprisingly, nobody in her party wished to accompany her, so she requisitioned her friend Court Dewes's servant for the adventure, walking along the beach while "the vast curve of those fierce waves, that burst down with a deafening roar, scarce three yards from me, sufficiently gratified my rage for the terrific." Clambering up to the fort despite the tide enveloping its lower steps, Seward gloried in the sublime vista:

> By this time, the last gloom of the night had fallen, and the white foam of the thundering waters made their "darkness visible." It seemed scarce possible that an unconscious element could wear such horrid appearances of living rage. Each billow seemed a voraginous monster, as it came roaring on, and dashed itself against the repelling walls. The spray of each flashing wave flew over my head, and wet me on its descent. The pealing waters, louder than thunder, made it impossible for me or the servant to hear each other speak. . . . I stood at least half an hour upon the wild promontory's top, almost totally encircled by the dark and furious main.[47]

Seward's description anticipates J. M. W. Turner's claim to have had himself lashed to a ship's mast in 1842 so that he might be able to paint accurately the impression of a snowstorm at sea.⁴⁸ She, like the later painter, wished to expose herself to the storm both to "gratify [her] rage for the terrific" and to acquire firsthand knowledge, as a poet, of its effects. Her report to Saville attempts to capture verbally details that an artist might depict with paint. Seward's quotation of Milton's description of hell's "darkness visible" conjures the essence of sublime obscurity. Her vivid comparison of the waves to nightmarish monsters from the abyss, her account of being wet through and unable to hear due to the waves' thundering noise, appeal to the senses and the imagination. The reader is invited to stand beside her, like Dewes's stoic, borrowed servant, within the tempest, tasting sublimity. Throughout her published letters, there is no better example of Seward's quest for the sublime in landscape or her passionate emotional encounters with the natural world.

The figure of the silent, unnamed servant reminds us that Seward rarely experienced even such rapturous moments by herself. Like Johnson, she traveled with companions but often described solitary landscapes as if she were alone. Servants, especially, tended to disappear from her accounts. Not until September 1796, when she was fifty-three, did Seward report being alone for a short period. She found herself stranded from her usual hotel at Harrowgate, obliged to take rooms a quarter-mile away and too ill to travel further. "There, during an whole week, I lived, unknowing and unknown, in a seclusion never in my whole preceding life experienced. A total solitude on the verge of so busy a little world, pleased me at once by its novelty, and by the leisure it gave me." She related to Lady Elinor Butler her delight in being "not so ill as to be insensible to the luxury of uninterrupted leisure, and abstract contemplation."⁴⁹ Although her maid was nursing her throughout the week, Seward describes herself as alone, and solitude as if it were a "luxury" feature of her summer tour. Of course, as soon as she was able, Seward made acquaintances and resumed her accustomed social life. Solitude was a rare event, not especially welcome except as a "novelty," despite her quest for the glories of isolated landscapes. The following summer found Seward at Hoyle Lake (now known as Hoylake), confiding to Mrs. Childers that she was surrounded by genteel young people but finding no intellectual stimulation, "little, for which I could desire to change my lonely musings, as, leaning on my maid's arm, I rove, several times a day, the soft green downs."⁵⁰ She was evidently not eager to repeat the past year's seclusion, despite her claim to have found it a rewarding change of pace.

Seward's poems often transmute the material of her correspondence into celebrations of desolate but sublime landscapes. Inspired by Whalley's epistolary travel narratives, for example, she composed in 1785 a poem of 102 four-line stanzas entitled "Alpine Scenery." Near the poem's outset, she praises former travel writers such as Sir Nathaniel William Wraxall, Daniel Coxe, and Francis Moore, whose accounts illuminate the climate, history, and laws of obscure lands.⁵¹ She also praises Laurence Sterne, whose *Sentimental Journey* (1768) "Winds through the labyrinths of the human heart."[52] and Captain James Cook, whose voyages and tragic death inspired her first printed poem, the "Elegy on Captain Cook" (1780). But Whalley's travels have fired her imagination with visions of how

> the Alps, huge in embattled pride,
> A clust'ring Phalanx, meet the wintry gales;
> Or where, dispers'd, they seem, with giant stride,
> To chase each other to the gloomy vales.[53]

Seward employs personification, a favorite technique of poets aspiring to sublimity, to characterize mountains obscured by clouds as gigantic beings that "Wrap their stupendous heads from mortal eyes." While a storm rages, "The savage Graces o'er the mountains stalk."[54] Seward later devotes ten stanzas to Whalley's trip to Vaucluse, but her imagination—and poem—are soon drawn back to the Savoy region, with its images of forlorn castles and overwhelming scenery. Her most intriguing adjustment to Whalley's letters fictionalizes an episode developed at length in her letters. On March 1, 1785, she wrote Whalley condoling with him on "the anguish of losing your tenderly valued friend, in the flower of his youth."[55] The Whalleys had been hosted by a gracious Savoyard, the Baron de Châtillon, but learned of his death before their planned return visit. Seward expresses sympathy but is pleased that Mr. and Mrs. Whalley "are together, and have the power of devoting a portion of every day to the remembrance of him whom you have lost."[56] In her poem, Seward substitutes the death of the Baron's mother for that of the Whalleys' young friend. Despite the presence of the matron's three sons and daughter, Seward imagines Whalley kneeling by her bedside as "On thee the expiring lips their blessings pour, / Mix'd with the accents of immortal hope!"[57] Seward never commented on this apparently imaginary scene; perhaps she felt the Whalleys' grief was too strong to confront a poetic version of their friend's death. Or she may have felt the expiration of an aged matron was more likely to evoke sentiment. Earlier in the poem, she imagines Whalley at his friend's decayed ancestral castle, listening while a storm howls outside, but

> if a wish in softer scenes to rove
> Stole through his breast, amid that awful gloom,
> 'Twas for the murmurs of a cypress grove,
> 'Twas for the silence of a sister's tomb.[58]

By portraying Whalley mourning the death of his beloved sister, which Seward's note places two year earlier, and portraying him—perhaps in his clerical role—as the last recipient of an aged mother's blessing, Seward has cast him in the role of an exemplary hero of sensibility, a man of fraternal and filial piety.

"Alpine Scenery" is a wide-ranging poem, exploring sublime topics from landscape description to political liberty. Seward positions herself "on the rocks of Savoy,"[59] transported by Whalley's inspired pen, and describes the terrain as if she were alone on their peaks or invisibly witnessing Whalley's experiences. The poem concludes by imagining the Whalleys' return to Britain, welcomed by "Albion's tutelary Genius."[60] It is hard not to identify that Genius with Seward herself, based on similarly suggestive portraits of the Genius-as-Muse in her elegies for Cook and Major John André (1781).[61] Her poetic tour necessarily differs from the use Johnson made of his letters and journal in producing his *Journey*, but her emphasis on herself as the lone observer of scenes stupendous or sentimental indicates their widely differing views of solitude, whether as place or state of being. A second example from later in her career underscores this distinction. Seward pared her lengthy, vivid account of self-exposure to an oceanic storm in a letter of 1793 to a sonnet included in *Original Sonnets on Various Subjects* (1799). Instead of her scrambling ascent to the fort assisted by a servant, the sonnet's speaker wanders "Lonely" on the shore or reclines "Beneath a rock" witnessing the scene. Seward describes the sounds of wind, waves, and shrieking seabirds and the sight of "the boiling, the tumultuous waste" as it lashes the promontory. Surprisingly, however, in the sonnet's conclusion, the furious storm

> delight has cast
> O'er my rapt spirit, and my thrilling heart,
> Dear as the softer joys green vales impart.[62]

Seward does not claim the singularity of her personal "taste for the terrible graces." She assumes a readership keen to imagine themselves alone on a storm-lashed beach, their hearts equally thrilled by this sublime natural manifestation. This brief poem captures the distance between Johnson's and Seward's tastes and their objectives in describing the natural world.

JOHNSON, SEWARD, AND POETIC EVOCATIONS OF SOLITARY SUBLIMITY

Such widely differing tastes and aims likewise distinguished Johnson's and Seward's respective approaches to literary criticism. For *The Lives of the Most Eminent English Poets* (1779–1781), Johnson prepared fairly terse assessments of most writers. His critiques serve as a practical guide to the British canon, assisting readers by acknowledging the failures as well as the achievements of each poet. Johnson's approach resembles that of his scenic descriptions in the published *Journey*; he rarely expresses an emotional response but rationally evaluates, then draws conclusions. He praises James Thomson, for example, as "a man of genius" who "looks round on nature and on life, with the eye which nature bestows only on a poet" (Yale *Works*, 23:1291–92). After extolling Thomson's imagination and his ability to impress the reader, who "wonders that he never saw before what Thomson shews him, and that he never yet has felt what Thomson impresses," Johnson modifies his praise. "The great defect of the *Seasons* is want of method," he observes. "His diction is to the highest degree florid and luxuriant," he adds; "It is too exuberant" (Yale *Works*, 23:1292–93). Thomson, he concludes, is sometimes more concerned with the sound than the sense of his verse. Seward, predictably, loved Thomson's poems as exemplars of "poetic landscape. Those enchanting compositions, the Seasons, are almost wholly descriptive; yet I know not any poetry more capable of exalting the imagination, and expanding the heart."[63] Johnson's praise echoes Pope's admonitions, in the *Essay on Criticism* (1711) that "Men must be *taught* as if you taught them *not*, / And Things *unknown* proposed as Things *forgot*" and that "*True Wit*" conveys "What oft' was *Thought*, but ne'er so well *Exprest*."[64] Seward's expresses her generation's preference for verse that inspires the imagination and touches the heart with sublime images and musical effects.

Writers so unlike were bound to disagree; Johnson's critical principles were not Seward's. Johnson may have been surprised to learn that Seward most admired his *Journey* for its "picturesque style" and "imagery,"[65] not its information. To Hayley she declared her opinion in 1787 that Johnson was a good but not great poet, "able to rouse and fire, though not to exhilarate and melt the soul."[66] Since for Seward, the poet's task was to "exhilarate and melt" her reader, she was inevitably outraged by Johnson's insufficient admiration of Thomas Gray. In *The Lives of the Poets*, Johnson had been especially hard on Gray's "The Bard," following Goldsmith in supposing it derived from a Horatian ode. The poem therefore "disgusts us with apparent and unconquerable falsehood," since it is not historically accurate (Yale *Works*, 23:1467). "The Bard" had not disgusted most contemporaries. It had inspired readers and visual artists such as Thomas Jones, who painted "The Bard" in 1774. It would soon be illustrated by William Blake (1797–1798) and painted by John Martin (1817), whose portrayal of the lone surviving bard amid towering Welsh peaks is the best known today. Johnson eviscerates the ode, finding its stanzas overlong, its alliteration misguided, its personification obscure. Gray's borrowings are inept and some lines, chiefly "Give ample room and verge enough," egregiously bad. Johnson's antipathy was probably roused by his failure to perceive any "truth, moral or political" in the ode. He concludes by finding the bard's dramatic leap a bad moral example, "but suicide is always to be had, without expence of thought" (Yale *Works*, 23:1468–70). Of all Gray's poems, Johnson wholeheartedly approves only the "Elegy Written in a Country Churchyard." The "Elegy" fulfills Pope's requirement that a poem recall "What oft' was thought, but ne'er so well expressed." Johnson does not add that the "Elegy" exudes Christian humility and piety; of all his poems, Gray's "Elegy" fulfilled Johnson's moral expectations.

Seward was distressed by Johnson's critique of Gray. She affirmed to Mrs. Piozzi that she had anonymously published "in The Gentleman's Magazine of October 1784," a poem admonishing the Rev. William Mason "for his silence over Johnson's malignant injustice to the greatest lyric poet the world ever produced."[67] She no doubt felt Mason, Gray's biographer and known opponent of Johnson, was better able than she to protest publicly on behalf of his deceased mentor. Mason had remained silent regarding *The Lives of the Poets* despite Johnson's manifest injustice toward a poet she believed Pindar himself "could not . . . excel . . . in the sublimity of his imagery, or in the grandeur and variety of his numbers; and our translations of Pindar show me that the Greek poet's subjects were less elevated, less interesting."[68] Seward, like many in a generation that, to paraphrase Ralph Cohen, "returned to the ode," found Johnson's strictures indefensible.[69] One of many poets who delighted in the ode's freedom from "an overabundance of . . . moralizing," its "specialized" allusive diction, "experiments with meter and rhyme," and musicality,[70] Seward found Johnson's disparagement of Gray's techniques, such as alliteration, preposterous. Valuing sublimity, varied metric patterns, and melodious sound, she rejected Johnson's complaints. His objection to the bard's triumphant suicide would have seemed obtuse. Her "Verses to the Rev. William Mason . . . Written in 1782" is an irregular ode, opening with a sublime image, as Gray's aggrieved muse thrusts her pen toward Mason. By his silence, Mason has allowed "rude malicious hands" to tear Gray's laurel wreath from her head. Johnson is identified as "that Philistine critic" assaulting the "armies of the heavenly muse." Seward's pun on the word "philistine" connects Johnson both with a failure of taste and with the giant slain by David. She reproaches Mason with not having sunk "Truth's victor pebbles . . . deep buried in [Johnson's] haughty brow!" If Mason persists in ignoring Johnson's vulture-like assault on Gray, figured as a dead eagle, his own reputation will be blighted as if by mildew "With the disgraceful spots of cold and selfish fears."[71] With its mix of classical and biblical imagery, varied stanzaic patterns and rhyme schemes, and elevated diction, Seward's poem challenges Johnson's poetic standards with those of herself and Gray. In Mason's absence, she steps forward as the David opposing Johnson's Goliath.

Perhaps the best illustration of Johnson's and Seward's opposed literary principles was their contrasting opinions of James Macpherson's Ossian poems. Between 1760 and 1765, Macpherson published a series of fragments supposedly from an ancient epic by the bard Ossian. Macpherson claimed to have collected and translated the episodes from ancient Gaelic manuscripts. The Ossian cycle, narrating a series of ancient wars, was immediately both popular and controversial. As part of a generational shift away from Roman models and toward recovery of pre-Roman and medieval British culture, Ossian held immense appeal for many readers, writers, and artists.[72] Contemporaries such as Angelica Kauffman and James Barry painted scenes from Ossian; among writers, Macpherson influenced Romantic-era poets such as Blake and Wordsworth and, on the Continent, Goethe. Ossian's fascination extended through the Romantic period in music as well, inspiring Schubert and Mendelssohn. Seward was therefore responding to Ossian in the spirit of her time. She especially admired the poems' evocations of bleak, mist-shrouded scenery: the very terrain she identified with her Peak District childhood. We have already encountered her remark to Christopher Smith in 1792 that her love of Derbyshire's "lonely and romantic grandeur" still caused her eyes to brim with "the dews of pensive transport" whenever she read Ossian.[73]

Johnson instinctively suspected Macpherson of fraudulently claiming to have recovered previously unknown Erse manuscripts. Ossian's admirers, however, were outraged by his dismissal of the poems' literary value. To James Blair's query in 1763 whether "any man of a modern age could have written such poems," Johnson retorted, "Yes, Sir, many men, many women, and many children" (*Life*, 1:396). During his Scottish tour with Boswell, Johnson became convinced that Macpherson could not have found ancient transcriptions because Erse was an unwritten language. He doubted the probability of the epics having been orally transmitted over many centuries. "Yet I hear the father of Ossian boasts of two chests more of ancient poetry, which he suppresses, because they are too good for the English" (Yale *Works*, 9:117). Johnson's resistance to Ossian resembles his dislike of Gray's "The Bard." He found the latter poem lacking in moral truth and particularly disliked its final, sublime image of the lone bard's suicidal leap from a Welsh peak. The chief reason for Johnson's dismissal of Ossian was that he disbelieved Macpherson's reiterated claim to possess authentic manuscript sources.[74] When, after the *Journey*'s publication in 1775, Macpherson threatened Johnson with legal action and worse due to his printed rejection of the epic, Johnson replied, "I thought your book an imposture from the beginning, I think it upon yet surer reasons an imposture still." He demanded proof of Macpherson's sources, adding, "what I have heard of your morals disposes me to pay regard not to what you say, but to what you can prove" (*Letters*, 2:169).

Johnson was perplexed by Ossian's popularity: "But this is the age in which those who could not read, have been supposed to write; in which the giants of antiquated romance have been exhibited as realities. If we know little of the ancient Highlanders, let us not fill the vacuity with Ossian" (Yale *Works*, 9:119). Since the purpose of Johnson's travel narrative was to transmit accurate information about the Hebrides, Macpherson's fanciful representation of ancient Scottish warriors resembled populating "the Magellanick regions . . . with Patagons" (Yale *Works*, 9:119). Johnson vigorously opposed such inaccuracy. He did not of course abjure all imaginative language, but objected to what he thought improbable or misleading inventions such as Macpherson's Ossian and Gray's legendary Welsh bard (Yale *Works*, 23:1469). Seward admired Ossian for qualities completely distinct from those observed by Johnson. An early believer in the epic's authenticity, she was not prepared until 1791 to believe that Macpherson had invented Ossian after collecting "oral traditions."[75] For Seward, Ossian's value resided not in authenticity but in its depictions of landscape. "The scenic painting in Ossian's works gives them their high and exquisite value. They represent, in every variety possible, amidst an uncultivated and naturally barren country, its wild and solemn features."[76] Seward's reflections on Ossian epitomize her differences with Johnson, drawing together the themes of solitude as place and state of mind, of sensibility, and of sublimity. Johnson evaluated Macpherson in terms of veracity and probability. Since the poems, presented as genuine, were a hoax, and their representations unlikely, the works of Ossian were worthless. Heir of a tradition that valued urban refinement, and that considered barren landscapes possible sites of commercial or agricultural development, Johnson would in any case have failed to apprehend the appeal of Ossian's "lonely scenery."[77] Seward opened the same pages and found herself transported, in imagination, to the solitary peaks she yearned toward but so rarely visited except in a chaise or with companions.

NOTES

1. I developed these arguments in Kairoff, "Anna Seward, Samuel Johnson, and the End of the Eighteenth Century," in *Anna Seward and the End of the Eighteenth Century* (Baltimore: Johns Hopkins University Press, 2012), 240–65.
2. Howard D. Weinbrot's study, *Augustus Caesar in "Augustan" England* (Princeton, NJ: Princeton University Press, 1978), demonstrated the wide range of purposes served by ubiquitous references to Caesar, by sycophants and satirists alike, throughout the period.
3. Alexander Pope, "Epistle 4," *An Essay on Man*, ed. Maynard Mack, in *The Twickenham Edition of the Poems of Alexander Pope*, ed. John Everett Butt et al. (New Haven, CT: Yale University Press, 1939–1969), 3.1:160, line 332.

4. Samuel Johnson, "Life of Pope," in Yale *Works*, 23:1219.
5. Jerome McGann, *The Poetics of Sensibility: A Revolution in Literary Style* (Oxford: Clarendon Press, 1996), is an especially useful study of the sensibility phenomenon.
6. Anna Seward, *The Collected Poems of Anna Seward*, ed. Lisa L. Moore (London: Routledge, 2016), 1:68. Moore's edition prints "my" as "by," an apparent misprint.
7. See, for one of several examples in James Boswell's *Life*, 2:238.
8. I refer here to Seward's letters to the *Gentleman's Magazine* in 1793 disputing Boswell's characterization of Johnson in his *Life*, and Boswell's published rebuttals, although her personal correspondence contains many similar examples of Seward's dislike of Johnson's supposed hypocrisy. See Sylvanus Urban [pseud.], ed., the *Gentleman's Magazine* 63, no. 2 (October 1793): 875; and 63, no. 2 (November 1793): 1009–11.
9. Hester Thrale also attributed keen sensibility to Johnson throughout her *Anecdotes*, although specifying that his sensibility was primarily associated with his piety and not activated by trivial matters. See Hester Lynch Piozzi, *Anecdotes of the Late Samuel Johnson, LL.D., During the Last Twenty Years of His Life* (London, 1786), 186, 190, 200, 301.
10. Johnson to Hester Thrale, Monday, November 8, 1779, in *Letters*, 3:211.
11. For example, when Moll persuades her Lancashire husband to plead for transportation instead of hanging, she joins to her argument "that known Womans Rhetorick . . . that of Tears," in Daniel Defoe, *The Fortunes and Misfortunes of the Famous Moll Flanders* (London, 1722), 319.
12. Frances Burney, entry for June 13, 1779, in *The Early Journals and Letters of Fanny Burney*, ed. Lars E. Troide et al. (Montreal and Kingston, ON: McGill-Queen's University Press, 1988–2012), 3:304.
13. Ibid., 3:316.
14. Anna Seward to George Hardinge, November 11, 1787; in *Letters of Anna Seward: Written between the Years 1784 and 1807*, ed. Archibald Constable. (Edinburgh: Archibald Constable, 1811): 1:349–350.
15. Lyle Larsen, *Dr. Johnson's Household* (Hamden, CT: Archon Books, 1985), provides an overview of Johnson's tenants. Michael Bundock, *The Fortunes of Francis Barber: The True Story of the Jamaican Slave Who Became Samuel Johnson's Heir* (New Haven, CT: Yale University Press, 2015), traces the biography of Johnson's trusted servant.
16. Teresa Barnard identifies Elizabeth Fern in *Anna Seward: A Constructed Life* (Burlington: Ashgate, 2009), 152–53.
17. Samuel Johnson, *Rasselas*, ed. Gwin J. Kolb, in Yale *Works*, 16:50.
18. Seward, *Poems*, 2:176.
19. Ibid., 2:179.
20. Seward, "To William Hayley, Esq. on Leaving Eartham . . . ,"in Seward, *Poems*, 2:188.
21. Seward, *Poems*, 1:146–47.
22. Seward, "To Mrs Skerett, Written, Nov. 1805," in Seward, *Poems*, 2:298.
23. Samuel Johnson, *A Journey to the Western Islands of Scotland*, ed. Mary Lascelles, in Yale *Works*, 9:xiv.
24. Martin Martin, *A Description of the Western Islands of Scotland* (London, 1703), 1:1.
25. Daniel Defoe, *A Tour Thro' the Whole Island of Great Britain* (London, 1724), 3:6.
26. Defoe, *Tour*, 3:7.
27. Ibid., 3:9.
28. Thomas Pennant, *A Tour in Scotland, and Voyage to the Hebrides* (Chester, 1771), 40–41.
29. Ibid., 41.
30. See David Fairer's tribute, "J. D. Fleeman: A Memoir," *Studies in Bibliography* 48 (1995): 1–24, in which he describes Johnson's reminiscence of Iona as one in which "memory and imagination, recollection and hope, relieve momentarily the struggle of the present, and

Johnson in that spot senses a kind of eternity" (12); Fairer recalls that Fleeman found the same passage an instance of Johnson's complete devotion to the power of language (12). Anthony W. Lee, in *Dead Masters: Mentoring and Intertextuality in Samuel Johnson* (Bethlehem, PA: Lehigh University Press, 2011), calls the Iona narrative an instance of "the Johnsonian sublime," observing its ability to wring tears from the eyes of contemporary readers such as Lord Monboddo (101). Lee defines Johnson's framing of the Iona visit as "a typically Johnsonian gesture: he does not countenance sentimentality, or indulge in bathos; yet the soberness of his reserve makes his brief, incisive incursion into the transcendental realm all the more valuable, compelling, and poignant" (102).

31. See *Life*, 5:334, and Seward, *Letters*, 2:9.
32. Samuel Johnson, *The Idler and The Adventurer*, ed. W. J. Bate, John M. Bullitt, and L. F. Powell, in Yale *Works*: 2:300.
33. Susan Lamb, *Bringing Travel Home to England: Tourism, Gender and Imaginative Literature* (Newark: University of Delaware Press, 2009), 116.
34. Joseph Addison urged readers to appreciate sublimity in his *Spectator* essays on "the Pleasures of the Imagination," in June 1712. Edmund Burke published *A Philosophical Inquiry into the Origin of Our Ideas of the Sublime and Beautiful* in 1757, when Seward was fifteen; Rousseau's *Julie; ou La nouvelle Heloïse* (1761) was published that same year in an English translation, *Eloisa*, when Seward was nineteen.
35. Lamb, *Bringing Travel Home*, 166.
36. Seward to Rev. T. S. Whalley, November 7, 1784; in Seward, *Letters*, 1:9.
37. Whalley, quoted by Seward, March 15, 1785, in Seward, *Letters*, 1:26–27.
38. Lamb, *Bringing Travel Home*, 116.
39. Seward to Sophia Weston, September 6, 1783, in Seward, *Letters*, 2:72.
40. Ibid.
41. Ibid., 2:71.
42. Seward to Sophia Weston, in Seward, *Letters*, 2:76.
43. Ibid., 2:76.
44. Seward to Christopher Smith, April 1792, in Seward, *Letters*, 3:131–32.
45. Johnson to Hester Thrale, September 21, 1773, in *Letters*, 2:78–79.
46. Seward, *Letters*, 3:99.
47. Seward to John Saville, July 28, 1793, ibid., 3:289–90.
48. Luke Herrmann describes Turner's claim as "apocryphal" in his "Turner, James W. M.," s.v. *Oxford Dictionary of National Biography* article, but it has become part of Turner's legend (http://www.oxforddnb.com/).
49. Seward to Lady Elinor Butler, September 1796, in Seward, *Letters*, 4:248–49.
50. Seward to Mrs. Childers, Summer, 1777, in Seward, *Letters*, 4:378.
51. In her notes on the poem, Francis Moore identifies two of these figures as Hannah More and Peter Coxe. I consider it likely that Seward refers instead to Daniel Coxe (1640–1730), author of *A Description of the English Province of Carolana* (1722; see Michael Hunter, "Daniel Coxe," s.v. *Oxford Dictionary of National Biography Online*); and to Francis Moore, author of *Travels in the Inland Parts of Africa* (1755?). Sir Nathaniel William Wraxall (1751–1831) had published *Cursory Remarks Made in a Tour through some of the Northern Parts of Europe* (1775), which Katherine Turner observes achieved popularity due to contemporaries' relative ignorance of Scandinavia and Russia (see "Sir Nathaniel William Wraxall," s.v. *Oxford Dictionary of National Biography Online*).
52. Seward, *Poems*, 2:224.
53. Ibid., 2:225.
54. Ibid.
55. Seward to Whalley, March 1, 1785, in Seward, *Letters*, 1:21.

56. Ibid.
57. Seward, *Poems*, 2:234.
58. Ibid., 2:230.
59. Ibid., 2:225.
60. Ibid., 2:234.
61. See Kairoff, *Anna Seward and the End of the Eighteenth Century*, 96.
62. Seward, *Poems*, 1:226.
63. Seward, *Letters*, 1:70.
64. Alexander Pope, *An Essay on Criticism*, ed. E. Audra and Aubrey Williams, in *Twickenham Edition*, 1:297–98, lines 574–75.
65. Seward, *Letters*, 4:55–56.
66. Ibid., 1:304–5.
67. Seward to Mrs. Piozzi, in Seward, *Letters*, 2:42.
68. Ibid.
69. Ralph Cohen, "The Return to the Ode," in *The Cambridge Companion to Eighteenth-Century Poetry*, ed. John Sitter (Cambridge: Cambridge University Press, 2001), 203–24.
70. Ibid., 220.
71. Seward, *Poems*, 2:190–91.
72. Tim Fulford has discussed the popularity of natural imagery in poetry written after 1745: "New in their primitiveness, Macpherson's ancient poets made rural imagery the sign of authenticity." See Fulford, "'Nature' Poetry," in *The Cambridge Companion to Eighteenth-Century Poetry*, ed. John Sitter (Cambridge: Cambridge University Press, 2006), 126.
73. Seward, *Letters*, 3:131–32.
74. In his biography, Derick S. Thomson states that Macpherson collected Gaelic ballads, but added much classical material and scenic description. Thomson believes Johnson's contention that Macpherson had no manuscript sources was wrong, but confirms an ongoing controversy over the Ossian poems' degree of authenticity. See "James Macpherson," s.v. *Oxford Dictionary of National Biography Online*.
75. Seward, *Letters*, 3:128.
76. Ibid., 1:240–41.
77. Seward, *Letters*, 3:128.

10
JOHNSON, WARTON, AND THE POPULAR READER

Christopher Catanese

IT IS A SALUTARY ENTERPRISE to consider a figure like Samuel Johnson among a larger field of correspondents, collaborators, disciples, and rivals. Because he is often taken as metonymic for his age, we risk allowing him to become monolithic in our understanding of it, and embedding him once more among his circle may allow us to better read against the grain of his own, prolific self-fashioning. Johnson and Thomas Warton, for example, though for many years colleagues and close friends, nevertheless considered themselves to inhabit quite different worlds in their day. And yet, treating these two otherwise dissimilar authors as responding to the common exigencies of their changing literary milieu—and in particular to the demands of the eighteenth century's growing popular reading public—reveals unexpected facets of their respective vocational comportments.

If Johnson perhaps resented his younger colleague's scholarly sinecure, he also reveled in maintaining a position from which to scoff at it: during the final stages of the *Dictionary* project the city-dwelling Johnson visited Oxford to make use of Warton's access to philological resources,[1] and it takes no great leap to imagine that Johnson may have had the successful young Warton in his crosshairs when he wrote in the Preface that his own linguistic labors had proceeded "not in the soft obscurities of retirement, or under the shelter of academic bowers" but amid the "inconvenience and distraction" of the commercial literary sphere (Yale *Works*, 18:112). Indeed, in many ways Johnson's sometimes hardscrabble career as a London commercial writer could not have been more different than Warton's scholarly post; as Jack Lynch has recently noted, the very term "bookseller's project"—with its implied denigration of projects undertaken for financial gain rather than the free dictates of authorial vision—was actually coined in a 1767 satire on Johnson and his notoriously close ties to the book trades.² And yet despite the very real differences that are captured in the easy opposition between commercial metropolis and ivory tower, in many ways Johnson and Warton did inhabit very much the same world. And therefore I hope that, despite their differences in style, emphasis, and temperament, the critical task of teasing out the two writers' shared concerns will allow us to consider certain central categories of eighteenth-century literary history—the market, the romance, historicism—more profitably than if we were to address each author individually.

The biographical contrast of market impresario and academy intellectual that we find in the juxtaposition of Johnson and Warton can in turn be found reproduced in an analogous methodological split—between what we might call "book" history and "intellectual" history—that largely continues to operate in Johnson criticism today, and indeed in literary criticism more generally. For some scholars, and especially for an earlier generation of twentieth-century literary historians such as Bertrand Bronson, it was Johnson's elegance of style, his "moral responsibility," and his integrated religious, political, and aesthetic sensibility that continued to make him worthy of close study two centuries after his death.³ By contrast, at least in the decades since Alvin Kernan's landmark work on eighteenth-century print culture (and drawing significant energy from the ascendency of new historicist methodologies among literary scholarship in general) much recent Johnson criticism has focused on his important role within the material culture of the era's book trades and social-literary coteries.⁴ The situation is of course only symptomatic of a larger methodological divide among literary scholars today,⁵ and yet these two distinct approaches seems to render especially variable results when applied to the eighteenth century, as David Fairer has persuasively demonstrated in the context of debates over the formation of the English canon. Different methodological emphases, Fairer shows—whether "aesthetic/ philosophical," or "cultural materialist," or some combination of the two—tend to produce widely divergent and sometimes even disjunctive scholarly narratives from the same basic historical materials.⁶ Here I will argue that treating Johnson and Warton together as producing different but parallel authorial responses to a shared stimulus—the more general eighteenth-century anxiety over the effects of a rapidly growing popular readership—not only generates a richer conceptual field within which to read their individual works but in turn encourages a more dialectical critical methodology that offers a constructive challenge to more partisan scholarly orientations.

So rather than treating Johnson's concern with popular reception and Warton's concerns with historicist genre theory as epiphenomenal of two separate worlds, Grub Street and the antiquarian's study, respectively, I consider both in the context of the larger eighteenth-century shift in emphasis from textual production to textual consumption.[7] First, I briefly review a selection of influential literary, historical, and historiographical criticism that has tended to treat—from one angle or the other—the ascendancy of aesthetic historicism and the transformation of the commercial literary market as separate trends. Then, I offer readings of certain brief passages from Warton's 1754 *Observations on the Faerie Queene of Spenser* and from several early installments of Johnson's *Rambler* in order to draw out in each the contours of a projected relationship between author and reader, and specifically, the figure of what I call the "disarticulating reader," to highlight certain shared anxieties and strategies for mitigating such anxieties. In particular, I claim that Warton's historicist critical strategies for assimilating the postclassical romance form of *The Faerie Queene* to the aesthetic expectations of eighteenth-century readers represents an analogue to the strategies employed by commercial literary writers such as Johnson in their confrontation with the "popular" reading public of mid-century. Understanding how two quite different figures grappled with the era's paradigm shift in the concept of reading offers insights into the phenomenology of modern reading practices that are still relevant today.

There is a consensus among scholars that the development of a new kind of "historical sense" became central to the literary criticism of the mid-eighteenth century, and yet, although the particular contours of such a sense have been shown to be quite variable,[8] an influential line of reasoning locates the causes of this development in the internal filiations of intellectual history. The historian Reinhardt Koselleck, for example, treats this development—which he calls the "temporalization of history," to distinguish the eighteenth-century historicism from earlier notions of history as natural chronology, sacred narrative, or reservoir of ethical exempla—as if it emerges from latent tensions within the relatively recondite historical writing of the era, in a gradual process of scholarly elaboration from Vico to Hegel.[9] Similarly, Nicholas Halmi, who has usefully extended Koselleck's insights to a more granular account of the era's artistic, literary, and architectural works, sees this phenomenon as primarily internal to the "aesthetic realm," with an emphasis on theorists of literary genre like Thomas Warton.[10] Warton himself, likewise, did not link these aesthetic changes to "changes in underlying historical conditions," but to a "single, essentially psychological causal principle, the advancement of human reason."[11] If the causes of the emergent aesthetic historicism lay in the assiduous labor of enlightened minds, its effect was to destabilize traditional standards of beauty and decorum which had previously been considered universal and authoritatively underwritten by the example of an idealized Antiquity. In short, eighteenth-century aesthetics faced a crisis in which traditional forms and categories no longer seemed adequate to the tasks of literary criticism and were displaced by historicist narratives of formal development.

Koselleck and Halmi's own scholarly narrative of the emergence of eighteenth-century historicism offers great explanatory power and utility, and yet when weighed upon the scales of the Johnson-Warton opposition with which we began, it skews definitively toward an image of intellectual history peopled by a procession of solitary scholars working incrementally through philosophical puzzles—in other words, it reproduces the vision of history that it discovers in Warton. Therefore, while Halmi does occasionally gesture toward details of material history, such as the differences between print and manuscript circulation, his model of intellectual history is primarily concerned with the processes that Edward W. Said has collected under the rubric of "filiation," that "utopian domain of texts connected serially, seamlessly, and immediately only with other texts." There are other models of history, however, and if we were instead to shift our emphasis to the complementary features of what Said collectively names "affiliation"—the extra-textual processes of production, circulation, and repetition that "give materiality back to the strands holding the text to society, author, and culture"—a different type of narrative may come into focus, and what has so far been rendered as a crisis of aesthetic form may perhaps just as easily be described as a crisis of readership.[12]

If the eighteenth-century "aesthetic realm" confronted a broad crisis in the theorization of form, eighteenth-century *writers* faced an analogous crisis in the use of literary form, deriving at least in part from the rapidly changing nature of their reading audience. English readers, at least since the Elizabethan era, had mostly consisted of a stable, learned, male, and courtly audience—what, in the context of Ben Jonson's poetry, Stanley Fish has referred to as a "community of the same"— and Bertrand Bronson has even made the case that up until the time of Pope a poet's readership would still have been understood as "roughly commensurate" with their (largely homogeneous) social world.[13] And yet around that time a wave of urbanization and the growth of the periodical press after the lapse of the *Licensing Act* began to rapidly transform the scale and composition of English readerships. Susan Stewart has argued that by the early decades of the eighteenth century, "the classical public sphere of letters was beginning to disintegrate under pressures from private commercial interest, from the dissemination of literacy, from the expansion of wealth and population, and from the rise of a professional writing"—and that in such an alien literary milieu the formerly familiar relationship implicit between author and reader had largely become "one of speculation."[14] Recent scholarship has elaborated the significant ways in which the uncertain conditions of readerly reception marked Johnson's thinking in particular,[15] but Johnson himself tackled this theme quite directly in his *Life of Savage*, which might be read as a kind of cautionary tale about a modern writer destroyed by the overlapping but incommensurable demands of literary patronage and market economies (Yale *Works*, 22:968).

In his personal authorial foray into this speculative literary milieu with the *Rambler*, Johnson strategically imports a figure of the "popular" from classical rhetoric to contextualize his own particular choice of literary form—the periodical essay—and I believe that it is precisely this figure of the "popular" that haunts the mid-century writing of *both* Johnson and Warton. While in Warton's Spenser criticism the popular as such is the animating force behind the heterodox or postclassical poetic genre of romance, in the *Rambler* it appears as the Ciceronian rhetorical trope of the *aura popularis*, which Johnson translates as "the gale of favour" (Yale *Works*, 3:8). Despite differences of inflection in the two works, for both writers the figure of the popular manifests a readerly force that is openly disruptive of, or even potentially threatening to, the author figure. The appearance of this trope—what I call the disarticulating reader—in both Johnson and Warton therefore cuts across the market/academy distinction and provides a specific topos for the larger claim advanced by Trevor Ross that the eighteenth century witnessed an overall shift in power—or perhaps investment—from authors to readers. "The emergence of literature in its modern sense," Ross writes, "reflects . . . a change in how literary value was perceived, a change from production to consumption, invention to reception, writing to reading."[16] In what follows, then, I offer a brief close reading of Warton's *Observations on the Faerie Queene* and selections from the *Rambler* in order to substantiate the claim that the eighteenth-century emergence of historicism can profitably be understood—both from the perspective of a material history of the reading public as well as of an intellectual history of genre theory—as a function of the confrontation between the world of letters and the newly important figure of the popular reader.

THE PROBLEM OF POPULAR ROMANCE

The mid-century literary phenomenon that would most directly focalize the twofold shift narrated above—within aesthetic theory and within the literary marketplace—was the proliferation of antiquarian and nationalistic "old canon" anthology projects, which collected and juxtaposed selections from different historical epochs of "British" poetry in a popular and widely accessible print form.[17] The most famous of these projects was Percy's *Reliques*, which first appeared in 1765, but at least as influential was the related and ongoing antiquarian research of

Thomas Warton, which would culminate in the 1774 publication of *The History of English Poetry* but which began as far back as two decades earlier with the publication of his *Observations on the Faerie Queene of Spenser*. The *Observations* is one of the great and enthusiastic pieces of doublespeak in the history of literary criticism, as Warton exhaustively enumerates the aesthetic heterodoxies of Spenser's romance and its many deviations from much-cherished classical norms of unity and decorum, all the while tacitly valorizing the poem's powerful appeal to "the affection of the heart, rather than the applause of the head"—not just in spite of its supposed defects but because of them. Warton's assessment of Spenser's romance therefore involves a descriptive phenomenology of reading, which takes the form of a kind of sliding scale of autonomy, distributed between author and reader (whether equally or unequally), with regard to their interaction with the poetic text.

It will first be helpful to establish just how fully Warton associates the form of the verse romance with the idea of the popular reader. For Warton, as for many of his precursors, the touchstone for the topic is Ariosto's *Orlando Furioso*, probably the single most popular poem of the sixteenth century, a significant influence on Spenser, and an unapologetically un-Aristotelian work that created confusion among generations of Italian literary critics who either bent over backwards to assimilate the sprawling romance to their privileged classical models or who instead attempted to legitimate the popular poem upon a variety of other, sometimes paradoxical, grounds.[18] Warton begins the first section of his own *Observations* with a discussion of the problem that Ariosto poses as a formal model for *The Faerie Queene*, and he speculates about the plight of later Renaissance authors like Tasso in Italy and Spenser in England, who found themselves forced to make concessions to the "prevailing taste" for "allegories, enchantments, and romantic adventures": writing "in the midst of this bad taste," Warton notes, Spenser can hardly be faulted for adopting a style that was, at the time, admittedly "the most celebrated and popular." Warton's position here, at least in his general skepticism about the romance form, if not in his tacit, germinally historicist defense of it, is consistent with that of other eighteenth-century literary critics, for whom the idea of romance as a poetic category became a kind of metonymy for the conflict between what had been understood as an earlier stable, unified, and rational order, and an emergent, heterodox, and even "unnatural" set of ideas and values.[19] As Ian Duncan has glossed this phenomenon: "From the mid-18th century, romance denoted a variable (and unstable) antithetical category: the discredited stories of the 'other,' beginning with the *ancient régime* and its continental avatars, but soon including women, adolescents, aliens, the colonized, and the common people."[20] Just as the Renaissance's demographic "community of the same" tended to valorize and reproduce the classical poetic genres with which a courtly audience would have been familiar, the newly rediscovered allure of romance's sheer otherness in the eighteenth century can, at a broad level, be understood as part of a collective process of assimilating a larger and more diverse popular reading public into the mutual activity of determining aesthetic values.

For most eighteenth-century critics, including Johnson and Warton, the problem posed by the popular romance most often manifested itself as a concern *for* readers—as a matter of the only questionably didactic uses to which such works of writing might be put[21]—but in a subtler register we can see that this anxiety cuts the opposite direction as well, as the defense of formal unity can also at times be read as concern for the integrity of authorship itself. In this light, the delicate balance of power between author and reader can be seen as a significant part of Warton's analysis; indeed, the most famous and perhaps most revolutionary moment in Warton's judgment, that "in the *Faerie Queene* we are not satisfied as critics, yet we are transported as readers,"[22] theorizes a reading experience in which the creative imagination of the poet holds the willing reader in a kind of delightful thrall. Although the shift in emphasis from "critics" to "readers" is itself telling in the context of my argument, I would argue that it is the emphasis on readerly affect and imagination that makes this judgment novel for its time—not the simple fact of enthrallment. Johnson himself used such terms in describing his admiration for Dryden, "the [only] master to keep the mind in pleasing captivity,"[23] and the even the exemplar of poetic didacticism that Addison found in the *Georgics* involved using heightened language to render a reader passive so that improving precepts could be delivered more effectively.

Though influential in its subtle departure from earlier "neoclassical" poetics, Warton's pronouncement really only modulates the old Horatian dictum that poetry should "instruct and delight" into the more affective register of the creative imagination; as Warton himself demonstrates, to completely untether the popular romance from the norms of classical unity could become potentially dangerous for both reader and poet. In other words, he only endorses this experience of enraptured reading because of Spenser's limited and generally judicious use of the romance form. For Warton, *The Faerie Queene* is, in general, much more classical in its overall delineations than the "general indigested medley" of romantic entanglements depicted in, for example, *Orlando Furioso*.[24] Ariosto's thoroughly nonclassical romance, by contrast, creates a variety of potential problems in the distribution of power between poet and reader: at times, Warton writes, Ariosto's narrative becomes so "extravagant and absurd" that "the imagination of the reader is not so much involv'd in, as it is oppressed" by the narrative.[25] This imbalance relates to the more often commented-upon issue mentioned earlier, of the propriety of romance and of its potential dangers to readerly morality.

The more relevant danger for my argument, however, involves the problems that ensue when the balance of power swings too far in the opposite direction, when the reader becomes a threat to the author. Here, Warton objects to the romance reader's disregard for the formal integrity of the work, with the rather uncharacteristic vehemence of the plaint manifesting in a parenthetical interjection: "This poet is seldom read twice in order; that is, by passing from the first canto to the second, and from the second to the rest successively; but by perusing (without any regard to the order of the books, or the stanzas) the different stories."[26] In this scenario, Ariosto's failure to establish a classical sense of unity in the poem ultimately licenses readers to literally take the matter into their own hands, without regard for the formal shape or order of the poem. Ultimately, in the *Observations*, Warton executes a brief but decisive change in the image of the reader: no longer a critic characterized by judgment and decorum, but rather a popular figure motivated by the promises of transport, enchantment, and delight; at the edges of this portrait, however, lies the threat of a readership unconcerned with formal unity or authorial intentions, paging errantly through their books, subject only to romantic appetite and desire.

THE PERIODICAL WRITER AND THE GALE OF FAVOUR

In intellectual histories it is common to characterize Warton as a kind of pre-Romantic, but I would argue that Warton's revisionary image of the popular reader not only represents a foreshadowing of the gothic revival to come, but also and less obviously that he registers a change that is already well underway in the eighteenth century: namely, the growth of what would eventually come to be understood as the mass reading public. Warton and Johnson are both writing in the middle of a long eighteenth-century shift in literary milieu, from an Augustan market in which normative aesthetic values are disseminated confidently from author to reader, to a very different Romantic market—which Jerome Christensen memorably referred to as a "self-reflexive publishing machine"—in which texts are understood as the site of a historically conditioned and market-driven negotiation of values.[27] In broad strokes, this shift is evident enough if you compare, for example, the *Spectator*'s optimistically confident project of regulating and improving the taste of its large and aspirational readership through the implementation of the regular periodical press, to, a century later, the kind of rearguard reactionary gatekeeping against the excesses of popular taste that would become Francis Jeffrey's trademark style in the *Edinburgh Review*. I would suggest that, despite the image of the insulated scholar that features most prominently in intellectual histories, Warton's intimations of anxiety regarding the potentially overpowering autonomy of the romance reader in fact reflects an awareness of this shift, and it is for this reason that Johnson's more extensive discussion of readers and readerships in his own mid-century serial publication (which, as we will see, present their own picture of the disarticulating reader) represents such an important textual foil.

As a writer working, as he claimed, far from the "academic bowers" of scholarly retreat and instead fully entrenched within the commercial system of the London book trades, Samuel Johnson was directly engaged—as the arch-academic Warton was not—with the practical effects of the transformations underway in the eighteenth-century literary milieu. Originally published serially and eventually collected in a single volume just before the appearance of Warton's *Observations*, Johnson's *Rambler* is characteristic of such a milieu, one in which the popular reader is perceived as presenting new kinds of dangers for the commercial writer. In *Rambler* 23, for example, Johnson contrasts the traditional, old-fashioned, and reverent reader of the printed book—who willingly "accommodates his mind to the author's design"—with the modern reader of popular periodicals who feels himself licensed to blithely offer whatever censures, admonitions, criticisms, and instructions first come to mind (Yale *Works*, 3:127). For Johnson, the popular periodical-writer, the reader could no longer be assumed to submit to the authority of the writer, and even the format of modern commercial writing seemed to contribute to the erosion of authorial integrity: as early as in the 1743 proposal for the *Harleian Miscellany* he had complained that "a multitude of valuable productions, published in small pamphlets, or in single sheets, are in a short time, too often by accidents, or negligence, destroyed or entirely lost."[28] This image in a sense literalizes the fear of the disarticulated text, and in his production of the *Rambler*, as if to preemptively protect himself against such negligence or indeed against the very sort of errant readerly perusing that had so alarmed Warton, Johnson had the individual numbers of the *Rambler* printed with a running cumulative pagination, intending from the outset to protect their eventual integrity as an ordered formal whole.[29]

If Johnson indeed intended to give the *Rambler* the overall shape of a "deliberately constructed classic,"[30] it is worth dwelling on the peculiar manner in which he performs and performatively mitigates his reception anxiety through a meditation on the nature of popular taste—via a Horatian allusion to the *aura popularis*—in the apologia of his introductory installment. In *Rambler* 1, Johnson introduces and recommends himself to his readers with exquisite self-awareness, reflecting at length on the minefield of hazards faced by an author upon first presenting himself "before the publick," and especially "those dangers which the desire of pleasing is certain to produce" (Yale *Works*, 3:4). In a series of metaphors portraying the relationship between author and audience, Johnson then depicts the popular reader successively as skeptical judge, vain or wary lover, and impatient investor before cannily proceeding to "try the event of [his] first performance" (Yale *Works*, 3:7). Compared to the book-writer, he finally begins, the periodical-writer is largely spared the anxiety of wondering whether his work is timely enough to engage the public: "He who is confined to no single topick," he writes, "may follow the national taste through all its variations, and catch the *Aura popularis*, the gale of favour, from what point soever it shall blow" (Yale *Works*, 3:8). Johnson's assessment of the relative merits of book- and pamphlet-writing here seems to reverse the anxieties we have already seen him express—a point to which I return below—but the figure of the *aura popularis* itself is a common enough one among Latin writers (it appears in Livy, Virgil, Cicero, and Horace, among others) and is often and most simply translated as "popular favor."[31] By contrast, Johnson's inline translation of the phrase as the "gale of favour" is notable for a few reasons.

An indication of Johnson's particular source comes in the third installment of the *Rambler* a week later, which is prefixed by an ode from Horace in which the truly virtuous man is not swayed by the fickleness of popular favor; the English translation is attributed to Elphinston and reads,

> With native honours virtue shines;
> Nor takes up pow'r, nor lays it down,
> As *giddy rabbles* smile or frown" (Yale *Edition*, 3:14).

Elphinston's original translation in fact read "giddy critics," however, and so with the decision to alter the line Johnson clearly establishes an image of a popular readership that is both dangerously dynamic and marked by the general debasement of an ignorant and even morally questionable station. Johnson's *Dictionary* proposes the definition of *rabble* as "a tumultuous croud; an assembly of low people" by way of Addison's image of treasonous political agents putting "the dregs of the people in a ferment," along with a further series of quotations that together create a semantic field featuring "mobs," "ravishments," "betrayings," "scurrility," "profanity," "barbarity," "baseness," "cowardice," etc. (*Dictionary*, s.v. "rabble"). By endorsing the idea that a writer of class should stand aloof from the vicissitudes of popular opinion in *Rambler* 3, then—which seeks to defend the dignity of authorship against the "Prejudice and False-Taste" of facile criticism in the popular periodical press (Yale *Works*, 3:18)—Johnson shrewdly imports Roman political rhetoric in the service of an eighteenth-century literary anxiety. And yet in *Rambler* 1, by contrast, the narrator does not stand aloof from the rabble but expects—or at least hopes—to somehow harness it for his own purposes.

On a second level, then, Johnson's allusion to the *aura popularis* is part of an ironic persona and rhetorical strategy meant to acknowledge and to humorously minimize the effects of what he considered to be legitimate dangers facing his project. For example, whereas in both of the aforementioned quotations from the *Harleian Miscellany* and from *Rambler* 23 Johnson had compared the plight of the pamphlet-writer unfavorably with that of the book-writer, here he instead presents the pampleteer's ability to "catch the *Aura popularis*" as a decided advantage. That this is in fact part of a rhetorical strategy in keeping with the ironic tone of the piece becomes clear in the next paragraph, where Johnson likewise recasts his earlier judgment about the fragility and instability of the pamphlet's physical format instead as a boon to the writer for whom "the shortness of every single paper is a powerful encouragement"; here Johnson's self-deprecating humor—the author that "fears to be lost in a complicated system," he writes, "may yet hope to adjust a few pages without perplexity"—makes his strategic irony unmistakable (Yale *Works*, 3:8). In fact, here Johnson can be seen as parodically engaging in one of the very authorial tactics that he had described in the piece's opening salvo of metaphors, in which certain writers may choose "to recommend their own labours" in the hopes that their "deviation from modesty" will be adequately compensated by the appeal of their "spirit and intrepidity" (Yale *Works*, 3:5). In the context of all this irony, then, the purpose of the *aura popularis* trope is to sharpen the lampoon of the commercial writer who, cynically matching the fickleness of the popular reading audience stroke for stroke, chooses the periodical essay as the format which will "soonest give him an opportunity of hearing the voice of fame" (Yale *Works*, 3:7).

Granting Johnson's irony in this passage, we are still left with both his image of the *aura popularis* and the fact that it represents a real challenge for the serious and aspiring writer—like Johnson, for example, at this early moment in his career—who is unwilling merely to cater to popular favor. And yet while in Johnson's use of the figure it seems to retain its traditional rhetorical connotations at least in part, his English rendering of the Latin as a "gale of favour" somewhat alters the image. With its definition having been established since at least the sixteenth century as "a wind of considerable strength," the word *gale* in fact seems to shift in its precise connotations over the course of the eighteenth century toward an ever-more-disruptive and powerful force. In fact, the shifting definition of the word *gale* seems to exhibit a trajectory analogous to that of the ever-more-threatening figure of the reader that I trace in this piece. For example, while in Dryden's Virgil and Thomson's *Seasons* gales are without exception pleasing, auspicious, and friendly—one might almost say "polite"—by the time of the Romantic era the word had come to connote a dangerous storm at sea.[32] As if to highlight the very shift in connotation that I describe, Johnson's own mid-century definition for "gale" is given as "a wind not tempestuous, but stronger than a breeze" (*Dictionary*, s.v. "gale"). If, then, we take Johnson's rendering of the popular reading public as a "gale of favour" seriously, the resulting image is of a formidable source of power, one that can potentially be harnessed for a directed purpose but that contains—whether through semantic *différence,* linguistic prolepsis, or through Johnson's choice of "giddy rabble," with all its aristocratic suspicion of the mob—the unmistakable trace of a threat.

The eventual manifestation of this incipient readerly threat does not appear until *Rambler* 16, the letter from Misellus on "the dangers and miseries of literary eminence," where Johnson gives us the fullest portrait of the disarticulating reader as a threat to authorial integrity. The piece begins as a light farce on the self-importance of a newly published author who is beset by a deluge of praise from friends and acquaintances (as long as he is buying the claret for celebratory toasts), and yet by turns the farce becomes gradually darker and finally even surreally nightmarish before its conclusion. Misellus soon finds that his popular reception prevents him from moving freely in the social world of the coffeehouse, then becomes paralyzed by his self-consciousness around any kind of audience whatsoever, and is finally driven out of his own house by the fear of profiteering intruders who will have his "closets rifled" and his "cabinets broke open at the instigation of piratical booksellers" (Yale *Works,* 3:90). Eventually not only his private papers and belongings are subject to the threat of disruption and dispersion, but even his physical *corpus*: he is "haunted" wherever he goes, he says, with "good reason to believe that eleven painters are now dogging me [in an attempt to] get my face," and he spends his days and nights in fear of becoming one of those authors "whose likenesses must have been certainly stolen when their names made their faces vendible" (Yale *Works,* 3:91). "Thus I live," he concludes at the end of his letter, "in the solitude of a hermit, with the anxiety of a miser, and the caution of an outlaw; afraid to show my face, lest it should be copied; afraid to speak, lest I should injure my character, and to write lest my correspondents should publish my letters; always uneasy lest my servants should steal my papers for the sake of money, or my friends for that of the publick" (Yale *Works,* 3:91).

In Johnson's portrait of the popular writer we begin with some good-natured abuse among close friends, but end with a paralyzed and paranoid hostage of public favor. Although the successive amplification is certainly a function of the piece's humor, Johnson's Misellus provides a kind of neat parable for the changing role of the reader over the course of the eighteenth century, from convivial breeze to a gale entirely tempestuous. The opening scene with toasts and claret with friends represents a lightly parodic portrait of the fictionalized conversation circle that was the implicit scene of Addison's *Spectator*. From there we move into the semi-public space of the coffeehouse and then finally out into the anonymous multitude of the open public. While liberals like Bentham would later seek to harness the energy of this gale for popular governance in the form of a "regime of publicity," the ravenous rabble of Johnson's Misellus letter is much closer to an equally influential and very different image of the mass public—the "swinish multitude"—that would come to haunt Burke at the scene of the French Revolution.[33] The final passages of the Misellus letter, especially, can also be read as an uncanny foreshadowing of the Byron phenomenon, still seventy years out, in which an ambitious young writer—upon the first publication of *Childe Harold* in 1812—truly did wake one morning to find himself a celebrity of overwhelming proportions. Though Johnson's grotesque joke on the literal dismemberment involved in stealing someone's face may perhaps be indebted to Swift's Celia, Misellus's worries prefigure the actual trafficking in pirated woodplates and forged portraits that would become a common epiphenomenon of Byron's literary fame. Such forgeries appeared on the frontispieces of the many pirated editions of *Don Juan*, for example, not to mention the case of the engraver Thomas Blood, who stole the face from Westall's portrait of Byron and stuck it onto a different body altogether for his low-cost reproductions.[34] The image of the disarticulating reader that worried Warton—the errant reader who takes the author apart and puts him back together at will—is literalized first in Johnson's mid-century parody, and then in Romantic-era reality.

TASTE AND READERLY TRANSPORT

The overall gesture of this chapter has been to suggest that reading the "academic" Warton and the "commercial writer" Johnson in parallel can illuminate the way that both the professional crisis of writerly authority in the literary market and the historicist crisis of aesthetic form in literary criticism can each in their own way be understood as a confrontation with the figure of the popular reader. Considered in this larger light, both facets of this crisis were comprehended in the eighteenth-century concern for establishing a new and more flexible concept of "taste"—whose gustatory origin itself foregrounds the shift toward readerly consumption. Regarding the canonization project to which both Johnson and Warton contributed, Ross has argued that the historical works of Shakespeare or Spenser could only be understood as suitable for the popular reader "at the moment when they were no longer thought useful models for composition but rather things people ought to know in order to help sharpen their taste and judgment."[35] If, as Ross suggests, the century witnessed a fundamental change in how individuals understood what we might call the scene of reading, a shift in the balance of power from author to reader, then the figure of the disarticulating reader that haunts both Warton and Johnson can be seen as a manifestation of the anxiety that such a shift might engender in those within the most elite inner circles of literary production, whether academic or commercial.

Of course such a sea change generates new possibilities and opportunities at the same time that it creates new types of problems, and viewing Warton and Johnson as engaged in a common task allows us get a sense for what those might be as well. Ross's account emphasizes that most eighteenth-century literary critics tended to project an idealized image of the "disinterested" or "impartial" reader quite unlike the image of the affective, imaginative reader that appears in Warton's *Observations*;[36] and yet he also notes an important contrapuntal strain within this discourse, one closer to Warton's position in that it supposes and even requires the existence of a "more engaged reader." After all, Ross writes, the average eighteenth-century reader who for the first time encountered the centuries-old text of Spenser would necessarily be forced to "confront squarely the alterity, or unsettling otherness, of the aged texts": "opening up the canon," he continues, "means coming to terms with cultural and historical difference, a process that is never easy and is often dismaying."[37] In other words, in light of the newly necessary faculty of critical relativity required for simultaneously valorizing both antique Classical and native English works, the cultivation of popular taste could not proceed along the lines of the old didacticism, in which the immutable precepts of decorum were transmitted without friction; instead it required theorizing a communicable *method* of reading able to flexibly engage different historical epochs and styles. In fact, later in his career Johnson would confront the problem of historical alterity directly, when in his *Life of Dryden* he offered his readers advice on fruitfully engaging out-of-date Augustan criticism: "To judge rightly of an author we must transport ourselves to his time, and examine what were the wants of his contemporaries, and what were his means of supplying them" (Yale *Works*, 21:436). As it turns out, translating the antiquarian textual techniques of the emergent scholarly historicism into the domain of the popular readership can itself take the form of readerly "transport."

In a sense, then, the reading public's taste for romances provides the solution to the very problem that it creates: even if the confrontation with the popular and postclassical form of the romance disrupted the ability to reliably judge works according to accepted classical standards, it turns out that the readerly experience of imaginative transport (to, say, the distant faerie lands of romantic enchantment) could actually rather usefully prepare the same readers for an imaginative engagement with the historical standards of distant eras (like Restoration London, or even the Elizabethan court). Along these very lines—decades before he would write his *Life of Dryden*—in a letter thanking Warton for a copy of the newly published *Observations*, Johnson praised his younger friend's scholarly approach to the "ancient authors" through "the perusal of the books which those authors had read."[38] Warton evidently took the compliment to heart, because in the postscript to the second edition of the *Observations* in 1762, Warton added that one of his primary goals was to consider the particular "customs and genius" of Spenser's age: "I have searched his contemporary writers," he writes, "and examined the books on which the peculiarities of his style, taste, and composition, are confessedly founded."[39] Rather than equating the "popular" and "prevailing" interests of Spenser's contemporaries simply with "bad taste" as he had eight years earlier, Warton here finds a "peculiarity" that can be isolated and used as an explanatory principle—just as Johnson would recommend to his readers with regard to Dryden. What we now consider a historicist model of interpretation—considering aesthetic values pluralistically and constructing a totalizing background context for each work—arises not simply from theoretical antiquarian concerns but also from the readerly experiences of popular romance reading.

It is perhaps not too remote to draw a real parallel between Warton's account of romantic transport and our own scholarly reading practices today. For Warton, "transport" implied a kind of healthy equilibrium between author and reader: on the one hand, in exhibiting "regard" for the integrity of the author, the transported reader submitted some degree of their autonomy to the experience of imaginative enthrallment; on the other hand, an author who abused this voluntary submission and "oppressed" the reader with willful obtuseness or impenetrability risked disrupting the experience of transport and therefore devolving power to the reader to reconstruct the text according to their own needs.[40] As scholarly readers navigating the spectrum of methodological options today, from the most utopian of intellectual histories to the most exhaustively suspicious of historicisms, we could choose worse models than Johnsonian transport for a critically informed and yet sympathetic and even imaginative participation in the texts we engage. Walter Scott, that great theorist of the romance, would attempt to articulate this same imaginative, readerly poise in his assessment of Walpole, a man who literally inhabited (at Strawberry Hill House) his studies in Gothic antiquarianism: "These are studies, indeed, proverbially dull; but it is only when they are pursued by those whose fancies nothing can enliven. A Horace Walpole, or a Thomas Warton, is not a mere collector of dry and minute facts, which the general historian passes over with disdain. He brings with him the torch of genius, to illuminate the ruins through which he loves to wander."[41] In assessing the relative careers and concerns of Warton and Johnson, two eighteenth-century figures who can be shown to have lived in historically distinct milieux, we should not fail to imaginatively consider what was shared in the lived experience of the two: let us not be so eager to satisfy ourselves as critics that we forget ourselves as readers.

NOTES

1. John A. Vance, "Samuel Johnson and Thomas Warton," *Biography* 9, no. 2 (1986): 95.
2. Jack Lynch, "Generous Liberal-Minded Men: Booksellers and Poetic Careers in Johnson's *Lives of the Poets*," *Yearbook of English Studies* 45 (January 2015): 95–96.
3. Bertrand Bronson, "The Double Tradition of Dr. Johnson," *English Literary History* 18, no. 2 (June 1951): 90–106, see esp. 95–99.
4. Alvin Kernan, *Printing Technology, Letters, & Samuel Johnson* (Princeton, NJ: Princeton University Press, 1987), repr. published as *Samuel Johnson and the Impact of Print*, 1989.
5. As Andrew Kopec's "The Digital Humanities, Inc.: Literary Criticism and the Fate of a Profession," *PMLA* 131, no. 2 (March 2016): 324–39, has recently pointed out, the growing importance of the digital humanities represents a further turn of the screw for this already significant divide, which I would suggest gives additional weight to methodological considerations undertaken here.
6. David Fairer, "Historical Criticism and the English Canon: A Spenserian Dispute in the 1750s," *Eighteenth-Century Life* 24, no. 2 (2000): 43. Fairer's article offers a deft account of the different uses to which "historicism" could be put in the eighteenth century; both his reading of Warton and his helpful review of the recent literature greatly aided me in the development of this chapter. Fairer has also directly treated the relationship between Johnson and Warton in another essay, and his account there of the "mutual stimulus and fruitful provocation" created by the "uneasy distance" between their respective critical positions dovetails nicely with my emphasis on the productively dialectical interplay that is set in motion in a comparison of the two. See David Fairer, "Johnson and the Warton Brothers," in *Samuel Johnson: The Arc of the Pendulum*, ed. Freya Johnston and Lynda Mugglestone (Oxford: Oxford University Press, 2013), 181.
7. Here, as I discuss more concretely below, I tap into a much broader reading of the eighteenth-century literary milieu that has been articulated most prominently by Trevor Ross, *The Making of the English Literary Canon: From the Middle Ages to the Late Eighteenth Century* (Montreal: McGill-Queen's University Press, 1998).
8. Quotation from Fairer, "Historical Criticism," 43. Fairer's article on the scholarly dispute between Warton and Thomas Upton demonstrates the very different uses to which "historicist" readings of Spenser could be put; a useful third term on this subject is provided by Kristine Haugen's article on the Spenserian criticism of Richard Hurd ("Chivalry and Romance in the Eighteenth Century: Richard Hurd and the Disenchantment of the *Faerie Queene*," *Prose Studies* 23, no. 2 [August 2000]: 45–60). Philip Smallwood's *Johnson's Critical Presence: Image, History, Judgement* (Burlington: Ashgate, 2004), offers an

excellent take on the somewhat paradoxical historicizing impulse in the Shakespeare scholarship of Johnson himself.
9. Reinhart Koselleck, *Futures Past: On the Semantics of Historical Time* (Cambridge, MA: MIT Press, 1985), 31–38.
10. Nicholas Halmi, "Romanticism, the Temporalization of History, and the Historicization of Form," *Modern Language Quarterly* 74, no. 3 (January 2013): 369.
11. Ibid., 375.
12. Edward W. Said, *The World, the Text, and the Critic* (Cambridge, MA: Harvard University Press, 1983).
13. Stanley Fish, "Authors-Readers: Jonson's Community of the Same," *Representations* 7 (July 1984): 26–58; Bertrand Bronson, "The Writer," in *Man versus Society in Eighteenth-Century Britain: Six Points of View*, ed. James L. Clifford (London: Cambridge University Press, 1968), 107.
14. Susan Stewart, *Crimes of Writing: Problems in the Containment of Representation* (Durham, NC: Duke University Press, 1994), 37.
15. See, for example, Jacob Sider Jost, "The *Gentleman's Magazine*, Samuel Johnson, and the Symbolic Economy of Eighteenth-Century Poetry," *Review of English Studies* 66, no. 277 (November 2015): 915–35, on the speculative entrepreneurship of taste exhibited by Cave's poetry contests, and Jack Lynch ("Liberal-Minded Men") on the importance of commercial detail to the Johnsonian biographical style.
16. Trevor Ross, "The Emergence of 'Literature': Making and Reading the English Canon in the Eighteenth Century," *English Literary History* 63, no. 2 (1996): 397.
17. The question of nationalism (which I do not address here) plays a central role in the discourse surrounding canon formation. The *Reliques of Ancient English Poetry* included much Scottish material that, Bishop Thomas Percy argued, dated from an earlier, unified British culture. A variety of nationalistic Scottish figures like David Herd, Walter Scott, and Robert Jamieson would later dispute such an assignation in a variety of ways. See Suzanne Gilbert, "Scottish Ballads and Popular Culture," *Bottle Imp* 5 (May 2009): 1–3.
18. The classic reference work in English for these debates is Bernard Weinberg, *A History of Literary Criticism in the Italian Renaissance* (Chicago: University of Chicago Press, 1961). Halmi also gives a synopsis ("Temporalization of History," 373–74).
19. The term is Warton's, along with "barbaric," "improbable," "ignorant," "irregular," etc. Thomas Warton, *Observations on the Faerie Queene of Spenser* (London, 1754), 1–2.
20. Ian Duncan, "Romance," in *Encyclopedia of the Novel*, ed. Paul Schellinger (New York: Routledge, 2014), 2:1113.
21. Johnson's most extensive discussion of the romance in *Rambler* 4, of course, follows just this line of thought.
22. Warton, *Observations*, 13.
23. Johnson, quoted in Leopold Damrosch, "Samuel Johnson and Reader-Response Criticism," *Eighteenth Century* 21, no. 2 (Spring 1980): 99.
24. Warton, *Observations*, 10.
25. Ibid., 11.
26. Ibid., 12.
27. Jerome Christensen, *Lord Byron's Strength: Romantic Writing and Commercial Society* (Baltimore: Johns Hopkins University Press, 1993), 147. Also see his discussion of the implied scene of reading in the *Spectator* (6–7).
28. Johnson, quoted in Betty Schellenberg, "The Second Coming of the Book, 1740–1770," *Producing the Eighteenth-Century Book: Writers and Publishers in England, 1650–1800*, ed. Laura L. Runge and Pat Rogers (Newark: University of Delaware Press, 2009), 34.

29. This detail comes from Schellenberg, who also incorporates Paul Tankard's argument that the physical details of the *Rambler*'s production imply "a periodical designed from the start with permanence in view," and Paul Korshin's claim the *Rambler* was intended to establish authorial power: to "create a following and, through publication in a collected version, widen the author's reputation" (Schellenberg, "Second Coming," 34–35).
30. Ibid.
31. Thomas Harbottle, *Dictionary of Quotations (Classical)* (London: Swan Sonnenschein, 1906), 215.
32. James Capper, *Observations on the Winds and Monsoons* (London: Whittingham, 1801), xxiii.
33. Jeremy Bentham, *The Works of Jeremy Bentham* (Edinburgh: Tait, 1843), 2:311; Edmund Burke, *Reflections on the Revolution in France* (London, 1790), 117.
34. Tom Mole, *Byron's Romantic Celebrity: Industrial Culture and the Hermeneutic of Intimacy* (Basingstoke, UK: Palgrave Macmillan, 2007), 84.
35. Ross, "Emergence," 410–11.
36. On this subject, see Ross's interesting selections from Defoe, Archibald Alison, and Vicesimus Knox (ibid., 410–12).
37. Ibid.
38. *Letters*, 1:81.
39. Thomas Warton, "Observations on the Fairy Queen of Spenser: Postscript," 2nd ed. (London, 1762), http://spenserians.cath.vt.edu/TextRecord.php?action=GET&textsid=34629.
40. For Johnson, too, the meaning of texts "emerged as part of an exchange between author and audience." See Linda Zionkowski, *Men's Work: Gender, Class, and the Professionalization of Poetry, 1660–1784* (Basingstoke, UK: Palgrave Macmillan, 2001), 188.
41. Horace Walpole and Sir Walter Scott, *The Castle of Otranto: A Gothic Story* (Edinburgh: Ballantyne, 1811), xi–xii.

ACKNOWLEDGMENTS

I wish to thank all the contributors to this collection for their hard work and generosity in making the book possible. Christine Jackson-Holzberg was indispensable in many ways, from moral to practical, and many points between. Thanks also to Jim May and Lance Wilcox for reading and correcting numerous errors in the introduction. Dr. Greg Clingham's enthusiastic support and encouragement of this book also demand acknowledgment here. An anonymous reader for the Bucknell University Press carefully read over the manuscript and offered numerous invaluable suggestions. Many thanks to Debbie McCarson for her thoroughness in preparing the index. I dedicate my own labors in bringing this book to fruition over the past three years to a pair of fine young men who will likely never read it—my two sons—but that's OK.

On a rather different personal note, I learned the morning after sending the complete manuscript for this book to the Press that John Radner, one of our contributors, had died. For a number of years I have enjoyed John's smiling company at various ASECS and EC/ASECS gatherings. He was always eager to talk about Boswell (whose work he knew like the back of his own hand) and Johnson, and I always came away from our conversations happier and better informed than before. He will be missed by many in the eighteenth-century community.

Finally I wish also to add that *Community and Solitude* has a companion volume, *Revaluation: New Essays on Samuel Johnson*, published this year by the University of Delaware Press; the latter focuses upon some important texts by and themes concerning Johnson at this moment in time. Both books were conceived and undertaken simultaneously, and it is my hope that both may prove useful to students of Johnson, Johnson's circle, and the wider eighteenth-century universe that they—and we—all inhabit.

BIBLIOGRAPHY

ARCHIVES AND COLLECTIONS
Beinecke Rare Book & Manuscript Collection. Yale University Library, New Haven, CT.
John Rylands University Library. English Manuscripts. Manchester, United Kingdom.
Northamptonshire Archives. Northamptonshire County Council Record Office. Fitzwilliam Milton Estates. Northampton, United Kingdom.

SOURCES
Baldwin, Louis. "The Conversation in Boswell's *Life of Johnson*." *Journal of English and Germanic Philology* 51, no. 4 (October 1952): 492–506.
Barnard, Teresa. *Anna Seward: A Constructed Life*. Burlington, VA: Ashgate, 2009.
Basker, James. "Johnson and Slavery." In *Johnson After Three Centuries: New Light on Texts and Contexts*, edited by Thomas A. Horrocks and Howard D. Weinbrot, 29–50. Cambridge, MA: Harvard University Press, 2011.
Bate, W. Jackson. *Samuel Johnson*. New York: Harcourt Brace Jovanovich, 1975.
Beal, Joan C. "Elphinston" s.v. *Oxford Dictionary of National Biography Online*. http://www.oxforddnb.com/.
Bell, Robert H. "Boswell's Notes Toward a Supreme Fiction: From *London Journal* to *Life of Johnson*."*Modern Language Quarterly* 38, no. 2 (June 1977): 132–48.
Benedict, Barbara M. *Making the Modern Reader: Cultural Mediation in Restoration and Eighteenth-Century Literary Anthologies*. Princeton, NJ: Princeton University Press, 1996.
Bentham, Jeremy. *The Works of Jeremy Bentham*. 11 vols. Edinburgh, Tait, 1843.
Bernardin de Saint-Pierre, Jacques-Henri. *Études de la nature*. Paris, 1788.
Black, Ronald. *To the Hebrides: Samuel Johnson's Journey to the Western Islands of Scotland and James Boswell's Journal of a Tour to the Hebrides*. Edinburgh: Birlinn, 2007.
Bloom, Edward A. "'As Fly Stings to a Stately Horse': Johnson under Satiric Attack." *Modern Language Studies* 9, no. 3 (Autumn 1979): 137–49.
Bloom, Harold, ed. *Modern Critical Interpretations: James Boswell's* Life of Samuel Johnson. New Haven, CT: Chelsea House Publishers, 1986.
Boileau-Despréaux, Nicolas. *Boileau, Œuvres Complètes*. Edited by Françoise Escal. Paris: Pléiade, 1966.
———. *The Satires of Boileau Despréaux and his Address to the King,* Translated by Hayward Porter. Illustrated by James Magnus. Glasgow: James MacLehose, 1904.
———. *The Works of Monsieur Boileau*. 3 vols. London, 1712–1714.
Bonnell, Thomas F. *The Most Disreputable Trade: Publishing the Classics of English Poetry, 1765–1810*. Oxford: Oxford University Press, 2008.
Bossuet, Jacques Benigne. *An Universal History*. London, 1748.
Boswell, James. *Boswell for the Defence, 1769–1774*. Edited by William Wimsatt Jr. and Frederick A. Pottle. London: William Heinemann; New York: McGraw-Hill, 1959.

———. *Boswell in Extremes: 1776–1778*. Edited by Charles M. Weis and Frederick A. Pottle. New York: McGraw-Hill, 1970.
———. *Boswell in Search of a Wife: 1766–1769*. Edited by Frank Brady and Frederick A. Pottle. New York: McGraw-Hill, 1956.
———. *Boswell: Laird of Auchinleck, 1778–1782*. Edited by Joseph W. Reed and Frederick A. Pottle. New York: McGraw-Hill, 1977.
———. *Boswell on the Grand Tour: Italy, Corsica, and France, 1765–1766*. Edited by Frank Brady and Frederick A. Pottle. New York: McGraw-Hill, 1955.
———. *Boswell's Journal of a Tour to the Hebrides with Samuel Johnson, LL. D., now first published from the original manuscript*. Edited by Frederick A. Pottle and Charles H. Bennett. New York: Viking, 1936.
———. *Boswell's Journal of a Tour to the Hebrides with Samuel Johnson, LL.D., 1773*. Edited by Frederick A. Pottle and Charles H. Bennett. 2nd ed. New York: McGraw-Hill, 1961.
———. *Boswell: The Applause of the Jury, 1782–1785*. Edited by Irma S. Lustig and Frederick A. Pottle. New York: McGraw-Hill, 1981.
———. *Boswell: The English Experiment, 1785–1789*. Edited by Irma S. Lustig and Frederick A. Pottle. New York: McGraw-Hill, 1986.
———. *Boswell: The Great Biographer, 1789–1795*. Edited by Marlies K. Danziger and Frank Brady. New York: McGraw-Hill, 1989.
———. *Boswell: The Ominous Years, 1774–1776*. Edited by Charles Ryskamp and Frederick A. Pottle. New York: McGraw-Hill, 1963.
———. *Boswelliana: The Commonplace Book of James Boswell*. Edited by Charles Rogers. London, 1874.
———. *The Correspondence of James Boswell with Certain Members of the Club*. Edited by Charles N. Fifer. New York: McGraw-Hill, 1976.
———. *The Correspondence of James Boswell with David Garrick, Edmund Burke, and Edmond Malone*. Edited by James M. Osborn and Peter S. Baker. London: Heinemann, 1986.
———. *The Correspondence and Other Papers of James Boswell Relating to the Making of the Life of Johnson*. Edited by Marshall Waingrow. 2nd ed. New Haven, CT: Yale University Press, 2002.
———. *The General Correspondence of James Boswell, 1757–1763*. Edited by David Hankins and James J. Caudle. Edinburgh: Edinburgh University Press, 2006.
———. *The Journal of a Tour to the Hebrides, with Samuel Johnson, LL.D.* 1st ed. London, 1785.
———. *The Journal of a Tour to the Hebrides, with Samuel Johnson, LL.D. By James Boswell. . . . The Second Edition, Revised and Corrected*. 2nd ed. London, 1785.
———. *The Journal of a Tour to the Hebrides with Samuel Johnson, LL.D. By James Boswell. . . . The Third Edition, Revised and Corrected*. 3rd ed. London, 1786.
———. *The Life of Samuel Johnson, LL.D.* Edited by George B. Hill, with Revised ed. by Lawrence F. Powell. 6 vols. Oxford: Clarendon Press, 1934–1964.
———. *London Journal: 1762–1763*. Edited by Frederick A. Pottle. New York: McGraw-Hill, 1950.
———. *London Journal 1762–1763*. Edited by Gordon Turnbull. New York: Penguin, 2010.
———. *London Journal, 1762–1763, Together with Journal of my Jaunt, Harvest, 1762*. Deluxe ed. London: Heineman, 1951.
———. *No Abolition of Slavery or the Universal Empire of Love, A Poem*. London, 1791. http://www.gutenberg.org/ebooks/20360.
———. *Private Papers of James Boswell from Malahide Castle in the Collection of Lt.-Colonel Ralph Heyward Isham*. Edited by Geoffrey Scott and Frederick A. Pottle. 18 vols. Privately printed, 1928–1934.
Botting, Ronald B. "The Textual History of Murphy's *Gray's-Inn Journal*," *Research Studies of the State University of Washington* 25 (1957): 33–48.

Brack, O M, Jr. "Attack and Mask: James Boswell's Indebtedness to Sir John Hawkins' *Life of Samuel Johnson*." In *The Interpretation of Samuel Johnson*, edited by J. C. D. Clark and Howard Erskine-Hill, 43–71. Basingstoke, UK: Palgrave Macmillan, 2012.

———. ed. *Journal Narrative Relative to Doctor Johnson's Last Illness Three Weeks before his Death*. Iowa City: Windhover Press, 1972.

Brack, O M, Jr., and R. E. Kelley, eds. *The Early Biographies of Samuel Johnson*. Iowa City: University of Iowa Press, 1974.

Bradford, C. B. "The Edinburgh 'Ramblers.'" *Modern Language Review* 34 (1939): 241–44.

Brady, Frank. *James Boswell: The Later Years, 1769–1795*. New York: McGraw-Hill, 1984.

Brewer, David. *The Afterlife of Character, 1726–1825*. Philadelphia: University of Pennsylvania Press, 2005.

Briggs, Peter. "Laurence Sterne and Literary Celebrity in 1760." *Age of Johnson: A Scholarly Annual* 4 (1991): 251–80.

Brock, Claire. *The Feminization of Fame, 1750–1830*. Basingstoke, UK: Palgrave Macmillan, 2006.

Bronson, Bertrand. "The Double Tradition of Dr. Johnson." *English Literary History* 18, no. 2 (June 1951): 90–106.

———. "The Writer." In *Man Versus Society in Eighteenth-Century Britain: Six Points of View*. By James L. Clifford, 102–32. London: Cambridge University Press, 1968.

Brookes, Richard, MD. *A New and Accurate System of Natural History*. 6 vols. London: J. Newbery, 1763-[1764].

Brown, Christopher Leslie. *Moral Capital: Foundations of British Abolitionism*. Chapel Hill: University of Carolina Press, 2006.

Bundock, Michael. *The Fortunes of Francis Barber: The True Story of the Jamaican Slave Who Became Samuel Johnson's Heir*. New Haven, CT: Yale University Press. 2013.

Burke, Edmund. *The Correspondence of Edmund Burke*. Edited by Thomas W. Copeland et al. 10 vols. Cambridge: Cambridge University Press, 1958–1978.

———. *The Early Life, Correspondence and Writings of the Rt. Hon. Edmund Burke*. Edited by Arthur Purefoy Irwin Samuels and Arthur Warren Samuels. Cambridge: Cambridge University Press, 1923.

———. *Reflections on the Revolution in France*. London, 1790.

———. *The Writings and Speeches of Edmund Burke*. Edited by Paul Langford and William Todd. 9 vols. Oxford: Oxford University Press. 1981–2016.

Burke, John J., Jr. "But Boswell's Johnson Is Not Boswell's Johnson." In *Boswell's Life of Johnson: New Questions, New Answers*, edited by John A. Vance, 172–203. Athens, GA: University of Georgia Press, 1985.

Burney, Frances. *The Court Journals and Letters of Frances Burney*. Edited by Peter Sabor. 4 vols. to date. Oxford: Clarendon Press, 2011–.

———. *Diary and Letters of Madame D'Arblay*. Edited by Charlotte Barrett. 7 vols. London, 1842–1846.

———. *The Early Journals and Letters of Fanny Burney*. Edited by Lars E. Troide, with Stewart J. Cooke and Betty W. Rizzol. 5 vols. Montreal and Kingston, ON: McGill-Queen's University Press, 1988–2012.

———. *The Journals and Letters of Fanny Burney (1791–1840)*. Edited by Joyce Hemlow et al. 12 vols. Oxford: Clarendon Press, 1972–1984.

———. *The Wanderer*. Edited by Margaret Anne Doody, Robert L. Mack, and Peter Sabor. Oxford: Oxford University Press, 2001.

Burney D'Arblay, Frances. *The Memoirs of Dr. Burney*. London, 1832.

Butt, John Everett. *James Boswell*. University of Edinburgh Inaugural Lecture 3. Edinburgh: Oliver and Boyd, 1959.

Campbell, Thomas. *Dr. Campbell's Diary of a Visit to England in 1775*. Edited by James L. Clifford. Cambridge: Cambridge University Press, 1947.
Capper, James. *Observations on the Winds and Monsoons*. London: Whittingham, 1801.
Catalogue of the Private Papers of James Boswell at Yale University. Edited by Marion S Pottle, Claude Colleer Abbott, and Frederick A. Pottle. 3 vols. Edinburgh: Edinburgh University Press, 1993.
Caudle, James J. "'O Rare Sam Jonson': James Boswell's Journal of a Tour to Hawthornden Castle with Samuel Johnson and Ben Jonson, 1773." *Age of Johnson: A Scholarly Annual* 22 (2012): 23–71.
Cervantes, Miguel Cervantes. *The History and Adventures of the Renowned Don Quixote*. Translated by Tobias Smollett. London, 1755.
Chapman, R. W. "Mrs. Piozzi's Omissions from Johnson's Letters to Thrales." *Review of English Studies* 22, no. 85 (1946): 17–28.
Chisholm, Kate. *Wits and Wives: Dr. Johnson in the Company of Women*. London: Chatto and Windus, 2011.
Christensen, Jerome. *Lord Byron's Strength : Romantic Writing and Commercial Society*. Baltimore: Johns Hopkins University Press, 1993.
Churchill, Charles. *The Ghost*. 4 books. London, 1762–1763.
Clark, A. F. B. *Boileau and the French Classical Critics in England*. New York: Burt Franklin, 1970.
Clarke, Norma. *Brothers of the Quill: Oliver Goldsmith in Grub Street*. Cambridge, MA: Harvard University Press, 2016.
———. *Dr. Johnson's Women*. London: Hambledon, 2000.
Clarkson, Thomas. *The History of the Rise, Progress, and Accomplishment of the Abolition of the Slave-Trade by the British Parliament*. 3 vols. New York, 1836.
Clifford, James L. "The Authenticity of Anna Seward's Published Correspondence." *Modern Philology* 39, no. 2 (November 1941): 113–22.
Clingham, Greg, ed. *The Cambridge Companion to Samuel Johnson*. Cambridge: Cambridge University Press, 1997; 2005.
———, ed. *New Light on Boswell: Critical and Historical Essays on the Occasion of the Bicentenary of the Life of Johnson*. Cambridge: Cambridge University Press, 1991.
Cohen, Ralph. "The Return to the Ode." In *The Cambridge Companion to Eighteenth-Century Poetry*, edited by John Sitter, 203–24. Cambridge: Cambridge University Press, 2001.
Collings, Samuel. "Revising for the Second Edition" In *Picturesque Beauties of Boswell Parts I and II*, engraved by Thomas Rowlandson. London, 1786.
Corum, Robert T., Jr. *Reading Boileau: An Integrative Study of the Early Satires*. West Lafayette, IN: Purdue University Press, 1998.
Cradock: Joseph. *Literary and Miscellaneous Memoirs*. London, 1826.
Croker, John Wilson, ed., *Johnsoniana, or, Supplement to Boswell: Being Anecdotes and Sayings of Dr. Johnson. . . .* London, 1836.
Curley, Thomas M. *Sir Robert Chambers: Law, Literature, and Empire in the Age of Johnson*. 2 vols. Madison: University of Wisconsin Press, 1998.
Cutting-Gray, Joanne. *Woman as Nobody and the Novels of Fanny Burney*. Gainesville: University Press of Florida, 1992.
Daghlian, Philip B., ed. *Essays in Eighteenth-Century Biography*. Bloomington: Indiana University Press, 1968.
Dallas, Robert Charles. "Biographical Memoir of James Elphinston, Esq." *European Magazine* 56 (1809): 361–68.
Damrosch, Leopold. "Samuel Johnson and Reader-Response Criticism." *Eighteenth Century* 21, no. 2 (Spring 1980): 91–108.

Davidson, Virginia Spencer. "Johnson's *Life of Savage:* The Transformation of a Genre." In *Studies in Biography*, edited by Daniel Aaron, 57–72. Cambridge, MA: Harvard University Press, 1978.
Davie, Donald. *Purity of Diction in English Verse and Articulate Energy*. Manchester: Carcanet, 2006.
Defoe, Daniel. *The Fortunes and Misfortunes of the Famous Moll Flanders*. London, 1722.
———. *A Tour Thro' the Whole Island of Great Britain*. 3 vols. London, 1724.
DeMaria, Robert, Jr. *The Life of Samuel Johnson: A Critical Biography*. Cambridge, MA: Blackwell Publishers, 1993.
DeMaria, Robert, Jr., and Gwin J. Kolb. "Johnson's *Dictionary* and Dictionary Johnson." *Yearbook of English Studies* 28 (1998): 19–43.
Donoghue, Frank. *The Fame Machine: Book Reviewing and Eighteenth-Century Literary Careers*. Stanford, CA: Stanford University Press, 1996.
Doody, Margaret Anne. *Frances Burney: A Life in the Works*. New Brunswick, NJ: Rutgers University Press, 1988.
Dryden, John. *The Works of John Dryden*, ed. Edward Niles Hooker et al. 20 vols. Berkeley and Los Angeles: University of California Press, 1956–2000.
Dun, John. *Sermons, in Two Volumes, by John Dun, V.D.M.* Kilmarnock, 1790.
———. "To Edmund Burke, Esq. on his 'Reflections.'" *Whitehall Evening Post* 6716 (August 30, 1791-September 1, 1791).
———. "To Thomas Paine, Esq., Letter I." *Whitehall Evening Post* 6720 (September 8–10, 1791).
———."To Thomas Paine, Esq., Letter II."*Whitehall Evening Post* 6721 (September 10–13, 1791).
———. "To Thomas Paine, Esq., Letter III."*Whitehall Evening Post* 6722 (September 13–15, 1791).
Dunbar, Howard H. *The Dramatic Career of Murphy*. New York: Modern Language Association of America, 1946.
Duncan, Ian. "Romance." In *Encyclopedia of the Novel*, edited by Paul Schellinger, vol. 2, 1113–17. New York: Routledge, 2014.
Eccles, Mary Hyde. *The Impossible Friendship: Boswell and Mrs. Piozzi*. Cambridge, MA: Harvard University Press, 1972.
Ellis, David. "Biography and Friendship: Johnson's *Life of Savage*." In *Imitating Art: Essays in Biography*, edited by David Ellis, 19–35. London: Pluto Press, 1993.
Elphinston, James. *The Analysis of the French and English Languages*. London, 1756; 1763.
———. *An Apology for the Monthly Review, with an Appendix in Behalf of the Critical*. London, 1763.
———. *Correspondance Française-Anglaise causée par une lettre trouvée en mer dans une bouteille sur la côte normande; avec la lettre même*. . . . London, 1789.
———. *Education, in Four Books*. London, 1763.
———. *Fifty Years' Correspondence, Inglish, French, and Lattin, in Proze and Verse; Between Geniusses ov Boath Sexes, and James Elphinston*. . . . London, 1794.
———. *Forty Years' Correspondence Between Geniusses ov Boath Sexes, and James Elphinston*. 8 vols. London, 1791; 1794.
———. *The Hypercritic*. London, 1783.
———. *Proposals for Printing by Subscription . . . the Epigrams of M. V. Martial*. London, 1778.
———. *Religion, a Poem: From the French of the Younger Racine*. London, 1754.
———. *Six Pocket-Vollumes: Foar ov Oridginal Letters, Two' ov Poetry*. London, 1791.
Emery, John Pike. *Arthur Murphy: An Eminent English Dramatist of the Eighteenth Century*. Philadelphia: University of Pennsylvania Press, 1946.
Engel, Laura. *Fashioning Celebrity: Eighteenth-Century British Actresses and Strategies for Image Making*. Columbus: Ohio State University Press, 2011.

Engel, Laura, and Elaine M. McGirr, eds. *Stage Mothers: Women, Work, and the Theater, 1660–1830*. Lewisburg, PA: Bucknell University Press, 2014.
Erwin, Timothy. *Textual Vision: Augustan Design and the Invention of Eighteenth-Century British Culture*. Lewisburg, PA: Bucknell University Press, 2015.
Ezell, Margaret. *The Patriarch's Wife: Literary Evidence and the History of the Family*. Chapel Hill: University of North Carolina Press, 1987.
Fairer, David. "Historical Criticism and the English Canon: A Spenserian Dispute in the 1750s." *Eighteenth-Century Life* 24, no. 2 (2000): 43–64.
———. "J. D. Fleeman: A Memoir." *Studies in Bibliography* 48 (1995): 1–24.
———. "Johnson and the Warton Brothers." In *Samuel Johnson: The Arc of the Pendulum*. edited by Freya Johnston and Lynda Mugglestone, 181–94. Oxford: Oxford University Press, 2013.
Feather, John. *The Provincial Book Trade in Eighteenth-Century England*. Cambridge: Cambridge University Press, 1985.
Fish, Stanley. "Authors-Readers: Jonson's Community of the Same." *Representations* 7 (July 1984): 26–58.
Flavell, Julie. *When London Was Capital of America*. New Haven, CT: Yale University Press, 2010.
Fleeman, David. *A Bibliography of the Works of Samuel Johnson*. Edited by James McLaverty. 2 vols. Oxford: Clarendon Press, 2000.
Folkenflik, Robert. *Samuel Johnson, Biographer*. Ithaca, NY: Cornell University Press, 1978.
Fong, David. "Johnson, Goldsmith, and *The Traveller*." *New Rambler* (Autumn 1971): 22–30.
Formey, Henri Samuel. *Histoire Abrégée de la Philosophie* [*A Concise History of Philosophy and Philosophers*]. Translated by Oliver Goldsmith. London: F. Newbery, 1766.
Forrester, James. *The Polite Philosopher*. Edinburgh, 1736.
Francklin, Thomas. *A Dissertation on Antient Tragedy*. London, 1760.
Free, Melissa. "Un-Erasing *Crusoe*: *Farther Adventures* in the Nineteenth Century." *Book History* 9 (2006): 89–130.
Fulford, Tim. "'Nature' Poetry." In *The Cambridge Companion to Eighteenth-Century Poetry*, edited by John Sitter, 109–31. Cambridge: Cambridge University Press, 2006.
Gallagher, Catherine. *Nobody's Story: Vanishing Acts in the Marketplace, 1670–1820*. Berkeley: University of California Press, 1995.
Gilbert, Suzanne. "Scottish Ballads and Popular Culture." *Bottle Imp* 5 (May 2009): 1–3.
Gillray, James. "Apollo and the Muses, Inflicting Penance on Dr. Pomposo, round Parnassus." London, 1783.
Glendenning, John. "Young Fanny Burney and the Mentor." *Age of Johnson: A Scholarly Annual* 4 (1991): 281–312.
Goldsmith, Oliver. *The Citizen of the World, Or, Letters from a Chinese Philosopher*. 2 vols. London: J. Newbery, 1762.
———. *The Collected Letters of Oliver Goldsmith*. Edited by Katharine C. Balderston. Cambridge: Cambridge University Press, 1928.
———. *Collected Works of Oliver Goldsmith*. Edited by Arthur Friedman. 5 vols. Oxford: Clarendon Press, 1966.
———. *A Compendium of Biography*. vols. 1–4. London: J. Newbery, 1762.
———. *The Deserted Village, A Poem*. London, 1770.
———. *Essays. By Oliver Goldsmith. Collecta Revirescunt*. London, 1765.
———. *Essays. By Oliver Goldsmith. Collecta Revirescunt*. 2nd ed. London, 1766.
———. *The Grecian History*. London: J. and F. Rivington, 1774.
———. *A History of England, in a Series of Letters from a Nobleman to His Son*. 2 vols. London: J. Newbery, 1764.

———. *A History of the Earth and Animated Nature*, 8 vols. London: J. Nourse, 1774.
———. *The Life of Richard Nash Esq.; Late Master of the Ceremonies at Bath . . . The Second Edition*. London, 1762.
———. *The Martial Review; Or, A General History of the late Wars*. London: J. Newbery 1763.
———. *The Roman History*, 2 vols. London: S. Baker & G. Leigh et al., 1769.
———. *The Traveller, Or A Prospect of Society. A Poem*. London, 1765 [1764].
———. *The Traveller 1765 and The Deserted Village 1770 with "A Prospect of Society" (1764)*. Facsimile. Menston, UK: Scolar Press, 1970. Available online at *Eighteenth Century Collections Online (ECCO)*, https://www.gale.com/primary-sources/eighteenth-century-collections-online.
Greene, Donald. "Do We Need a Biography of Johnson's 'Boswell' Years?" *Modern Language Studies* 9, no. 3 (Autumn 1979): 128–36.
Greene, Jody. *The Trouble with Ownership: Literary Property and Authorial Liability in England, 1660–1730*. Philadelphia: University of Pennsylvania Press, 2005.
Grundy, Isobel. "Samuel Johnson as Patron of Women." *Age of Johnson: A Scholarly Annual* 1 (1987): 59–77.
Habermas, Jürgen. *The Structural Transformation of the Public Sphere: An Inquiry into a Category of Bourgeois Society*. Translated by Thomas Burger, with Frederick Lawrence (1962). Cambridge, MA: MIT Press, 1991.
Halmi, Nicholas. "Romanticism, the Temporalization of History, and the Historicization of Form." *Modern Language Quarterly* 74, no. 3 (January 2013): 363–89.
Hamilton, Kate. "Frances Burney and Celebrity." PhD diss., Carnegie Mellon University, 2016.
Hanson, L. W. Review of *Studies in Bibliography* 7 (1955). *Library* 5th ser., 10 (1955): 297–98.
Harbottle, Thomas. *Dictionary of Quotations (Classical)*. London: Swan Sonnenschein, 1906.
Haugen, Kristine. "Chivalry and Romance in the Eighteenth Century: Richard Hurd and the Disenchantment of the *Faerie Queene*." *Prose Studies* 23, no. 2 (August 2000): 45–60.
Hawkins, Sir John. *The Life of Samuel Johnson, LL.D.* Edited by O M Brack, Jr. London and Athens, GA: University of Georgia Press, 2009.
Heiland, Donna. "Swan Songs: The Correspondence of Anna Seward and James Boswell." *Modern Philology* 90, no. 3 (February 1993): 381–91.
Herrmann, Luke. "Turner, James W. M." s.v. *Oxford Dictionary of National Biography Online*. http://www.oxforddnb.com/.
Hill, Bridget. *Women, Work, and Sexual Politics in Eighteenth-Century England*. London: Blackwell, 1989.
Hilles, Frederick W. *The Literary Career of Sir Joshua Reynolds*. Cambridge: Cambridge University Press, 1936. Reprint. Hamden, CT: Archon Press, 1967.
Holmes, Richard. *Dr. Johnson & Mr. Savage*. New York: Pantheon Books, 1993.
Hopkins, Robert H. *The True Genius of Oliver Goldsmith*. Baltimore: Johns Hopkins University Press, 1969.
Hunter, Michael. "Daniel Coxe." s.v. *Oxford Dictionary of National Biography Online*. http://www.oxforddnb.com/.
Jennings, Judith. *Gender, Religion, and Radicalism in the Long Eighteenth Century: [Mary Knowles] The "Ingenious Quaker" and Her Contemporaries*. Aldershot, UK: Ashgate, 2006.
Johnson, Claudia. "'Let Me Make the Novels of a Country': Barbauld's 'The British Novelists' (1810/1820)." *Novel: A Forum on Fiction* 34, no. 2 (Spring 2001): 163–79.
Johnson, Samuel. *Diaries, Prayers, and Annals*. Edited by Edward L. McAdam, Jr., with Donald and Mary Hyde. New Haven, CT: Yale University Press, 1958.
———. *A Dictionary of the English Language*. 2 vols. London, 1755.

———. *Johnsonian Miscellanies*. Edited by George B. Hill. 2 vols. Oxford: Clarendon Press, 1897.
———. *A Journey to the Western Isles of Scotland*. Edited by J. D. Fleeman. Oxford: Clarendon Press, 1985.
Princeton University Press, 1992–1994.
———. *The Life of Mr. Richard Savage*. Edited by Nicholas Seager and Lance Wilcox. Peterborough, ON: Broadview Press, 2016.
———. *Life of Savage*. Edited by Clarence Tracy. Oxford: Clarendon Press, 1971.
———. *The Lives of the Most Eminent English Poets: With Critical Observations on Their Works*. Edited by Roger H. Lonsdale. 4 vols. Oxford: Oxford University Press, 2006.
———. *The Poems of Samuel Johnson*. Edited by David Nichol Smith and Edward L. McAdam, Revised by J. D. Fleeman. 2nd ed. Oxford: Clarendon Press, 1974.
———. *The Works of Samuel Johnson*, 11 vols. Oxford, 1825.
———. *The Yale Edition of the Works of Samuel Johnson*. Edited by Robert DeMaria, Jr. 23 vols. New Haven, CT: Yale University Press, 1958–2018.
Jost, Jacob Sider. "The *Gentleman's Magazine*, Samuel Johnson, and the Symbolic Economy of Eighteenth-Century Poetry." *Review of English Studies* 66, no. 277 (November 2015): 915–35.
Justice, George. *The Manufacturers of Literature: Writing and the Literary Marketplace in Eighteenth-Century England*. Newark: University of Delaware Press, 2002.
Kairoff, Claudia Thomas. *Anna Seward and the End of the Eighteenth Century*. Baltimore: Johns Hopkins University Press, 2012.
Kennedy, Deborah. *Poetic Sisters: Early Eighteenth-Century Women Poets*. Lewisburg, PA: Bucknell University Press, 2012.
Kenney, William. "Parodies and Imitations of Johnson in the Eighteenth Century." *Studies in Eighteenth-Century Culture* 7 (1978): 463–73.
Kernan, Alvin. *Samuel Johnson and the Impact of Print*. Princeton, NJ: Princeton University Press, 1987. Paperback ed., 1989. First published as *Printing Technology, Letters, & Samuel Johnson*. Princeton, NJ: Princeton University Press, 1987.
Keymer, Thomas, and Peter Sabor. *Pamela in the Marketplace: Literary Controversy and Print Culture in Eighteenth-Century Britain and Ireland*. Cambridge: Cambridge University Press, 2005.
Kinsella, Thomas. "The Pride of Literature: Arthur Murphy's *Essay on Johnson*." *Age of Johnson: A Scholarly Annual* 16 (2005): 129–56.
Kopec, Andrew. "The Digital Humanities, Inc.: Literary Criticism and the Fate of a Profession." *PMLA* 131, no. 2 (March 2016): 324–39.
Korshin, Paul. "Johnson's Conversation in Boswell's *Life of Johnson*. In *New Light on Boswell: Critical and Historical Essays on the Occasion of the Bicentenary of the Life of Johnson*, edited by Greg Clingham, 174–93. Cambridge: Cambridge University Press, 1991.
Koselleck, Reinhart. *Futures Past: On the Semantics of Historical Time*. Cambridge, MA: MIT Press, 1985.
Lamb, Susan. *Bringing Travel Home to England: Tourism, Gender and Imaginative Literature*. Newark: University of Delaware Press, 2009.
Lambert, Elizabeth. "Boswell's Burke: The Literary Consequences of Ambivalence." In *The Age of Johnson: A Scholarly Annual* 9 (1998): 201–35.
———. "Johnson on Friendship: The Example of Burke." In *Johnson After Two Hundred Years*, edited by Paul J. Korshin, 111–23. Philadelphia: University of Pennsylvania Press, 1986.
Lamont, Claire. "James Boswell and Alexander Fraser Tytler." *Bibliotheck* 6 (1971):1–16.
Larsen, Lyle. "Dr. Johnson's Friend, the Worthy Bennet Langton." *Age of Johnson: A Scholarly Journal* 20 (2010): 145–72.

———. *Dr. Johnson's Household*. Hamden, CT: Archon Books, 1985.
Lee, Anthony W. "Allegories of Mentoring: Johnson and Frances Burney's *Cecilia*," *Eighteenth-Century Novel* 5 (2006): 249–76.
———. *Dead Masters: Mentoring and Intertextuality in Samuel Johnson*. Bethlehem, PA: Lehigh University Press, 2011.
———. *Mentoring Relationships in the Life and Writings of Samuel Johnson: A Study in the Dynamics of Eighteenth-Century Literary Mentoring*. Lewiston, NY: Edwin Mellen Press, 2005.
Leslie, Charles Robert, and Tom Taylor. *The Life and Times of Sir Joshua Reynolds*. 2 vols. London, 1865.
Leyburn, Ellen Douglas. "The Translations of the Mottoes and Quotations in the *Rambler*." *Review of English Studies* 16 (1940): 169–76.
Lipking, Lawrence. *Samuel Johnson: The Life of an Author*. Cambridge, MA: Harvard University Press, 1998.
Lonsdale, Roger, ed. *The Poems of Thomas Gray, William Collins, and Oliver Goldsmith*. London: Longmans, 1969; 1976.
Lustig, Irma S. "Fact into Art: James Boswell's Notes, Journals, and the *Life of Johnson*." In *Biography in the 18th Century*, edited by John D. Browning, 128–46. New York: Garland Publishing, 1980.
Lynch, Jack. "Generous Liberal-Minded Men: Booksellers and Poetic Careers in Johnson's *Lives of the Poets*." *Yearbook of English Studies* 45 (January 2015): 93–108.
Marteilhe, Jean. *The Memoirs of a Protestant Condemned to the Galleys of France, for his Religion . . . Translated . . . By James Willington*. Edited by Oliver Goldsmith. Translated by James Willington. London: R. Griffiths, 1758.
Martin, Martin. *A Description of the Western Islands of Scotland*. 2 vols. London, 1703.
Martin, Peter. *Samuel Johnson: A Biography*. Cambridge, MA: Harvard University Press, 2008.
McCarthy, William. "The Composition of Johnson's *Lives*: A Calendar." *Philological Quarterly*. 60 (1981): 53–67.
McGann, Jerome. *The Poetics of Sensibility: A Revolution in Literary Style*. Oxford: Clarendon, 1996.
McGuffie, Helen Louise. *Samuel Johnson in the British Press, 1749-1784: A Chronological Checklist*. New York: Garland, 1976.
McKeon, Michael. *The Secret History of Domesticity*. Baltimore: Johns Hopkins University Press, 2005.
Mengel, Elias F. "Pope's Imitation of Boileau in *Arbuthnot*." *Essays in Criticism* 38, no. 4 (October 1988): 295–307.
Miller, Stephen. *Three Deaths and Enlightenment Thought*. Lewisburg, PA: Bucknell University Press, 2001.
Mole, Tom. *Byron's Romantic Celebrity: Industrial Culture and the Hermeneutic of Intimacy*. Basingstoke, UK: Palgrave Macmillan, 2007.
Morrison, Sarah R. "Toil, Envy, Want, the Reader, and the Jail: Reader Entrapment in Johnson's *Life of Savage*." *Age of Johnson: A Scholarly Annual* 9 (1998): 145–64.
Murphy, Arthur. *An Essay on the Life and Genius of Samuel Johnson, LL.D.* London, 1792.
———. *The Life of David Garrick*. 2 vols. London, 1801.
———. *New Essays by Murphy*. Edited by Arthur Sherbo. East Lansing: Michigan State University, 1963.
———. *A Poetical Epistle to Mr. Samuel Johnson, A.M.* London, 1760.
———. *The Works of Arthur Murphy*. 7 vols. London, 1786.
Noyes, Edward S., ed. *The Letters of Tobias Smollett, M.D.* Cambridge, MA: Harvard University Press, 1926.

Nussbaum, Felicity. *Rival Queens: Actresses, Performance, and Eighteenth-Century British Theater*. Philadelphia: University of Pennsylvania Press, 2010.

Odell, Jonathan. *An Essay on the Elements, Accents, and Prosody of the English Language*. London, 1805.

Oxford Dictionary of National Biography Online (*ODNB*). 2018. http://www.oxforddnb.com/.

Parke, Catherine N. "Johnson and the Arts of Conversation." In *The Cambridge Companion to Samuel Johnson*, edited by Greg Clingham, 18–33. Cambridge: Cambridge University Press, 1997; 2005.

Paterson, James. *History of the County of Ayr: With a Genealogical Account of the Families of Ayrshire*. 2 vols. Edinburgh, 1847. Reprint. 1895.

Pennant, Thomas. *A Tour in Scotland, and Voyage to the Hebrides*. Chester, 1771.

Pindar, Peter [John Wolcot]. *A Poetical and Congratulatory Epistle to James Boswell, Esq. on his Journal of a Tour to the Hebrides. With the Celebrated Dr. Johnson*. London, 1786.

———. *A Poetical, Supplicating, Modest, and Affecting Epistle to Those Literary Colossuses the Reviewers*. London, 1778.

Piozzi, Hester Lynch. *Anecdotes of the Late Samuel Johnson, LL.D., During the Last Twenty Years of His Life*. London, 1786.

———. *Anecdotes of Samuel Johnson, LL.D.* In *Memoirs and Anecdotes of Dr. Johnson*. Edited by Arthur Sherbo. London and New York: Oxford University Press, 1974.

———. *Thraliana: The Diary of Mrs. Hester Lynch Thrale (Later Mrs. Piozzi), 1776–1809*. Edited by Katherine C. Balderston. 2nd ed. 2 vols. Oxford: Oxford University Press, 1951.

Pittock, Murray G. H. *James Boswell*. Aberdeen: AHRC Centre for Irish and Scottish Studies, 2007.

———. "Johnson and Scotland." In *Samuel Johnson in Historical Context*, edited by Jonathan Clark and Howard Erskine-Hill, 184–96. Basingstoke, UK: Palgrave Macmillan, 2002.

Pocock, Gordon. *Boileau and the Nature of Neo-Classicism*. Cambridge: Cambridge University Press, 1980.

Pope, Alexander. *The Twickenham Edition of the Poems of Alexander Pope*. Edited by John Everett Butt et al. 11 vols. New Haven, CT: Yale University Press, 1939–1969.

Pottle, Frederick A. "The Adequacy as Biography of Boswell's *Life of Johnson*." In *Boswell's Life of Johnson: New Questions, New Answers*, edited by John A. Vance, 147–60. Athens, GA: University of Georgia Press, 1985.

———. "The Dark Hints of Sir John Hawkins and Boswell." *Modern Language Notes* 56, no. 5 (May 1941): 325–29.

———. *The Literary Career of James Boswell, Esq.; Being the Bibliographical Materials for A Life of Boswell*. Oxford: Clarendon Press, 1929.

———. "The Power of Memory in Boswell and Scott." In *Essays on the Eighteenth Century: Presented to David Nichol Smith in Honour of His Seventieth Birthday*, 168–89. Oxford: Clarendon Press, 1945.

Powell, Manushag N. *Performing Authorship in Eighteenth-Century English Periodicals*. Lewisburg, PA: Bucknell University Press, 2012.

Quintana, Ricardo. "*The Deserted Village*: Its Logical and Rhetorical Elements." *College English* 26, no. 3 (1964): 204–6, 211–14.

———. *Oliver Goldsmith: A Georgian Study*. New York: Macmillan, 1967.

Rader, Ralph. "Literary Form in Factual Narrative." In *Boswell's Life of Johnson: New Questions, New Answers*, edited by John A. Vance, 25–52. Athens: University of Georgia Press, 1985.

Radner, John B. *Johnson and Boswell: A Biography of Friendship*. New Haven, CT: Yale University Press, 2012.

Raven, James. *Publishing Business in Eighteenth-Century England*. Woodbridge: Boydell, 2014.

Redford, Bruce. *Designing the Life of Johnson: The Lyell Lectures, 2001–2*. Oxford: Oxford University Press, 2002.
Reynolds, Sir Joshua. *Portraits by Sir Joshua Reynolds*. Edited by Frederick W. Hilles. New York: McGraw-Hill, 1952.
Rider, William. *An Historical and Critical Account of the Lives and Writings of the Living Authors of Great-Britain*. London: For the author, 1762.
Roach, Joseph. *It*. Ann Arbor: University of Michigan Press, 2007.
Roberts, William. *Memoirs of the Life and Correspondence of Mrs. Hannah More*. 3rd ed. 4 vols. London, 1835.
Rojek, Chris. *Celebrity*. London: Reaktion Books, 2001.
Ross, Trevor. "The Emergence of 'Literature': Making and Reading the English Canon in the Eighteenth Century." *English Literary History* 63, no. 2 (1996): 397–422.
———. *The Making of the English Literary Canon: From the Middle Ages to the Late Eighteenth Century*. Montreal: McGill-Queen's University Press, 1998.
Rousseau, G. S., ed. *Goldsmith: The Critical Heritage*. London: Routledge & Kegan Paul, 1974.
Rudd, Niall. "Variation and Inversion in Pope's *Epistle to Dr. Arbuthnot*." *Essays in Criticism* 34, no. 3 (July 1984): 216–28.
Said, Edward W. *The World, the Text, and the Critic*. Cambridge, MA: Harvard University Press, 1983.
Schellenberg, Betty. "The Second Coming of the Book, 1740–1770." In *Producing the Eighteenth-Century Book: Writers and Publishers in England, 1650–1800*, edited by Laura L. Runge and Pat Rogers, 30–52. Newark: University of Delaware Press, 2009.
Scherwatzky, Steven D. "'Complicated Virtue': The Politics of Samuel Johnson's *Life of Savage*." *Eighteenth Century Life* 25, no. 3 (2001): 80–93.
Schwalm, David E. "Johnson's *Life of Savage*: Biography as Argument." *Biography* 8, no. 2 (Spring 1985): 130–44.
Schwartz, Richard B. "Epilogue: The Boswell Problem." In *Boswell's Life of Johnson: New Questions, New Answers*, edited by John A. Vance, 248–59. Athens, GA: University of Georgia Press, 1985.
Scott, Geoffrey. "The First Records." In *Private Papers of James Boswell From Malahide Castle*, edited by Geoffrey Scott and Frederick A. Pottle, vol. 6, 15–27. Privately printed, 1929.
———. "The Making of the *Life of Johnson* as Shown in Boswell's First Notes." In *Twentieth Century Interpretations of Boswell's Life of Johnson*, edited by James L. Clifford, 27–39. Englewood Cliffs, NJ: Prentice Hall, 1970.
Scott, Hew, ed. *Fasti Ecclesiae Scoticanae: The Succession of Ministers in the Church of Scotland from the Reformation*. 2nd ed. 10 [9] vols. Edinburgh: Oliver and Boyd, 1915–1981.
Scott, Temple. *Oliver Goldsmith Bibliographically and Biographically Considered: Based on the Collection of Material in the Library of W. M. Elkin, Esq.* New York: Bowling Green Press, 1928.
Seward, Anna. *The Collected Poems of Anna Seward*. Edited by Lisa L. Moore. 2 vols. London: Routledge, 2016.
———. *Letters of Anna Seward: Written between the Years 1784 and 1807*. Edited by Archibald Constable. 6 vols. Edinburgh and London, 1811.
Seymour, Terry. *Boswell's Books: Four Generations of Collecting and Collectors*. New Castle, DE: Oak Knoll Press, 2016.
[Shaw, Cuthbert]. *The Race*. London, 1765.
Shaw, William. *Memoirs of the Life and Writings of the Late Dr. Samuel Johnson*. In *The Early Biographies of Samuel Johnson*. Edited by O M Brack, Jr. and R. E. Kelley, 137–86. Iowa City: University of Iowa Press, 1974.

Sher, Richard B. "Dun, John (1723/4–1792)." s.v. *Oxford Dictionary of National Biography Online*, 2004. http://www.oxforddnb.com/.

Siebenschuh, William R. "Boswell's Second Crop of Memory: A New Look at the Role of Memory in the Making of the Life." In *Boswell's Life of Johnson: New Questions, New Answers*, edited by John A. Vance, 94–109. Athens, GA: University of Georgia Press, 1985.

Siskin, Clifford. *The Work of Writing: Literature and Social Change in Britain, 1700–1830*. Baltimore: Johns Hopkins University Press, 1999.

Sledd, James H., and Gwin J. Kolb. *Dr. Johnson's Dictionary: Essays in the Biography of a Book*. Chicago: University of Chicago Press, 1955.

Small, Miriam. *Charlotte Ramsay Lennox: An Eighteenth Century Lady of Letters*. London and New Haven, CT: Yale University Press and Oxford University Press, 1935.

Smallwood, Philip. "The Johnsonian Monster and the *Lives of the Poets*: James Gillray, Critical History, and the Eighteenth-Century Satirical Cartoon." *British Journal for Eighteenth-Century Studies* 25 (2002): 217–24.

———. *Johnson's Critical Presence: Image, History, Judgment*. Burlington: Ashgate, 2004.

Smith, Chloe Wigston. *Women, Work, and Clothes in the Eighteenth-Century Novel*. Cambridge: Cambridge University Press, 2013.

Smith, John Thomas. *Nollekens and His Times: A Life of that Celebrated Sculptor and Memoirs of Several Contemporary Artists, from the Time of Roubiliac, Hogarth and Reynolds to that of Fuseli, Flaxman and Blake*. 2nd ed. London, 1829.

Smith, Robert W. "Edmund Burke's Negro Code." *History Today* 26, no. 11 (November 1976): 715–24.

Snipes, Wilson. "Authorial Typology in Literary Biography." *Biography* 13, no. 3 (Summer 1990): 235–50.

Sodeman, Melissa. *Sentimental Memorials: Women and the Novel in Literary History*. Stanford, CA: Stanford University Press, 2014.

Spector, Robert D. *Arthur Murphy*. Boston: Twayne, 1979.

Springer-Miller, Fred. "Johnson and Boileau." *Notes & Queries* 196 (November 10, 1951): 497.

Stephens, John. "Henry Mayo." s.v. *Oxford Dictionary of National Biography Online*, 2008. http://www.oxforddnb.com/.

Stewart, Susan. *Crimes of Writing: Problems in the Containment of Representation*. Durham, NC: Duke University Press, 1994.

Strawhorn, John. "Master of Ulubrae: Boswell as Enlightened Laird." In *Boswell: Citizen of the World, Man of Letters*, edited by Irma S. Lustig, 117–34. Lexington: University Press of Kentucky, 1995.

Suarez, Michael F., and Michael L. Turner, eds. *The Cambridge History of the Book in Britain. Volume 5 1695–1830*. Cambridge: Cambridge University Press, 2009.

Tadmor, Naomi. *Family & Friends in Eighteenth-Century England: Household, Kinship, Patronage*. Cambridge: Cambridge University Press, 2001.

Tankard, Paul. "Nineteen More Johnsonian Designs: A Supplement to 'That Great Literary Projector.'" *Age of Johnson: A Scholarly Annual* 23 (2015): 141–57.

———. "'That Great Literary Projector': Samuel Johnson's *Designs*, or Catalogue of Projected Works." *Age of Johnson: A Scholarly Annual* 13 (2002): 103–80.

Taylor, Richard C. *Goldsmith as Journalist*. Rutherford, NJ: Fairleigh Dickinson University Press, 1993.

———. "James Harrison, *The Novelist's Magazine*, and the Early Canonizing of the English Novel." *Studies in English Literature* 33, no. 3 (Summer 1993): 629–43.

Thomson, Derick S. "James Macpherson." s.v. *Oxford Dictionary of National Biography Online*, 2006. http://www.oxforddnb.com/.

Todd, William B. "Quadruple Imposition: An Account of Goldsmith's *The Traveller*." *Studies in Bibliography* 7 (1955): 103–11.
Tomarken, Edward. *Genre and Ethics: The Education of an Eighteenth-Century Critic*. Newark: University of Delaware Press, 2002.
Turnbull, Gordon. "Boswell and Sympathy: The Trial and Execution of John Reid." In *New Light on Boswell: Critical and Historical Essays on the Occasion of the Bicentenary of the Life of Johnson*, edited by Greg Clingham, 104–15. Cambridge: Cambridge University Press, 1991.
Turner, Katherine. "Sir Nathaniel William Wraxall." s.v. *Oxford Dictionary of National Biography Online*, 2008. http://www.oxforddnb.com/.
Vance, John A., ed. *Boswell's Life of Johnson: New Questions, New Answers*. Athens, GA: University of Georgia Press, 1985.
———. "Samuel Johnson and Thomas Warton." *Biography* 9, no. 2 (1986): 95–111.
Vermeule, Blakey. *The Party of Humanity: Writing Moral Psychology in Eighteenth-Century Britain*. Baltimore: Johns Hopkins University Press, 2000.
Vickery, Amanda. *The Gentleman's Daughter: Women's Lives in Georgian England*. New Haven, CT: Yale University Press, 1998.
Walker, Hallam. *Molière*. Boston: Twayne, 1971.
Walpole, Horace, and Sir Walter Scott. *The Castle of Otranto: A Gothic Story*. Edinburgh, Ballantyne, 1811.
Wardle, Ralph. *Oliver Goldsmith*. Lawrence: University of Kansas Press, 1957.
Warton, Thomas. *Observations on the Faerie Queene of Spenser*. London, 1754.
———. "Observations on the Fairy Queen of Spenser: Postscript." 2nd ed. London, 1762. http://spenserians.cath.vt.edu/TextRecord.php?action=GET&textsid=34629.
Watt, James. "Dallas." s.v. *Oxford Dictionary of National Biography Online*. http://www.oxforddnb.com/.
Weinberg, Bernard. *A History of Literary Criticism in the Italian Renaissance*. 2 vols. Chicago: University of Chicago Press, 1961.
Weinbrot, Howard D. *Augustus Caesar in "Augustan" England*. Princeton, NJ: Princeton University Press, 1978.
Williams, Iolo A. *Seven XVIIIth Century Bibliographies*. London: Dulau, 1924.
Withrington, Donald J., and Ian R. Grant, eds. *Statistical Account of Scotland*. 20 vols. East Ardsley, UK: E. P. Publishing, 1975–. Reprint of Edited by Sir John Sinclair, 1791–1799.
Woolley, James D. "Johnson as Despot: Anna Seward's Rejected Contribution to Boswell's *Life*." *Modern Philology* 70, no. 2 (November 1972): 140–45.
Wright, Charles H. C. *French Classicism*. Cambridge, MA: Harvard University Press, 1920.
Yarrow, William. "Boswell's Debt to Mrs. Piozzi." Paper presented at the East-Central/American Society for Eighteenth Century Studies Annual Conference, Philadelphia, 1992.
Zionkowski, Linda. *Men's Work: Gender, Class, and the Professionalization of Poetry, 1660–1784*. Basingstoke, UK: Palgrave Macmillan, 2001.

ABOUT THE CONTRIBUTORS

CHRISTOPHER CATANESE received an MA from the English Department at Duke University in 2013. His article "Refinement and Romantic Genre" was awarded the 2016 Ralph Cohen Prize and published in *New Literary History*. He is an editor at Duke University Press and coedits Golias Books in New York.

JAMES J. CAUDLE, research associate at the Centre for Robert Burns Studies at the University of Glasgow, worked for over two decades with the Yale Boswell Editions, most recently as their Associate Editor from 2000 to 2017. He has collaborated with Richard B. Sher on Sher's edition of the correspondence of Boswell and William Forbes of Pitsligo. His scholarship focuses on the history of the book, especially censorship and copyright, on sociability and social verse, and on mass communications of political ideas through the media of newspaper and magazine essays, pamphlets, and sermons. His recent essays on Boswell include "Affleck Generations: The Libraries of the Boswells of Auchinleck, 1695–1825," in *Before the Public Library: Reading, Community, and Identity in the Atlantic World, 1650–1850*; and "'Soaping' and 'Shaving' the Public Sphere: James Boswell's 'Soaping Club' and Edinburgh Enlightenment Sociability," in *The Need to Belong: Associationalism in Enlightenment Scotland*.

MARILYN FRANCUS is professor of English at West Virginia University, where she teaches Eighteenth-Century British Literature and Women's Studies. Marilyn is the author of *Monstrous Motherhood: 18th-Century Culture and the Ideology of Domesticity* (2012); and *The Converting Imagination: Linguistic Theory and Swift's Satiric Prose* (1994). She has published articles in a variety of journals, including *ELH*, *Eighteenth-Century Life*, and *Persuasions*. She is the editor of *The Burney Journal*.

CHRISTINE JACKSON-HOLZBERG is an independent scholar based in Munich, Germany. The main focus of her research is on the third Earl of Shaftesbury, specifically his unpublished manuscripts and his correspondence. She belongs to a small team of editors responsible for the *Standard Edition* of Shaftesbury's complete writings and is currently annotating his letters for publication.

ABOUT THE CONTRIBUTORS

CLAUDIA THOMAS KAIROFF is professor of English at Wake Forest University, where she has taught since 1986. She is the author of *Alexander Pope and His Eighteenth-Century Women Readers*; *Anna Seward and the End of the Eighteenth Century*, and numerous articles on Pope and on women writers. With Jennifer Keith, she is coeditor of a two-volume critical edition of *The Works of Anne Finch, Countess of Winchilsea*, forthcoming from Cambridge University Press. She is currently working on a monograph about Anne Finch's poetics of disguise.

ELIZABETH LAMBERT is professor of English emeriti at Gettysburg College. She is the author of *Edmund Burke of Beaconsfield*; and has published articles on various aspects of Burke's life and thought, including his religion, his Irish connections, his friendship with Samuel Johnson, and the ways James Boswell's portrayal of Burke in *The Life of Johnson* was influenced by their personal relationship. She is president of the Edmund Burke Society of North America and coeditor of *Studies of Burke and His Time*.

ANTHONY W. LEE's research interests center on Samuel Johnson and his circle, mentoring, and intertextuality. He has published three books and more than thirty essays on Johnson and eighteenth-century literature and culture. He has two books forthcoming, *Revaluation: New Essays on Samuel Johnson* (University of Delaware Press, 2018); and *"Modernity Johnson": Samuel Johnson Among the Modernists* (Clemson University Press, 2019). Anthony has taught at a number of colleges and universities, including the University of Arkansas, Arkansas Tech University, Kentucky Wesleyan College, the University of the District of Columbia, and the University of Maryland University College, where he also served as director of the English and Humanities Program.

JAMES E. MAY (Penn State University, emeritus) has for over two decades surveyed rare book and manuscript sales for *The Scriblerian*, edited *The Eighteenth-Century Intelligencer* newsletter, and compiled Section One (Bibliographical and Print History Studies) for *ECCB: The Eighteenth-Century Current Bibliography*. He has written on bibliographical and textual problems in early editions of Tobias Smollett, Jonathan Swift, and Edward Young. He is presently writing a descriptive bibliography of Edward Young (to 1775), and identifying the ornament stocks of early eighteenth-century Dublin and London printers.

The late JOHN RADNER was associate professor of English (emeritus) at George Mason University. His *Johnson and Boswell: A Biography of Friendship* (Yale University Press, 2013) was co-winner of the 2015 Annabel Jenkins Biography Prize awarded by the American Society for Eighteenth-Century Studies.

ABOUT THE CONTRIBUTORS

LANCE WILCOX is professor of English and holder of the Theophilus Mueller Chair at Elmhurst College, Illinois, where he teaches courses in British literature and modern drama. He has published articles on Samuel Johnson and Elizabeth Inchbald, among others. In 2016, Broadview Press published an edition of Samuel Johnson's *Life of Richard Savage*, which he coedited with Nicholas Seager, Keele University, United Kingdom.

INDEX

Page numbers in bold italic indicate references to Table 1.

Addison, Joseph, 132, 157, 201, 212, 220, 223
African Company, 179, 186
Allen, Ralph, 127n9
Anstey, Christopher, *The New Bath Guide*, 115
Arbuthnot, John, 156, 161, 165n42
Ariosto, *Orlando Furioso*, 219–221
Auchinleck, Lord, 55–56
Auchinleck, Scotland, 54, 56, 62, 66, 68, 69, 70, 119
Augustanism, 162
aura popularis, 218, 222–224

Balderston, Katharine C., 87
Ballitore, Ireland, 178
Barber, Elizabeth, 168
Barber, Frances, 167, 168, 171, 178, 187, 194
Baretti, Giuseppe, 10, 12, 23, 27, 29n4, 149; "Ode to Charlotte Lennox," 155
Barry, James, 149, 209
Basker, James, 169, 171
Bate, W. Jackson, 134
Bathurst, Allen Lord, 127n9
Beaconsfield, Buckinghamshire, 174, 185
Beattie, Dr. James, 26, 193
Beauclerk, Topham, 16, 149
Bentham, Jeremy, 226
Bernardin de Saint-Pierre, Jacques-Henri, 31; *Paul et Virginie,* 45
Blackwater River, County Cork, 177
Blair, James, 209
Bluestockings, 108, 125, 127n9, 185
Boileau, 156–161, 164n21, 164n28, 165n44; *Art poétique*, 158; *Second Satire (La rime et la raison) (Épître à Molière)*, 4, 156, 157, 159
Bolingbroke, Henry St. John 1st Viscount, 127n9

Bond, Phineas (the younger), 37
Booth, Wayne, 135
Bossuet, Jacques Benigne, 48n10
Boswell, James, **28**, 125, 148–149, 152n32, 153, 155–156, 167–187, 188n27, 189n38, 191, 193, 197, 199, 211n8, 233; *The Journal of a Tour of the Hebrides,* 53, 55–56, 65; *Life of Johnson,* 9–29, 29n4, 30n10, 31, 37, 43, 48n12, 53–71, 75nn37–38, 75n51, 85, 100, 103, 124, 132, 168, 250
Bradshaigh, Lady Dorothy, 127n9
Brewer, David, 127n7
Bristol, England, 133, 142–143, 17–180, 185–186
British Magazine, 181
Brock, Claire, 130n33
Brocklesby, Dr. Richard, 149, 168
Brookes, Richard, MD, *A New and Accurate System of Natural History,* 80
Brown, Christopher, 186
Bunbury, Mrs. Catherine, 87, 113
Bundock, Michael, 171
Burke, Edmund, 18, 22, 62, 70, 125, 131n45, 149, 167–168, 173–187, 188n31, 189n50, 189n59, 201, 226; *Reflections on the Revolution in France,* 62; *Sketch for a Negro Code,* 180–187
Burke, William, 178, 184
Burney, Charles, 51n64, 111, 118, 127n14, 131n47, 149, 154; *A General History of Music,* 111
Burney, Frances, 67–68, 108–126, 127n11, 127n14, 128nn17–18, 128nn20–22, 129n29, 130nn33–36, 149, 153, 194; *A Busy Day,* 130n37; *Camilla,* 126, 130n37; *Cecilia,* 112, 118, 123; *Evelina,* 108–114, 123, 125, 128n17, 128nn20–21, 129n29; *Love and Fashion,* 130n37;

[253]

Burney, Frances (cont.)
  Memoirs of Dr. Burney, 126; *The Wanderer,* 126, 131n47, 139; *The Witlings,* 118; *The Woman Hater,* 130n37
Burney, Susan, 118
Bute, Lord, 38
Byron, Augusta, 128n22, 193
Byron, Lord, 49n19, 226

Cambridge, George Owen, 122, 125
Carlyle, Thomas, 50n34
Carnan, Thomas, 84
Carte, Thomas, 48n5
Carter, Elizabeth, 118, 149
Cartwright, Edmund, 43n59
Case, Arthur, 83
Chalmers, James, 55
Chambers, Catherine, 21
Chambers, Robert, 10–29, **28**, 30n17, 149
Chamier, Anthony, 22
Chapone, Hester, 118
Charles I, king of Great Britain, 94
Chesterfield, Lord, 110, 133, 147–148, 151n27, 161
Cholmondeley, Mrs. Mary, 112
Churchill, Charles, 110, 153, 161
Cibber, Colley, 122
Clarke, Norma, 97, 106n45, 109
Code Noir, 180
Cohen, Ralph, 208
Collings, Samuel, 64–65
Colqhoun, Sir James, 57
Conway, Henry Seymour, 174
Cooke, William, 82
Courtney, John, 173
Cowley, Abraham, 116, 118
Cradock, Joseph, 53
Crane, R. S., 83
Crewe, Frances, 118
Crisp, Samuel, 118, 128n23, 130n35
The Critical Review, 89, 92, 123
Cromwell, Oliver, 55
Cumberland, Richard, 129n24; *The West Indian,* 115
cursus honorum, 162

Dallas, Robert Charles, 40, 49n19, 50n37, 51n52
Davidson, Virginia Spencer, 133

Davie, Donald, 27, 161
Davies, Thomas, 11, 23, 149
DeFoe, Daniel, 110, 194, 196–197, 200; *Robinson Crusoe,* 110; *Tour Thro' the Whole Island of Great Britain,* 196
Delleville, Jean Francois Philippe, Sieur de, 44–46
Dellingham, Mrs. Susannah, 113
Denham, John, 116
Dilly, Charles, 70
Dilly brothers, 54
Dobell, Bertram, 105n23
Dobson, Mrs. Susanna, 113
Dodsley, Richard, 15
Dolben, William, 172, 180–181, 185
Drummond, Alexander-Munro, 36
Drummond, James, 36, 39, 44, 49n31
Drummond, William, 36
Dryden, John, 157, 162, 164n28, 192, 195, 220, 228
Dun, John, 53–71, 72n5, 73n12
Duncan, Ian, 219
Dundas, Henry, 180–183

Effen, Justus Van, 80
Ellis, David, 138
Elphinston, Charlotte, 31, 44
Elphinston, James, 31–47, 48n5, 48n10, 48n14, 49n19, 51n63, 223; *Apology,* 40, 51n51; and the critics, 39–40; *Forty Years' Correspondence,* 31; *Fifty Years' Correspondence,* 37, 41; *Hypercritic,* 51n51; translation for Charlotte Lennox, 39; translation of Martial, 43; translation of Racine, 39
Elphinston, Margaret, 32. *See also* Strahan, Margaret
Elphinston, Rachel, 43
Erwin, Timothy, 133
The Essex Head Club, 149
Eyam, 195, 201–202

Fairer, David, 199, 215, 229n6, 229n8
Falconar, James, 44–45
Farquhar, Alexander, 55
Fielding, Henry, 116, 125, 153, 194
Finch, Dr. Robert, 113
Flavell, Julie, 178
Fleeman, David, 34, 199, 211n30
Folkenflik, Robert, 139
Fong, David, 103

[254]

Foote, Samuel, 153
Formey, Jean Henri Samuel, *A Concise History of Philosophy and Philosophers (Histoire Abrégée de la Philosophie)*, 80
Forrester, Col. James, *The Polite Philosopher*, 37
Francis, Phillip, 186
Francklin, Thomas, 155–156; *Dissertation on Ancient Tragedy*, 155
Franklin, Benjamin, 36–37
Franklin, William Temple, 37
Friedman, Arthur, 79–83, 86–89, 104n16, 107n67

Gallagher, Catherine, 109
Garrick, David, 42, 149, 153, 161
Garth, Samuel, 116
Gay, John: *Beggar's Opera*, 110; *Polly*, 110
Gentleman's Magazine, 43, 93–94, 96, 99, 102, 132, 137, 169, 208
Gibbon, Edward, 49n19
Glorious Revolution, 94
Goldsmith, Oliver, 22, 79–103, 104n8, 107n61, 149, 153, 161, 207; "Assem, the Man Hater," 107n61; *The Captivity: An Oratorio*, 87; *The Deserted Village*, 79–80, 82–94; *An Enquiry into the State of Polite Learning*, 80, 102; *She Stoops to Conquer*, 79, 161; *The Traveller; Or, A Prospect of Society*, 82, 94–103
Gray, Thomas, 121, 207–210
Gregory, Dorothea, 108, 126n4
Greville, Frances, 118
Griffin, William, 80, 87, 105n24
Grignion, Charles, the elder, 91
Grub St., 132, 142, 147, 159, 160, 215

Halmi, Nicholas, 216
Hastings, Warren, 181, 184
Hawkesworth, John, 92, 103, 149
Hawkins, John, 53, 66, 68, 154
Hayley, William, 195, 201, 207
Haywood, Eliza, 142
Hervey, Lord, 159
Hill, Aaron, 132, 144
Hillarians, 132, 142
Holmes, Richard, 132–133, 145
Hopkins, Robert H., 82, 91
Horace, 36, 40, 223

Howard, Martin, 37, 42
Huddesford, George, *Warley: A Satire Addressed to the First Artist in Europe*, 117
"An Imitation of the Second Satire of Boileau, inscribed to Pylades," 157
The Ivy Lane Club, 149

Johnson, Samuel: "The Celebrated Letter", 147; *Dictionary*, 32, 37, 41, 63, 114, 125, 126n4, 195, 214, 223; *False Alarm*, 38–39; *Gnōthi Seauton ["Know Thyself"]*, 155; *Harleian Miscellany*, 222–224; *Journey to the Western Islands of Scotland*, 196, 199–200, 207, 209; *Life of Dryden*, 227–228; *Life of Savage*, 132–150; *Lives of the Most Eminent English Poets*, 206; *Lives of the Poets*, 207–208; *Parliamentary Debates*, 154; *Plan of a Dictionary*, 147; *Prayers and Meditations*, 43; *The Rambler*, 9, 14, 32–36, 148, 218, 222–226; *Rasselas*, 9, 195; *Shakespeare edn.*, 18, 110; Shakespeare proposals, 36, 154; *Taxation No Tyranny*, 39, 169; *Thoughts on the . . . Falkland Islands*, 22, 39; *The Vanity of Human Wishes*, 200. See also Pope, Alexander: *Rambler* series
Jortin, John, 50n37
Justice, George, 135, 105n2

Knight, Joseph, 169, 171
Knowles, Mary, 53
Koselleck, Reinhardt, 216–217

La Beaumelle, Laurent Angliviel de, 39
Lamb, Susan, 201
Langhorne, John, 94–99, 103
Langton, Bennet, 9–29, **28**, 172, 186
Lascelles, Mary, 196–197, 200
Lawrence, Dr. Thomas, 15
Lee, Anthony W., 150n7, 151n15, 199, 211n30
Lennox, Charlotte, 39–40, 149
Levett, Robert, 12
Lewis, Francis, 34
licensing act, 217
Lipking, Lawrence, 151n20
The Literary Chronicle, 118
Literary Magazine, 12, 153
Lloyd's Evening Post, 92
London Chronicle, 92–93, 103, 84–85, 92–93

Lonsdale, Roger H., 81, 91, 119
Lort, Michael, 168
Lucas, F. L., 82

Macclesfield, Countess of, 135–146
Mackenzie, Henry, 38, 40–41
Macpherson, James, 41, 192, 209–211; *Ossian,* 65, 209
Malone, Edmond, 57–59, 177
Mansfield, 1st Earl of, 181
Marivaux, Pierre, 125
Marteilhe, Jean, 79
Martial, M. V., 42
The Martial Review; Or, A General History of the Late Wars, 80
Martin, Martin, 196, 200
Martin, Peter, 151n19
Maxwell, Dr. William, 154
Menzies, John, 185
Milton, John, 116, 191, 204
Misellus, 225–226
Molière, 156, 160–161, 165n44; *L École des femme* [The School for Wives], 157
Montague, Elizabeth, 108–125, 130n41, 131n42
The Monthly Review, 65, 94, 103, 110, 123, 153
More, Hannah, 113, 118, 126n4, 131n45
Morrison, Sarah R., 133
Murphy, Arthur, 15, 47, 118, 125, 153–162; *Essay on the Life and Genius of SJ,* 154; *A Poetical Epistle to Mr. Samuel Johnson, A.M.,* 153–162; *Ode to the Naiads of Fleet Ditch,* 161; *The Orphan of China,* 15, 155

Newbery, John, 79, 82
"The Newgate Biography," 150n9
"Nobody," 115–119

Odell, Jonathan, 37, 50n38
Oldham, John, "Letter from the Country to a Friend in Town," 157
Ossian, 40–41, 65, 197, 202, 209–210

Paine, Thomas, *Rights of Man,* 62
Palmer, Miss Mary, 112, 184
Peace of Paris, 187
Penal Laws, 177–178
Pennant, Thomas, 196; *A Tour in Scotland,* 197

Pepys, William Weller, 119–124
Percy, Thomas, 22, 82
Pindar, Peter, 161; *Poetical and Congratulatory Epistle to James Boswell,* Esq., 65
Piozzi, Hester Lynch, 53, 67, 118, 168. *See also* Thrale, Hester
Pitt, William, 172–173
Pomfret, John, 116
Pope, Alexander, 101, 121–123, 132, 142, 156–162, 192, 199, 207–208; *The Dunciad,* 122, 142, 165n46; *Epistle to Arbuthnot,* 158–159; *Rambler* series: #3, 40; #16, 225; #23, 222; #52, 33; #54, 33; #134, 35; #145, 147; #159, 34, 208
Portland, 2nd Duke of, 185
Public Ledger, 80–81

Quiller-Couch, A. T., 83
Quintana, Ricardo, 81–82, 91–92

Reid, John, 171
Reynolds, Frances, 113, 149
Reynolds, Sir Joshua, 15, 32, 37, 87, 115, 117, 149, 172
Richardson, Samuel, 39, 15, 155; *Pamela,* 110
Rider, William, 79
Robertson, William, 176
Rockingham, Marchioness of, 180, 189n59
Ross, Trevor, 218
Rothes, Lady Jane, 22, 121
Rousseau, Jean-Jaques, 192, 201
Rowlandson, Thomas, 64–65
Ruffhead, Owen, 40, 153

Said, Edward, 217
Savage, Richard, 132–150; *Sir Thomas Overbury,* 141, 144; *An Author to be Let,* 142, 147
Schwalm, David E., 143
Scots Magazine, 33, 43
Scott, Jeffrey, 68
Scott, Temple, 80
Scott, Walter, 228
The Scriblerians, 132
Seward, Anna, 53, 191–210; "Alpine Scenery," 204, 206; "Elegy on Captain Cook," 205; *Louisa,* 192–193; *Original Sonnets on Various Subjects,* 206
Shackleton, Abraham, 178

[256]

Shaw, Cuthbert, 47
Shaw, William, 37–38
Sheridan, Thomas, 9, 16, 118
Smith, Robert W., 185
Smollett, Tobias, 63, 67, 93, 153, 250
Somerset, James, 180–181
The Spectator, 72n5, 212n34, 226
Spenser, Edmund, 219, 227–228; *The Faerie Queen*, 220
Steele, Richard, 132, 136, 137, 142
Sterne, Laurence, 114, 124, 205; *Tristram Shandy*, 124
Stewart, Charles, 181
Stewart, Susan, 217
Strahan, Margaret, 32–33, 35, 52n73. *See also* Elphinston, Margaret
Strahan, William, 32, 36, 39, 42
Streatfield, Sophia, 118
Swift, Jonathan, 110, 122, 132, 162, 165n46, 192; *The Battle of the Books*, 119

Thomson, James, 201, 207, 225
Thrale, Henry, 153
Thrale, Hester, 20, 26, **27**, 42, 108, 117–119, 121, 149, 153, 185, 187, 193–194, 203. *See also* Piozzi, Hester Lynch
Thurlow, Edward, 172
Todd, William B., 83, 105n24
Tomarken, Edward, 137

Tracy, Clarence, 137
The Turk's Head Club, 149
Turner, J. M., 203
Tyrconnel, Lord, 134, 136, 138, 148
Tytler, William, 40–41

Voltaire, 80; *L'Orphan de la Chine*, 155

Wale, Samuel, 91
Walpole, Horace, 119, 166, 228–229
Walpole, Sir Robert, 138–139
Wardle, Ralph, 79–80, 98, 102
Warton, Thomas, 12, 214–229; *Observations on the Faerie Queen of Spenser*, 218–221
Whalley, Rev. T. S., 201–206
White, William (Bishop of Pennsylvania), 37
Whitehall Evening Post, 62–70
Wilberforce, William, 172
Wilkes, John, 54
Williams, Anna, 12, 113, 195
Willington, James, 79
Wilmot, John, 164n28
Wilson, John, 35
Windham, William, 172–173, 186–187
Wolcot, John, 65. *See also* Pindar, Peter
Wordsworth, William, 193, 209

Yearlsey, Ann, 126n4

Printed in the United States
By Bookmasters